The Association of University Presses

Directory 2019

The Association of University Presses
1412 Broadway, Suite 2135
New York, NY 10018

1775 Massachusetts Avenue, NW
Washington, DC 20036

Phone: 212.989.1010
Website: www.aupresses.org
Email: info@aupresses.org
Twitter: @aupresses

Published by the Association of University Presses
1412 Broadway, Suite 2135
New York NY 10018
© 2018 by the Association of University Presses, Inc.
All rights reserved.
Printed in the United States of America

International Standard Book Number: 978-0-945103-40-0
Library of Congress Catalog Number 54-43046

Distributed to the Trade by:
The University of Chicago Press
11030 South Langley Avenue
Chicago, Illinois 60628
USA

Publication of this *Directory* was assisted by a generous grant from Thomson-Shore.

Contents

PREFACE

This *Directory* serves as a guide to the publishing programs and personnel of the 147 distinguished scholarly presses that have met the membership standards of the Association of University Presses. Updated annually, the *Directory* provides the most comprehensive information on these publishers available from any source. It belongs on the reference shelf of anyone connected to scholarly publishing: scholars preparing materials for publication, booksellers, librarians, scholarly presses interested in joining the Association, and, of course, the Association's own members.

The *Directory* is organized particularly for the convenience of authors, librarians, and booksellers who require detailed information about Association members and their wide-ranging publishing programs. The "Subject Area Grid," for example, provides a quick overview of the many disciplines published by the presses, indicating those most likely to publish a work in a given area. "On Submitting Manuscripts" gives advice to potential authors on preparing and submitting a scholarly manuscript for publication.

For further detail, individual press listings provide information on their editorial programs, journals published, and key staff members. Addresses, ordering information, and information on international sales representatives are also included. Detailed information on Association Partners is also listed.

The last section of the *Directory* focuses on the association and its purposes, and includes its by-laws, guidelines for admission to membership, and the names of the Association's Board of Directors, committees and task forces, and staff.

GENERAL INFORMATION FOR AUTHORS

What University Presses Do

University Presses perform services that are of inestimable value to the scholarly establishment, and also to the broader world of readers, and ultimately to society. If you are considering publishing with a university or other non-profit scholarly press, the following list should give you a good understanding of the scholarly publishing community.

- University Presses make available to the broader public the full range and value of research generated by university faculty.

- University Press books and journals present the basic research and analysis that is drawn upon by policymakers, opinion leaders, and authors of works for the general public.

- University Presses contribute to the variety and diversity of cultural expression at a time of global mergers and consolidation in the media industry.

- University Presses make common cause with libraries and other cultural institutions to promote engagement with ideas and sustain a literate culture.

- University Presses help to preserve the distinctiveness of local cultures through publication of works on the states and regions where they are based.

- University Presses give voice to minority cultures and perspectives through pioneering publication programs in ethnic, racial, and sexual studies.

- University Presses bring the work of overseas scholars and writers to English-language audiences by commissioning and publishing works in translation.

- University Presses rediscover and maintain the availability of works important to scholarship and culture through reprint programs.

- University Presses encourage cultural expression by publishing works of fiction, poetry, and creative nonfiction and books on contemporary art and photography.

- University Presses sponsor work in specialized and emerging areas of scholarship that do not have the broad levels of readership needed to attract commercial publishers.

- University Presses, through the peer review process, test the validity and soundness of scholarship and thus maintain high standards for academic publication.

- University Presses add value to scholarly work through rigorous editorial development; professional copyediting and design; and worldwide dissemination.

- University Presses are based at a wide array of educational institutions and thus promote a diversity of scholarly perspectives.

- University Presses encourage and refine the work of younger scholars through publication of the first books that establish credentials and develop authorial experience.

- University Presses make the works of English-language scholars available worldwide by licensing translations to publishers in other languages.

- University Presses commit resources to long-term scholarly editions and multivolume research projects, assuring publication for works with completion dates far in the future.

- University Presses add to the richness of undergraduate and graduate education by publishing most of the non-textbook and supplementary material used by instructors.

- University Presses collaborate with learned societies, scholarly associations, and librarians to explore how new technologies can benefit and advance scholarship.

- University Presses extend the reach and influence of their parent institutions, making evident their commitment to knowledge and ideas.

- University Presses demonstrate their parent institutions' support of research in areas such as the humanities and social sciences that rarely receive substantial Federal or corporate funding.

- University Presses help connect the university to the surrounding community by publishing books of local interest and hosting events for local authors.

- University Presses generate favorable publicity for their parent institutions through news coverage and book reviews, awards won, and exhibits at scholarly conferences.

- University Press staff act as local experts for faculty and administrators, providing guidance on intellectual property, scholarly communication, and the publishing process.

- University Presses provide advice and opportunities for students interested in pursuing careers in publishing.

On Submitting Manuscripts

JOURNAL ARTICLES

University presses have always been associated with publishing books of merit and distinction. This remains as true today as in the past, but less well appreciated is the extent to which university presses are active in publishing scholarly journals.

Journals form a major part of the publishing program of many presses, and more than half of the Association's members produce at least one periodical. (See page 2 for a list of presses publishing journals.)

Authors submitting papers to a journal should check a current issue for information on where to submit manuscripts and for guidelines on length and format. Editors of journals often have very precise requirements for manuscript preparation and may return articles that do not meet their specifications.

BOOK MANUSCRIPTS

Selecting a Publisher

If you are looking for a publisher for a book-length manuscript, do some research on which press may be best for your book. You should consider the reputation in your field of various presses and their editors, the design and production quality of their books, and the range and strength of their marketing efforts. To take advantage of group promotions and past experience, presses tend to specialize in certain subjects. Occasionally a press may take on a title in an unfamiliar area, but you are more likely to be successful in your submission if you choose one that knows the field. Use the "Subject Area Grid," which begins on page 9, to find out which presses publish titles in your field. You can then find more specific information about their interests under the listings of individual presses or by consulting their catalogs. If your book has a strong regional interest, consider the lists of the university presses active in your state to determine what types of regional books they publish.

You can also learn more about the list of each publisher by studying brochures received in the mail, reading book advertisements in journals, and by visiting press exhibits at academic meetings. At these exhibits you can meet acquisitions editors from the presses most active in the discipline and talk with them about your manuscript. Such talks can be very helpful to you and the editor in deciding if your manuscript would be suitable for a particular press. If you have already decided which press you would prefer for your book, call the appropriate editor before the meeting to make an appointment.

Preparing a Manuscript Prospectus

If you have selected a publisher but do not know an editor, you can use this directory to find the appropriate editor at that press. If you are not sure which editor to approach, write to the director of the press or to its editor-in-chief. Many Association member presses describe their submission guidelines on their Websites. It is best not to send the complete manuscript until you have been invited to do so. Presses vary in the amount of material they want to receive on a first submission, but some or all of the following materials are usually provided:

- a short, informative cover letter including a clear and concise description of your book and its notable features, your opinion of the audience for the book, information on the current status of the manuscript and expected completion date, and some details on the physical characteristics of the manuscript, such as length, number of illustrations, tables, appendices, etc.

- a table of contents

- a preface, introduction, or other brief sample of your manuscript

- a curriculum vitae or biographical notes

If the press is interested, the editor will invite you to submit the complete manuscript or inform you that he or she can proceed to review the materials you sent.

Preparing Your Manuscript for Review

Presses vary in their requirements for manuscript preparation. In general, the manuscript you submit for review should be as accurate and complete as possible. If a manuscript is carelessly prepared, reviewers may take offense at typographical errors or careless citations and spend precious review space discussing these problems instead of attending to the substance of your manuscript. If, for good reasons, your manuscript is incomplete, you should indicate what material is missing and provide your schedule for completion.

Although some presses will accept a single-spaced manuscript for review, it is best to double-space your text. A double-spaced manuscript is easier to read and may be required when your manuscript reaches the copyediting stage. For book publication, every element of the text should be double-spaced (including quotations, notes, bibliographies, appendices, figure legends, and glossaries). Once your manuscript is accepted for publication, your editor will advise you on any special requirements imposed by that press's house style.

The Review Process

Some university presses may give advance (i.e., conditional) contracts to experienced authors on the basis of incomplete or unreviewed manuscripts. Most, however, must obtain one or more reviews of a completed manuscript before presenting a project for the approval of the press's editorial board. As review procedures differ from press to press, check with the editor when you first submit the manuscript to find out what will be involved. He or she should be able to give you a tentative schedule for the review process. It is difficult to predict exactly how long it will take to reach a decision, since often readers' reports encourage authors to make further revisions to the manuscript and the manuscript is usually reviewed again after the author makes the revisions. If your manuscript is also under review at another publisher, be sure to let the editor know. Some editors will not review manuscripts that are under simultaneous consideration elsewhere; others will not object.

Preparing Your Manuscript for Publication

Most publishers will want an electronic version of your manuscript. Your manuscript should be keyboarded as simply as possible. There is no need to change fonts, type styles, and formats to differentiate between sections; in fact, this is counterproductive. The press's copyediting or production department will insert the proper typesetting codes for formatting extracts, different levels of headings, and so on. And keep in mind that your book will be designed by a professional. Many presses will send you their own guidelines for submitting manuscripts.

FURTHER READING

Abel, Richard, Lyman W. Newlin, Katina Strauch, and Bruce Strauch, eds. *Scholarly Publishing: Books, Journals, Publishers, and Libraries in the Twentieth Century.* Indianapolis: Wiley, 2001.

American Psychological Association. *Publication Manual of the American Psychological Association.* 6th ed. Washington, DC: APA Books, 2010.

Appelbaum, Judith. *How to Get Happily Published: A Complete and Candid Guide.* 5th ed. New York: Collins Reference, 1998.

Becker, Howard S. *Writing for Social Scientists: How to Start and Finish Your Thesis, Book, or Article.* 2nd ed. Chicago: University of Chicago Press, 2007.

Belcher, Wendy Laura. *Writing Your Journal Article in Twelve Weeks: A Guide to Academic Publishing Success.* 2nd ed. Chicago: University of Chicago Press, 2019.

Day, Robert A. and Barbara Gastel *How to Write and Publish a Scientific Paper.* 8th ed. Westport, CT: Greenwood Publishing Group, Inc., 2016.

Derricourt, Robin. *An Author's Guide to Scholarly Publishing.* Princeton: Princeton University Press, 1996.

Germano, William. *From Dissertation to Book.* 2nd ed. Chicago: University of Chicago Press, 2013.

Germano, William. *Getting it Published: A Guide for Scholars and Anyone Else Serious about Serious Books.* 3rd ed. Chicago: University of Chicago Press, 2016.

Hacker, Diana and Nancy Sommers. *A Writer's Reference with 2016 MLA Update.* 8th ed. Boston & New York: Bedford/St. Martin's, 2016.

Harman, Eleanor, Ian Montagnes, Siobhan McMenemy, and Chris Bucci eds. *The Thesis and the Book: A Guide for First-Time Academic Authors.* 2nd ed. Toronto: University of Toronto Press, 2003.

Huff, Anne Sigismund. *Writing for Scholarly Publication.* Thousand Oaks, CA: SAGE Publications, 1998.

Jensen, Joli. *Write No Matter What: Advice for Academics.* Chicago: University of Chicago Press, 2017.

Kasdorf, William E. *The Columbia Guide to Digital Publishing.* New York: Columbia University Press, 2003.

Katz, Michael J. *Elements of the Scientific Paper: A Step-by-Step Guide for Students and Professionals.* New Haven: Yale University Press, 1986.
Kaufman, Roy S. *Publishing Forms and Contracts.* New York: Oxford University Press, 2008.

Luey, Beth. *Handbook for Academic Authors.* 5th ed. New York: Cambridge University Press, 2009.

Luey, Beth, ed. *Revising Your Dissertation: Advice from Leading Editors.* 2nd ed. Berkeley: University of California Press, 2007.

Modern Language Association. *MLA Handbook.* 8th ed. New York: Modern Language Association of America, 2016.

Moxley, Joseph M. and Todd Taylor. *Writing and Publishing for Academic Authors.* 2nd ed. Lanham, MD: Rowman and Littlefield, 1996.

Mulvany, Nancy C. *Indexing Books.* 2nd ed. Chicago: University of Chicago Press, 2005.

Parsons, Paul. *Getting Published: The Acquisition Process at University Presses.* Knoxville: University of Tennessee Press, 1989.

Powell, Walter W. *Getting into Print: The Decision-Making Process in Scholarly Publishing.* Chicago: University of Chicago Press, 1985.

Strong, William S. *The Copyright Book: A Practical Guide.* 6th ed. Cambridge, MA: MIT Press, 2014.

Strunk, William J. and E. B. White. *The Elements of Style.* 4th ed. New York: Pearson Higher Education, 1999.

Swain, Dwight V. *Techniques of the Selling Writer.* Norman: University of Oklahoma Press, 198.

Thompson, John. *Books in the Digital Age: The Transformation of Academic and Higher Education Publishing in Britain and the United States* Cambridge: Polity Press, 2005.

University of Chicago Press. *The Chicago Manual of Style.* 17h ed. Chicago: University of Chicago Press, 2017.

University of Chicago Press. *The Chicago Manual of Style Online.* 17th ed. Chicago: University of Chicago Press, 2017, www.chicagomanualofstyle.org/home.html

Wiser, James. *Open Book: A Librarian's Guide to Academic Publishing.* Santa Barbara, CA: Mission Bell Media, 2016.

Zerubavel, Eviator. *The Clockwork Muse: A Practical Guide to Writing Theses, Dissertations, and Books.* Cambridge, MA: Harvard University Press, 1999.

Subject Area Grid

This ten-page grid indicates the subject areas in which each press has a particularly strong interest.

Some presses are prepared to consider manuscripts of outstanding quality in areas other than those listed. For more detailed descriptions of press editorial programs, consult the individual listings in the "Directory of Members" section and contact the presses that interest you.

Legend and column headers for a press subject-area acquisition chart.

Subject	Abilene Christian	Akron	Alabama	Alaska	Alberta	A. Historical	A. Psychiatric	A. School Classical	Amherst	Amsterdam	UniAndes	Arizona	Arkansas	Army	Athabasca	Baylor	Beacon	British Columbia	Brookings	Bucknell	Cairo (American)	Calgary	California	Cambridge	Carnegie Mellon	Catholic	Central European	Chicago	Chinese
African Studies					●						●											●		●				●	
African American Studies		●								●	○		●				●			●			●	●				●	
American Studies		●	●							●	○						●			●			●	●				●	
Anthropology		●	●	●						●	●	●	●		●		●	●		●			●	●				●	●
Archeology		●	●					●		●	●	●			●					●		○		●					●
Arts		●								●												●		●				●	
Architecture			●				●	●	●	●		●								●		●	○	●				●	
Art Criticism								●		●					●		○			○		●		●				●	
Comics								●		○												●	○					●	
Dance	●							●		●													●					●	
Fashion and Textiles								●															○						
Folk Art		●						●		○					●								○					●	
Film		●		●			●	●	●	●					●					●		●	●	●				●	
Fine Arts and Art History		●			●	●	●	●		●		●			●					●		●	●	●	○		●	●	
Music & Music Theory							●	●		●					●							●	●	●				●	●
Photography		●	●	●				●		●												●	●	●				●	
Popular Culture							●	●		●					●	○						●	●	●				●	●
Television			○					●		●					●							○	●	●				●	
Theater							●	●		●					●					●			●	●	○			●	●
Asian Studies							●	●	○						●	●						●	●				●	●	
Biography and Memoir		●	●	●	●			●	●	●				●	●		●	○	●	●	●		●	○	●		●	●	
Business and Management								●	●						○			●		○			●				●	●	
Caribbean Studies		●						●		●					●			●		●		●		●				●	
Child Development			●					●							●								●				●	●	●
Classics						●	●	●	●					○				●				●	●			●	●	●	
Criminology								●						○			●					●	●					●	
Demography							●	●						●								●	●						●
Disability Studies							●	○			●			●	●	●						●					●		
European Studies							●	●	●					●			●	●	●			●					●		
Economics	●		●					●	●					●			●	●	●		●		●			●	●	●	
Education	●		●					●	●					●		●	●	●	●			●					●	●	●
Folklore			●						●		○			●			○					●					●		
Food & Agriculture		●	●	●					○					●	●					●	●								
Agriculture		●		●					○							●					●								
Cooking	●	●		●					○												●		○						
Food & Culture	●	●		●					○	●	●			●	●					●	○				●				
History of Food									○					●						●	○			●	●	●			
Geography		●					●		●					●			○			●		●	●				●		
Gender and Sexuality Studies		●	●	●			●	●	●					●		●	●	●				●				●	●	●	●
LGBTQIA Studies		●	●	●			●	●	○					●		●			●	●		●				●			
Women's Studies		●	●	●			●	●	●					●		●	●	●			●	●	●			●	●	●	
Health & Medicine		●			●			●						●								●					●		●
Addiction Studies									○					●		●	●	●					○						
Aging								●		○					●							●					●		
History of Medicine		●	●	●				●	○					○		●				●			●				●		
Public Health		●	●					●	●					●	●	●			●	●	●		●					●	
History		●		●				●	●					●	○	●	●				●		●				●	●	
African				●				●		○					●	●				●			●				●		
American	●	●	●	●				●		○	●	●	●	●	●	●						●	●	●	●		●		
Ancient		●				●	●	●	●	○					●				●			●	●				●		
Asian								●	●	○					●			●				●	●				●	●	
Australasian									○					●									●						
British								●		○					●		●	●				●	●				●		
Canadian			●	●				●		○					●		●	●				●	●						
Caribbean		●						●		●					●			●		●		●					●		
Central American								●		○	●				●							●	●				●		
Eastern European		●						●		○					●							●	●		●		●		
European								●	●	●			●	●					●			●	●	●	●		●		
Latin American		●						●		●	●				●		●			●		●	●	●			●		
Medieval								●		●					●							●	●	●	●	●	●		
Middle Eastern								●		○					●	●				●		●	●				●		
South American								●		●	●				●							●	●	●				●	

● press acquires in this area
○ press is NOT actively acquiring but has backlist

	Abilene Christian	Akron	Alabama	Alaska	Alberta	Amherst	A. Historical	A. Psychiatric	A. School Classical	Amsterdam	UniAndes	Arizona	Arkansas	Army	Athabasca	Baylor	Beacon	British Columbia	Brookings	Bucknell	Cairo (American)	Calgary	California	Cambridge	Carnegie Mellon	Catholic	Central European	Chicago	Chinese
Immigration							●	●			○	●			●		●	●	●				●	●		●	●		
Indigenous Studies			●	●		●						●	●		●		●	●	●			●	●					●	
Information and Communications			●	●			●				●	●			●			●	●				●	●					○
Information Science				●		●					○				●								●	●					
Internet Studies						●					○				●								●	●					
Journalism and Media Studies				●							●	●			●				●			●	●	●				●	●
International Relations											●				●				●				●						
Labor				●							●				●	●	●					●							
Language		●	●								●	●			○								●					●	●
Dictionaries and Lexicals			●	●							●						○							●				●	
Linguistic Theory		●	●							●	○				●								●					●	●
Language Texts			●								●				○			●		●					●				
Writing and Style Guides											●											●	●			●			
Latin American Studies		●			●					●	●			○			●	●		●	●	●				●			
Law and Legal Studies	○	●	●		●					●	●			●		●	●		●	●	●	●			●	○			
Literature (Creative)			●							●	●			●							○								
Creative Nonfiction	●	●	●	●						●	●			●	●	●			●			○	●			●			
Fiction		●	●	●						●	●			○					●	●	○								
Poetry	●		●	●						●	●	●	●	●		●			●		●	○	●		●			●	●
Drama		●								●				●								○	○						
Children's		●								○				○					●			○							
Translations		●								●				●					●			○	○			●	●		
Literature (Scholarly)		●		●			●	●		●	●			●	○			●			●						●		
Literary Criticism	●	●	●	●	●		●	●		●	●			●				●		●	●		●	●	●				
History				●			●	●		●	●			●		●		●	●	●	●		●	●	●				
Theater Studies				●						●	●			●				●		●	●		●						
Medieval Studies				●			●	●		○				○				●		●	●	●	●		●	●			
Military Studies		●	●						○			●	○			●	●					●							
Pacific Studies							●	○				○			○	●		●			●	●							
Philosophy							●	●			○	●						●			●		●	○	○	●	●		
Political Science/Public Policy	●		●	●	●		●	●		●	●	●	●	●	●		●	●		●	●	●			○	●	●		
Psychology	●					●		●	●		○	●			○	●	●				●							○	
Race and Class Studies	●		●	●	●					●	●	●			●	●	●				●				●	●			
Reference and Guidebooks			●							○				○		○			●			●				●			
Religion/Religious Studies	●		●	●		●				●	○			○	●	●	●	○		●	●				●				
Buddhism				●						○						●					●				●				
Christianity	●				●					○					●	●			●				●	●	●				
Hinduism				●						○						●					●				●				
Indigenous Religions			●	●						●					●	●	●				●				●				
Islam			●	●						○				●	●	●	○		●			●			●				
Judaism		●								○				●	●	●			●			●			●				
Renaissance Studies				●			●	○		○				○					●		●								
Science & Mathematics			●							●				○						●					●				
Astronomy			●							○	●									●					●				
Biological Science		●	●							●										●					●				
Botany		●	●							●	●									●					●				
Chemistry										○										●					●				
Computer Science										○		●				●				●					●				
Ecology and Conservation			●	●						●		●			●		●			●	●	●			●				
Earth and Environmental	○	●	●	●						●	●			●		●			●	●	●				●				
Engineering										●										●					●				
General		●								●			●						○		●				●			●	
History of Science	○	●						●	●					●						●					●			●	
Mathematics										●										●					●				
Neuroscience						●			○				●	●						●					●				
Physics										●										●					●				
Statistics										○										●					●				
Zoology		●		●						○						●				●					●			●	
Slavic Studies			●	●			●	○				○						●		●				●		●			
Sociology			●	●	●			●	○			●			●	●	●		●		●	●	●			●	●	●	○
Social Justice	●			●	●			●	●			●			●	●	●		●		●	●	●			●	●		
Sports		●	●		●	●					○		●		●			●				●	○						
Travel and Tourism		●		●	●						○				○			○		●			○						
Urban Studies			●	●						●	●				●		●	●			●	●	●	●			●	●	

● press acquires in this area
○ press is NOT actively acquiring but has backlist

-11-

Matrix of university press acquisition areas.

Legend:
● press acquires in this area
○ press is NOT actively acquiring but has backlist

	Cincinnati	Colorado	Columbia	Concordia	Cork	Cornell	Delaware	Duke	Florida	Fordham	Gallaudet	GBHEM Publishing	George Mason	Georgetown	Georgia	Getty	Harvard	Hawaii	Illinois	IMF	Indiana	INSTAP	IFPRI	Iowa	Johns Hopkins	Kansas	Kent State	Kentucky	Leuven	Lever	Liverpool	Louisiana
African Studies	●					●			●								●		●		●			●				●				
African American Studies	●					○		●	●	●	○				●		●		●							●	●		●		●	●
American Studies	●					○		●	●	●			●		●		●		●						●	●	●	●	●		●	●
Anthropology	●	●				●		●	●	●	●				●	●	●	●		●						○			●	●		
Archeology		●			●	●			●						●	●		●				●						●	●			
Arts			●					●							●	●	●								●	●		●	●			
Architecture			●				●		●	●				●	●	●	○				●					●	○	○	●	●	●	
Art Criticism			●					●	●						●														●	●	●	
Comics			●												●														●	●		
Dance			●				●		●							○	●												●	●		
Fashion and Textiles			●												●	●														●		
Folk Art			●					●							●				●											●		
Film	●	●	●		●	●		●		●					●			●	●		●				○	●		●	●	●		
Fine Arts and Art History		●	●	○	●	●									●	●		●	●		●					●		●	●	●		
Music & Music Theory		●	●	○	●	●									●		●	●	●		●							○	●	●		
Photography		●	●		●	●		●	●						●	●												○	●	●		
Popular Culture		●	●			●	●								●			●	●	●					●	●	●		●	●	●	
Television			●												●														●	●		
Theater			●				●	●	○							○								●				○	●	●	●	
Asian Studies	●	●	●			●	●	●		●				●			●	●						●				●	●	●	●	
Biography and Memoir		●			●		●	●	●	●	●		●		●		●	●	●		●			●	●	●	●	●				
Business and Management			●			●				●			●				●			●												
Caribbean Studies					●	●	●								●		●												●	●	●	
Child Development	●						●																	●								
Classics					●					●				●	●						●			●				●	●			
Criminology	●				●										●											●		●				
Demography																							●									
Disability Studies	●		●			●		●	●						●				●					●				●				
European Studies			●		●	●	●	●			●			●				●			●			●	○			●	●	●		
Economics		●				●				●		●			●			●		●		●		●	●			○				
Education	●		●	●	●	●		●	●	●	●				●				●	●	●			○	●	●						
Folklore	●		●	●	●		●								●		●							○							●	
Food & Agriculture														●			●	●			●	●			●	●	●				
Agriculture				●										●			●	●			●	●		●								
Cooking							●							●		○			●						●							
Food & Culture		●	●				●	●						●			●	●			●	●			●	●	●	●				●
History of Food		●	●											●	●		●	●			●	●			●	●	●					●
Geography			●	●		●	●							●			●	●	●						●			●		●		●
Gender and Sexuality Studies	●		●		○	●		●						●			●	●	●		●			●		●		●	●	●	●	
LGBTQIA Studies			●			●		●	●					●			●	●	●		●			●				●	●	●	●	
Women's Studies			●	●	●	●		●	●	○				●			●	●	●		●			●		●		●	●	●	●	
Health & Medicine	●					●								●										●								
Addiction Studies														●										●								
Aging		●												●										●								
History of Medicine				●				●						●										●	●	●		●				
Public Health			●	●		●		●					○		●									●	●	●		●				
History	●		●		●	●		●	●				●				●							●	●	●	●	●		●		
African					●				●						●						●								●	●	●	●
American		●	●		●	●	●	●	●	●	●		●		●		●	●		●				●	●	●	●	●		●	●	●
Ancient	●			●	●	●									●	●	●				●			●				●	●	●		
Asian		●			●		●						●		●	●	●											●	●	●		
Australasian					●										●														●			
British					●	●							●		●										●			●	●			
Canadian			●																										●			
Caribbean					●	●			●				●		●									●				●	●	●		
Central American	●				●	●			●				●		●									●				●	●	●		
Eastern European			●										●		●				●						●			●	●			
European			●	●	●	●			●				●	●	●									●	●			●	●	●		●
Latin American	●				●	●			●				●	●	●									○				●	●	●		
Medieval			●	●	●				●				●	●	●						●			○				●	●	●		
Middle Eastern	●	●			●	○			●				●		●				●									●	●			
South American	●				●	●			●				●		●																	

Subject acquisition matrix by university press. Legend: ● press acquires in this area; ○ press is NOT actively acquiring but has backlist.

Subject	Cincinnati	Colorado	Columbia	Concordia	Cork	Cornell	Delaware	Duke	Florida	Fordham	Gallaudet	GBHEM Publishing	George Mason	Georgetown	Georgia	Getty	Harvard	Hawaii	Illinois	IMF	Indiana	INSTAP	IFPRI	Iowa	Johns Hopkins	Kansas	Kent State	Kentucky	Leuven	Lever	Liverpool	Louisiana
Immigration	●	●	●			●		●	●	●				●			●	●	●					●	●				●		●	●
Indigenous Studies	●	●		●		●		●										●	●					●	●	●			●			
Information and Communications			●							●			●				●		●					●					●			
Information Science			●														●				●		●	●					●			
Internet Studies								●									●												●			
Journalism and Media Studies		●	●					●		●					●														●		●	
International Relations		●	●			●								●							●			●				●	●	●		
Labor	●		●			●		●	○												●			●	●			●				
Language									●	●				●			●	●														
Dictionaries and Lexicals										●				●				●														
Linguistic Theory										●				●			●															
Language Texts														●				●				●										
Writing and Style Guides		●															●							●								
Latin American Studies	●	●						●	●	●							●							●							●	●
Law and Legal Studies							●		●	●	●				○		●		●					●				●				
Literature (Creative)									●	●							●		●								●					
Creative Nonfiction		○							●								●							●	○			●				
Fiction										●							●	○						●	○			●				●
Poetry		○							○	●	●						●							●	○	●		●				●
Drama																																
Children's																	○															
Translations		●					●		●					●			●															
Literature (Scholarly)						●	●	●		●							●	●						●					○	●	●	
Literary Criticism		●	●	●	●	●	●	●	●	●					●		●	○			○			●	●		●	○	●	●	●	●
History		●	●	●	●	●	●	●	●	●					●		●	●						●	●			●	●	●	●	●
Theater Studies					●	●	○	●	●									○						●	○			●				
Medieval Studies						●	●	●	●							●	●				●			●	○				●		●	
Military Studies								●									●		●		●	●		●	●	●	●	●				●
Pacific Studies									●								●	●						●								
Philosophy		●		○				●	○	○							●	○							○			○	●	●		
Political Science/Public Policy	●	○	●	●		●		●	●			●		●	●	●	●				●				●	●	●	●				○
Psychology				●									●	○			●							●	○							
Race and Class Studies	●		●		●		●	●	●					●			●	●	●					●	●			●		●	●	●
Reference and Guidebooks	●								○					●			●	●	●					●	●			●				●
Religion/Religious Studies			●			●		●	●	●		●	●	○			●	●	●								○	●				
Buddhism		●		●													●	●														
Christianity								●	●	●		●					●												●			
Hinduism														●			●															
Indigenous Religions														●			●	●														
Islam		●		●					○								●				●								●			
Judaism									○	●				●			●				●											
Renaissance Studies						●		●	●							●	●								○			●				
Science & Mathematics				●													●							●								
Astronomy		●															●	●						●								
Biological Science	●	●		●					●								●							●								
Botany	●			●					●								●															
Chemistry																																
Computer Science																	●															
Ecology and Conservation	●	●				●		●	●						●		●	●						●		●		●	●			
Earth and Environmental	●	●				●	●		●	●							●	●						●		●		●	●			●
Engineering																																
General		●															●	●						●								
History of Science							●										●							●				●	●			
Mathematics																	●							●								
Neuroscience		●															●							●								
Physics																	●							●								
Statistics																							●	●								
Zoology					●												●							●								
Slavic Studies					●												●					●										
Sociology	●	●	●	●	●	●		●		●	●		●		●		●	●	●					●								
Social Justice	●	●	●			●		●						●			●	●	●		●						●	●	●	●	●	●
Sports				●				●	●	●					●					●				●	●	●	●	●				
Travel and Tourism		●				●			●	●					●											○						
Urban Studies	●		●	●		●		●	●						●		●	●	●						●			●				●

● press acquires in this area
○ press is NOT actively acquiring but has backlist

	Manchester	Manitoba	Marquette	Marine Corps	Massachusetts	McGill-Queen's	Medieval Institute	Mercer	Michigan	Michigan State	Minnesota	Minnesota Hist.	Mississippi	Missouri	MIT	MLA	MOMA	National Acad.	National Gallery	Naval	Nebraska	Nevada	New Mexico	New South Wales	New York	North Carolina	North Texas
African Studies	●					●			●	●	●					●		●			●						
African American Studies	●			●			●	●	●	●	●	●	●		●		●				●		●		●	●	
American Studies	●			●				●	○	●	●	●	●		●		●			●	●	●	●		●	●	●
Anthropology	●				●			○	●	●										●		●	○	●	●		
Archeology	●				●	●		●	○										●		●		●	○	○		
Arts		●	●			●			●			●	●	●							●				●		
Architecture	●			●	●			○	●	●	○	●	●	●		●	●	●					●	●		●	
Art Criticism				●				○	●				●		●	●	●						●			●	
Comics											●															●	
Dance	●			●				●	○	○			○		●												
Fashion and Textiles				●				○	●			○															
Folk Art				●				○		●			●				●				●				●		
Film	●			●			●		●		●	●	●		●						●		●				
Fine Arts and Art History	●	●		●	●	●	○	○	●			●		●		●				●	●					
Music & Music Theory			●	●	●	●	○	●	●	●	●							○					●	●	
Photography	●	●		●				○	●	●	●		●		●		●		●						
Popular Culture	●			●	●	●	●	●	○	●	●	●	●	●							●	●	●	●	
Television				●				○	●		●	●	○									●			
Theater	●			●				●	○	○	●		●								●				
Asian Studies	●			●				●	○	●			●		●		●				●	●			
Biography and Memoir	●		○	●	●		●	○	○	●	●	●	●		●			●	●	●	●		●	●	●
Business and Management	●			●				○					●		●									
Caribbean Studies	●			○	●			○	●		●		●		●		●				●			●	
Child Development								○			●	●	●											
Classics				○	●	●	●	●	○				●										○	
Criminology				●				●			●		●		●				●		●	●
Demography				●				○		●			●									
Disability Studies				●	●		●		●		●		○		●		●			●	●	
European Studies	●			○	●			○	●		●		●		●		●					
Economics	●			●				○			●		●		●							
Education				●	●			●	●		●	●	●				●		●		
Folklore				●				○	●		●	●	●			●	●		●	●	○
Food & Agriculture				●	●			●		●	●		●		●	●	●	
Agriculture				●	●			○	○	●	●		●		●		○	
Cooking				●				●	●	●			●			●	●
Food & Culture		●		●	●		●	●	●	●		●			●	●	●	●
History of Food		●		●	●			●		●	●			●	●	●	●	●
Geography		●		○	●			○	●		●			●	●	○
Gender and Sexuality Studies	●			●	●			●	●	●	●	●	●		●		●	●	●
LGBTQIA Studies	●			●	●			●	●	●	●	●		○	●	●	●	●
Women's Studies	●			●	●			●	●	●	●	●	●	○	●	●	●	●
Health & Medicine				●	●			○	●		●		●	
Addiction Studies				●				○			○		●	
Aging				●				○			○		●	●
History of Medicine	●	●		●	●		○	○	●		●		●	●
Public Health	●			●			○	○	●	○	●		●	●	●	●	●
History	●		○	●	●	●			●	●	●		●	●	●	●	●	●	●
African	●			●			●	●			●	●	●
American	●		●	●	●		●	●	●		●	●		●	●	●	●	●	●
Ancient				●	●	●	●	○			●	●
Asian	●			●			●	○	●		●	●	●
Australasian				●			○		●	●
British	●	●		●			○	●		●	●	●
Canadian	●	●		●			○		●	●
Caribbean				●			●	●	●	●	●	●
Central American				●			○		●	●
Eastern European				●			○		●
European	●		○	●			●	●	●	●	●
Latin American	●			●			○	●	●	●	●
Medieval			●	●	●		●	○
Middle Eastern				●			○	●
South American				●			○	●	●	●

● press acquires in this area
○ press is NOT actively acquiring but has backlist

-14-

	Manchester	Manitoba	Marquette	Marine Corps	Massachusetts	McGill-Queen's	Medieval Institute	Mercer	Michigan	Michigan State	Minnesota	Minnesota Hist.	Mississippi	Missouri	MIT	MLA	MOMA	National Acad.	National Gallery	Naval	Nebraska	Nevada	New Mexico	New South Wales	New York	North Carolina	North Texas
Immigration		●			●	●		○	●	●	●							●						●		●	●
Indigenous Studies		●			●	●		○	●	●	●	●	●		●			●			●			●	●		●
Information and Communications	●			●	●	●				●				●	●			●			●						
Information Science					●					○					●			●									
Internet Studies					●				●	○	●				●			●					●				
Journalism and Media Studies	●			●	●	●			●	●	●		●	●	●						●				●		●
International Relations			●		●											○		●									
Labor					●	●			●	●	●		○		●	●		●							●		
Language					●				●	●					●						●						
Dictionaries and Lexicals					●					○	○				●						●						
Linguistic Theory					●					○					●												
Language Texts					●				●	●					●						●						
Writing and Style Guides									●	○				●									●				
Latin American Studies	●				●				○	○	○	●			●		●			●	●		●		●		
Law and Legal Studies	●			●	●				○	●	●				●			●		●	●	●	●		●	○	●
Literature (Creative)					●											○					●	●			●		
Creative Nonfiction					●	●	○		○			○	●		●						●	●	●	●		●	●
Fiction					●		●		○	○	●				○						●	●	●		●		●
Poetry	●				●	●		●	○	○											●	●	●				●
Drama									○	○	○																
Children's										○							●								●		
Translations	●				●	●			○	●	●				●						●		●				
Literature (Scholarly)	●				●	●						●	●	●	●						●		●			●	●
Literary Criticism	●	●			●	●	●		○	○	●		●	●	●	●					●		●		●	●	●
History	●				●	●	●	●		○	●		●	●	●										●	●	●
Theater Studies					●	●			○	●	●		○	●	●										●		
Medieval Studies	●		●		●	●	●	●	○	○					●												
Military Studies			●	●	●					●		○	●	●				●			●	●		●	●	●	●
Pacific Studies					●				○	●							●	●			●						
Philosophy	●		●		●		●		●	●			●	●				○									
Political Science/Public Policy	●		●	●	●				●	●	●	●		●	●			●			●	●			●	●	
Psychology					●					○					●			●									
Race and Class Studies					●	●		●	●	●	●	●	●	●	○			●			●				●	●	
Reference and Guidebooks	●								○		○				●			●		●			○			●	
Religion/Religious Studies			●			●		●																		●	●
Buddhism					●			●	●		○																
Christianity					●	●		●	●	●	○															●	●
Hinduism					●			●	●	●	○															●	
Indigenous Religions										●	○												●			●	
Islam					●	●		●	●	●	○											●				●	●
Judaism					●	●		●	●	●	○	○													●	●	●
Renaissance Studies			●		●	●	●		○	○	○							●							●		
Science & Mathematics					●					●						●		●					●				
Astronomy										○						●		●				●					
Biological Science					●											●		●				●					
Botany					●				●	○						●		●				●					
Chemistry					●					○						●		●									
Computer Science					●					○						●		●									
Ecology and Conservation					●	●			●	●	●	●	●	●		●				●		●		●	●	●	○
Earth and Environmental					●	●				●		●	●	●		●					●	●		●	●	●	○
Engineering										○						●		●									
General					●					○						●						●					
History of Science	●				●	●				●	●			●	●			●					●				
Mathematics										○						●		●									
Neuroscience					●					○						●		●				●					
Physics					●					○						●		●									
Statistics									○	○						●		●			●						
Zoology					●					●						●		●									
Slavic Studies					●					○							●										
Sociology	●				●				○	●	●					○		●							●	●	
Social Justice		●	○		●	●			●	●	●			●				●					●		●	●	
Sports	●				●	●		●	○	○	●	●						●				●		●		●	
Travel and Tourism					●	●			○	●	○												●	●		●	
Urban Studies	●	○	●	●	●				●	●	●			●	●			●					●	●		●	

● press acquires in this area
○ press is NOT actively acquiring but has backlist

	Northern Illinois	Northwestern	Notre Dame	Ohio	Ohio State	Oklahoma	Oregon State	Otago	Ottawa	Oxford	Pennsylvania	Penn State	Pittsburgh	Princeton	Puerto Rico	Purdue	RAND	Regina	RIT	Rochester	Rockefeller	Russell Sage	Rutgers	St. Josephs	SBL Press	South Carolina	South Dakota Hist.	Southern Illinois	Stanford	SUNY
African Studies					●					●		●		●						●			○							
African American Studies		●	●	●	●	●	●				●	●		●	●					●		●	●	●		○	●	○	●		●
American Studies	○	●		●	●	●				●	●	●	●		●					●		●	●	●					●	●
Anthropology	○			●		●	●			●			●	●	●		●	○				●	●						●	
Archeology				●		●	●	●		●	●	●	●		●									●				○		
Arts	○						●	●	●	●		●		●																
Architecture	○			●		●				●	●	●	●	●	●			●		●							●			
Art Criticism		●		●		●				●		●		●															●	
Comics				●	●							●		●						●				●						
Dance										●																				
Fashion and Textiles				●						○			●																	
Folk Art				○		●				○																				
Film		●	●	●	●					●		●	●	○	●		●		●	●	●		●					○	●	
Fine Arts and Art History	●		●	○		●		●		●	○	●	●	●	●		●	○	●			●	●			○		●		
Music & Music Theory				●						●		●		○	●				●									●		
Photography				●		●				●		●		●	●		○	●	●									○		
Popular Culture		●	●	●	●	●		●		●		●	●						●	●		●								●
Television				●	●					●									●	●		●								
Theater	○	●		○				●		●								●	●	●		○					●			
Asian Studies	●		●				●		●	●	●		●			●				○							●		●	●
Biography and Memoir	●	○	●	●	●	●	●	●	●	●				●	●		●	●	●				○			●	●	●	●	●
Business and Management			●	●	○					●			●	●		●		●											●	
Caribbean Studies			●	○	●					●			●			●														●
Child Development				○				○		●				●		●	●	●		●										
Classics		●	●		●	●				●	●			●	●			●		●			○		●			○		
Criminology				○					●	●				●				●		●		●					●			
Demography										●			○	●	●		●		●		●		●							
Disability Studies				○	●					●	●		●			●	●	●					○							
European Studies	○	●	●		○					●	●	●	●		●		●		●			●								
Economics										●			●	●		●	●	●		●			●						●	
Education				○					●	●			●	●		●	●	●		●		●	●			○			○	●
Folklore			○		●		●			●				●														●		
Food & Agriculture					●					●							●			●			●				●			
Agriculture	○			●	○					●				●	●	●														
Cooking				●						●																				
Food & Culture		●		●			●			●		●						●				●								
History of Food				●		●				●								●				●								
Geography					●					●			●		●		●			●			●							
Gender and Sexuality Studies		●		●			●			●				●		●	●	●		●			●						●	●
LGBTQIA Studies			○	●	●	●	●	●		●				●		●	●			●										●
Women's Studies	○	●		●	●	●	●	●		●				●		●	●	●		●		●	●	●		●	●	●	●	●
Health & Medicine										●	●					●	●			●			●							
Addiction Studies				●						●								●					●							
Aging										●							●					●	●	●						
History of Medicine				●	○				○	●	●	●	●	●			●		●			●	●			○			○	
Public Health				●	○					●		●		●	●	●	●		●			●	●			○				
History	●		●							●		●		●	●								○			●		●		
African				●						●		●		●						●										
American	●	●	●	●	○	●	●			●	●	●	●	●		●		●		●			●	●		●	●	●	●	●
Ancient					●					●	●	●		●									●		●					
Asian	●			●						●				●															●	●
Australasian							●			●				●																
British	○		●	○	○					●		●	●																●	
Canadian								●	●	●			●					●												
Caribbean										●		●	●										●							
Central American			○		●					●		●	●										●					●		
Eastern European	●	●		●	○					●		●	●		●					●			●					●		
European	●	●	●		○					●		●	●	●	●					●			●					●		
Latin American		●	●	●		●				●		●	●	●	●	●				●			●					●	●	●
Medieval	●									●	●	●		●																
Middle Eastern										●		●	●										●		●				●	●
South American			●							●		●	●		●								●						●	

● press acquires in this area
○ press is NOT actively acquiring but has backlist

Subject	Northern Illinois	Northwestern	Notre Dame	Ohio	Ohio State	Oklahoma	Oregon State	Otago	Ottawa	Oxford	Pennsylvania	Penn State	Pittsburgh	Princeton	Puerto Rico	Purdue	RAND	Regina	RIT	Rochester	Rockefeller	Russell Sage	Rutgers	St. Josephs	SBL	South Carolina	South Dakota Hist.	Southern Illinois	Stanford	SUNY
Immigration			●	●						●	●											●	●					●	●	
Indigenous Studies	○	●		●	●	●	●	●	●	●	●							●					●					●		●
Information and Communications			●							●		●	●	●																
Information Science										●			●		●															
Internet Studies							●	●		●			●																	
Journalism and Media Studies		○	●	●		●				●	●		●		●	●							●					○		●
Labor										●			●																	●
International Relations						●				●			●							●	●					●	○			
Language										●			●	●																
Dictionaries and Lexicals				○		○				●			●																	
Linguistic Theory					○	○				●	●		●																○	
Language Texts	○			○	●					●			●																	
Writing and Style Guides				○						●			●															●		
Latin American Studies	●	●	○	●	●					●				●	●	●		●		●			●						●	●
Law and Legal Studies	○		●	○	●			●	●	●			●	●		●			●	○								●	●	
Literature (Creative)	○			●		●					●															○			●	
Creative Nonfiction		●	●	●	●		●	●	●							●										●			●	●
Fiction	○	●	●	●	●	●	●						●													○			●	●
Poetry	○	●	●	●	●	○		●			●	●	●			●							○			○		●		
Drama		●	○																											
Children's																										○	●			
Translations	●	●	○	●				●			●					●														
Literature (Scholarly)	●	●	●			●		●		●	●		●													●		●		
Literary Criticism	●	●	●	●	●	○		●	●	●	●	●	●	●	●					●			●			●		●	○	●
History	●	●	●	○	●			●	●	●	●	●	●							●			●			●		●		
Theater Studies	○	●		○	○			●	●	●																		●		
Medieval Studies			●		●				○	●	●	●		●																
Military Studies			●		●	●				●			○			●							●			○	●	●		●
Pacific Studies							●	●	●															○						
Philosophy	○	●	●	●						●	●		●	●	●		●		●	○								○	●	●
Political Science/Public Policy	●		●	●	○	●			●	●	●		●	●	●		●		●			●	●			●	●	●	●	●
Psychology								○	●	●			●	●								●								●
Race and Class Studies		●		●	●	●				●	●		●	●						●		●	●			●	●	●	●	●
Reference and Guidebooks		●	●		●		●			●	●		●	●	●											●	●			
Religion/Religious Studies	●		●							●	●		●		●					●		●			●	●	○		●	●
Buddhism										●	●				●															●
Christianity	●		●							●	●	●	●		●					●		●	●		●	●	○		●	●
Hinduism										●					●															●
Indigenous Religions							●	●		●					●					●						○				●
Islam			●							●	●				●							●				●		●	●	
Judaism										●	●	●	●		●		●					●			●	●	○		●	●
Renaissance Studies		○		●					○	●	●									●			●							
Science & Mathematics										●	●			●	●	●														
Astronomy										●	●			●	●															
Biological Science					●					●				●	●						●	●								
Botany					●					●				●	●														○	
Chemistry										●					○															
Computer Science										●					●			●	●	●										
Ecology and Conservation			●		●					●				●	●	●	●	●	●				●							●
Earth and Environmental				○		●	●			●	●		●	●	●		●	●					●							●
Engineering			●							●										●										
General										●				●																
History of Science	○	●	●			●		●	●	●	●			●	●			●		●			●	●						
Mathematics										●				●																
Neuroscience										●				●																
Physics										●				●																
Statistics										●				●								●								
Zoology										●																				
Slavic Studies	●	●		●						●	●			●	●		●		●		●		●							
Sociology			●	○						●	●		●	●	●		●						●	●					●	●
Social Justice	●	●		●				●	●	●	●									●		●	●			●		●	●	●
Sports	○		●	●									●									●				●		●	○	
Travel and Tourism			●	○		●				●	●											●				●	●	●		●
Urban Studies	○		●	○	●	●				●	●		●	●	●		●					●	●				○		●	●

● press acquires in this area
○ press is NOT actively acquiring but has backlist

	Syracuse	Teachers	Temple	Tennessee	Texas	Texas A&M	TCU	Texas Review	Texas Tech	Tokyo	Toronto	Trinity	UCL	U.S. Inst. Peace	Upjohn	Utah	Vanderbilt	Virginia	Washington	Wash. State	Wayne State	Wesleyan	West Indies	West Virginia	Wilfrid Laurier	Wisconsin	Wits	Woodrow Wilson	Yale
African Studies													●	●			●	●								●	●	●	●
African American Studies	●		●	●	●	●			●								●	●	●			●	○		●		●		●
American Studies	●		●	●	●			●	●			●					●	●	●	●	●	○				○			●
Anthropology	●		●	●	●	●			●	●		●			●	●	●		●	●	●			●	○	●	●		●
Archeology			●	●	●				●	●		●			●	●			●	○						●			●
Arts			●	●	●				●	●		●					●		●										●
Architecture			●	●	●	●		●	●	●	●	●		●			●		●	●		○							●
Art Criticism								●	●			●										●					●		●
Comics			●						●																	●			●
Dance									●												●				○				●
Fashion and Textiles					●																								●
Folk Art																									●				●
Film	●			●				●	●			●			●			●	○			●	●	●					●
Fine Arts and Art History	●			●	●			●	●	●		●			●		●	○				●		●					●
Music & Music Theory			○	●	●	●		●	●			●			●		●	●				●		●					●
Photography			●	●			●	●	●	●					●			●				●		●					●
Popular Culture	●		●	●			●		●			●			●		●					●	○	●					●
Television	●		●					●							●			●				●							●
Theater								●	●															●					●
Asian Studies		●			●	●		●			●						●							●		●		●	●
Biography and Memoir	○		●	●	●	●	●	●	●		●	●	●			●	●	●	●	●	●		●		●	●	●		●
Business and Management								●	●			●					●				●		●	●		●			●
Caribbean Studies			○	●					●			●			●	●		○		●	●		●			●			●
Child Development		●					●	●				●					●							●					●
Classics			●					●	●	●		●							○					●		●			●
Criminology			●				●		●		●				●						●		●						●
Demography								●	●																				●
Disability Studies	●	●						●	●						●	●		●											●
European Studies	●							●	●		●				●	●						●	●			●	●		●
Economics								●	●	●	●	●					●				●		●	●		○		●	●
Education	●	●	●		●		●	●	●	●	●		●		●	●					●	●	●	●		○		●	●
Folklore	●		●	●		●	●	●	●	●	●		●						●					●					●
Food & Agriculture			●	●				●	●											●				●					
Agriculture				●				●										●					○					●	
Cooking			●				●	●	●					●	○						●			●					
Food & Culture		●	●	●		●	●		●	●	●		●		●	●			●	●	●						○		●
History of Food								●	●								●	●											
Geography	●		●	●	●				●	●	●	●		●		●				●	●			●					●
Gender and Sexuality Studies		●		●				●	●		●		●		●	●	●		●	●		●	●	●					
LGBTQIA Studies	●	●	●					●	●				●			●	●					●	●						●
Women's Studies	●	●	●		●	●	●		●	●	●		●	●		●	●		●	●				●	○	●	●		●
Health & Medicine				●					●	●	●		●				●									○			
Addiction Studies									●				●				●												
Aging				●				●	●				●				●												
History of Medicine				●				●	●				●	●			●								○				●
Public Health				●				●	●				●				●			●		●				●			●
History	●			●	●	●	●		●			●	●				●				●				●		●	●	●
African															●			●	●						●	●		●	●
American	●		●	●	●	●	●	●	●	●		●				●	●	●	●	●	●		○		●		●	●	●
Ancient				●					●	●															●			●	●
Asian					●	●		●			●							●							●		●	●	●
Australasian																													●
British								●	●		●	●					●								●	○		●	●
Canadian								●	●											●					●			●	●
Caribbean			○	●					●						●	●						●				○			●
Central American				●					●					●		●										○			●
Eastern European								●	●		●	●							●							●			●
European	●		●					●	●	●	●	●				●	●		●							●		●	●
Latin American				●		●		●	●	●	●		●		●	●										○		●	●
Medieval									●							●			●										●
Middle Eastern	●			●					●				●		●	●	●	●			●								●
South American				●					●				●		●											○			●

● press acquires in this area
○ press is NOT actively acquiring but has backlist

	Syracuse	Teachers	Temple	Tennessee	Texas	Texas A&M	TCU	Texas Review	Texas Tech	Tokyo	Toronto	Trinity	UCL	U.S. Inst. Peace	Upjohn	Utah	Vanderbilt	Virginia	Washington	Wash. State	Wayne State	Wesleyan	West Indies	West Virginia	Wilfrid Laurier	Wisconsin	Wits	Woodrow Wilson	Yale
Immigration		●		●						●			●		●		●	●	●		●					●			
Indigenous Studies	●	●		●	●	●	●		●	●	●		●			●	●	●	●	●	●				●	○	●		●
Information and Communications					○														●					●			●		
Information Science										●																			
Internet Studies										●	●		●																●
Journalism and Media Studies	○			●							●		●						●			●		●	●	○	●	●	●
Labor		●	●	●						●				●		●			●	●						●		●	●
International Relations										●	●																		
Language				●						●	●		●																
Dictionaries and Lexicals										●	●		●		●		●		●							●			
Linguistic Theory										●	●		●													●			
Language Texts										●	○															○			●
Writing and Style Guides										●	○																		
Latin American Studies		●	○	●		●			●		●		●	●		●	●	●		●	●					○		●	●
Law and Legal Studies										●	●	●	●		●			●	●					●		●	○		●
Literature (Creative)	●				●		●																			●			
Creative Nonfiction				●					●	●	●			●			●			●		●		●	●	●	●		●
Fiction	○					●	●														●	●		●	●	●	○		
Poetry	○				●	●	●		●				●			●					●	●		●	●	●	●		●
Drama	○												●						○					●		●			●
Children's																				●									
Translations	●			●							●						●			●	●			●	●				●
Literature (Scholarly)	●		●	●		●	●		●	●	●						●		○					●	●	●			●
Literary Criticism	●	●	●	●		●	●	●	●	●	●						●	●		○	●	●		●	●	●	●	●	●
History	●			●		●	●	●	●	●	●						●	●		●	●	●		●	●		●		●
Theater Studies										●																●			●
Medieval Studies										●	●		●							●				●	○				●
Military Studies			●		●				●		●					●			○	○			●			●			●
Pacific Studies										●			●		●				●							●		●	●
Philosophy	●			●					●	●	●		●			○	○							●		●	●		○
Political Science/Public Policy	●		●	○	●	●			●	●	●		●	●	●		●	●		●			●		●	●	●	●	●
Psychology	○									●	●		●				●			●				●		●		●	●
Race and Class Studies		●	●	●	●	●	●		●		●		●				●	●	●		●		●	●		●		●	●
Reference and Guidebooks										●					●		●	●	●	●		●			●				○
Religion/Religious Studies	●		●	●	●				●		●		●		●		●	●	●	●					●	●		●	●
Buddhism										●							●	●											●
Christianity	●										●					●	●		●			○							●
Hinduism																		●											●
Indigenous Religions				●						●	●					●	●			●									●
Islam	●			●							●				●		●	●	●										●
Judaism	●			●							●							●	●		●								●
Renaissance Studies										●	●		●							○									●
Science & Mathematics							●		●	●	●																		
Astronomy										●	●															○			●
Biological Science				●						●	●	●																	●
Botany	○			●						●	●	●																	●
Chemistry										●	●																		
Computer Science										●	●																		
Ecology and Conservation	○					●			●	●	●	●				●				●				●			●	●	●
Earth and Environmental	○				●	●	●		●	●	●	●				●			●	●	●			●		●	●	●	●
Engineering										●	●																		
General										●	●																		●
History of Science										●	●	●	●		●				●							○			●
Mathematics										●	●																		●
Neuroscience										●	●																		●
Physics										●	●																		●
Statistics										●	●																		
Zoology							●			●	●	●														○			●
Slavic Studies										●	●		●											●				●	●
Sociology	●	●	●		●				●		●		●		●			●	●		●	●		●	●	●	○	●	●
Social Justice	●	●	●	●	●			●		●	●	●					●		●		●		●			●	●		
Sports	●		●	●	●	●	●		●								●			●				●					
Travel and Tourism					●	●					●								●					●					
Urban Studies		●	●		●	●				●	●		●	●		●				●						●	●	●	

● press acquires in this area
○ press is NOT actively acquiring but has backlist

-19-

Presses Publishing Journals

University presses have always been associated with publishing books of merit and distinction. This remains as true today as in the past, but less well appreciated is the extent to which university presses are active in publishing scholarly journals.

Journals form a major part of the publishing program of many presses, and more than half of the association's members produce at least one periodical. University presses publish several hundred scholarly periodicals, including many of the most distinguished in their respective fields.

Each individual press listing also gives the number of journals, if any, that a press publishes and usually lists the titles of journals under the press's editorial program. Many journals are available in both print and electronic versions. For information concerning a specific periodical, readers are advised to consult a copy of the publication before communicating with the press concerned.

The following Association member presses publish journals.

University of Akron Press
The University of Alabama Press
American Historical Association
American Psychiatric Association Publishing
The American School of Classical Studies at Athens
The American University in Cairo Press
Amsterdam University Press
The University of Arkansas Press
Army Press
Athabasca University Press
Brookings Institution Press
University of California Press
Cambridge University Press
The Catholic University of America Press
The University of Chicago Press
The Chinese University Press
University of Cincinnati Press
Cork University Press
Duke University Press
University Press of Florida
Fordham University Press
Gallaudet University Press
George Mason University Press
Georgetown University Press
Getty Publications
University of Hawai'i Press
University of Illinois Press
IMF Publications
Indiana University Press
The Johns Hopkins University Press
The Kent State University Press
Leuven University Press
Liverpool University Press
Manchester University Press
Marine Corps University Press
Marquette University Press
Medieval Institute Publications
Michigan State University Press
Minnesota Historical Society Press

University of Minnesota Press
The MIT Press
Modern Language Association of America
Naval Institute Press
University of Nebraska Press
The University of North Carolina Press
University of North Texas Press
Ohio State University Press
Otago University Press
University of Ottawa Press
Oxford University Press
University of Pennsylvania Press
Pennsylvania State University Press
University of Puerto Rico Press
Purdue University Press
RAND Corporation
RIT Press
The Rockefeller University Press
Russell Sage Foundation
SBL Press
South Dakota Historical Society Press
State University of New York Press
Temple University Press
University of Texas Press
Texas Review Press
Texas Tech University Press
University of Toronto Press, Inc.
UCL Press
Washington State University Press
Wayne State University Press
Wesleyan University Press
The University of the West Indies Press
West Virginia University Press
Wilfrid Laurier University Press
The University of Wisconsin Press

DIRECTORY OF MEMBERS

This section includes a wealth of information on the Association's member presses, including current street and mailing addresses, phone and fax numbers, email addresses, websites, and social media participation. Most presses also list their sales representatives/distributors for Canada, the UK, and Europe. (Addresses for these representatives are included on page 216)

Each entry contains important information describing that press's editorial program. This includes a list of disciplines published, special series, joint imprints, copublishing programs, and the names of journals published, if any.

Press staff are listed, wherever possible, by the following departments/order: director and administrative staff, acquisitions editorial, electronic publishing, manuscript editorial, design and production, marketing, journals, business, and information systems. In most cases the first person listed within a department is its head. Readers should note, however, that this method of organization is intended to promote ease of use, and is not always indicative of the lines of authority within an individual press.

Information on each press's membership status follows the staff listing. This includes date of press founding, type of membership (regular, affiliate, or introductory), year admitted to the Association, title output for 2017 and 2018, the number of journals published, and the total number of titles currently in print.

Abilene Christian University Press

ACU Box 29138
Abilene, TX 79699

Phone: 325.674.2720
Fax: 325.674.6471

Orders:
Phone: 325.674.2720 or 877.816.4455
Email: orders@acupressbooks.com

Websites and Social Media:
Website: www.acupressbooks.com;
www.leafwoodpublishers.com; www.acupressbookclub.com
Facebook: Facebook.com/ACUPress
Twitter: @ACUPress
YouTube: www.youtube.com/user/leafwoodpublishers

Staff
Director ACU Press & Leafwood Publishers: Jason Fikes (325.674.2720;
    email: jason.fikes@acu.edu)
Director of Sales & Operations: Duane Anderson (325.674.2720;
    email: duane.anderson@acu.edu)
Managing Editor: Managing Editor: Rebecka Scott (325.674.2761; email: rrs12c@acu.edu)
Office Manager: Taylor Humphrey (325.674.2720; email: taylor.humphrey@acu.edu)

Number of Press Staff: 4

Regular Member
Established: 1984

Admitted to the Association: 2008
(intro. member)
Admitted to the Association: 2012
(full member)

Title output 2018: 27
Titles currently in print: 601

Title output 2018: 33

Editorial Program
Religion in American culture; biblical studies and Christian spirituality theology; Texas regional studies; history and theory of higher education (with an emphasis on faith-based education); international and multicultural studies; literary works.
Book series: Christianity and Literature; Faith-Based Higher Education; History and Theology of the Stone-Campbell Movement; Texas History and Culture
Imprints: Leafwood Publishers

The University of Akron Press

120 E. Mill Street, Suite 415
Akron, OH 44308

Cust. Service/Order Fulfillment:
Toll-free: 800.247.6553
Fax: 419.281.6883
Email: orders@btpubservices.com

Website and Social Media:
Website: www.uakron.edu/uapress
Facebook: www.facebook.com/UAkronPress
Twitter: @uakronpress
Instagram: @uakronpress

Canadian Representative:
Magenta Entertainment

UK Representative:
Roundhouse Group

Staff
Director: Jon Miller (330.972.6202; email: mjon@uakron.edu)
Editorial & Design: Amy Freels (330.972.5342; email: afreels@uakron.edu)
Production & Manufacturing: Thea Ledendecker (330.972.2795; email: thea@uakron.edu)
Marketing Manager: Julie Gammon (330.972.6962; email: jgammon@uakron.edu)

Number of Press Staff: 4

Regular Member
Established: 1988
Title output 2017: 10
Titles currently in print: 204

Admitted to the Association: 1997
Title output 2018: 11
Journals published: 1

Editorial Program
Regional trade books, scholarly books, and poetry, with special interests in applied politics, contemporary poetics, psychology, and regional culture and history. The Press distributes the publications of Principia Press. Submissions of poetry are only accepted during the annual poetry prize.
Journal: *The International Journal of Ethical Leadership*
Book series: Akron Series in Contemporary Poetics; Akron Series in Poetry; Bliss Institute Series; Center for the History of Psychology Series; Critical Editions in Early American Literature; & Law; and Ohio History and Culture

The University of Alabama Press

Street Address:
200 Hackberry Lane
Tuscaloosa, AL 35401

Mailing Address:
Box 870380
Tuscaloosa, AL 35487-0380

Phone: 205.348.5180
Fax: 205.348.9201
Email: (user I.D.)@uapress.ua.edu

Website and Social Media:
Website: www.uapress.ua.edu
Facebook: www.facebook.com/
UniversityALPress
Twitter: @univofalpress
Instagram: @univofalpress

Order Fulfillment:
The University of Alabama Press
Chicago Distribution Center
11030 South Langley Avenue
Chicago, IL 60628
Phone: 773.568.1550
Fax: 773.660.2235

UK/European Distributor:
Eurospan

Canadian Representative:
Codasat Canada

Staff
Director: Linda Manning (205.348.1560; email: lmanning)
Assistant to the Director: Kristen Hop (205.348.5180; email: khop)
Rights and Permissions Coordinator: TBA (205.348.1561; email: rights)
Acquisitions Editorial: Dan Waterman, Editor-in-Chief and Acquisitions Editor, Humanities (litera-
    ture and criticism, rhetoric and communication, African American studies, public administration,
    theater, law and legal studies) (205.348.5538; email: waterman)
    Senior Acquisitions Editors: Wendi Schnaufer (archaeology, anthropology, ethnohistory, Native
    American studies, food studies) (205.348.1568; email: wschnaufer); Claire Lewis Evans (history,
    natural history and the environment, history of science, technology, agriculture, and medicine)
    (205.348.7108; email: cevans)
Manuscript Editorial: Jon Berry, Managing Editor (205.348.9708; email: jberry)
    Assistant Managing Editor: Joanna Jacobs (205.348.1563; email: jjacobs)
    Project Editor: Kelly Finefrock-Creed (205.348.1565; email: kcreed)
    Editorial Assistant: Carol Connell (205.348.5183; email: cconnell)
Design and Production: Rick Cook, Production Manager (205.348.1571; email: rcook)
    Art Director and Designer: Michele Quinn (205.348.1570; email: mquinn)
    Book Designer and Production Assistant: David Nees (205.348.9665; email: dnees)
Marketing: Clint Kimberling, Director of Sales and Marketing (205.348.1566; email: ckimberling)
    Sales Manager: Kristi Henson (205.348.9534; email: khenson)
    Marketing Coordinator: Blanche Sarratt (205.348.5180; email: bsarratt)
Business: Rosalyn Carr, Business Manager (205.348.1567; email: rcarr)
    Accounting Specialist: Allie Harper (205.348.1564; email: aharper)

Number of Press Staff: 17

Regular Member
Established: 1945
Title output 2017: 71
Titles currently in print: 1,800

Admitted to the Association: 1964
Title output 2018: 64
Journals published: 3

Editorial Program
African American studies; American history; American literature and criticism; American religious
history; American social and cultural history; anthropology; archaeology, American, Caribbean,
southern and historical; creative non-fiction; ethnohistory; Judaic studies; Latin-American studies;
linguistics, esp. dialectology; maritime history; military history; Native American studies; natural
history and environmental studies; public administration; regional studies; rhetoric and communi-

cation; southern history and culture; sports history; theatre. Submissions are not invited in poetry, fiction, or drama.
Journals: *Theatre History Studies; Theatre Symposium*
Book series: Alabama: The Forge of History; American Writers Remembered; Archaeology of the American South: New Directions and Perspectives; Atlantic Crossings; Caribbean Archaeology and Ethnohistory; Classics in Southeastern Archaeology; Contemporary American Indian Studies; Gosse Nature Guides; Historical Archaeology in South America; Jews and Judaism: History and Culture; Library of Alabama Classics; Modern and Contemporary Poetics; The Modern South; NEXUS: New Histories of Science, Technology, the Environment, Agriculture, and Medicine; NGOgraphies: Ethnographic Reflections on NGOs; Public Administration: Criticism and Creativity; Religion and American Culture; Rhetoric, Culture, and Social Critique; Rhetoric, Law, and the Humanities; Studies in American Literary Realism and Naturalism; War, Memory, and Culture
Imprints: Fiction Collective Two

University of Alaska Press

Mailing Address:
PO Box 756240
Fairbanks, AK 99775-6240

Street Address:
1760 Westwood Way
Fairbanks, AK 99709

Phone: 907.474.5831
Fax: 907.474.5502

Website and Social Media:
Website: www.uapress.alaska.edu
Facebook: www.facebook.com/pages/
    University-of-Alaska-Press/44832289241
Twitter: @ualaskapress

Orders:
Chicago Distribution Center
11030 South Langley Avenue
Chicago, IL 60628-3892
Phone: 800.621.2736
Fax: 800.621.8476

Staff
Director/Acquisitions Editor: Nate Bauer (907.474.5832; email: nate.bauer@alaska.edu)
Production Editor: Krista West (907.474.6413; email: krista.west@alaska.edu)
Publicity Coordinator: Dawn Montano (907.474.6544; email: dawn.montano@alaska.edu)
Sales and Marketing Manager: Laura Walker (907.474.5831; email: laura.walker@alaska.edu)
Editorial Assistant: Elizabeth Laska (907.474.6389; email: eplaska@alaska.edu)

Number of Press Staff: 5

Regular Member
Established: 1967
Title output 2017: 13
Titles currently in print: 268

Admitted to the Association: 1992
Title output 2018: 13

Editorial Program
The University of Alaska Press is recognized as the premier scholarly publisher of books relating to Alaska, the Pacific Rim, and circumpolar North. The Press publishes on topics that include history, politics, and literature; anthropology; Native American studies and art; science and natural history; energy and conservation; environmental studies; geography; biography and memoir; humanities and health; poetry and international poetry; photography; field guides; and children's literature. Submissions are invited in poetry, fiction, and literary nonfiction and should have a strong connection to Alaska or the circumpolar North.
    The Press distributes publications for the following University of Alaska entities: UA Foundation; UA Museum of the North; Alaska Sea Grant College Program; Alaska Native Knowledge Network; and Alaska Native Language Center. The Press also serves as a distributor for various independent publishers.

Book series: Alaska Literary Series; Alaska Writer Laureate; Classic Reprint; Oral Biography; and Rasmuson Library Historical Translation
Imprints: Snowy Owl (trade books)

The University of Alberta Press

Ring House 2
Edmonton AB T6G 2E1
Canada

Phone: 780.492.3662
Fax: 780.492.0719
Email: (user I.D.)@ualberta.ca

Website and Social Media:
Website: www.uap.ualberta.ca
Blog: sites.library.ualberta.ca/ualbertapressblog
Facebook: www.facebook.com/pages/
  University-of-Alberta-Press-UAP/
  18764314500
Twitter: @UAlbertaPress

UK/European Distributor:
Gazelle Academic

Canadian Distributor:
University of Toronto Press
5201 Dufferin Street
Toronto ON M3H 5T8 Canada

Phone: 800.565.9523
Fax: 800.221.9985
Email: utpbooks@utpress.utoronto.ca

US Distributor:
Wayne State University Press
The Leonard N. Simons Building
4809 Woodward Avenue
Detroit MI 48201-1309
Phone: 800.978.7323
313.577.6120
Fax: 313.577.6131
Email: bookorders@wayne.edu

Staff
Director: Douglas Hildebrand (780.492.0717; email: dhildebr)
Business Administrator: Basia Kowal (780.492.3662; email: bkowal)
Senior Editor (Acquisitions): Peter Midgley (780.492.7714; email: pmidgley)
Editor (Production): Mary Lou Roy (780.492.9488; email: marylou.roy)
Digital Coordinator: Duncan Turner (780.492.4945; email: duncan.turner)
Design/Production: Alan Brownoff (780.492.8285; email: alan.brownoff)
Associate Director/Manager Planning & Operations: Cathie Crooks (780.492.5820; email: ccrooks)
Sales/Marketing Assistant: Monika Igali (780.492.7493; email: monika.igali)

Number of Press Staff: 8

Regular Member
Established: 1969
Title output 2017: 18
Titles currently in print: 888

Admitted to the Association: 1983
Title output 2018: 20

Editorial Program
UAlberta Press publishes in the areas of Indigenous studies, Canadian history, arctic and circumpolar studies, literature, anthropology, urban studies, African studies, Islamic studies, race and gender studies, biography, natural history and environmental studies, regional interest, travel narratives, and reference books.
Book series: Mountain Cairns—a series on the history and culture of the Canadian Rockies; Patterns of Northern Traditional Healing;; Robert Kroetsch: Canadian creative writing, short stories and poetry; Wayfarer—literary travel; CLC Kreisel Lecture Series (co-published with the Canadian Literature Centre / Centre de littérature canadienne)
Imprints: Pica Pica Press (textbooks); Gutteridge Books (trade books); Polynya Press (books on the circumpolar north)

American Historical Association

400 A Street, S.E.
Washington, DC 20003-3889

Phone: 202.544.2422
Fax: 202.544.8307
Email: aha@historians.org

Orders:
Oxford University Press
Phone: 800.445.9714
Email: orders.us@oup.com

Website and Social Media:
Website: www.historians.org
Blog: www.historians.org/perspectives
Facebook: www.facebook.com/AHAhistorians
Twitter: @AHAhistorians
YouTube: www.youtube.com/user/historiansorg

Staff
Executive Director: James R. Grossman (202.544.2422; email: jgrossman@historians.org)
Editor, *American Historical Review*: Alex Lichtenstein (812.855.0027; email: ahredit@indiana.edu)
Director of Scholarly Communication and Digital Initiatives: Seth Denbo (202.544.1118 email: sdenbo@historians.org)
Editor, *Perspectives on History*: Allison Miller (202.450.5617; email: amiller@historians.org)
Managing Editor, *Perspectives on History*: Kritika Agarwal (202.544.2422 ext. 133; email: kagarwal@historians.org)
Associate Editor, Web Content and Social Media: Elyse Martin (202.544.2422 ext. 117; emartin@historians.org)
Editorial Assistant: Zoë Jackson (202.544.2422 ext. 119; email: zjackson@historians.org)

Number of Press Staff: 20

Regular Member
Established: 1884
Title output 2017: 2
Titles currently in print: 65

Admitted to the Association: 2005
Title output 2018: 5
Journals published: 1

Editorial Program
The AHA publishes a wide variety of periodical, annual, and other publications of service and interest to the historical profession and the general public. Primary publications are the journals, the *American Historical Review* (published by Oxford University Press) and the monthly news magazine *Perspectives on History*. The Association's other major publication is the annual *Directory of History Departments, Historical Organizations, and Historians*. Beyond that, the AHA publishes a wide range of topical booklets on the practice of history and historical topics. Both the booklets and the annual Directory are distributed by Oxford University Press. On the Web, the Association publishes articles, directories, and documentary materials. The AHA also maintains a daily blog for those interested in the study of the past and the practice of history, and a wiki on archives for history researchers.

American Psychiatric Association Publishing

800 Maine Avenue, SW
Washington, DC 20024

Phone: 703.907.7322
Fax: 703.907.1092
Email: appi@psych.org
Indiv: (user I.D.)@psych.org

Orders:
Phone: 800.368.5777; 888.357.7924
Fax: 703.907.1091

Website and Social Media:
Website: www.appi.org
Facebook: www.facebook.com/AmericanPsychiatricPublishing
Twitter: @APP_Publishing

European Distributor:
NBN International

Canadian Representative:
Login Brothers Canada

Staff
Publisher: John J. McDuffie (202.559.3960; email: jmcduffie)
Acquisitions Manager: Erika Parker (202.609.7114; email: eparker)
Editor-in-Chief: Laura Roberts, M.D., M.A. (202.609.7114)
Director, Digital Publishing and Product Development: Tim Marney (202.559.3468; email: tmarney)
Managing Editor, Books: Greg Kuny (202.609.7083; email: gkuny)
Director of Production: Andrew Wilson (202.683.8310; email: awilson)
Director of Marketing and Sales: Patrick Hansard (202.559.3662; email: phansard)
Associate Director of Marketing: Christie Couture (202.609.7227; email: ccouture)
Editorial Director, Journals: Michael Roy (202.559.3718; email: mroy)
Director of Publishing and Business Operations: Debra Eubanks (202.609.7125; email: deubanks)

Number of Press Staff: 45

Regular Member
Established: 1981
Title output 2017: 32
Titles currently in print: 650

Admitted to the Association: 1993
Title output 2018: 30
Journals published: 5

Editorial Program
Clinical books and monographs in psychiatry and related fields; research monographs; medical textbooks; study guides; and journals. *Diagnostic and Statistical Manual of Mental Disorders, 5th Edition*
Journals: *American Journal of Psychiatry; FOCUS; Journal of Neuropsychiatry; Psychiatric News; Psychiatric Services*
Book series: Clinical Manuals
Imprints: American Psychiatric Association

The American School of Classical Studies at Athens

Publications Office:
6–8 Charlton Street
Princeton, NJ 08540-5232
Phone: 609.683.0800
Fax: 609.924.0578

Orders:
Casemate Academic
Phone: 610.853.9131
Fax: 610.853.9146
Email: info@casemateacademic.com

Website and Social Media:
Website: www.ascsa.edu.gr/publications
Twitter: @ascsapubs

UK Representative:
Oxbow Books
Phone: (44) 1226-734350
Email: orders@oxbowbooks.com

Canadian Representative:
Casemate Academic

Staff
Director of Publications: Carol A. Stein (ext. 16; email: castein@ascsa.org)
Editor of *Hesperia*: Jennifer Sacher (ext. 22; email: jsacher@ascsa.org)
Senior Project Editor: Colin Whiting (ext. 17; email: cwhiting@ascsa.org)
Project Editor: Destini Price (ext. 21; email: dprice@ascsa.org)
Production Manager: Sarah George Figueira (ext. 18; email: sgf@ascsa.org)
Editorial Assistant: Megan R. M. Mendonça (ext. 26; email: mmendonca@ascsa.org)

Number of Press Staff: 6

Regular Member
Established: 1881

Admitted to the Association: 2008
(Introductory Member)
Admitted to the Association: 2012
(Assoc. Member)

Title output 2017: 7
Titles currently in print: 160

Title output 2018: 5
Journals published: 2

Editorial Program
All fields of Greek archaeology, art, epigraphy, history, materials science, ethnography, and litera-
ture, from earliest prehistoric times onward. A particular focus is on publishing the work of the
American School of Classical Studies at Athens, a research and teaching institutions founded in
1881 and based in Athens, Greece.
Journals: *Hesperia, The New Griffon*
Book series: Agora Picture Books; Ancient Art and Architecture in Context; The Argive Heraion;
The Athenian Agora; Corinth; Gennadeion Monographs; Hesperia Supplements; Isthmia; Lerna;
Nemea Valley Archaeological Project; Samothrace

The American University in Cairo Press

113 Kasr el Aini Street
PO Box 2511
Cairo, Egypt 11511

US Office:
420 Fifth Avenue
New York, NY 10018-2729

Phone: 202.2797.6926
Fax: 202.2794.1440
Email: aucpress@aucegypt.edu
Indiv: (user I.D.)@aucegypt.edu

Phone: 212.730.8800
Fax: 212.730.1600

Website and Social Media:
Websites: www.aucpress.com, www.hoopoefiction.com
Facebook: www.facebook.com/aucpress
Twitter: @aucpress
YouTube: www.youtube.com/user/aucpress

North American Distributor:
Ingram Academic Services

UK and European Distributor:
I.B.Tauris
6 Salem Road
Phone: +44.20.7243.1225
Email: pdavighi@ibtauris.com

Staff
Director: Nigel Fletcher-Jones (202.2797.6888; email: nigel)
Executive Assistant to the Director: Sylvia Maher (email: sylvia)
Associate Director for Editorial Programs and Production: Miriam Fahmy (email: miriam)
Senior Commissioning Editor: Nadia Naqib (email: nnaqib)
Managing Editor: Nadine El-Hadi (email: nadine.elhadi)
Senior Online Editor: Ingrid Wassmann (email: wassmann)
Associate Director, Sales and Marketing: Trevor Naylor (email: trevornaylor)
Marketing and International Rights Manager: Basma El Manialawi (email: basma.manialawi)
North America Marketing Manager (NY City): Tarek El-Elaimy (202.730.8800, ext. 4546; email: telaimy)
North America Senior Acquisition Editor (NY City): Anne Routon (email: anne.routon)

Number of Press Staff: 13

Regular Member
Established: 1960
Title output 2017: 70
Titles currently in print: 800

Admitted to the Association: 1986
Title output 2018: NR
Journals published: 2

Editorial Program
The Press is recognized as the leading English-language publisher in the Middle East, and publishes a wide range of scholarly monographs, texts and reference works, and general interest books on ancient and modern Egypt and the Middle East, as well as Arabic literature in English translation (under the Hoopoe imprint), most notably the works of Egyptian Nobel laureate Naguib Mahfouz.
Journals: *Alif: Journal of Comparative Poetics; Cairo Papers in Social Science*
Copublishing programs: Numerous copublishing programs with US, UK, and European universities and trade publishers

Amherst College Press

Robert Frost Library, Amherst College
61 Quadrangle Drive
Amherst, MA 01002
Phone: 413.542.5709
Fax: 413.542.2662

Website and Social Media:
Website: acpress.amherst.edu
Blog: acpress.amherst.edu/blog/
Twitter: @amcollpress

Staff
Director: Mark Edington (413.542.5709; email: medington@amherst.edu)
Editor-in-Chief: Beth Bouloukos (413.542.5519; email: bbouloukos@amherst.edu)
Editor-in-Chief, New Books Network: Marshall Poe (email: mpoe@amherst.edu)
Social Media Marketing Manager: Leann Wilson (email: lwilson@amherst.edu)

Number of Press Staff: 4

Introductory Member
Established: 2014   Admitted to the Association: 2014
Title output 2017: 3   Title output 2018: 2

Editorial Program
The Amherst College Press produces pathbreaking, peer-reviewed studies by scholars and makes it available to readers everywhere as digital, open-access work. Digital forms of all of our work—new studies, interviews with authors, and reviews of digital scholarly resources—is provided for use without cost through Creative Commons (4.0) licenses.
Book series: Laws | Literatures | Cultures; Public Works: Insights from the Humanities on Issues in the Public Square; Studies in Ethnomusicology

Amsterdam University Press

Nieuwe Prinsengracht 89
1018 VR Amsterdam
The Netherlands

Phone: +31.20.4200050
Fax: +31.20.4203214
Email: info@aup.nl
Indiv: (user I.D.)@aup.nl

Website and Social Media:
Website: www.aup.nl
Facebook (English): www.facebook.com/
   AUPAcademic
Twitter: @AmsterdamUPress

US and Canadian Sales Representative:
Baker & Taylor Publisher Services
Phone: 567.215.0030

China and Hong Kong Representative:
China Publishers Service
Phone: +86(0)852 24911 436

Japan Representative:
MHM Limited
+81(0)3 3518 9449

India Representative:
MAYA Publishers PVT Ltd.
Phone: + 91 (0) 9811 555 197

Staff
Director: Jan-Peter Wissink (email: wissink)
Finance and Administration: Wendy van Diepen, Head of Finance (email: wvandiepen@uvaventures.nl); Daniela Pinnone, Finance (email: d.pinnone)

Acquisition Editors: Saskia Gieling (Asian studies; Islam studies; social & political sciences; language and linguistics) (email: s.gieling); Maryse Elliott (film, media and communication) (email: m.elliott); Inge van der Bijl (educational textbooks) (email: i.vd.bijl); Julie Benschop-Plokker (modern history) (email: j.benschop); Shannon Cunningham (Asian studies US & Canada; Medieval studies) (email: s.cunningham); Loretta Lou (Asian studies UK) (email: l.lou); Louise Visser (language studies) (email: l.visser); Erika Gaffney (early modern history; Dutch golden age history); (email: erika.gaffney@arc-humanities.org); Katrien de Vreese (history) (email: k.de.vreese); Rixt Runia (educational textbooks) (email: r.runia); Erin Dailey (Medieval history) (email: e.t.dailey); Tyler Cloherty (Medieval studies) (email: tcloherty@arc-humanities.org); Nada Zečević (Medieval history) (email: Nada.Zecevic@rhul.ac.uk)
Managing Editor: Louise Visser (email: l.visser)
Manuscript Editorial: Chantal Nicolaes, Head of Desk Editing and Production (email: c.nicolaes); Jaap Wagenaar, Desk Editor (email: j.wagenaar)
Production: Rob Wadman (email: r.wadman)
International Sales, Marketing and PR: Vanessa de Bueger, International Sales and Marketing Director (email: v.de.bueger); Lucia Dove, International Marketing Coordinator (email: l.dove)
Journals and Educational Textbook Marketing: Jeroen Hoogerwerf (email: j.hoogerwerf)
Orders & Customer Service: Femke Sudmeijer (email: orders; f.sudmeijer)

Number of Press Staff: 15

Regular Member

Established: 1992	Admitted to the Association: 2000
Title output 2017: 113 ENG	Title output 2018: 117 ENG; 1 FR
Titles currently in print: 758 (688 ENG; 4 FR; 66 DE)	Journals published: 16

Editorial Program
Scholarly titles in English in the humanities and social sciences, specializing in Asian studies, film, media and communication, history, language and literature, and social and political sciences. Additional publishing program of Journals, MRW, and textbooks for universities and higher education. Titles published in paper and e-format.
Journals: AUP Advances; Algemeen Nederlands Tijdschrift voor Wijsbegeerte (ANTW Journal of Philosophy); E-data & Research; FORUM+ voor Onderzoek en Kunsten (for Research and Arts); Internationale Neerlandistiek (International Dutch Studies); Mens en Maatschappij (People and Society); NECSUS. European Journal of Media Studies; Nederlandse Letterkunde (Dutch Literature); Nederlandse Taalkunde (Dutch Linguistics); NTT Journal for Theology and the Studies of Religion; Pedagogiek (Pedagogy); Sociologie (Sociology); Taal en Tongval (Language and Dialects); Tijdschrift voor Genderstudies (Journal of Gender Studies); Tijdschrift voor Geschiedenis (Journal of History); Tijdschrift voor HRM (Journal of HR); Tijdschrift voor Taalbeheersing (Journal of Communications)
English series: Amsterdam Archaeological Studies; Amsterdam Studies in the Dutch Golden Age; Asian Borderlands; Asian Cities; Asian Heritages; Asian History; Asian Visual Cultures; Central European Medieval Studies; China: From Revolution to Reform; China's Environment and Welfare; Church, Faith and Culture in the Medieval West; Cities and Cultures; Comprehensive Grammar Resources; Consumption and Sustainability in Asia; Crossing Boundaries: Turku Medieval and Early Modern Studies; Cultures of Play, 1300-1700; Early Christianity in the Roman World; Early Modern Court Studies; Eastern European Screen Cultures; Environmental Humanities in Pre-modern Cultures; Film Culture in Transition; Film Theory in Media History; Food Culture, Food History (13th-19th centuries); Framing Film; Games and Play; Gendering the Late Medieval and Early Modern World; Global Asia; Global Chinese Histories, 250-1650; Golden Age Lectures; Hagiography beyond Tradition; Heritage and Memory Studies; History of Science and Scholarship in the Netherlands; Knowledge Communities; Landscape and Heritage Studies; Languages and Culture in History; Late Antique and Early Medieval Iberia; Maritime Humanities, 1400-1800: Cultures of the Sea; MediaMatters; Monsters and Marvels: Alterity in the Medieval and Early Modern Worlds; New Mobilities in Asia; North East Asian Studies; Perspectives on Interdisciplinarity; Premodern Crime and Punishment; Premodern Health, Disease, and Disability; Protest and Social Movements; Recursions; Religion and Society in Asia; Renaissance History, Art and Culture; Scientiae Studies; Social Histories of Work in Asia; Social Studies in Asian Medicine; Social Worlds of Late Antiquity and the Early Middle Ages; Sources of Anglo-Saxon Literary Culture; Spatial

Imageries in Historical Perspective; Televisual Culture; The Early Medieval North Atlantic; The Key Debates: Mutations and Appropriations in European Film Studies; Transforming Asia; Transmedia; Visual and Material Culture, 1300-1700; War, Conflict and Genocide Studies; Work around the Globe: Historical Comparisons
Dutch series: De kleine filosoof; Europa; Filmjaarboek; Tekst in Context
German series: Justiz und NS-Verbrechen
Copublications: Princeton University Press (USA); University of California Press (USA); MIT Press (USA); Thames & Hudson (UK); Brandeis University Press (USA); Actes Sud (France); Lannoo Uitgeverij (Belgium); Uitgeverij Davidsfonds (Belgium); Mercatorfonds (Belgium); Arc Humanities Press (USA); Geradbukaya (Malaysia), ISEAS (Singapore), NUS (Singapore)

Ediciones Uniandes

Street Address:
Calle 19 # 3-10, of. 1401
Bogotá 110311
Colombia, South America

Mailing Address:
Carrera 1 # 18A-12
Bogotá 111711
Colombia, South America

Phone: (57.1) 3394949, ext. 2133
Email: infeduni@uniandes.edu.co
Indiv. email: (user I.D.)@uniandes.edu.co

Orders:
Librería y Tienda Uniandes
Phone: (57.1) 3394949, ext. 2181
Email: gimoral@uniandes.edu.co
Online sales: libreria.uniandes.edu.co/

Website and Social Media:
Website: ediciones.uniandes.edu.co
E-books platform: ebooks.uniandes.edu.co
Facebook: www.facebook.com/ediciones.uniandes/
Twitter: @Ed_Uniandes
Instagram: @ediciones.uniandes

Staff
Editor-in-Chief: Julio Paredes (ext. 2159; email: j.paredes189)
Publications Coordinators: Adriana Delgado (ext. 3741; email: ab.delgado); María Ortiz (ext. 3689; email: ma.ortiz); Josefina Marambio (ext. 4861; email: j.marambio)
Administrative Coordinators: Julián Cortés (ext. 3190;email: jcortes); Carolina Mazo (ext. 2198; email: cmazo)
Marketing Coordinator: María Victoria González (ext. 2274; email: mgonzale)
Administrative Assistant: Stibaliz Vanegas (ext. 3890; email: lavanega)
Sales and Marketing Assistant: John Mario Rodríguez (ext. 3748; email: jm.rodriguez138)
Assistant to the Editor: Diana Muñoz (ext. 2133; email: do.munoz210)

Number of Press Staff: 10

Regular Member
Established: 1988
Title output 2017: 90
Titles currently in print: 822

Admitted to the Association: 2018
Title output 2018: 100

Editorial Program
Scholarly books in social sciences and the humanities: history, political science, anthropology, philosophy, cultural studies, literature and literary criticism, music, journalism, arts; architecture; design; Latin American studies (with an emphasis on Colombia); women's studies; public admin-istration; management; law; economics; education; engineering; biological sciences; medicine; publishing studies.
Book series: Relecturas (revival of classic Colombian literature and essay); Labirinto (literature and essay in translation, originally written in Portuguese, from authors from Portugal, Brazil and

former Portuguese colonies in Africa); La Biblioteca Editorial (publishing studies); Tándem (books in translation on social sciences and the humanities); Séneca (general-interest essay on a wide range of topics)

The University of Arizona Press

1510 E. University, 5th Floor
P.O. Box 210055
Tucson, AZ 85721-0055

Phone: 520.621.1441
Fax: 520.621.8899
Email: uapress@uapress.arizona.edu
Indiv: (user I.D.)@uapress.arizona.edu

Website and Social Media:
Website: www.uapress.arizona.edu
Facebook: www.facebook.com/AZpress
Twitter: @AZpress

Orders:
Chicago Distribution Center
Phone: 800.621.2736
Email: orders@press.uchicago.edu

Canadian Representative:
University of British Columbia Press

European Representative:
Eurospan

Staff
Director: Kathryn M. Conrad (520.621.1441; email: kconrad)
Assistant to the Director/Permissions: Julia Balestracci (520.621.3911; email: jbalestracci)
Editor-in-Chief: Kristen Buckles (Native American and Indigenous studies, Latin American studies, Border studies, Latina/o studies, history, regional) (520.621.7921; email: kbuckles)
Senior Editor: Allyson Carter (anthropology, archaeology, ecology, natural history, Native American and Indigenous studies, Latin American studies, environmental science, astronomy and space sciences, regional) (520.621.3186; email: acarter)
Assistant Editor: Scott DeHerrera (literature) (520.621.5919; email: sdeherrera)
Editing, Design, and Production Manager/Production Editor: Amanda Krause (520.621.5915; email: akrause)
Production Coordinator: Sara Thaxton (520.621.7916; email: sthaxton)
Art Director and Book Designer: Leigh McDonald (520.621.5824; email: lmcdonald)
Marketing and Sales Manager: Abby Mogollón (520.621.8656; email: amogollon)
Publicity Manager: Rosemary Brandt (520.621.3920; email: rbrandt)
Exhibits Manager/Marketing Assistant: Savannah Grace Hicks (520.621.4913; email: shicks)
Accounts Payable: Susan Fasciani (520.626.3041; email: sfasciani)

Number of Press Staff: 13

Regular Member
Established: 1959
Title output 2017: 103
Titles currently in print: 1,603

Admitted to the Association: 1962
Title output 2018: 59

Editorial Program
Specialties strongly identified with the universities in the state and other significant nonfiction of regional and national interest. Especially strong fields include anthropology and archaeology; environmental science; history; Latin American studies; Latina/o studies and literature; Native American and Indigenous studies and literature; and space sciences.

The Press also distributes titles from Ironwood Press; the Arizona State Museum; Statistical Research, Inc.; SWCA, Inc.; Center for Desert Archaeology; Center for Sustainable Environments; Crow Canyon Archaeological Center; and The Gila River Indian Community.
Book series: Amerind Studies in Anthropology; Anthropological Papers of the University of Arizona; Archaeology of Indigenous-Colonial Interactions in the Americas; Arizona-Sonora Desert Museum Studies In Natural History; Biodiversity in Small Spaces; Camino del Sol; Critical Green Engagements; Critical Issues in Indigenous Studies; The Feminist Wire Books; La Frontera:

People and Their Environments in the U.S.-Mexico Borderlands; Global Change / Global Health; Latin American Landscapes; Latinx Pop Culture; The Mexican American Experience; Modern American West; Native Peoples of the Americas; Southwest Center Series; Space Science Series; Sun Tracks; Women's Western Voices
Imprints: Sentinel Peak Books

The University of Arkansas Press

McIlroy House
105 North McIlroy Avenue
Fayetteville, AR 72701-1201

Phone: 800.626.0090
Email: info@uapress.com
Indiv: (user I.D.)@uark.edu

Website and Social Media:
Website: www.uapress.com
Facebook: www.facebook.com/UARKPRESS
Twitter: @uarkpress

Customer Service/Orders:
University of Arkansas Press
c/o Chicago Distribution Center
11030 South Langley Avenue
Chicago, IL 60628
Phone: 800.621.2736
Fax: 773.702.7212
Email: orders@press.uchicago.edu

Canadian Representative:
Scholarly Book Services

UK/European Representative:
Eurospan

Staff
Director: Mike W. Bieker (479.575.3859; email: mbieker)
Editor-in-Chief: David Scott Cunningham (479.575.5767; email: dscunnin)
Production Manager: Liz Lester (479.575.6780; email: lizl)
Project Editor: Molly Rector (479.575.4724; email: mbrector)
Director of Marketing and Sales: Melissa King (479.575.7715; email: mak001)
Marketing/Advertising Designer: Charlie Shields (479.575.7258; email: cmoss)
Business Manager: Sam Ridge (479.575.3858; email: sridge)
UAP Distribution Services:
Distribution Services Manager: Sam Ridge (479.575.3858; email: sridge)

Number of Press Staff: 7

Regular Member
Established: 1980
Title output 2017: 25
Titles currently in print: 675

Admitted to the Association: 1984
Title output 2018: 27
Journals published: 1

Editorial Program
African American history, art, civil rights studies, food studies, Middle East studies, Ozarks studies, poetry, political science, regional studies, Southern history, sports studies, Civil War studies, women's studies
Journal: *Philosophical Topics*
Book series: The Arkansas Character; CantoMundo Poetry Series; The Civil War in the West; Etel Adnan Poetry Series; Fay Jones Collaborative Series; Food and Foodways; Miller Williams Poetry Series; Ozarks Studies; Portraits of Conflict; The Simms Series; Sport, Culture, and Society

Army University Press

290 Stimson, Unit 1
Fort Leavenworth, KS 66027

Phone: 913.684.9327/2127
General Info: usarmy.leavenworth.tradoc.
mbx.csi-rp@mail.mil

Websites and Social Media
Website: www.armyupress.army.mil/
Twitter: @ArmyUPress
Youtube: www.youtube.com/channel/UCX9G3c6jkROVZ0tXr4gvUKQ/videos%20

Book Orders
Amy Castillo 913.684.2127
amy.k.castillo.civ@mail.mil

Journal Orders
Linda Darnell 913.684.9327
linda.j.darnell.civ@mail.mil

Staff
Director/Editor-in-Chief: COL Kate Guttormsen (913.684.9331; email: Katherine.p.guttormsen.
  mil@mail.mil)
Deputy Director: Dr. Donald P. Wright (913.684.2088; email: donald.p.wright.civ@mail.mil)
Administrative Officer: Amy Castillo (913.684.2127; email: amy.k.castillo.civ@mail.mil)

Introductory Member
Established 2015 (merger of Combat Studies Institute Press and Military Review)
Admitted to the Association: 2015
Title output 2017: 8   Title output 2018: 8
Titles currently in print: 50   Journals published: 2

Editorial Program
Established to publish on topics for military professionals. Areas of emphasis include history,
strategy, leadership, doctrine, training, military education and general policy issues.
Journals: *Military Review* (3 Versions; English, Portuguese, and Spanish); *Journal of Military
Learning*
Book series: Occasional Papers on Global War on Terror, Leavenworth Papers, Art of War Papers.

Athabasca University Press

Peace Hills Trust Tower
1200, 10011–109 Street
Edmonton, AB T5J 3S8 Canada

Phone: 780.497.3412
Fax: 780.421.3298
Email: aupress@athabascau.ca

Website and Social Media:
Website: www.aupress.ca
Facebook: www.facebook.com/AUPress1
Twitter: @au_press
YouTube: www.youtube.com/user/aupresst
Instagram: au_press

UK, Europe, Middle East, & Africa Orders:
Combined Academic Publishers
Windsor House
Email: enquiries@combinedacademic.co.uk

Canadian Orders:
University of British Columbia Press
c/o UTP Distribution

Phone: 800.565.9523/416.667.7791
Fax: 800.221.9985/416.667.7832
Email: utpbooks@utpress.utoronto.ca

US Orders:
University of Washington Press
c/o Hopkins Fulfillment Service
Phone: 800.537.5487/410.516.6965
Fax: 410.516.6998
Email: hfscustserv@press.jhu.edu

Asia and Pacific:
East West Export Books

China, Hong Kong, Taiwan, and Korea:
Asia Publishers Services Ltd.

Staff
Director: Megan Hall (780.428.2067; email: mhall@athabascau.ca)
Marketing and Editorial Assistant: Karyn Wisselink (780.497.3408; email: kwisselink@athabascau.ca)
Senior Editor, Acquisitions: Pamela Holway (780.428.7278; email: pholway@athabascau.ca)
Associate Editor: Connor Houlihan (780.392.1204; email: connorh@athabascau.ca)
Journals and Digital Coordinator: Kathy Killoh (780.421.2528; email: kathyk@athabascau.ca)

Number of Press Staff: 8

Regular Member
Established: 2007

Admitted to the Association:
2008 (intro. member)
Admitted to the Association:
2011 (full member)

Title output 2017: 15
Titles currently in print: 138

Title output 2018: 14
Journals published: 7

Editorial Program
AU Press has cultivated a strong list of publications in the areas of online education, labour studies, Métis and Indigenous studies, gender studies, and the environment. However, we welcome superior works of scholarship, regardless of subject area. We also have a particular interest in often neglected forms of social and cultural history, including oral history and memoir, and in works that are broadly iconoclastic—that experiment with narrative form and/or challenge received wisdom.
Journals: *Alternate Routes, The Canadian Journal of Learning and Technology (CJLT); International Review of Research in Open and Distributed Learning (IRRODL); The Journal of Distance Education; Journal of Research Practice (JRP); Labour/Le Travail; Oral History Forum d'histoire orale; The Trumpeter*
Web-based publications: Aurora; Canadian Theatre Encyclopedia
Book series: Canadian Plays; Cultural Dialectics; Global Peace Studies; Issues in Distance Education; Mingling Voices; OPEL: Open Paths to Enriched Learning; Our Lives: Diary, Memoir, and Letters; Recovering the Past: Studies in Archaeology; The West Unbound: Social and Cultural Studies; Working Canadians: Books from the CCLH

Baylor University Press

Street Address:
1920 South 4th Street
Waco, TX 76706-2529

Mailing Address:
One Bear Place # 97363
Waco, TX 76798-7363

Phone: 254.710.3164
Fax: 254.710.3440
Email: (user I.D.)@baylor.edu

Website and Social Media:
Website: www.baylorpress.com
Facebook: www.facebook.com/BaylorPress
Twitter: @Baylor_Press

UK Representative:
Gazelle

Orders:
Baylor University Press
c/o Longleaf Services, Inc.
116 South Boundary Street
Chapel Hill, NC 27514-3808
Phone: 800. 848.6224 ext. 1
(US & Canada)
or 919.966.7449 (rest of the world)
Fax: 800.272.6817 (US and Canada) or
919.962.2704 (rest of the world)
Email: orders@longleafservices.org

Staff
Director: Carey Newman (254.710.3522; email: carey_newman)
Business: Madeline Wieters, Finance and Operations Manager (254.710.1285; email: madeline_wieters)
Assistant Editor: Cade Jarrell (254.710.4116; email: cade_jarrell)
Production/Digital Publishing: Jenny Hunt , Director of Digital Publishing (254.710.3236; email: jenny_hunt)
Design Manager: Savanah Landerholm (254.710.2563; email: savanah_landerholm)
Marketing and Sales Manager: David Aycock (254.710.1465; email: david_aycock)

Number of Press Staff: 9

Regular Member
Established: 1897
Title output 2017: 42
Titles currently in print: 501

Admitted to the Association: 2007
Title output 2018: 44

Editorial Program
Established in 1897, Baylor University Press publishes forty new academic titles each year. The list focuses on scriptural, historical, and theological studies of Christianity, Judaism, and Islam. Press publications also investigate the relationship between religion and politics, sociology, anthropology, literature, philosophy, history, and culture.
Book series: Baylor-Mohr Siebeck Studies in Early Christianity; Baylor Handbook on the Greek New Testament; Baylor Handbook on the Hebrew Bible; Baylor Handbook on the Septuagint; Documents of Anglophone Christianity Series; Library of Early Christology; Papyrology and the New Testament; Studies in Religion, Theology, and Disability; Studies in World Christianity
Imprints: Baylor University Press; 1845 Books; Big Bear Books

Beacon Press

24 Farnsworth Street
Boston, MA 02210

Phone: 617.742.2110
Fax: 617.723.3097
Marketing/Sub Rights Fax: 617.742.2290
Email: permissions@beacon.org
Indiv: (user I.D.)@beacon.org

<u>Website and Social Media:</u>
Website: www.beacon.org
Blog: www.beaconbroadside.com
Facebook: www.facebook.com/beaconpress
Twitter: @BeaconPressBks
YouTube: www.youtube.com/user/BeaconBroadside

<u>UK Representative:</u>
Publishers Group UK

<u>Canadian Representative:</u>
Penguin Random House Canada

Staff
Director: Helene Atwan (email: hatwan)
  Assistant to the Director: Haley Lynch (hlynch)
Editorial: Gayatri Patnaik, Editorial Director (email: gpatnaik)
  Executive Editor: Amy Caldwell (email: acaldwell)
  Senior Editors: Rakia Clark (email: rclark); Joanna Green (email: jgreen)
  Contracts Director and Director of Beacon Press Audio: Melissa Nasson (email: mnasson)
  Editors: Rachael Marks (email: rmarks)
Production: Marcy Barnes, Production Director & Digital Publishing Director (email: mbarnes)
Managing Editor: Susan Lumenello (email: slumenello)
Creative Director: Carol Chu (email: cchu)
Director of Sales and Marketing: Sanj Kharbanda (email: skharbanda)
  Director of Communications: Pamela MacColl (email: pmaccoll)
  Publicity Manager: Caitlin Meyer (email: cmeyer)
  Associate Marketing Manager: Emily Powers (email: epowers)
Business: Cliff Manko, Chief Financial Officer (email: cmanko)
  Business Manager: Jill Dougan (email: jdougan)

Number of Press Staff: 30

Regular Member
Established: 1854
Title output 2017: 57
Titles currently in print: 1,792

Admitted to the Association: 1988
Title output 2018: 56

<u>Editorial Program</u>
Beacon Press, the non-profit publisher affiliated with the Unitarian Universalist Association, publishes works for the general reader, specializing in African American, Native American, and Asian American studies; anthropology; current affairs; education; environmental studies; LGBTQ studies; public health; religion; and women's studies.
Book series: The Beacon Press/Simmons College Series on Race, Education, and Democracy; The King Legacy; Queer Action/Queer Ideas, Revisioning American History; Celebrating Black Women Writers

Brandeis University Press

Website: www.brandeis.edu/library/bup.html

Orders:
Chicago Distribution Center
(800) 621-2736

Additional Information: TBA

University of British Columbia Press

2029 West Mall
University of British Columbia
Vancouver, BC V6T 1Z2 Canada

Phone: 604.822.5959
Toll-free (in Canada): 877.377.9378
Fax: 604.822.6083
Toll-free fax (in Canada): 800.668.0821
Email: (user I.D.)@ubcpress.ca

Website and Social Media:
Website: www.ubcpress.ca
Facebook: UBC Press
Twitter: @UBCPress
YouTube: UBCPressChannel
Instagram: instagram.com/ubcpress

Canadian Orders and Returns:
University of Toronto Press
5201 Dufferin Place
Toronto, ON M3H 5T8 Canada
Phone: 416.667.7791
Fax: 416.667.7832
Email: utpbooks@utpress.utoronto.ca

US Orders and Returns:
University of Washington Press
C/O Hopkins Fulfillment Service
PO Box 50370
Baltimore, MD 21211-4370 USA
Phone: 800.537.5487; 410.516.6956
Email: hfscustserv@press.jhu.edu

Distributors
The University of Washington Press (US); Combined Academic Publishers (UK, Europe, Middle East, Africa, China, Taiwan, and Hong Kong); East West Export Books (Asia [excluding China, Hong Kong, and Taiwan] and Pacific)

Staff
Director: Melissa Pitts (604.822.6376; email: pitts)
Assistant to the Publisher and Permissions Manager: Valerie Nair (604.822.4161; email: nair)
Acquisitions Editorial: Darcy Cullen, Assistant Director—Acquisitions (Vancouver) (BC studies, Canadian history, gender & sexuality studies, Indigenous studies) (604.822.5744; email: cullen); Randy Schmidt, Senior Editor (Kelowna) (Asian studies, diplomatic history, law and socio-legal studies, military history, political history, political science) (250.764.4761; email: schmidt); James MacNevin, Senior Editor (Toronto) (communications & media studies, environmental history, environmental and resource studies, health and food studies, sociology, transnational and multicultural studies, urban studies and planning) (289.779.2414; email: macnevin); Nadine Pedersen, Editorial Coordinator (604.827.1795; email: pedersen)
Production Editorial: Holly Keller, Assistant Director—Production and Editorial Services (604.822.4545; email: keller)
Editors: Ann Macklem (604.822.0093; email: macklem); Megan Brand (604.822.5885; email: brand); Katrina Petrik (604.822.6436; email: petrik); Michelle van der Merwe (604.822.4548; email: vandermerwe)
Marketing and Sales: Laraine Coates, Marketing Manager (604.822.6486; email: coates)
Academic Marketing Manager: Harmony Johnson (604.822.1978; email: johnson)
Digital Publishing Coordinator: Krista Bergstrom (604.822.5790; email: bergstrom)
Publicist and Events Manager: Kerry Kilmartin (604.822.8244; email: kilmartin)
Catalogues and Advertising Manager: Alexa Love (604.822.4546; email: love)
Agency and Digital Marketing Coordinator: Megan Malashewsky (604.822.8226; email: malashewsky)
Inventory and Distribution Coordinator: Liz Hudson (604.328.8923.; email: hudson)
Marketing Assistant and Awards: David Ly (604.822.5959; email: ly)
Finance: Steve Young, Assistant Director—Finance and Operations (604.822.8938; email: young)
Finance Assistant: Derick Chan (604.822.5370; email: chan)

Number of Press Staff: 23

Regular Member
Established: 1971
Title output 2017: 62
Titles currently in print: 1,083

Admitted to the Association: 1972
Title output 2018: 48

Editorial Program
Scholarly books and serious nonfiction, with special interest in First Nations culture politics and linguistics, Canadian history, environmental history and policy, resources, Canadian politics, globalization, multiculturalism, urban planning, Asian studies, and sexuality and gender studies.
Book series: Asia Pacific Legal Culture and Globalization; Asian Religions and Society; Brenda and David McLean Canadian Studies; Canada and International Relations; Canadian Democratic Audit; Canadian Yearbook of International Law; Communication, Strategy, and Politics; Contemporary Chinese Studies; Disability Culture and Politics; Equality|Security|Community; Ethnicity and Democratic Governance; First Nations Languages; Globalization and Autonomy; Histories of Substance; Law and Society; Legal Dimensions; Nature|History|Society; Pacific Rim Archaeology; Purich's Aboriginal Issues Series; RBCM Handbooks; Sexuality Studies; Shared: Oral and Public History; Studies in Canadian Military History; Sustainability and the Environment; The C.D. Howe Series in Canadian Political History, The Pioneers of British Columbia, Urbanization in Asia; Women and Indigenous Studies; Women's Suffrage and the Struggle for Democracy
Imprints: UBC Press; On Point Press; Purich Books; On Campus; and Pacific Educational Press

Brookings Institution Press

1775 Massachusetts Avenue, N.W.
Washington, DC 20036-2103

Phone: 202.797.6429
Email: books@brookings.edu
Indiv: firstinitiallastname@brookings.edu

Customer Service/Orders:
Ingram Publisher Services
210 American Drive
Jackson, TN 38301
Phone: 1.800.343.4499
Fax: 1.800.351.5073

Website and Social Media:
Website: www.brookings.edu/press
Twitter: @BrookingsPress

UK Representative:
Eurospan Group

Canadian Representative:
Perseus Distribution

Staff
Director: William Finan (202.536.3637)
Financial Manager: Ben Cahen (202.797.6163)
Digital and Marketing Manager: Steven Roman (202.536.3609)
Rights Manager and Editorial Associate: Kristen Harrison (202.536.3604)
Production Coordinator: Elliott Beard (202.536.3618)
Assistant Director: Yelba Quinn (202.536.3619)
Media Relations Manager: Carrie Engel (202.797.4364)
Marketing Coordinator: Adam Juskewitch (202.540.7773)
Distribution Manager: Laura Baida (202.741.6557)
Bookstore Manager: Frederick King (202.797.6429)

Number of Press Staff: 8

Regular Member
Established: 1916
Title output 2017: 40
Titles currently in print: 1,698

Admitted to the Association: 1958
Title output 2018: 33
Journals published: 3

Editorial Program
Economics, government, and international affairs, with emphasis on the implications for public policy of current and emerging issues confronting American society. The Press publishes books written by the Institution's resident and associated staff members, as well as manuscripts acquired from outside authors.

The Institution also publishes three journals: *Brookings Papers on Economic Activity*, *Economia* (copublished with the Latin American and Caribbean Economic Association), and *Behavioral Science and Policy*, the Journal of the Behavioral Science and Policy Association.

The Press distributes publications for organizations such as the Asian Development Bank Institute, the American Chamber of Commerce to the European Union, the Bertelsmann Foundation, the Carnegie Endowment for International Peace, the Centre for Economic Policy Research, the Century Foundation Press, Economica, the Center for Global Development, the Institute for the Study of the Americas, the International Labor Organization, the Japan Center for International Exchange, the OECD, the Royal Institute for International Affairs, the Trilateral Commission, the United Nations University Press, and the World Trade Organization.

Bucknell University Press

Street Address:
Hildreth-Mirza Hall
Bucknell University
Lewisburg, PA 17837

Mailing Address:
1 Dent Drive
Lewisburg, PA 17837

Phone: 570.577.3674
Email: universitypress@bucknell.edu
Indiv.: (User I.D.)@bucknell.edu

Website and Social Media:
Website: www.bucknell.edu/universitypress
Blog: upress.blogs.bucknell.edu
Facebook: www.facebook.com/BucknellUP
Twitter: @BucknellUPress

UK:
Rowman & Littlefield

Europe:
Durnell Marketing Ltd.

Australia, New Zealand and Papua New Guinea:
Co Info Pty Ltd

UK/European/Asian Representative:
Eurospan

Orders (USA and Canada):
For titles published 1968-2018
Rowman & Littlefield
Blue Ridge Summit, PA 17214
Phone: 800.462.6420
Fax: 800.338.4550
Website: www.rowman.com
Email: orders@rowman.com

Orders:
For titles published 2018--
In conjunction with Rutgers UP
c/o Chicago Distribution Center
11030 S Langley Ave, Chicago, IL 60628
Phone: 773.702.7010
Fax: 800.621.8476

Canadian Representative:
Scholarly Book Services

Staff
Director: Greg Clingham (570.577.1552; email: clingham)
Managing Editor: Pamelia Dailey (570.577.3674; email: pad024)
Acquisitions Editorial: Greg Clingham (Transits, Apercus, 17th-19th century studies, Hispanic studies) (email: clingham); Logan J. Connors (French and Francophone theater) (email: logan.connors@miami.edu); Carmen Gillespie (Griot) (email: gillespie); Anibal Gonzalez (Latin American studies) (email: anibal.gonzalez@yale.edu); Richard B. Sher (18th-century Scotland) (email: rbsher6@gmail.com); Karin Schutjer (Studies in the Age of Goethe) (email: kschutjer@ou.edu); Alfred Siewers (Susquehanna River) (email: asiewers)
Editorial Assistant: Nate Freed (email: nsf005)
Design: Adrienne Beaver (email: abeaver)

Number of Press Staff: 2

Introductory Member
Established: 1968
Title output 2017: 26
Titles currently in print: 1,200

Admitted to the Association: 2016
Title output 2018: 25

Editorial Program

Comparative eighteenth-century studies; English and American literary criticism, especially early modern to mid nineteenth century; cultural studies; Luso-Hispanic studies; Latin American literature and theory; contemporary Irish writers; French and Francophone theatre; Africana studies; environmental studies; literary memoirs; poetry (occasionally).

Book series: Aperçus: Histories Texts Cultures; Bucknell Studies in Latin American Literature and Theory; Contemporary Irish Writers; Griot Project Book (in association with the Griot Institute for Africana Studies at Bucknell); New Studies in the Age of Goethe (in association with the Goethe Society of North America); Scènes francophones: Studies in French and Francophone Theater; Stories of the Susquehanna Valley (in association with the Center for Sustainability and the Environmental at Bucknell); Studies in Eighteenth-Century Scotland (in association with the Eighteenth-Century Scottish Studies Society); Transits: Literature, Thought & Culture 1650-1850.

University of Calgary Press

2500 University Drive N.W.
Calgary, AB T2N 1N4 Canada

Phone: 403.220.7578
Fax: 403.282.0085
Email: ucpress@ucalgary.ca

Website and Social Media:
Website: www.press.ucalgary.ca
Facebook: www.facebook.com/UCalgaryPress
Twitter: @UCalgaryPress
YouTube: www.youtube.com/channel/UCmpSYUJVXlHG6p8mn-Ps4hw

Canadian Distribution & Orders:
UTP Distribution
Phone: 800.565.9523

US Distribution & Orders:
Longleaf Services, Inc.
116 S. Boundary St, Chapel Hill, NC
27514-3808 USA
Phone: 800.272.6817
Orders@longleafservices.org
Email inquiries: customerservice
@longleafservices.org

UK/Africa/Middle East/European
Distributor:
Gazelle Book Services, Ltd.
White Cross Mills, High Town, Lancashire
LA1 4XS UK

Phone: 011 44 (0)1524 63232
Email: sales@gazellebooks.co.uk

Staff

Director: Brian Scrivener (403.220.3511; email: brian.scrivener@ucalgary.ca)
Operations Manager: Michelle Lipp (403.220.8221; email: mlipp@ucalgary.ca)
Editorial (Acquisitions) & Marketing Coordinator: Helen Hajnoczky (403.220.4208; email: helen.hajnoczky@ucalgary.ca)
Graphic Design & Print Management: Melina Cusano (403.220.8719; email: macusano@ucalgary.ca)
Marketing Specialist: Alison Cobra (403.220.3979; email: alison.cobra@ucalgary.ca)
Digital Services & Fulfilment Coordinator/Accounts: Ethel Cuesta (403.220.7736; email: ucpmail@ucalgary.ca)

Regular Member

Established: 1981

Title output 2017: 17
Titles currently in print: 372

Admitted to the Association: 2002
(Affiliate member: 1992-95)
Title output 2018: NR

Editorial Program
At the University of Calgary Press we publish peer-reviewed scholarly books that connect local experience to the global community, helping to create a deeper understanding of human dynamics in a changing world. Through Open Access publishing, we make our authors' research accessible to the widest possible audience.

Publishing interests include: Arctic and northern studies; foreign affairs and public policy; energy, environment & ecology; environmental history; Indigenous and Métis studies; Canadian literature; contemporary Canadian art & architecture; African studies; Latin American & Caribbean studies; Western Canada; media & communications; gender studies; urban studies.

Book series: Africa: Missing Voices; Art in Profile; Arts in Action; Beyond Boundaries (Canadian Defense and Strategic Studies); Brave & Brilliant (poetry & fiction); Canadian History and Environment; Cinemas Off Centre; Energy, Ecology, and Environment; Global Indigenous Issues; Latin American and Caribbean Studies; Northern Lights (arctic & circumpolar studies); Small Cities Studies in Community & Cultural Engagement; The West (western history)

Co-publishing programs: The Arctic Institute of North America; Latin American Research Centre; Centre for Military, Security & Strategic Studies; Mount Royal University, Faculty of Arts

University of California Press

155 Grand Avenue, Suite 400
Oakland, CA 94612-3758
Phone: 510.833.8232
Fax: 510.836.8910
Email: askucp@ucpress.edu
Indiv: firstname.lastname@ucpress.edu

Order Fulfillment:
Ingram Content Group LLC
One Ingram Blvd.
La Vergne, TN 37086
Phone: 866.400.5351
Email: ips@ingramcontent.com

Website and Social Media:
Website: www.ucpress.edu
Journals website:
www.ucpress.edu/journals
Blog: www.ucpress.edu/blog
Facebook: www.facebook.com/ucpress
Twitter: @ucpress
YouTube: UCPressVideo

UK/European Office:
The University Press Group (US), Ltd.
LEC-1, First Floor Office
New Era Estates
Oldlands Way
Bognor Regis
PO22 9NQ UK
Phone: +44 (0) 1243 843291
Fax: +44 (0) 1243 843302
Toll free: (0800) 243407
Email: customer@wiley.com

Staff
Executive Director: Timothy Sullivan (510.883.8240)
Executive Assistant: Susan Owen (510.883.8319)
Director of Finance and Operations: Denise Feinsod (510.883.8323)
Director Journals and Open Access: Erich van Rijn (510.883.8264)
Digital Science Publisher/OA Journals: Dan Morgan (510.883.8330)
Journals Publisher: David Famiano (510.883.8270)
Editorial Director: Kim Robinson (regional studies, geography, Mark Twain) (510.883.8283)
    Sponsoring Editors: Stacy Eisenstark (environmental studies) (510.883.8245) Niels Hooper (US History, American studies, Pacific world, western history, world history, Middle East studies) (510.883.8300); Nadine Little (art history, museum copublications) (510.883.8284); Reed Malcolm (Asian studies, global studies, Luminos/Open Access) (510.883.8313); Kate Marshall (anthropology, food studies, Latin American studies) (510.883.8285); Raina Polivka (music, cinema, media studies) (510.883.8242); Maura Roessner (criminology, law and society, criminal justice) (mroessner@ucpress.edu); Eric Schmidt (classical studies, medieval studies, pre-modern history, the ancient world to late antiquity) (510.883.8263); Naomi Schneider (sociology, contemporary social issues, global health) (510.883.8302); Lyn Uhl (communication) (617.905.3681)
Director of Editing, Design, and Production: Scott Norton (510.883.8320)
Managing Editor: Kate Warne (510.883.8289)

Lead Production Coordinator: Angela Chen (510.883.8233)
Art Director: Lia Tjandra (510.883.8292)
Journals Production & Publishing Technology Manager: Gabe Alvaro (510.883.8266)
Director of Marketing and Sales: Elena McAnespie (510.883.8262)
Director of PR & Communications: Peter Perez (510.883.8318)
Human Resources: Denise Feinsod (510.883.8323)

Number of Press Staff: 80

Regular Member
Established: 1893   Admitted to the Association: 1937
Title output 2017: 185   Title output 2018: 195
Titles currently in print: 6,056   Journals published: 32

Editorial Program
Anthropology, art history, Asian studies, communication, Latin American studies, Middle Eastern studies, ethnic studies, classical studies, environmental studies, film, food studies, geography, history; late antiquity, law & society, media studies, medieval studies, music, natural history, global health, criminology, criminal justice, regional studies, religion, sociology. Submissions are not invited in original poetry or fiction.

Journals: *19th Century Music; Asian Survey; California History; Case Studies in the Environment; Civic Sociology; Classical Antiquity; Collabra: Psychology; Contemporary Arab Affairs; Departures in Critical Qualitative Research; Elementa: Science of the Anthropocene; Ethnic Studies Review; Federal Sentencing Reporter; Feminist Media Histories, Film Quarterly; Gastronomica; Historical Studies in the Natural Sciences; International Review of Qualitative Research; Journal of Medieval Worlds; Journal of Musicology; Journal of Palestine Studies; Journal of Popular Music Studies; Journal of the American Musicological Society; Journal of the Society of Architectural Historians; Journal of Vietnamese Studies; Latin American and Latinx Visual Culture; Mexican Studies/Estudios Mexicanos; Music Perception; New Criminal Law Review; Nineteenth-Century Literature; Nova Religio; Pacific Historical Review; Representations; Rhetorica; Sociology of Development; Southern California Quarterly; Studies in Late Antiquity; The American Biology Teacher; The Public Historian*

Book series: American Crossroads; American Studies Now; Ancient Philosophies; The Anthropology of Christianity; Asia Pacific Modern; Asia: Local Studies/Global Themes; Berkeley Series in British Studies; California Natural History Guides; California/Milbank Books on Health and the Public; California Series in Law, Politics, and Society; California Series in Public Anthropology; California Studies in 19th-Century Music; California Studies in 20th-Century Music; California Studies in Food and Culture; California World History Library; Communicating Social Justice; Islamic Humanities; The Clark Kerr Lectures on the Role of Higher Education in Society; Criminology Explains; Critical Refugee Studies; Defining Moments in American Photography; Documents of Twentieth Century Art; Ernest Bloch Lectures; Feminist Media Histories; Franklin D. Murphy Lectures; Ethnographic Studies in Subjectivity; From Indochina to Vietnam: Revolution and War; Global Korea; Global Perspective; Gender and Justice; Great Perspectives; Hellenistic Culture and Society; Hip Hop Studies; New Interventions in Japanese Studies; The Marcus Garvey and Universal Negro Improvement Association Papers; Mark Twain Papers; The Middle Awash Series; Music of the African Diaspora; New Perspectives on Chinese Culture and Society; The Norman and Charlotte Strouse Edition of the Writings of Thomas Carlyle; Palestinian Studies; The Phillips Books Prize Series; Reproductive Justice: A New Vision for the 21st Century; Rhetoric and Public Culture; Sather Classical Lectures; Sociology in the 21st Century; South Asia Across the Disciplines; Sport in World History; The Works of Mark Twain; Transformation of the Classical Heritage; Western Histories; Wildavsky Forum Series

Cambridge University Press

North American Office:
One Liberty Plaza
New York, NY 10006

Phone: 212.337.5000
Fax: 212.691.3239
Email: firstinitiallastname@cambridge.org

Head (UK) Office:
University Printing House
Cambridge CB2 8BS UK

Customer Service:
Email: customer_service@cambridge.org
Phone: 1.800.872.7423

Website and Social Media:
Website: www.cambridge.org
Blog: www.cambridgeblog.org
Facebook: www.facebook.com/CambridgeUniversityPress
Twitter: @CambridgeUP
YouTube: www.youtube.com/user/CambridgeUP
LinkedIn: www.linkedin.com/company/cambridge-university-press

Staff
Chief Executive: Peter Phillips (UK)
Managing Director, Academic Publishing: Amanda Hill (UK)
NY Office:
Senior Vice President for Academic, Americas & Director of Scholarly Communications Research
   and Development: Brigitte Shull (212.337.5965)
Academic Publishing:
Book Editors: Matthew Bennett (Director of Higher Education Publishing); Sara Doskow (political
   science); David Repetto (Executive Publisher, psychology); John Berger (law); Lauren Cowles
   (math, computer science); Robert Dreesen (politics, sociology); Steve Elliott (engineering); Matt
   Gallaway (law); Deborah Gershenowitz (American and Latin American history and politics);
   Diana Gillooly (math and statistics); Kaitlyn Leach (mathematical sciences); Matt Lloyd (Execu-
   tive Publisher, earth sciences); Karen Maloney (Executive Publisher, economics and finance);
   Beatrice Rehl (Publisher, classics, religion, archaeology); Ray Ryan (literature); Stephen Acerra
   (psychology and economics)
Journals:
STM Publishers: Aaron Johnson & Ann Avouris
STM Journal Editors: Jessica Bradley; Marissa Murray-Harrison
HSS Publisher: Mark Zadrozny & Ann Avouris
HSS Journal Editors: Chris Robinson; Amy Laurent; Lisa Arrington
Sales and Marketing:
Vice President of Business Development: Al Cascio
Institutional Sales Managers: Stephanie Kaelin; Kellie O'Rourke
Head of Sales, Retail and Wholesale Accounts: Thomas Willshire
Senior Rights Sales Representative: Adam Hirschberg
Business Development Representatives: Christina Ko and Valeria Guagnini
Senior Marketing Manager, End User Marketing: Michael Duncan, Marketing Manager: Danny
   Bean
Head of Higher Education Sales, Americas: Pam Cooper
Associate Marketing Director, Americas: Larry Grodsky
Marketing Manager, Library Marketing: Susan Soule
Production:
Production Director, Journals: Edward Carey
ELT Publishing:
Associate Business Unit Director: Jeff Krum
Project Manager: Danielle Power
North American Sales Director: Michelle Velissariou
Associate Business Unit Director: John Ade

Sales Manager: Mike Woods
Senior Business Performance Manager: Aniko Banfi
Publishing Manager - ELT Dictionaries: Wendalyn Nichols
Associate Director of Global Market Research: Jose Antonio Mendez
Operations:
HR: Giuseppe Rotella and Topher Payne
Associate Director Customer Services: Marianne Headrick
Global Warehousing Manager: Edward Galante
IT:
IT Director, Americas: Carlos Rivera
Technical Associate: Thomas Haggerty
Desktop Support Analyst: Cristian Mendoza

Number of Press Staff: 2,813

Regular Member
Established: 1534
American Branch: 1949   Admitted to the Association: 1950
Title output 2017: 1,378   Title output 2018: 2,700
Titles currently in print: 55,000   Journals published: 360

Editorial Program
A broad range of academic books, journals, digital and online products in the humanities, social sciences, science, engineering, technology, engineering, medical and health sciences; including pre-eminent lists in social and political sciences; biological, physical and earth sciences; mathematics; psychology, psychiatry and neuroscience; law, history and religious studies. Cambridge also publishes for the global education market and is one of the world's leading English language teaching/ESL publishers.

Carnegie Mellon University Press

5032 Forbes Avenue   Order Fulfillment/Customer Service:
Pittsburgh, PA 15289-1021   Carnegie Mellon University Press
                                                Chicago Distribution Center
                                                11030 S. Langley Avenue
Phone: 412.268.2861   Chicago, IL 60628
Fax: 412.268.8706   Phone: 773.702.7010
Email: Fax: 800.621.8476
cmupress@andrew.cmu.edu.com

Website and Social Media:
Website: www.cmu.edu/universitypress
Facebook: www.facebook.com/CarnegieMellonUniversityPress

Staff
Director: Gerald Costanzo (poetry editor) (email: gc3d@andrew.cmu.edu)
Senior Editor: Cynthia Lamb (nonfiction acquisitions) (email: cynthial@andrew.cmu.edu)
Production Manager: Connie Amoroso (email: camoroso@andrew.cmu.edu)
Accounts Administrator: Vicky McKay (email: vm29@andrew.cmu.edu)

Number of Press Staff: 5

Regular Member
Established: 1972
Title output 2017: 12
Titles currently in print: 190

Admitted to the Association: 1991
Title output 2018: 13

Editorial Program
Carnegie Mellon University Press' particular strength lies in literary publishing: Carnegie Mellon Poetry Series, Carnegie Mellon Classic Contemporaries Series (the reissuing of significant early poetry and fiction collections by important contemporary writers), Carnegie Mellon Series in Short Fiction, Poets in Prose Series (memoir in the form of poets writing about their writing lives, poetry criticism, guidebooks and handbooks about the writing of poetry, and Carnegie Mellon Series in Translation. Additionally, the Press publishes in regional social history (titles that explore the rich history of Pittsburgh and Western Pennsylvania), art history, the performing arts (original plays and adaptations), literary analysis, education, and Carnegie Mellon University history.

The Catholic University of America Press

240 Leahy Hall
620 Michigan Avenue, N.E.
Washington, DC 20064

Customer Service:
HFS
PO Box 50370
Baltimore, MD 21211

Phone: 202.319.5052
Fax: 202.319.4985
Email: (user I.D.)@cua.edu

Phone: 800.537.5487
Fax: 410.516.6998

Website and Social Media:
Website: cuapress.org
Facebook: www.facebook.com/pages/
    The-Catholic-University-of-America-Press/232124655084
Twitter: @CUAPress

Warehouse (Returns only):
HFS
RETURNS
c/o Maple Press Co.
Lebanon Dist. Center
704 Legionaire Drive
Fredericksburg, PA 17026

UK Representative:
Eurospan

Canadian Representative:
Brunswick Books

Staff
Director: Trevor Lipscombe (email: lipscombe)
    Assistant to the Director: Libby Newkumet (email: newkumet)
Acquisitions Editors: John Martino (philosophy, theology) (email: martinoj); Trevor Lipscombe (all other fields)
Managing Editor: Theresa Walker (email: walkert)
    Editorial Assistant: Tanjam Jacobson (email: jacobsot)
Design and Production: Anne Kachergis (Kachergis Book Design, 14 Small Street North, Pittsboro, NC 27312)
Marketing Manager: Brian Roach (email: roach)
    Marketing Assistant: Catherine Szczybor (email: szczyborc)
Journals Coordinator: Emma Heck (email: heck)

Number of Press Staff: 9

Regular Member
Established: 1939
Title output 2017: 40
Titles currently in print: 1,050

Admitted to the Association: 1985
Title output 2018: 40
Journals published: 13

Editorial Program

American and European history (both ecclesiastical and secular); American and European litera-ture; philosophy; political theory; theology. Periods covered range from late antiquity to modern times, with special interest in late antiquity, early Christianity, and the medieval period.

Journals: *Newman Studies Journal; The Thomist: A Speculative Quarterly Review; Antiphon: A Journal for Liturgical Renewal; Nova et Vetera; The Catholic Historical Review; Pierre d'Angle; The Jurist: Studies in Church Law and Ministry; U.S. Catholic Historian; The Bulletin of Medieval Canon Law; Quaestiones Disputatae; Catholic Biblical Quarterly; Old Testament Abstracts;* and *Saint Anselm Journal*

Book series: *Sacra Doctrina*; Catholic Moral Thought; The Fathers of the Church: A New Transla-tion; Library of Early Christianity; Medieval Texts in Translation; Publications of the American Maritain Association (distributed); Studies in Philosophy and the History of Philosophy; Thomas Aquinas in Translation; IPS Monograph Series of the Institute for the Psychological Sciences (distributed); Sapientia Press (distributed); Franciscan University Press (distributed); Association of American Franciscan History (distributed); Humanum Academic Press (distributed).

Imprints: Catholic Education Press

Central European University Press

Street Address:
H-1051 Budapest
Oktober 6 utca 14.
Hungary

Mailing Address:
H-1051 Budapest,
Nador utca 11
Hungary

Phone: +36 1 327 3138
Fax: +36 1 327 3183
Email: ceupress@press.ceu.edu
Indiv.: (user ID)@ceu.hu

US and Canadian Orders:
Books International
Phone: 703.661.1500
Email: todd@booksintl.com

Website and Social Media:
Website: www.ceupress.com
Blog: ceupress.blogspot.hu
Facebook: www.facebook.com/ceupress
Twitter: @CEUPress

European Orders:
NBN International

UK Representative:
Oxford Publicity Partnership

Asia and the Pacific:
East West Export Books
Phone: 808.956.8830

Staff

Director: Krisztina Kos (36.1.327.3844; email: kosk)
Deputy Director: Peter Inkei (36.1.327.3181; email: inkeip)
Editors: Jozsef Litkey (36.1.327.3000/2096; email: litkeij); Nora Voros (36.327.3136; email: vorosn); Linda Kunos (36.327.3136; email: kunosl)
Financial Manager: Noemi Szabo (36.1.327.3141; email: szabon)
US Sales Manager: Abel Meszaros (732.763.8816; email: meszarosa)
Marketing Manager: Agnes Barla-Szabo (36.1.327.3138; email: barla-szaboa)

Regular Member

Established: 1993
Title output 2017: 27
Titles currently in print: 345

Admitted to the Association: 2014
Title output 2018: NR

Editorial Program

Reflecting the intellectual strengths and values of its parent institution, the press publishes books on the political philosophy and practices of open society, history, legal studies, nationalism, human rights, conflict resolution, Jewish studies, economics, medieval studies, literature, and international relations.

The publishing program of CEU Press focuses on issues of Central and Eastern Europe; it is also committed to the past and present history, society, culture and economy of the countries of the former Soviet Union and its neighbors. In the last couple of years, the Press has been expanding its list to include books in the field of higher education policy, gender studies, media studies and art history.

Book series: Central European Medieval Texts; CEU Medievalia; CEU Press Classics; CEU Studies in the History of Medicine; Discourses of Collective Identity in Central and Southeast Europe 1770–1945: Texts and Commentaries; Historical Studies in Eastern Europe and Eurasia; Natalie Zemon Davies Annual Lecture Series; The National Security Archive Cold War Readers

The University of Chicago Press

1427 E. 60th Street
Chicago, IL 60637-2954

Phone: 773.702.7700
Fax: 773.702.2705 (Books Acquisitions)
    773.702.9756 (Books Marketing)
    773.753.4247 (Journals Production)
Email: (user I.D.)@uchicago.edu

Chicago Distribution Center
11030 South Langley Avenue
Chicago, IL 60628
Phone: 773.702.7000

Website and Social Media—Books:
Website www.press.uchicago.edu
Chicago Blog: pressblog.uchicago.edu
Twitter: @UChicagoPress
Facebook: facebook.com/UniversityofChicagoPress
Tumblr: uchicagopress.tumblr.com
Instagram: UChicagoPress
Goodreads: goodreads.com/UChicagoPress
LibraryThing: www.librarything.com/profile/UChicagoPress

Website and Social Media—Journals:
Website: www.journals.uchicago.edu
Facebook: www.facebook.com/UChicagoJournals
Twitter: @ChicagoJournals

UK Representative:
Yale Representation Ltd.

Canadian Representative:
The University Press Group

Staff
Director: Garrett P. Kiely (773.702.8878; email: gkiely)
Deputy Director: Christopher Heiser (773.702.2998; email: cheiser)
Assistant to the Director and Deputy Director: Ellen M. Zalewski (773.702.8879; email: emz1)
Executive Director of Information Technology: Patti O'Shea (773.702.8521; email: poshea)
IT Operations Manager Information Technology Support: Derek Simmons (773.702.0510; email: dcsimmons)
Human Resources Manager: Alice Lloyd (773.702.7303; email: alloyd)
Digital Publishing Manager: Krista Coulson (773.702.5862; email: kcoulson)
Books Division
Acquisitions Editorial:
Editorial Director: Alan Thomas (773.702.7644; email: athomas2)
    Editors: Susan Bielstein (art, architecture, ancient archeology, classics, film studies) (773.702.7633; email: smb1); Timothy Mennel (American history, regional publishing) (773.702.0158; email: tmennel); Elizabeth Branch Dyson (sociology, ethnomusicology, education) (773.702.7637; email: ebd); Marta Tonegutti (music) (773.702.0427; email: mtonegut);

Randolph Petilos (medieval studies, poetry) (773.702.7647; email: rpetilos); Karen Darling (history, philosophy, and social studies of science) (773.702.7641; email: darling); Jane Macdonald (economics, business, finance) (773.702.7638; email: janem); Chuck Myers (political science, law and society) (773.702.7648; email: myersc); Priya Nelson (anthropology, history) (773.702.4759; email: pnelson); Kyle Wagner (religious studies) (773.702.1006; email: kwagner); Mary Laur (reference, writing guides) (773.702.7326; email: mlaur) Scott Gast (life sciences) (773.702.0162; email sgast); James Toftness (contemporary art, media and technology studies) (773.702.8826; email: toftness); Rachel Kelly Unger (geography, cartography) (773.702.5870; email: rachelkelly)

Paperback Editor: Margaret Hivnor (773.702.7649; email: mhivnor1)

Director of Intellectual Property: Laura Leichum (773.702.6096; email: lleichum)

Manuscript Editorial: Jenni Fry, Managing Editor (773.702.5328 email: jennifry)

Design and Production: Jill Shimabukuro, Design and Production Director (773.702.7653; email: jshimabu)

Marketing: Levi Stahl, Marketing Director (773.702.0289; email: levi)

Associate Marketing Director and Promotions Director: TBA

Senior Promotions Managers: Melinda Kennedy (773.702.2945; email: mkennedy1); Nick Lilly (773.702.7740; email: nlilly); Kristen Raddatz (773.702.1964; email: kraddatz)

Promotions Managers: Mollie McFee (773.702.7740; email: mmcfee) Tristan Bates (773.702.0279; email: thbates); Tyler McGaughey (773.702.4216; email: tmcaughey)

Promotion Assistant: Adrienne Meyers (adriennem; 773.702.7740)

Advertising Manager: Anne Osterman (773.702.7897; email: abwolver)

Senior Exhibits Manager: Eric DeTratto (773.834.7201; email: edetratto)

Marketing Design Manager: Mary Shanahan (773.702.7697; email: meshanah)

Graphic Artist: Brian Beerman (773.702.7849; email: bbeerman)

Sales: John Kessler, Associate Marketing Director/Sales Director (773.702.7248; email: jck1)

Sales and Distribution Associate: Robert Hoffman (773.702.0340; email: rmh)

Special Sales and Inventory Manager: Joseph Peterson (773.702.7723; email: jpeterson)

Sales Representatives: Bailey Walsh (Midwest) (email: bgw); Gary Hart (West Coast) (email: ghart)

International Sales Manager: Micah Fehrenbacher (773.702.7898; email: micahf)

E-commerce/Direct-to-Consumer Sales: Dean Blobaum, Electronic Marketing Manager (773.702.7706; email: dblobaum)

Marketing Systems Coordinator: Tom McGraw (773.702.6674; email: tmcgraw)

Direct Mail Associate: Teresa Fagan (773.702.7887; email: tfagan)

Reference Marketing: Jenny Ringblom, Reference Marketing Manager (773.702.3233; email: ringblom)

Reference Special Sales and Senior Promotions Manager: Lauren Salas (773.702.0890; email: lsalas)

Client Relations Specialists, Reference: Laureen Keene (773.702.0377; email: lskeene1); Brian Carroll (512.669.3857; email: carrollb)

Marketing Client Distribution: Levi Stahl, Marketing Director (773.702.0289; email: levi)

Distribution Client Manager: Steven Pazik (773.834.1916; email: spazik)

Journals Division

Director, Journals Division: Ashley Towne (773.753.4241; email: atowne)

Director, Journals Acquisitions and Publisher: Kari Roane (773.702.7362; email: kroane)

Director of Strategic Partnerships: Katharine Duff (773.702.7688; email: kduff)

Senior Publisher: Gordon Rudy (773.702.2448; email: grudy)

Publishers: Valerie Bajorat (773.702.7521; email: vbajorat) and Andrew Seagram (773.702.4673; email: aseagram)

Associate Marketing Director: Tiffany Adams (773.834.0432; email: tiffanyadams)

Marketing Managers: Marsha Ross (773.702.8185; email: mar); Rose Rittenhouse (773.834.4075; email: rittenhouse).

Marketing Associate: Mallory Gevaert (773.834.5912; email: mgevaert)

Production and Operations Manager: Sarah Gardiner (773.702.2490; email: sgardiner)

Assistant Chief Manuscript Editors: Brendan Carrick (773.702.7676; email: bjc); Devon Ritter (773.702.7518; email: ritterd); Larry Wethington (773.702.0199; email: lwething)
Electronic Publishing Technology Manager: Michael Boudreau (773.753.3298; email: mboudrea)
Institutional Licensing Manager: Chaz Oreshkov (773.834.1793; email: oreshkov)
Subscription Fulfillment and Sales Manager: Rich Connelly (773.753.3601; email: rec1)
Chicago Distribution Center Services
Director, Chicago Distribution Services: Joseph D'Onofrio (773.702.7020; email: jdonofrio)
Senior Operations Manager: Mark Stewart (773.702.7024; email: stewart44)
Director, Clients Services and Business Operations: Saleem Dhamee (773.702.7014; email: sdhamee)
Customer Service Manager: Karen Hyzy (773.702.7109; email: khyzy)
Business Metadata Manager: Latrice Allen (773.702.7112; email: lallen)
Credit and Collections, A/R Manager: Cynthia Bastion (773.702.7167; email: cab9)
Director of Accounting: Bob Peterson (773.702.7036; email: xrwp)
Manager, Chicago Digital Distribution Center: Kewon Bell (773.702.7238; email: kewonbell)
M.I.S. Manager: Christopher Jones (773.702.7229; email: cdjones)
Royalty/Rights Manager: Cassandra Wisniewski (773.702.7062; email: cwisniew)
Warehouse Office Manager: Gail Candreva-Szwet (773.702.7080; email: gcandrev)
Production Manager: Tammy Paul (773.702.7081; email: tpaul)
Journals Warehouse Manager: Don P. Collins (773.702.7245; email: dpcollins)
Returns Manager: Jenn Stone (773.834.3687; email: jstone1)
Inventory Control Manager: Dennis Kraus (773.834.3499; email: kraus)
BiblioVault
BiblioVault Manager: Kate Davey (773.834.4417; email: kdavey)

Number of Press Staff: 279

Regular Member

Established: 1891   Admitted to the Association: 1937
Title output 2017: 329   Title output 2018: 311
Titles currently in print: 7,232   Journals published: 73

Editorial Program
Scholarly, course, and general-interest works in: Anthropology; Art and Architecture; Asian Studies; Business; Cartography and Geography; Classics; Economics and Finance; Education; Film and Media Studies, History; Law; Life Sciences; Linguistics; Literary Criticism; Musicology; Philosophy; Political Science; Reference; Religious Studies; Science Studies; Sociology; Writing and Publishing. Closed to submissions in fiction and poetry.
Journals: *Afterall; American Art; American Journal of Education; American Journal of Sociology; The American Naturalist; American Political Thought; Archives of American Art Journal; Art Documentation; The Biological Bulletin; Bulletin of the American Schools of Oriental Research; Bulletin of the Detroit Institute of Art; The China Journal; Classical Philology; Comparative Education Review; Critical Historical Studies; Critical Inquiry; Current Anthropology; Economic Development and Cultural Change; The Elementary School Journal; English Literary Renaissance; Ethics; Freshwater Science; Gesta; Getty Research Journal; HAU: Journal of Ethnographic Theory; History of Humanities; History of Religions; HOPOS; International Journal of American Linguistics; International Journal of Plant Sciences; Isis; The Journal of African American History; Journal of Anthropological Research; Journal of the Association for Consumer Research; The Journal of the Association of Environmental and Resource Economists; Journal of Cuneiform Studies; The Journal of Geology; Journal of Human Capital; Journal of Labor Economics; Journal of Law and Courts; The Journal of Law and Economics; The Journal of Legal Studies; The Journal of Modern History; Journal of Near Eastern Studies; Journal of Political Economy; The Journal of Politics; The Journal of Religion; Journal of the Society for Social Work and Research; KNOW: A Journal on the Formation of Knowledge; The Library Quarterly; Marine Resource Economics; Metropolitan Museum Journal; Modern Philology; Near Eastern Archaeology; The Papers of the Bibliographical Society of America; Philosophy of Science; Physiological and Biochemical Zoology; Polity; Portable Gray; The Quarterly Review of Biology; Renaissance Drama; Res: Anthropology and Aesthetics; Schools; Signs; Signs and Society; The Social History of Alcohol and Drugs; Social Service Review; Source: Notes in the History of Art; Speculum; I Tatti Studies in the Italian Renaissance; West 86th; Winterthur Portfolio; The Wordsworth Circle*

Annuals: *Crime and Justice; Innovation Policy and the Economy; NBER Macroeconomics Annual; Osiris; Spenser Studies; Supreme Court Economic Review; The Supreme Court Review; Tax Policy and the Economy*

The Chinese University Press

The Chinese University of Hong Kong
Sha Tin
New Territories, Hong Kong

North American Distributor:
Columbia University Press
c/o Perseus Distribution
Phone: 800.944.8648/731.988.4440
Email: cup_book@columbia.edu

Phone: +852.3943.9800
Fax: +852.2603.7355
Email: cup@cuhk.edu.hk
Indiv: (user I.D.)@cuhk.edu.hk

UK and European Distributor:
Eurospan Group
c/o Turpin Distribution
Phone: +44 (0) 1767 604972
Email: eurospan@turpin-distribution.com

Website and Social Media:
Website: www.chineseupress.com
Facebook: www.facebook.com/
    TheChineseUniversityPress
Weibo: weibo.com/cupress
Twitter: @CUHKPress

Other Areas:
(Customer Service and Orders)
The Chinese University Press
Phone: +852 39439800
Fax: +852 26037355
Email: cup-bus@cuhk.edu.hk

Australian Distributor:
Footprint Books

Staff
Director: Qi GAN (+852.3943.9818; email: ganqi)
Secretary to the Director: Tina Chan (+852.3943.9810; email: tinachan)
Editorial: Ying LIN, Managing Editor (+852.3943.9811; email: linying)
Acquisitions Editor: Minlei YE (+852.3943.9812; email: minleiye)
Business/Marketing: Angelina Wong, Manager (+852.3943.9822; email: laifunwong)

Number of Press Staff: 24

Regular Member
Established: 1977
Title output 2017: NR
Titles currently in print: 1,032

Admitted to the Association: 1981
Title output 2018: 86
Journals published: 8

Editorial Program
Bilingual publication of academic and general trade titles. Areas of interest include Chinese studies in literature, history, philosophy, languages, arts and contemporary Chinese history. The Press also publishes books on business, government, medicine, as well as dictionaries and general books in both the English and Chinese languages.
Journals: *Asian Journal of English Language Teaching; The China Review; Communication & Society; Daoism: Religion, History and Society; Journal of Chinese Studies; Journal of Translation Studies, International Journal for the Study of Humanistic Buddhism*
Book series: Bibliography and Index Series; Bilingual Series on Modern Chinese Literature; Ch'ien Mu Lectures in History and Culture; Educational Studies Series; Hong Kong Taxation; Institute of Chinese Studies Monograph Series; International Poetry Nights in Hong Kong Series (IPNHK); Jintian Series of Contemporary Chinese Writing; Young Scholars Dissertation Awards, Translation Series
Imprints: The Chinese University Press

University of Cincinnati Press

Street Address:
Rieveschl 503C
Cincinnati OH 45221-0033
Phone: 513.556.1515
Email: ucincinnatipress@ucmail.uc.edu

Mailing Address:
Langsam Library
2911 Woodside Dr
ML 0033
Cincinnati OH 45221-0033

Website and Social Media:
Website: ucincinnatipress.uc.edu/
Twitter: @ucincipress
Instagram: @ucincipress
Facebook: University of Cincinnati Press

Staff
Director: Elizabeth Scarpelli (513.556.1494; email: Elizabeth.Scarpelli@uc.edu)
    Staff Executive Asst: Kathi Miniard (513.556.1515; email: miniarkn@ucmail.uc.edu)
Scholarly Communications, Cincinnati Library Publishing Services (CLiPS) Coordinator: Mark
    Konecny (513.556.2511; email: mark.konecny@uc.edu)
Assistant Managing Editor: Sarah Muncy (513.556.6276; email: muncysh@ucmail.uc.edu)
Editorial Assistant GA: Daniel Mattox (email: ucincinnatipress@uc.edu)
Marketing Intern: DQuez Carr (email: ucpressmktg@uc.edu)
Library Staff Accountant: Dorcas Gichuru (513.556.1463; email: Dorcas.Gichuru@uc.edu)
Library and Press Technical Development Lead: Sean Crowe (513.556.1899; email:
    sean.crowe@uc.edu)

Introductory Member
Established: 2016
Title output 2017: 1
Titles currently in print: 7

Admitted to the Association: 2017
Title output 2018: 5
Journals published: 3

Editorial Program
Serious works of non-fiction in social justice across HSS, STEM and business, transdisciplinary
works in community engagement and collective impact. The press publishes scholarly monographs and serious works for a wide audience of scholars and practitioners which move beyond
discipline-specific approaches to create new rigorous perspectives across HSS, STEM and Business. Our books focus on issues, solutions and strategies which highlight and improve underserved and underrepresented populations and disparities in access, equity, and privilege throughout the world. Additionally, the Press publishes in all areas and all subjects related to Regional
Studies in the Greater Cincinnati area. The press invites open and subscription model journals
related to areas of publication to submit proposals.
Joint imprints and co-publishing programs: University of Cincinnati Library Publishing Services
(CLiPS)

University Press of Colorado/Utah State University Press

Colorado Address:
245 Century Circle
Suite 202
Louisville, CO 80027

Phone: 720.406.8849
Fax: 720.406.3443
Email: (user I.D.)@upcolorado.com

Utah Address:
3078 Old Main Hill
Merrill-Cazier Library
Logan, UT 84322-3078
Phone: 720.406.8849
Fax: 720.406.8849

Distributor:
Chicago Distribution Center
11030 South Langley Ave.
Chicago, IL 60628

Phone: 800.621.2736
Fax: 800.621.8476

European and International Representative:
National Book Network International

Websites and Social Media:
Websites: www.upcolorado.com; www.usupress.com
Facebook: www.facebook.com/pages/The-University-Press-of-Colorado/347439013387;
www.facebook.com/pages/Utah-State-University-Press/164439110276267
Twitter: @UPColorado

Staff
Director: Darrin Pratt (email: darrin)
Assistant Director/Managing Editor: Laura Furney (email: laura)
Acquisitions Editor (USUP Imprint): Rachael Levay (email: rachael@usupress.com)
Acquisitions Editor (Colorado Imprint): Charlotte Steinhardt (email: charlotte)
Production Manager: Dan Pratt (email: dan)
Marketing & Sales Manager: Beth Svinarich (email: beth)

Number of Press Staff: 8

Regular Member
Established: 1965
Title output 2017: 48
Titles currently in print: 812

Admitted to the Association: 1982
Title output 2018: 44

Editorial Program
Physical sciences; natural history; ecology; American history; Western history; anthropology; archaeology; composition studies; folklore studies; Native American studies; Western women's history; Mormon history; and regional (Mountain West) titles.
    The Press also copublishes with and distributes titles for the Denver Museum of Natural History, the Colorado Historical Society Colorado State University's Cooperative Extension, the Center for Literary Publishing, History Colorado, the Institute for Mesoamerican Studies, the International Association for Society and Natural Resources (Social Ecology Press), the WAC Clearinghouse, and Western Press Books.
Book series: Atomic History & Culture; The George and Sakaye Aratani Nikkei in the Americas Series; Leonard J. Arrington Lecture Series; Life Writings of Frontier Women; Mining the American West; Timberline Books

Columbia University Press

61 West 62nd Street, Fl. 3
New York, NY 10023-7015

Phone: 212.459.0600
Fax: 212.459.3677
Email: (user I.D.)@columbia.edu

Distributor:
Ingram Academic Services:
210 American Drive
Jackson, TN 38301
Phone: 800.343.4499
Email: IPSJacksonOrders@ingramcontent.com

Website and Social Media:
Website: cup.columbia.edu
Blog: cupblog.org
Facebook: www.facebook.com/
ColumbiaUniversityPress
Twitter: @ColumbiaUP
Pinterest: ColumbiaUP

UK Office:
University Press Group
LEC 1 – New Era Estate
1 Oldlands Way, Bognor Regis
West Sussex PO22 9SA
Phone: +44 1243 842165
Fax: +44 1243 842167

Staff
Administration
Associate Provost and Director: Jennifer Crewe (ext. 7145; email: jc373)
Executive Assistant to the Director: Sheniqua Larkin (ext. 7163; email: sl2805)
Associate Director and Director of Operations and Sales: Brad Hebel (ext. 7130; email: bh2106)
Editorial Director: Eric I. Schwartz (ext. 7118; email: es3387)
Financial Manager: Robert Abrams (ext. 7119; email: ra2555)
Director of Human Resources: James Pakiela (ext. 7109; email: jp2483)
Director of Rights and Contracts: Justine Evans (ext. 7128; email: je2217)
Director, Editing, Design, and Production: Marielle Poss (ext. 7155; email: mtp2147)
IT Director: Greg Lara (ext. 7132; email: gl2298)
Development and Grants Manager: Alanna Duncan (ext. 7131; email: ad3212)
Acquisitions
Editorial Director: Eric I. Schwartz (sociology, Columbiana) (ext. 7118; email: es3387)
 Publisher, Columbia Business School Publishing and Economics: Myles Thompson (ext. 7161; email: mt2312)
 Publisher for Philosophy and Religion: Wendy Lochner (ext. 7121; email: wl2003)
 Editors: Philip Leventhal (literary studies, film studies, journalism) (ext. 7159; email: pl2162); Christine Dunbar (Asian humanities, Asian and Russian literature in translation) (ext. 7141; email: cd2654); Caelyn Cobb (global history and politics) (ext. 7107; email: cc4141); Stephen Wesley (American history and politics; social work) (ext 7203; email: sw2729); Miranda Martin (life and physical science) (ext 7154: email: mm5451)
EDP (Editing, Design, and Production)
Director, Editing, Design, and Production: Marielle Poss (ext.7155, email: mtp2147)
 Production Editing Manager: Leslie Kriesel (ext. 7110; email: lrk11)
 Production Editor: Susan Pensak (ext. 7139; email: srp4)
 Manufacturing Director: Jennifer Jerome (ext. 7177; email: jj352)
 Production Manager: Jessica Schwarz (ext. 7114; email: js2447)
 Design Director: Julia Kushnirsky (ext. 7102; email: jk3151)
 Senior Designers: Lisa Hamm (ext. 7105; email: lh400); Milenda Lee (ext. 7103; email: ml2657); Chang Jae Lee (ext. 7140; email: chl32)
 Designer: Noah Arlow (ext. 7178; email: na2407)
Marketing and Sales
Associate Director and Director of Operations and Sales: Brad Hebel (ext. 7130; email: bh2106)
 Promotions Director: Meredith Howard (ext. 7126; email: mh2306)
 Assistant Marketing Director/Direct Marketing Manager: Todd Lazarus (ext. 7152; email: tdl10)
 Advertising Manager: Elena Iaffa (ext. 7124; email: ei2131)
 Sales Consortium Manager/Southeast Sales Representative: Catherine Hobbs (email: catherinehobbs@earthlink.net)

Mid-West Sales Representative: Kevin Kurtz (email: kkurtz5@earthlink.net)
West Coast Sales Representative: William Gawronski (email: wgawronski@earthlink.net)
Northeast Sales Representative: Connor Broughan (email: cb2476)
Digital Products Representative: Herbert Plummer (ext. 7112; email: hp2356)
Metadata and Social Media Manager: Maritza Herrera-Diaz (ext. 7115; email: mh3850)
Finance and Operations
Financial Manager: Robert Abrams (ext. 7119; email: ra2555)
   Assistant Manager, Finance: Louis Gabriele (ext. 7108; email: lmg2210)
   IT Director: Greg Lara (ext. 7132; email: gl2298)
   Network Operations Technician: Iain Scott (ext. 7106; email: is2588)
   Publishing Systems Manager: Michael Haskell (ext. 7162; email: mh2100)
   Managing Editor for Reference and Electronic Publishing: Stephen Sterns (ext. 7148; email: ss724)

Regular Member

Established: 1893	Admitted to the Association: 1937
Title output 2017: 185	Title output 2018: 170
Titles currently in print: 4,361	

Editorial Program
Scholarly, general interest, and upper-level textbooks in the humanities; social sciences; sciences; and professional disciplines. Subjects include animal studies; Asian studies; behavioral science; botany; conservation and environmental science; criminology; ecology; evolutionary studies; film; finance and business economics; gender studies; history; international relations; journalism; literary and cultural studies; media studies; Middle East studies; philosophy; political philosophy; political science; religion; social work; and sociology. General reference works in print and electronic formats. The Press publishes poetry, fiction, and drama in translation only.

   Columbia University Press is the distributor in the United States, Canada, and Latin America for American Institute of Buddhist Studies; Agenda Publishing; Auteur Publishing; Barbara Budrich Publishers; Chinese University Press; Columbia Books on Architecture and the City; East European Monographs/Maria Curie-Skłodowska University Press; Harrington Park Press; Hong Kong University Press; ibidem Press; Jagiellonian University Press; Peterson Institute for International Economics; Social Science Research Council; Transcript Verlag; Tulika Books; and University of Tokyo Press.
Book series, joint imprints, and/or co-publishing programs: American Academy of Religion Lectures on the History of Religions; Arts and Traditions of the Table; Asia Perspectives; Biology and Resource Management; Columbia Business School Publishing; Columbia Classics in Philosophy; Columbia Classics in Religion; Columbia History of Urban Life; Columbia Journalism Review Books; Columbia Readings of Buddhist Literature; Columbia Series in Race, Inequity, and Health; Columbia Series in Science and Religion; Columbia Studies in the History of U.S. Capitalism; Columbia Studies in International History; Columbia Studies in Terrorism and Irregular Warfare; Columbia Themes in Philosophy, Social Criticism and the Arts; Complexity in Ecological Systems; Contemporary Asia In the World; Critical Moments in Earth History; Critical Perspectives on Animals; Cultures of History; Empowering the Powerless; End of Life Care; Energy Markets and Geopolitics; European Perspectives; Film and Culture; Foundations of Social Work Knowledge; Gender and Culture; Gender, Theory and Religion; Global Chinese Culture; History and Society of the Modern Middle East; Initiative for Policy Dialogue at Columbia; Introduction to Asian Civilizations; Insurrections: Critical Studies in Religion, Politics, and Culture; Kenneth J. Arrow Lecture Series; Leonard Hastings Schoff Lectures; Literature Now; The Middle Range; Modern Asian Literature; Modern Chinese Literature from Taiwan; New Directions in Critical Theory; Political Thought/Political History; Read Russia; Records of Western Civilization; Religion, Culture, and Public Life; Russian Library; Social Science Research Council Books; Society and the Environment, Translations from the Asian Classics; Weatherhead Books on Asia; Wellek Library Lectures; Woodrow Wilson Center Press.
Imprints: Columbia Business School Publishing, Wallflower Press

Concordia University Press

1455 de Maisonneuve Blvd. West, LB 331
Montreal, Quebec H3G 1M8

Phone: 514.848.2424 ext. 7748
Fax: 514.848.2882
Email: press@concordia.ca

Website and Social Media:
Website: www.concordia.ca/press
Twitter: @ConcordiaPress

Staff
Interim Director: Geoffrey Little (email: geoffrey.little@concordia.ca)
Managing and Production Editor: Meredith Carruthers (email: meredith.carruthers@concordia.ca)
Editorial Assistant: Charles Gonsalves (charles.gonsalves@concordia.ca)

Number of Press Staff: 3

Introductory Member
Established: 2016   Admitted to the Association: 2015

Editorial Program
Concordia University Press publishes books and pamphlets in the arts, humanities, and social sciences that engage with the themes of life, knowledge, and creation.

Life, including lifespan and aging; gender and sexuality; migration and diaspora; indigeneity; disability; the natural environment and sustainability; sense, emotion and affect; human and non-human rights; risk studies; cities and urban centers; and industrial and post-industrial communities. Knowledge, including memory, the past, and the future; digital and post-digital environments; the creation, formation, and curation of knowledge publics; oral history and storytelling; media; and translation and translation studies. Creation, including making and maker cultures; sculpture; painting; photography; fibre arts; literature; poetics; theatre; performance; cinema; video arts; and games and gaming studies.

Cork University Press

Youngline Industrial Estate, Pouladuff Road
Cork, Ireland

Phone: +353 21 490 2980
Fax: + 353 21 431 5329
Email: corkuniversitypress@ucc.ie

Website and Social Media:
Website: www.corkuniversitypress.com
Blog: corkuniversitypress.org
Facebook: www.facebook.com/CorkUP
Twitter: @CorkUP

UK Representative:
Marston Book Services

US Representative:
Longleaf Services
116 South Boundary Street
Chapel Hill, NC 27514-3808
Phone: 800.848.6224
Fax: 800.272.6817
Email: customerservice@longleafservices.org

Irish Representative:
Gill & MacMillan

Staff
Director: Mike Collins (email: mike.collins@ucc.ie)
Editorial and Production: Maria O'Donovan (email: maria.odonovan@ucc.ie)

Regular Member

Established: 1925
Title output 2017: 7
Titles currently in print: 200

Admitted to the Association: 2002
Title output 2018: 10
Journals published: 1

Number of Press Staff: 3

Editorial Program
While the Press specializes in the broad field of Irish Culture, its subject range extends across the fields of music, art history, literary criticism and poetry. However, the focus of our list is in the areas of Irish cultural history, archaeology and landscape studies.
Journal: *Irish Review*
Book series: Síreacht

Cornell University Press

Sage House
512 East State Street
Ithaca, NY 14850

Phone: 607.882.2219
Fax: 607.277.2374
Email: (user I.D.)@cornell.edu

Order Fulfillment:
Longleaf Services, Inc.
116 South Boundary Street
Chapel Hill, NC 27514-3808

Phone: 800.848.6224
Fax: 800.272.6817
Email: customerservice@longleafservices
org

Website and Social Media:
Website: cornellpress.cornell.edu; threehillsbooks.com
Twitter: @CornellPress
Blog: sagehouse.blog
Facebook: CornellPress
Instagram: cornelluniversitypress
YouTube: CornellPressNews

Distribution:
Codasat Canada, Ltd. — Canada
Footprint Books — Australia, New Zealand, Papua New Guinea, Fiji
Craign Falk — South and Central America
Combined Academic Publishers — Rest of World

Staff
Director: Dean J. Smith (607.882.2226; email: djs486)
Subsidiary Rights Manager: Tonya Cook (email: tcc6)
Acquisitions Editorial: Mahinder S. Kingra, Editor-in-Chief (humanities, medieval studies, literary studies) (607.882.2239; email: msk55)
Editorial Director, ILR Press: Frances Benson (workplace issues, labor, class studies, health care, sociology, anthropology of work, higher education) (607.882.2218; email: fgb2)
Executive Editor: Roger Haydon (international relations, comparative politics, East and Central Asian studies, Slavic/Eurasian studies, Middle East studies) (607.882.2236; email: rmh11)
Senior Editors: Emily Andrew (military history, modern European history, Asian history, law & society) (416.429.0322; email: ea424); James Lance (anthropology, geography, urban studies) (413.727.2265; email: jml554)
Editorial Director, Three Hills, and Senior Editor: Michael J. McGandy (US history and urban development & policy, New York region) (607.882.2250; email: mjm475)
Editor, Comstock Publishing Associates: Katherine H. Liu (natural history & nature writing, ornithology, herpetology & ichthyology, mammalogy, entomology, botany & plant sciences,

environmental studies) (607.882.2247; email: khl8)
Editor, Southeast Asia Program Publications: Sarah E. M. Grossman (Southeast Asian studies, anthropology, political science, history, cultural studies) (607.255.4359; email: sg265)
Assistant Editor: Bethany Wasik (classics, archaeology) (607.882.2218; email: bethany.wasik)
Acquisitions Assistants: Meagan Dermody (607.882.2255; email: mbd89); Ellen F. Murphy (607.882.2249; email: efm66)
Manuscript Editorial: Ange Romeo-Hall, Managing Editor (607.882.2257; email: asr8)
Digital Publishing Editor and Senior Production Editor: Karen Laun (607.882.2240; email: kml35)
Senior Production Editors: Karen T. Hwa (607.882.2237; email: kth9); Susan Specter (607.882.2259; email: sps19)
Production Editor: Jennifer Savran Kelly (607.882.2261; email: jds75)
Design and Production: Lynn Benedetto, Director of Finance and Production (607.882.2210; email: lad23)
Art Director: Scott Levine (607.882.2241; email: sel37)
Designer: Richanna Patrick (607.882.2253; email: rp12)
Senior Production Coordinator: Diana Silva (607.882.2258; email: drs68)
Production Coordinator: William L. Oates (607.882.2260; email: wlo6)
Marketing: Martyn Beeny, Marketing Director (607.882.2197; email: mb2545)
Social Media Coordinator: Adriana Ferreira (607.882.2202; email: af582)
Special Sales Rep & Metadata Specialist: Nathan Gemignani (607.882.2234; email: ndg5)
Digital Marketing Manager: Jonathan Hall (607.882.2235; email: jlh98)
Exhibits/Awards/Advertising Coordinator: David Mitchell (607.882.2251; email: dwm23)
Publicity Manager: Cheryl Quimba (607.882.2248; email: cq43)
Marketing Assistant: Carmen Torrado Gonzalez (607.882.2232; email cat223)
Business: Lynn Benedetto, Director of Finance and Production (607.882.2210; email: lad23)
Accounting: William O'Dell Wehling (607.882.2211; email: wvo3)
Administration, Royalties, Copyright: Michael Morris (607.882.2256; email: mam278)
Administrative Support: Katelyn Leboff (607.882.2238; email: kml329)
IT Administrator: Patrick Garrison (607.882.2233; email: plg6)
Permissions & Rights Coordinator: Stephanie Munson (607.882.2252; email: sm120)

Number of Press Staff: 38

Regular Member
Established: 1869   Admitted to the Association: 1937
Re-established in present form: 1930
Title output 2017: 126   Title output 2018: 148
Titles currently in print: 3,763

Editorial Program
Nonfiction, with particular strengths in anthropology, archaeology, Asian studies, classics, ge-ography, higher education, history (U.S., European, Asian, and military), law, literary and cultural studies, medieval studies, New York City and State, politics and international relations, religion, Slavic studies, sociology, and urban studies. Under the ILR Press imprint, books in labor relations, class and workplace issues, and health care policy. Books in the life sciences, environmental studies, and natural history are published under Comstock Publishing Associates imprint, and books on Southeast Asian history, culture, and society, as well as the journal Indonesia, are published under the Southeast Asia Program (SEAP) Publications imprint. Books about New York State for a trade audience are published under the Three Hills imprint. Submissions are not invited in poetry or fiction.
    Cornell University Press is the distributor in North America for Leuven University Press.
Book series, joint imprints and/or copublishing programs: Agora Editions; Battlegrounds: Cornell Studies in Military History; Brown Democracy Medal, Penn State; Cornell Global Perspec-tives; Cornell Series in Environmental Education; Cornell Series on Land; Cornell Studies in Clas-sical Philology; Cornell Studies in Money; Cornell Studies in Political Economy; Cornell Studies in Security Affairs; Corpus Juris: The Humanities in Politics and Law; The Culture and Politics of Health Care Work; Expertise: Cultures and Technologies of Knowledge; Histories of American Education; Islandica; Myth and Poetics II; Persian Gulf Studies; Police/Worlds: Studies in Security, Crime, and Governance; Religion and American Public Life; Signale: Modern German Letters,

Cultures, and Thought; Studies of the Weatherhead East Asian Institute; The United States in the World; Zona Tropical Publications
Imprints: Cornell University Press; ILR Press; Comstock Publishing Associates; Three Hills; Southeast Asia Program Publications; Cornell Publishing

The University of Delaware Press

Street/Mailing Address:
200A Morris Library
181 South College Avenue
Newark, DE 19717-5267

Phone: 302.831.1149
Fax: 302.831.6549
Email: joestrei@udel.edu
Website: library.udel.edu/udpress/

Orders:
Longleaf Services, Inc.
116 S. Boundary St.
Chapel Hill, NC 27514-3808
Phone: 800-848-6224
Fax: 800-272-6817
Email: orders@longleafservices.org
Online orders: library.udel.edu/udpress

Staff
Director: Julia Oestreich (302.831.1149; email: joestrei@udel.edu)

Introductory Member
Established: 1922
Title output 2017: 11
Titles currently in print: 700

Admitted to the Association: 2014
Title output 2018: 4

Number of Press Staff: 1

Editorial Program
The University of Delaware Press publishes mainly in the fields of literary studies, especially Early Modern, eighteenth- and nineteenth-century literature; Eighteenth-Century Studies; art history; French studies; and historical/cultural studies of Delaware and the Eastern Shore. Our publishing program in literary studies and art history has expanded, and submissions that deal with the Late Medieval period through the contemporary era are welcome, as are those that address literature, art, or culture in the United Kingdom, Continental Europe, Asia, the United States, Latin America, or the Caribbean. Our series focus on works that are interdisciplinary, transnational, and/or trans-temporal in nature.
Book series: Cultural Studies of Delaware and the Eastern Shore; Studies in Seventeenth- and Eighteenth-Century Art and Culture; Early Modern Exchange; Swift and His Contemporaries; Performing Celebrity; Early Modern Feminisms
Co-publishing partners: University Museums (of the University of Delaware)

Duke University Press

Street Address:
905 West Main Street
Suite 18-B
Durham, NC 27701

Mailing Address:
Box 90660
Durham, NC 27708- 0660

Phone: 919.687.3600
Faxes: 919.688.4574 (general)
Email: info@dukeupress.edu
Indiv:
firstinitiallastname@dukeupress.edu or
firstname.lastname@dukeupress.edu
(unless otherwise indicated)

Orders and Customer Service:
Phone: 888.651.0122; 919.688.5134
Fax: 888.651.0124; 919.688.2615

Warehouse:
Duke University Press
Distribution Center
120 Golden Drive
Durham, NC 27705
Phone: 919.384.0733

Website and Social Media:
Website: www.dukeupress.edu
Blog: dukeupress.wordpress.com/
Facebook: www.facebook.com/DukeUniversityPress
Twitter: @DUKEpress

UK/European Representative:
Combined Academic Publishers

Canadian Representative:
Lexa Publishers' Representatives

Staff
Director: Stephen A. Cohn (919.687.3606)
Office of the Director
   Administrative Assistant to the Director/Development Coordinator: Maria Volpe (919.687.3685)
Executive Support Group
   Associate Director for Digital Publishing: Allison Belan (919.687.3683)
   Assistant Director for Contracts and Licensing: Cathy Rimer-Surles (919.687.8005)
   Manager, Rights and Permissions: Diane Grosse (919.687.8020)
Administration
   Director of Administration: Robyn L. Miller, Manager (919.687.3633)
   Accounting Manager: Cynthia Durham (919.687.3661)
   Business Manager: Kevin Sook (919.687.8004)
   Central Administration Manager: Bonnie Conner (919.687.3693)
   HR Manager: Thomas Devine (919.687.8018)
   IT Manager: Nicholas Sullivan (919.687.3641)
   Warehouse Manager: Don Griffin (919.384.1244)
Books
   Editorial Director: Ken Wissoker (anthropology, cultural studies, Asian Studies, post-colonial theory, lesbian and gay studies, construction of race, gender and national identity, new media, literary theory and criticism, film and television, popular music, social studies of science, visual studies) (212.817.7248; email: kwiss@duke.edu)
   Executive Editor: Courtney Berger (social and political theory, transnational American studies, Native American and indigenous studies, gender and sexuality studies, African American studies, Asian American studies, critical ethnic studies, science and technology studies, media studies, literary studies, and geography) (919.687.3652)
   Editor: Gisela Fosado (anthropology, sociology, American and Atlantic World history, gender and sexuality studies, race and ethnicity, African American and Africana studies, environmental studies, and Latin American and Latinx Studies) (919.687.3632)
   Editor: Elizabeth Ault (African Studies, Urban Studies, Middle East Studies, Geography, Theory from the South, Black and Latinx studies, disability studies, trans studies, and critical prison studies) (919.687.8022)
   Associate Editor: Miriam Angress (religion, world history, women's studies, creative non-fiction, World Readers, Latin American Readers) (919.687.3601)

Journals Publishing & Partnerships
  Journals Director: Rob Dilworth (919.687.3624)
  Senior Editor: Erich Staib (919.687.3664)
  Director of Publishing Services, Project Euclid: Leslie Eager (919.687.3630)
Editing, Design, and Production
  Director of Editing Design and Production: Nancy Hoagland (919.687.3629)
  Editorial Production Manager: Jessica Ryan (919.687.3666)
Editing (Books)
  Senior Project Editor: Liz Smith (919.687.8006)
  Project Editors: Susan Albury (919.687.3669); Sara Leone (919.687.3681); Christi Stanforth
  (919.687.8016); Chris Catanese (919.687.8003)
Editing (Journals)
  Senior Managing Editor: Ray Lambert (919.687.3625)
  Senior Project Editor: Charles Brower (919.687.3688)
  Assistant Managing Editors: Roy Pattishall; Joel Luber; Chris Mazzarra; Jan Martin; Nick Knittel
Design (Books)
  Design Manager: Amy Buchanan (919.687.3651)
  Book Designers: Matt Tauch (919.687.3676); Courtney Baker (919.687.3607); Mindy Hill
  (919.687.3621)
Design (Journals)
  Designer: Heather Hensley (919.687.3658)
  Production (Books)
  Production Manager: Chris Critelli (919.687.3622)
  Production Specialists: Kelsea Smith (919.687.8019); Venus Bradley (919.687.3643)
Productions (Journals)
  Production Manager: Brooke Philpott (919.687.3619)
  Senior Production Coordinator: Cynthia Gurganus (919.687.3691)
  Production Coordinators: Nancy Sampson; Nathan Moore; Amy Walter; Lisa Savage; Erica
  Tucker Woods
  Production Assistant: Taylor Brock
Marketing and Sales
  Director of Marketing and Sales: Cason Lynley (919.687.3631)
Customer Relations
  Customer Relations Manager: Amanda Kolman (919.687.3602)
  Digital Access and Journals Coordinator: Amber Carey (919.687.3612)
  Digital Access and Books Coordinator: Patrick Coleff (919.687.3617)
Library Relations and Sales
  Library Relations and Sales Manager: Kim Steinle (919.687.3655)
  Digital Collections Sales Manager: Katja Moos (919.687.8014)
  Library Sales Coordinator: Kristen Twardowski (919.687.3627)
  Library Sales and Digital Access Coordinator: Danielle Thibault (919.687-3636)
  Library Research Coordinator: Evan Watson (919.687.3634)
  Data Analyst: George Black (919.687.3614)
Marketing (Books)
  Books Marketing & Sales Senior Manager: Michael McCullough (919.687.3604)
  Publicity and Advertising Manager: Laura Sell (919.687.3639)
  Books Sales Manager: Jennifer Schaper (919.687.3680)
  Marketing Designer and Awards Coordinator: Emily Lawrence (919.687.3650)
  Direct Marketing Manager and Sales Associate: Julie Thomson (919.687.3603)
  Exhibits Manager: Helena Knox (919.687.3647)
  Metadata and Digital Systems Manager: H. Lee Willoughby-Harris (919.687.3646)
  Copywriter: Christopher Robinson (919.687.3663)
  Senior Marketing Assistant: Chad Royal (919.687.3649)

Marketing (Journals)
Journals Marketing Manager: Jocelyn Dawson (919.687.3653)
Library Marketing Outreach Manager: Mandy Brannon (919.687.8027)
Publicist and Exhibits Coordinator: Jessica Castro-Rappl (919.687.3637)
Digital Marketing Coordinator: Kasia Repeta (919.687.8019)
Marketing Designer and Advertising Coordinator: Dan Ruccia (919.687.8013)
Marketing and Sales Specialist: Anna Fletcher (919.687.8029)

Number of Press Staff: 120

Regular Member

Established: 1921 (as Trinity College Press)
Title output 2017: 130
Titles currently in print: 2,807

Admitted to the Association: 1937
Title output 2018: 140
Journals published: 55

Editorial Program
Scholarly books in the humanities and social sciences, with lists in art criticism and history; visual studies; cultural studies; gay and lesbian studies; gender studies; American studies; American history; African American studies; Latinx studies; Asian American studies; Native American & indigenous studies; cultural anthropology; minority politics and post-colonial issues; Latin American and Caribbean studies; Asian studies; South Asian studies; African studies; Middle East studies; European studies; music; film, TV and media studies; literary theory and history; environmental studies; geography; political science and political theory; legal studies; religion; sociology and social theory; and science studies

Journals: *American Literary Scholarship; American Literature; American Speech; Annals of Functional Analysis; Archives of Asian Art; Banach Journal of Mathematical Analysis; boundary 2; Camera Obscura; Collected Letters of Thomas and Jane Welsh Carlyle; Common Knowledge; Comparative Literature; Comparative Studies of South Asia, Africa and the Middle East; Critical Times; Cultural Politics; differences; Duke Mathematical Journal; East Asian Science, Technology and Society; Eighteenth-Century Life; English Language Notes; Environmental Humanities; Ethnohistory; French Historical Studies; Genre; GLQ: A Journal of Lesbian and Gay Studies; Hispanic American Historical Review; History of Political Economy; Illinois Journal of Mathematics; Journal of Chinese Literature and Culture; Journal of Health Politics, Policy and Law; Journal of Korean Studies; Journal of Medieval and Early Modern Studies; Journal of Middle East Women's Studies; Journal of Music Theory; Kyoto Journal of Mathematics; Labor; Meridians; minnesota review; Modern Language Quarterly; New German Critique; Nka; Notre Dame Journal of Formal Logic; Novel; Pedagogy; Philosophical Review; Poetics Today; positions; Public Culture; Qui Parle; Radical History Review; Small Axe; Social Text; South Atlantic Quarterly; Theater; TSQ: Transgender Studies Quarterly; Twentieth-Century Literature*

Book series, joint imprints and/or copublishing programs: ANIMA; American Encounters: Global Interactions; Asia-Pacific: Culture, Politics and Society; Collected Letters of Thomas and Jane Welsh Carlyle; C. L. R. James Archives; Console-ing Passions; Body/Commodity/Text; Critical Global Health: Evidence, Efficacy, Ethnography; Design Principles for Teaching History; Ecologies for the Twenty-First Century; Elements; Experimental Futures; Global Insecurities; Improvisation, Community, and Social Practice; Latin America in Translation; Latin America Otherwise: Languages, Empires, Nations; Latin America Readers; The Morgan Lectures; Narrating Native Histories; New Americanists; Next Wave: New Directions in Women's Studies; Objects/Histories; Perverse Modernities; Post-Contemporary Interventions; Public Planet; Radical Perspectives: A Radical History Review Book Series; Refiguring American Music; SIC; Sign, Storage, Transmission; Social Text Books; Theory in Forms; Theory Q; The Visual Arts of Africa and its Diasporas; World Readers

University Press of Florida

2046 NE Waldo Road
Suite 2100
Gainesville, FL 32609

Phone: 352.392.1351
Fax: 352.392.0590
Email: (user I.D.)@upress.ufl.edu

Orders:
Phone: 800.226.3822
Fax: 352.392.7302
Toll free fax: 800.680.1955

Website and Social Media:
Website: upress.ufl.edu
Blog: Floridabookshelf.wordpress.com
Facebook: www.facebook.com/Floridapress
Twitter: @floridapress
YouTube: floridapress
Instagram: floridapress

UK Representative:
Eurospan

Canadian Representative:
Scholarly Book Services

Staff

Director: Meredith Morris Babb (352.294.6834; email: mb)
Editor-in-Chief/Deputy Director: Linda Bathgate (352.294.6800; email: lbathgate)
   Senior Acquisitions Editor: Sian Hunter (919.428.8813; email: sian)
   Acquisitions Editor: Stephanye Hunter (352.294.6802; email: sah)
   Acquisitions Coordinator: Jenny Wilsen (352.294.6805; email: jenny)
   Acquisitions Assistant: Kayla Gaines (3522946803; email: kgaines)
Editorial, Design & Production: Michele Fiyak-Burkley, Associate Director & EDP Manager (352.294.6814; email: mf)
   Assistant Director, Managing Editor: Marthe Walters (352.294.6809; email: marthe)
   Project Editor: Eleanor Deumens (352.294.6810; email: leanor)
   Editorial Assistant: Valerie Melina (352.294.6811; email: valerie)
   Design Director: Larry Leshan (352.294.6815; email: ll)
   Senior Designer: Robyn Taylor (352.294.6816; email: rt)
   Production Coordinators: Anja Jimenez (352.294.6817; email: anja); Marisol Amador (352.294.6818; email: marisol)
Associate Director of Sales and Marketing: Romi Gutierrez (352.294.6819; email: romi)
   Assistant Marketing Manager: Rachel Doll (352.294.6820; email: rd)
   Metadata and Digital Publishing Manager: Ale Gasso (352.294.6821; email: ale)
   Publicist and Rights Manager: Samantha Zaboski (352.294.6822; email: sz)
   Exhibits and Promotions Coordinator: Mary Puckett (352.294.6823; email: mary)
   Marketing Coordinator: Victoria Reynolds (352.294.6824; email: victoria)
Journals Manager: Lauren Phillips (352.294.6835; email: lauren)
Business: Peter Van Woerden, Director for Finance (352.294.6831; email: peter)
   AP/Credit/Collections Manager: Jackie Panetta (352.294.6832; email: jackie)
   Order Entry: Chris Warner (352.392.6867; email: orders)
   Warehouse and Shipping Manager: Charles Hall (352.392.6867; email: charles)
IT Manager: Bryan Lutz (352.294.6829; email: bryan)

Number of Press Staff: 35

Regular Member

Established: 1945
Title output 2017: 78
Titles currently in print: 3,500

Admitted to the Association: 1950
Title output 2018: 61
Journals published: 6

Editorial Program

Floridiana; New World archaeology; conservation biology; Latin American studies; Caribbean studies; African American studies; American history and culture; Native American studies; medieval and modernist literature and literary criticism; dance; natural history; humanities. Submissions are not invited in prose fiction, poetry, or memoirs.

Journals: *Bioarchaeology International; Journal of Global South Studies; Forensic Anthropology; Delos; Florida Tax Review; Rhetoric of Health & Medicine; Subtropics*
Imprints: University Press of Florida; University of Florida Press; Seaside Books; Orange Grove Texts

Fordham University Press

Joseph A. Martino Hall
45 Columbus Avenue, 3rd Floor
New York, NY 10023

Fax: 347.842.3083
Email: (user I.D.)@fordham.edu

Orders:
Ingram Content Group LLC
One Ingram Blvd.
La Verne, TN 37086
Phone: 866.400.5351
IPSOrders@ingramcontent.com
ipage.ingramcontent.com

Website and Social Media:
Website: www.fordhampress.com
Blog: www.fordhampress.com/blog/
Facebook: www.facebook.com/FordhamUP
Twitter: @fordhampress
Pinterest: www.pinterest.com/fordhampress
Empire State Editions: www.fordhampress.com/empire-state-editions/
Empire State Editions Twitter: @E_S_Editions
Empire State Editions Facebook: www.facebook.com/EmpireStateEditions
YouTube: www.youtube.com/fordhampress1

European Representative:
Combined Academic Publishers Ltd.

Canadian Representative:
Canadian Manda Group

Staff

Director: Fredric W. Nachbaur (646.868.4201; email: fnachbaur)
Editor, Rights and Permissions Manager: Will Cerbone (646.868.4203; email: wcerbone)
Editorial Director: Richard W. Morrison (646.868.4208; email: rmorrison7)
Acquisitions Editor: Thomas Lay (646.868.4209; email: tlay)
Managing Editor: Eric Newman (646.868.4210; email: ernewman)
Design and Production Manager: Mark Lerner (646.868.4202; email: mlerner7)
Associate Director: Marketing & Sales Director: Kate O'Brien-Nicholson (646.868.4204; email: bkaobrien)
Marketing Manager: Kathleen Sweeney Parmiter (646.868.4205; email: kasweeney)
Business Manager: Margaret M. Noonan (646.868.4206; email: mnoonan)
Assistant Business Manager: Marie Hall (646.868.4207; email: mhall21)

Number of Press Staff: 10

Regular Member
Established: 1907
Title output 2017: 91
Titles currently in print: 1,181

Admitted to the Association: 1938
Title output 2018: 90
Journals published: 1

Editorial Program

Fordham University Press publishes primarily in the humanities and social sciences, with emphasis on the fields of African American studies, American studies, anthropology, communication and media studies, education, gender studies, history, literature, philosophy, religion, theology, and urban studies. Additionally, the Press publishes books focusing on the New York region and books of interest to the general public.

The Press distributes the publications of Creighton University Press; University of San Francisco Press; St. Joseph's University Press; Rockhurst University Press; The Institution for Advanced Study in the Theater Arts (IASTA); Center for Migration Studies; St. Bede's Publications and The Refugee Press.

Journal: *Joyce Studies Annual*

Book series: American Philosophy; Berkeley Forum in the Humanities; Catholic Practice in North America; Commonalities; Critical Studies in Italian America; Comparative Theology: Thinking Across Traditions; Donald McGannon Research Center's Everett C. Parker Book Series; Flannery O'Connor Trust Series; Fordham Series in Medieval Studies; Forms of Living; The Future of the Religious Past; Groundworks: Ecological Issues in Philosophy and Theology; International Humanitarian Affairs; Just Ideas: Transformative Ideals of Justice in Ethical and Political Thought; Meaning Systems; Lit Z; Medieval Philosophy: Texts and Studies; The North's Civil War; Orthodox Christianity and Contemporary Thought; Perspectives in Continental Philosophy; POLIS: Fordham Series in Urban Studies; Poets Out Loud; Reconstructing America; Studies in the Catholic Imagination; Thinking Out Loud; Transdisciplinary Theological Colloquia; Verbal Arts: Studies in Poetics; and World War II: The Global, Human, and Ethical Dimensions

Imprints: Empire State Editions: Dedicated to publishing books about the New York region

Gallaudet University Press

800 Florida Avenue, N.E.
Washington, DC 20002-3695

Phone: 202.651.5488
Fax: 202.651.5489
Email: gupress@gallaudet.edu
Indiv: (user I.D.)@gallaudet.edu

Website and Social Media:
Website: gupress.gallaudet.edu
Facebook: GallaudetUniversityPress
Twitter: @GallaudetPress
YouTube: www.youtube.com/channel/ c/GallaudetUniversityPress

European Distribution:
John Wiley

UK Sales Representation:
Yale Representation

Orders:
Gallaudet University Press
c/o Chicago Distribution Center
11030 South Langley Avenue
Chicago, IL 60628
Phone: 800.621.2736
Fax: 800.621.8476
Email: orders@press.uchicago.edu

Asia and the Pacific Sales Representation:
East-West Export Books

Staff
Interim Director and Marketing: Angela Leppig (202.651.5661; email: angela.leppig)
Acting Acquisitions Editor: Katie Lee (202.448.6907; email: katie.lee)
Managing Editor: Deirdre Mullervy (202.651.5967; email: deirdre.mullervy)
Production Coordinator and Business Office: Donna Thomas (202.651.5154; email: donna.thomas)
Marketing Assistant: Valencia Simmons (202.651.5917; email: valencia.simmons)

Number of Press Staff: 6

Regular Member
Established: 1980
Title output 2017: 14
Titles currently in print: 433

Admitted to the Association 1983
Title output 2018: 15
Journals published: 2

Editorial Program
Scholarly books and serious nonfiction from all disciplines as they relate to the interests and culture of people who are deaf and hard of hearing. Particular areas of emphasis include American Sign Language reference and research, signed language communities, linguistics, translation and interpreting studies, deaf education, Deaf history, Deaf culture, and disability studies.
Journals: *American Annals of the Deaf; Sign Language Studies*
Book series: Deaf Education; Deaf Lives; Gallaudet Classics in Deaf Studies; Gallaudet Deaf Literature; Interpreter Education; Sociolinguistics in Deaf Communities; Studies in Interpretation
Imprints: Kendall Green Publications; Clerc Books

GBHEM Publishing

1001 19th Avenue, South
Nashville, TN 37212

Phone: 615.340.7393
Email: Publishing@gbhem.org

Websites/Social Media:
Website www.gbhem.org/about/publications
Facebook: business.facebook.com/GBHEMPublishing/?business_id=1012602028764357

Staff
Publisher: Kathy Armistead
Acquisitions: Kathy Armistead
Editorial, Design, and Production Manager: Jennifer Manley Rogers (email: jrogers@gbhem.org)

Number of Press Staff: 2

Affiliate Member
Established 2016   Admitted to the Association: 2018
Title output 2017: 14   Title output 2018: 21
Titles currently in print: 72

Editorial Program
Theological and religious studies, history of Methodism, cultural studies, interfaith studies, and pastoral care. Spanish and bilingual titles (Spanish/English).

George Mason University Press

4400 University Drive MS 2FL
Fairfax, VA 22030-4444

Phone: 703.993.3636
Email: gmupress@gmu.edu
Indiv. email: (user I.D.)@gmu.edu

Orders:
University of Virginia Press
Phone: 1.800.831.3406
Website: www.upress.virginia.edu/order
Email: vapress@virginia.edu

Website and Social Media:
Website: publishing.gmu.edu/
Blog: publishing.gmu.edu/news/
Twitter: @MasonPublish
GitHub: github.com/masonpublishing/

UK Representative:
Eurospan

Canadian Representative:
Scholarly Book Services

Staff
Director: Aaron S. McCollough (703.993.2544; email: amccollo)
Scholarly Communications and Copyright Officer: Claudia Holland (703.993.2544;
  email: chollan3)
Coordinator, University Dissertation & Thesis Services: Sally Evans (703.993.2222;
  email: sevans13)
Associate University Librarian for Digital Programs and Services: Wally Grotophorst
  (703.993.9905; email: wallyg)
Dean of Libraries and University Librarian: John Zenelis (703.993.2491; email: jzenelis)

Introductory Member
Established: 2007
Title output 2017: 3
Titles currently in print: 7

Admitted to the Association: 2014
Title output 2018: NR
Journals published: 6

Editorial Program
Mason Publishing Group provides support and resources to the George Mason University
community for creating, curating, and disseminating scholarly, creative, and educational works.
Mason Publishing Group consolidates robust digital publishing programs and services within the
University Libraries, which has been developing expertise and increased capacity in scholarly
publishing for several years. The George Mason University Press supports the academic mission
of George Mason University by publishing peer-reviewed, scholarly works for a diverse, world-
wide readership. Subject areas include regional titles including history of Northern Virginia and
Washington DC; education, online learning, research methods and technology; political science,
public policy, and global affairs; environmental studies and conservation.
Journals: *Journal of Mason Graduate Research; Narrative and Conflict; New Voices in Public Policy;
Philosophy and Public Policy;* and *The Writing Campus*
Conference Proceedings: *Open Scholarship Initiative Proceedings; Innovations in Teaching and
Learning*

Georgetown University Press

3520 Prospect Street, NW
Suite 140
Washington, DC 20007

Phone: 202.687.5889
Fax: 202.687.6340
Email: gupress@georgetown.edu
Indiv: (user I.D.)@georgetown.edu
Indiv: (First name.last name)@georgetown.edu

Orders:
US: c/o Hopkins Fulfillment Service
PO Box 50370
Baltimore, MD 21211
Phone: 800.537.5487
Fax: 410.516.6998
Email: hfscustserv@press.jhu.edu

Website and Social Media:
Website: www.press.georgetown.edu
Blog: georgetownuniversitypress.tumblr.com
Facebook: www.facebook.com/georgetownup
News blog: georgetownup.wordpress.com
Pinterest: pinterest.com/georgetownup
Twitter:@gupress
YouTube: www.youtube.com/user/GeorgetownUP
Tumblr: georgetownuniversitypress.tumblr.com

UK/European Distributor:
NBN International

Canadian Representative:
Brunswick Books

Staff

Director: Al Bertrand (202.687.5912; email: ab3643@georgetown.edu)
Director, Georgetown Languages, and Assistant Director of the Press: Hope LeGro (202.687.4704; email: hjs6@georgetown.edu)
Acquisitions Editor, Languages: Clara Totten (202.687.2988; email: cls86@georgetown.edu)
Senior Acquisitions Editor, Political Science and International Affairs: Donald Jacobs (202.687.5218; email: dpj5@georgetown.edu)
Editorial, Design, and Production Manager: Glenn Saltzman (202.687.6251; email: gls43@georgetown.edu)
Editorial and Production Coordinator: Kathryn Owens (202.687.0159; email: kao51@georgetown.edu)
Marketing and Sales Director: Virginia Bryant (202.687.9856; email: vvb6@georgetown.edu)
Publicity Manager: Jacqueline Beilhart (202.687.9298; email: jb594@georgetown.edu)
Digital Publishing and Rights Manager: Puja Telikicherla (202.687.7687; email: pt97@georgetown.edu)
Publishing Assistant: Jessica Flores (202.687.4462; email: Jessica.Flores@georgetown.edu)
Business Manager and Assistant Director of the Press: Ioan Suciu (202.687.5641; email: suciui@georgetown.edu)
Accountant: Sulah Kim (202.687.8151; email: slk33@georgetown.edu)

Number of Press Staff: 12

Regular Member
Established: 1964
Title output 2017: 42
Titles currently in print: 923

Admitted to the Association: 1986
Title output 2018: 44
Journals published: 2

Editorial Program
Disciplines: international affairs; languages and linguistics; religion and ethics; and regional.
Journals: *Al-cArabiyya: Journal of the American Association of Teachers of Arabic; Georgetown Journal of International Affairs*
Book series: Advancing Human Rights; American Governance and Public Policy; Georgetown Classics in Arabic Language and Linguistics; Georgetown Shorts; Georgetown Studies in Spanish

Linguistics; Georgetown University Round Table on Languages and Linguistics; Moral Traditions; Public Management and Change; Religion and Politics; South Asia in World Affairs

University of Georgia Press

Main Library, Third Floor
320 S. Jackson Street
Athens, GA 30602

Phone: 706.542.1007
Fax: 706.542.2558
Indiv: (user I.D.)@uga.edu

Website and Social Media:
Website: www.ugapress.org
Blog: ugapress.wordpress.com
Facebook: www.facebook.com/UGAPress
Goodreads: www.goodreads.com/UGAPress
Instagram: instagram.com/ugapress
Twitter: @UGAPress
YouTube: UGAPress

World Distributor:
Eurospan

Fulfillment:
University of Georgia Press
c/o Longleaf Services, Inc.
116 Boundary St.
Chapel Hill, NC 27514-3808

Returns:
Longleaf Services – Returns
c/o Ingram Publisher Services
1250 Ingram Drive
Chambersburg, PA 17202

Orders and Customer Service:
Phone: 800.848.6224 or 919.966.7449
Fax: 800.272.6817 or 919.962.2704
Orders: orders@longleafservices.org
Email: customerservice
@longleafservices.org

Staff
Director: Lisa Bayer (706.542.0027; email: lbayer)
Assistant to the Director: Katherine La Mantia (706.542.1007; email: katglm)
Intellectual Property Manager (Contracts & Rights): Jordan Stepp (706.542.7175; email: jstepp)
Director of Development: Chantel Dunham (706.542.0628; email: cdunham)
Acquisitions Editorial: Mick Gusinde-Duffy, Executive Editor for Scholarly and Digital Publishing (history; human geography/urban studies; American studies) (706.542.9907; email: mickgd)
Executive Editor: Walter Biggins (American literary & cultural studies; history of the Americas; African American studies; narrative/creative nonfiction, media studies) (706.542.4728; email: wbiggins)
Acquisitions Editor: Patrick Allen (popular/public history; regional interest; landscape architecture; environmental studies; foodways; music) (706.542.6004; email: pallen)
Assistant Coordinator: Beth Snead (animal studies) (706.542.7613; email: bsnead)
Editorial Assistant: Katherine La Mantia (706.542.1007; email: katglm)
Editorial Design and Production: Jon Davies, Assistant Director for Editorial, Design, and Production (706.542.2101; email: jdavies)
Assistant Editorial, Design, and Production Manager: Melissa Bugbee Buchanan (706.542.4488; email: melissa.buchanan)
Production Editor and Reprints Coordinator: Rebecca Norton (706.542.4643; email: ranorton)
Senior Designer and Art Director: Erin Kirk New (706.769.0879; email: ekirknew)
Senior Designer and Production Manager: Kaelin Broaddus (706.542.3889; email: kaelinb)
Production Editor: Thomas Roche (706.542.2491; email: thomas.roche)
Marketing and Sales: Steven Wallace, Director of Marketing and Sales (706.542.4145; email: smwallace)
Electronic Information and Promotions Manager: David Des Jardines (706.542.9758; email: ddesjard)
Publicity and Social Media Manager: Jason Bennett (706.542.9263; email: jason.bennett)

Marketing Content and Exhibits Manager: Christina Cotter (706.542.0134; email: ccotter)
Business: Phyllis Wells, Associate Director and Chief Financial Officer (706.542.7250; email: pwells)
Accounts Payable and Permissions Coordinator: Stacey Hayes (706.542.2606; email: sbhayes)
Distributor Liaison: Jeri Headrick (706.542.9921 email: headrick)
The New Georgia Encyclopedia Project (www.georgiaencyclopedia.org)
Managing Editor: Ed Hatfield (404.523.6220, ext. 121; email: edward.hatfield)

Number of Press Staff: 22

Regular Member
Established: 1938   Admitted to the Association: 1940
Title output 2017: 65   Title output 2018: 65
Titles currently in print: 1,865

Editorial Program
Humanities and social sciences with particular interests in Atlantic world, American, and southern history; civil rights history; legal history; environmental history; African American studies; geography; urban studies; creative nonfiction; international relations; natural history; environmental studies; American and southern literature; American studies; cinema and media studies; food studies; popular culture; and regional trade titles.
Series and imprints: Animal Voices/Animal Worlds; Children, Youth, and War; Critical Studies in the History of Landscape Design; Crux: The Georgia Series in Literary Nonfiction; Early American Places; Environmental History and the American South; Geographies of Justice and Social Transformation; Georgia Review Books; Georgia River Network Guidebooks; History in the Headlines; Masters of Modern Landscape Design; The Morehouse College King Collection Series on Civil and Human Rights; Music of the American South; New Perspectives on the Civil War Era; The New Southern Studies; Peabody Media History Series; Politics and Culture in the Twentieth-Century South; Print Culture and the South; Race in the Atlantic World, 1700-1900; Since 1970: Histories of Contemporary America; Sociology of Race and Ethnicity Series; The South on Screen; Southern Foodways Alliance Studies in Culture, People, and Place; Studies in Security and International Affairs; Southern Legal Studies; UnCivil Wars; The United States and the Americas; A Wormsloe Foundation Publication
Literary competitions: Flannery O'Connor Award for Short Fiction; Georgia Poetry Prize; The Association of Writers and Writing Programs Award for Creative Nonfiction; Cave Canem Poetry Prize; National Poetry Series
Lecture series: Mercer University Lamar Memorial Lectures; George H. Shriver Lecture Series in Religion in American History
Imprint: A Wormsloe Foundation Nature Book

Getty Publications

1200 Getty Center Drive
Suite 500
Los Angeles, CA 90049-1682

Phone: 310.440.7365
Fax: 310.440.7758
Email: pubsinfo@getty.edu
Indiv: (user I.D.)@getty.edu

Orders:
Chicago Distribution Center
11030 South Langley Avenue
Chicago, IL 60628
Phone: 800.621.2736
Fax: 800.621.8476
Email: custserv@press.uchicago.edu

Website and Social Media:
Website: www.getty.edu/publications
Facebook: www.facebook.com/GettyPublications
Twitter: @GettyPubs

UK/European Distributors:
Yale University Press UK

UK/Sales Representative:
Yale University Press UK

Canada Sales Representative:
Lexa Publishers Representatives

Staff
Publisher: Kara Kirk (310.440.6066; email: kkirk)
Getty Research Institute: Michele Ciaccio (310.440.7453; email: mciaccio)
Getty Conservation Institute: Cynthia Godlewski (310.440.6805; email: cgodlewski)
Editor-in-Chief: Karen Levine (310.440.6525; email: klevine)
Rights & Permissions: Leslie Rollins (310.440.7102; email: lrollins)
Design and Production: Karen Schmidt (310.440.6504; email: kschmidt)
Associate Publisher: Maureen Winter (310.440.6117; email: mwinter)
Digital Publications Manager: Greg Albers (310.440.6067; email: galbers)
Sales Manager: Joanne Kenny (310.440.6119; email: jkenny)

Number of Press Staff: 31

Regular Member
Established: 1982
Title output 2017: 35
Titles currently in print: 585

Admitted to the Association: 1989
Title output 2018: 35
Journals published: 1

Editorial Program
Scholarly and general interest publications on the visual arts; conservation and the history of art and the humanities; and areas related to the work of the Getty Research Institute, the Getty Conservation Institute, the Getty Foundation, and the collections of the J. Paul Getty Museum: antiquities, decorative arts, drawings, manuscripts, paintings, photographs, and sculpture.
Journal: *Getty Research Journal*
Imprints: Getty Research Institute; Getty Conservation Institute; J. Paul Getty Museum; and Getty Publications

Harvard University Press

79 Garden Street
Cambridge, MA 02138-1499

Phones: 617.495.2600 (General)
617.495.2611 (Editorial)
617.495.2606 (Sales/Marketing)
Fax: 617.495.5898
Email:
firstname_lastname@harvard.edu

Customer Service/Orders:
Harvard University Press
c/o TriLiteral-LLC
100 Maple Ridge Drive
Cumberland, RI 02864-1769
Phone: 800.405.1619 (US & Canada)
401.531.2800 (all others)
Faxes: 800.406.9145 (US & Canada)
401.531.2801 (all others)

Website and Social Media:
Website: www.hup.harvard.edu
Blog: harvardpress.typepad.com
Facebook: www.facebook.com/HarvardPress
Twitter: @Harvard_Press
Instagram: www.instagram.com/harvardpress
YouTube: www.youtube.com/user/harvardupress

European Office:
Harvard University Press
Vernon House
23 Sicilian Avenue
London WC1A 2QS United Kingdom
Email: info@harvardup.co.uk
Phone: 011.44.20.3463.2350

Staff

Director and Editor-in-Chief: George Andreou (617.495.2601)
Executive Coordinator, Office of the Director: Robin Bellinger (617.496.6269)
CFO/COO: Dan Wackrow (617.495.2613)
Intellectual Property Director: Stephanie Vyce (617.495.2603)
Acquisitions Editorial
  Executive Editor for Life Sciences: Janice Audet (617.495.2674)
  Executive Editor and Director of Belknap Publishing: Joy de Menil (617.496.6831)
  Executive Editor for Physical Sciences and Technology: Jeff Dean (617.495.1226)
  General Editor: Andrew Kinney (617.495.9015)
  Executive Editor-at-Large: Thomas LeBien (617.496.2681)
  Senior Executive Editor-at-Large (Europe) and Senior Executive Editor for Economics (Global):
  Ian Malcolm (011.44.7843.301.029)
  Executive Editor for History: Kathleen McDermott (617.495.4703)
  Executive Editor-at-Large: Sharmila Sen (617.495.8122)
  Executive Editor for the Humanities: Lindsay Waters (617.495.2835)
  Editor: James Brandt (617.495.3599)
Managing Editor: Christine Thorsteinsson (617.495.5951)
Design and Production Director: Tim Jones (617.495.2669)
  Assistant Production Director: Abigail Mumford (617.496.9421)
  Design Manager and Senior Designer: Lisa Roberts (617.495.5129)
Marketing Director: Ken Carpenter (617.496.1317)
  US Sales Director: Vanessa Vinarub (617.495.2650)
  National Account Sales Rep/South American and Latin American Rep Manager: Briana Ross
  (617.384.7515)
  Data Analysis Manager: Val Hunt (617.495.2607)
  Director of International Sales and Marketing: Richard Howells (011.44.20.3463.2350)
  Associate Director of International Publicity: Rebekah White (011.44.20.3463.2350)

Number of Press Staff: 77

Regular Member

Established: 1913
Title output 2017: 274
Titles currently in print: 8,500

Admitted to the Association: 1937
Title output 2018: 250

Editorial Program
Scholarly books and serious works of general interest in the humanities, the social and behavioral sciences, the natural sciences, medicine, and technology. The Press does not normally publish poetry, fiction, festschriften, memoirs, symposia, or unrevised doctoral dissertations.

The Press distributes publications for a number of Harvard University departments and affiliates: Archaeological Exploration of Sardis, Center for Hellenic Studies, Center for the Study of World Religions, David Rockefeller Center for Latin American Studies, Department of Celtic Languages and Literatures, Department of the Classics, Department of Comparative Literature, Department of English, Department of Music, Department of Near Eastern Languages and Civilizations, Department of South Asian Studies, Derek Bok Center, Dumbarton Oaks Research Library and Collection, FXB Center for Health and Human Rights, Harvard Center for Middle Eastern Studies, Harvard College Library, Harvard Divinity School, Harvard Global Equity Initiative, Harvard University Asia Center, Harvard University Center for Jewish Studies, Harvard University Graduate School of Design, Houghton Library of the Harvard College Library, Ilex Foundation, Islamic Legal Studies Program, Harvard Law School, Peabody Museum Press, Harvard School of Public Health, the Ukrainian Research Institute of Harvard University, and Villa I Tatti.
Book series, joint imprints, and/or copublishing programs: The Adams Papers; Bernard Berenson Lectures; Carl Newell Jackson Lectures; Charles Eliot Norton Lectures; Dumbarton Oaks Medieval Library; Edwin L. Godkin Lectures; Edwin O. Reischauer Lectures; Harvard Historical Studies and Monographs; Harvard Studies in Business History; I Tatti Renaissance Library; I Tatti Renaissance Monographs; John Harvard Library; Loeb Classical Library (print and digital); Loeb Classical Monographs; Mary Flexner Lectures; Murty Classical Library of India; Nathan I. Huggins Lectures; Oliver Wendell Holmes Lectures; Revealing Antiquity; Tanner Lectures; W.E.B. Du Bois Lectures; William E. Massey Sr. Lectures
Imprints: The Belknap Press

University of Hawai'i Press

2840 Kolowalu Street
Honolulu, HI 96822-1888

Phone: 808.956.8255
Fax: 800.650.7811
Email: (user I.D.)@hawaii.edu

Orders:
Phone: 888.UHPRESS; 808.956.8255
Fax: 800.650.7811; 808.988.5203

Website and Social Media:
Website: www.uhpress.hawaii.edu
Blog: uhpress.wordpress.com
Facebook: www.facebook.com/pages/University-of-Hawaii-Press/200519105362
Twitter: @UHPRESSNEWS
Instagram: @uhpress

European Distributor:
Eurospan

Canadian Distributor:
Scholarly Book Services

Staff
Interim Director: Joel Cosseboom (808.956.6292; email: cosseboo)

Administrative Assistant/Rights and Permissions: Alison Kleczewski (808.956.8257; email: alison38)
Acquisitions Editorial: Masako Ikeda, Interim Executive Editor (808.956.8696; email: masakoi)
Acquisitions Editor: Stephanie Chun (808.956.8695; email: chuns)
Associate Acquisitions Editor: Emma Ching (808.956.6426; email: emma6)
Associate Editor: Debra Tang (808.956.8694; email: dtang);
Digital Publishing: Trond Knutsen, Manager (808.956.6227; email: tknutsen)
Digital Projects Specialist: Noah Perales-Estoesta (808.956.6279; email: perales6)
Editorial, Design, and Production: Santos Barbasa, Manager (808.956. 8277; email: barbasa)
Managing Editors: Cheryl Loe (808.956.8276; email: cheryl.loe); Grace Wen (808.956.8834; email: gracewen)
Art Director: Mardee Melton (808.956.2858; email: mmelton)
Production Editor: Lucille Aono (808.956.6328; email: lucille)
Administrative Support Specialist: Terri Miyasato (808.956.8275; email: terrimiy)
Marketing and Sales: Royden Muranaka, Sales Manager/Interim Marketing Manager (808.956.6214; email: royden)
Promotion Manager: Carol Abe (808.956.8697; email: abec)
Product Manager: Steven Hirashima (808.956.8698; email: stevehir)
Digital Marketing Manager: Blaine Tolentino (808.956.6417; email: blainemt)
Sales and Publishing Partners Specialist: Kiera Nishimoto (808.956.8830; email: eweb)
Journals: Pamela J. Wilson, Manager (808.956.6790; email: pwilson6)
Subscriptions Manager: Norman Kaneshiro (808.956.8833; email: uhpjourn)
Production Editor: Alicia Upano (808.956.8398; email: aupano)
Production Editor: Donovan Kūhiō Colleps (808.956.4492; email: collepsd)
Managing Editor: Benjamin Fairfield (808.956.6210; email: cri@hawaii.edu)
East-West Export Books: Royden Muranaka, International Sales Manager (808.956.6214; email: royden)
Assistant: Kiera Nishimoto (808.956.8830; email: eweb)
Business: Kari Ann Hirata, Administrative Officer (808.956.6218; email: karis)
Fiscal Assistant/Royalty Clerk: Kyle S. Watanabe (808.956.6228; email: kyle.watanabe)
Customer Support Supervisor: Cindy Yen (808.956.8256; email: cyen)
Warehouse: Kyle Nakata, Clifford Newalu (808.956.3357; email: uhpwhse)
IT: Collin Wong (808.956.6209; email: cwong808)

Number of Press Staff: 30

Regular Member

Established: 1947   Admitted to the Association: 1951
Title output 2017: 90   Title output 2018: 96
Titles currently in print: 2,114   Journals published: 25

Editorial Program
Scholarly books in the humanities and social sciences in Asian, Southeast Asian, and Asian American studies; Pacific Islands, Hawaiian, and Indigenous studies. Within those areas we have particular interests in history, world history, religion, Buddhist studies, anthropology and sociology, fiction in translation, popular culture, the environment, and language. We also publish serious works of general interest, natural history, guide books, and maps on the Hawai'i region.
Journals: *Asian/Pacific Island Nursing Journal; Asian Perspectives; Asian Theatre Journal; Azalea; Biography; Buddhist-Christian Studies; China Review International; The Contemporary Pacific; Cross-Currents; The Hawaiian Journal of History; Journal of Daoist Studies; Journal of Korean Religions; Journal of the Southeast Asian Linguistics Society; Journal of World History; Korean Studies; Language Documentation and Conservation; Manoa; Oceanic Linguistics; Pacific Science; Palapala; Philosophy East and West; Rapa Nui Journal; Review of Japanese Culture and Society; U.S.-Japan Women's Journal; Yearbook of the Association of Pacific Coast Geographers*
Book series, joint imprints, and/or copublishing programs: ABC Chinese Dictionary; Asia Pacific Flows; Asia Pop!; Biography Monographs; The Collected Works of Wŏnhyo; Confucian Cultures; Contemporary Buddhism; Critical Interventions; Dimensions of Asian Spirituality; Food in Asia and the Pacific; Hawai'inuiākea; Hawai'i Studies on Korea; Indigenous Pacifics; Intersections: Asian and Pacific American Transcultural Studies; KLEAR Textbooks in Korean Language (Korean

Language Education and Research Center/Korea Foundation); Korean Classics Library: Histori-
cal Materials; Korean Classics Library: Philosophy and Religion; Kuroda Institute Classics in
East Asian Buddhism; Kuroda Institute Studies in East Asian Buddhism; Modern Korean Fiction;
Music and Performing Arts of Asia and the Pacific; Nanzan Library of Asian Religion and Culture;
New Daoist Studies; The New Oceania Literary Series; Oceanic Linguistics Special Publications;
Pacific Islands Archaeology; Pacific Islands Monographs; Perspectives on the Global Past; Pure
Land Buddhist Studies; Southeast Asia: Politics, Meaning, and Memory; Spatial Habitus: Making
and Meaning in Asia's Architecture; Studies of the Weatherhead East Asian Institute (Columbia
University); Topics in the Contemporary Pacific
Imprints: Latitude 20

University of Illinois Press

1325 S. Oak Street
Champaign, IL 61820-6903

Phone: 217.333.0950
Fax: 217.244.8082
Email: uipress@uillinois.edu
Journals: journals@uillinois.edu
Indiv: (user I.D.)@uillinois.edu

Website and Social Media:
Website: www.press.uillinois.edu
Blog: www.press.uillinois.edu/wordpress
Journals Blog: www.press.uillinois.edu/journals/blog
Facebook: www.facebook.com/UniversityofIllinoisPress
Twitter: @IllinoisPress
Instagram: @illinoispress

UK/European Representative:
Combined Academic Publishers

Asia Representative:
B.K. Norton

Warehouse Address and Orders:
University of Illinois Press
c/o Chicago Distribution Center
11030 South Langley Avenue
Chicago, IL 60628

Orders:
Books: 800.621.2736
Email: orders@press.uchicago.edu
Journals: 866.244.0626

Canadian Representative:
Scholarly Book Services

Australia & New Zealand:
Footprint Books Pty Ltd.

Staff
Director: Laurie Matheson (music) (217.244.4685; email: lmatheso)
Assistant to the Director: Kathy O'Neill (217.244.4691; email: oneill2)
Outreach & Development and Acquisitions Assistant: Julie R. Laut (217.300.4126; email: jlaut2)
Acquisitions Editorial
    Senior Acquisitions Editors: Dawn Durante (African American studies; women's, gender, and
    sexuality studies; American studies; religion) (217.265.8491; email: durante9); Daniel Nasset
    (communication and information studies, film and media, military history, Chicago politics and
    urban studies, sports history) (217.244.5182; email: dnasset)
    Acquisitions Editor: James Engelhardt (Appalachian studies, folklore, labor studies, Lincoln
    studies, regional trade) (217.244.1040; email: jengel04)
    Associate Acquisitions Editor: Marika Christofides (anthropology, food studies, science fiction
    studies) (217.300.7842; email: mchristo)
    Assistant Acquisitions Editor: Alison K. Syring Bassford (217.300.5933; email: asyring2)
Editorial, Design, and Production
    Assistant Director and EDP Manager: Jennifer Comeau (217.244.3279; email: jlcomeau)
    Assistant Managing Editor: Jennifer Clark (217.244.8041; email: jsclark1)
    Senior Editor: Tad Ringo (217.265.0238; email: tringo)
    Production Manager: Kristine Ding (217.244.4701; email: kding)

Production Coordinator: Tamara Shidlauski (217.265.0940; email: shidlaus)
Desktop Publishers: Lisa Connery (217.244.1311; email: lconnery); Kirsten Dennison
(217.244.9892; email: kdennisn); Jim Proefrock (email: proefroc)
Art Director: Dustin Hubbart (217.333.9227; email: dhubbart)
Designer: Jennie Fisher (217.244.7156; email: jholz)
Marketing
Marketing and Sales Manager: Michael Roux (217.244.4683; email: mroux)
Sales and Course Adoption Coordinator: Ami Reitmeier (217.244.4703; email: reitmeir)
Publicity Manager: Heather Gernenz (217.300.2687; email: gernenz2)
Exhibits Manager: Margo Chaney (217.244.6491; email: mechaney)
Rights & Permissions and Awards Manager: Angela Burton (217.300.2883; email: alburton)
Direct Marketing & Advertising Manager: Denise Peeler (217.244.4690; email: dpeeler)
Catalog & Copywriting Coordinator: Kevin Cunningham (email: rkcunnin)
Sales and Marketing Assistant: Roberta Sparenberg (217.333.6494; email: sparnbrg)
Journals
Journals Manager: Clydette Wantland (217.244.6496; email: cwantlan)
Associate Journals Manager: Jeff McArdle (217.244.0381; email: jmcardle)
Senior Production Editor: Heather Munson (217.244.6488; email: hmunson)
Journals Production Editors: Kate Kemball (217.244.7411; email: kemball2); Kristen
Dean-Grossmann (217.265.9186; email: kdeangro)
Journals Circulation Manager: Cheryl Jestis (866.244.0626; email: jestis)
Journals Marketing Manager: Alexa Colella (217.244.5610; email: acolella)
Information Systems
Electronic Publisher: Paul Arroyo (217.244.7147; email: parroyo)
Database Administrator: Bob Repta (217.244.0854; email: repta)
Web Programmer: Winston Jansz (217.300.0871; email: jansz)
Business
Chief Financial Officer: Alice Ennis (217.244.0091; email: atennis)
Accounts Receivable: Sandy Sullivan (217.244.0628; email: ssulliva)
Accounts Payable: Jennifer Barbee (217.244.7958; email: jjbarbee)

Number of Press Staff: 40

Regular Member

Established: 1918	Admitted to the Association: 1937
Title output 2017: 113	Title output 2018: 96
Titles currently in print: 2502	Journals published: 42

Editorial Program
Scholarly books and serious nonfiction, with special interests in African American studies, American history, American music, anthropology, Appalachian studies, Asian American studies, critical theory, cultural studies, communications, cinema studies, ethnic studies, folklore, food studies, Latino/a studies, Lincoln studies, military history, religious studies, sport history, women's studies, labor and working-class history
Journals: *American Journal of Psychology; American Journal of Theology & Philosophy; American Literary Realism; American Music; American Philosophical Quarterly; Black Music Research Journal; Bulletin of the Council for Research in Music Education; Connecticut History Review; Ethnomusicology; Feminist Teacher; History of Philosophy Quarterly; History of the Present; Illinois Classical Studies; Illinois Heritage; Jazz & Culture; Journal of the Abraham Lincoln Association; Journal of Aesthetic Education; Journal of American Ethnic History; Journal of American Folklore; Journal of Animal Ethics; Journal for the Anthropological Study of Human Movement; Journal of Appalachian Studies; Journal of Book of Mormon Studies; Journal of Civil and Human Rights; Journal of Education Finance; Journal of English and Germanic Philology; Journal of Film & Video; Journal of the Illinois State Historical Society; Journal of Mormon History; Journal of Olympic Studies; Journal of Sport History; Mormon Studies Review; Music and Moving Image; The Pluralist; Polish American Studies; The Polish Review; Process Studies, Public Affairs Quarterly; Scandinavian Studies; Visual Arts Research; Women, Gender and Families of Color; World History Connected*
Book series, joint imprints, and/or copublishing programs: African American Music in Global Perspective; American Composers; The Asian American Experience; Bach Perspectives; The

Beauvoir Series; Beethoven Sketchbook Series; Black Internationalism; Common Threads; Contemporary Film Directors; Disability Histories; Dissident Feminisms; Feminist Media Studies; Folklore Studies in a Multicultural World; The Geopolitics of Information; Global Studies of the United States; Heartland Foodways; The History of Communication; The History of Emotions; History of Military Occupations; Interpretations of Culture in the New Millennium; Introductions to Mormon Thought; The Knox College Lincoln Studies Center; Latinos in Chicago and the Midwest; Lemann Institute for Brazilian Studies Series; Modern Masters of Science Fiction; Music in American Life; The New Black Studies Series; New Perspectives on Gender in Music; NWSA/University of Illinois First Book Prize; Sport and Society; Studies in Sensory History; Studies in Sports Media; Studies of World Migrations; Topics in the Digital Humanities; Transformations: Womanist, Feminist, and Indigenous Studies; The Urban Agenda; Working Class in American History; Women Composers; Women and Film History International; Women, Gender, and Sexuality in American History; Women, Gender and Technology; Women in Print

IMF Publications (International Monetary Fund)

Street Address:
700 19th Street, NW
Washington, DC 20431

Mailing Address:
Publications Services
P.O. Box 92780
Washington, DC 20090

Phone: 202.623.7430
Fax: 202.623.7201
Email: publications@imf.org

Orders:
202.623.7430
202.623.7201
Website: www.bookstore.imf.org

Website and Social Media:
Websites: www.bookstore.imf.org; www.elibrary.imf.org; www.imf.org
Blog: blogs.imf.org
Twitter: @IMFNews
YouTube: www.youtube.com/user/imf
Facebook: www.facebook.com/imf

Canadian Representative:
Renouf Publishing Co. Ltd.

UK/European Representative:
Eurospan Group

Staff
Publisher: Jeffrey Hayden (202.623.8354; email: jhayden@imf.org)
Associate Publisher: TBA (202.623.4124)
Rights Manager/Acquisitions Editor/Conference Manager: Patricia Loo (202.623.8296; email: ploo@imf.org)
Editorial Assistant: Josh Hyoun Woo Park (202.623.4248; email: hpark@imf.org)
Electronic Publishing Officer: Jim Beardow (202.623.7899; email: jbeardow@imf.org)
Digital Publishing Officer: Akshay Modi (202.623.8964; email: amodi@imf.org)
Editors: Joseph Procopio (202.623.9258; email: jprocopio@imf.org); Gemma Diaz (202.623.7114; email: gdiaz@imf.org); Linda Long (202.623.6591; email: llong@imf.org); Rumit Pancholi (202.623.8126; email: rpancholi@imf.org
Production Associate: Houda Berrada (202.623.7035; email: hberrada@imf.org); Wala'a El Barrase (202.623.9898; email: welbarrasse@imf.org)
Marketing Associate: Sandra Carrollo (202.623.9554; email: scarrollo@imf.org)
Licensing and Contracts Agent: Alexa Smith (952.944.5729; email: asmith2@imf.org)
Finance Administrator: Madje Amega (202.623.7010; email: mamega@imf.org)
Process Management Consultant: John Brenneman (202.623.7092; email: jbrenneman@imf.org)

Regular Member

Established: 1948
Title output 2017: 66
Titles currently in print: 8883

Admitted to the Association: 2011
Title output 2018: 50
Journals published: 2

Editorial Program
The International Monetary Fund publishes a wide variety of books, periodicals, and electronic products covering economics, international finance, monetary issues, statistics, and exchange rates.
Journals: *Finance & Development; IMF Economic Review*
Book series: Departmental Papers; Occasional Papers; Staff Discussion Notes; Technical Notes and Manuals; World Economic and Financial Surveys (includes World Economic Outlook, Fiscal Monitor, Global Financial Stability Report, and Regional Economic Outlooks); Working Papers
Joint imprints and copublishing programs: Select titles copublished with John Wiley & Sons, MIT Press, Oxford University Press, Palgrave Macmillan, Princeton University Press, Routledge, and Yale University Press.

Indiana University Press

Office of Scholarly Publishing
Herman B Wells Library 350
1320 E. 10th Street
Bloomington, IN 47405

Fulfillment Center:
C/O Ingram Publisher Services
1280 Ingram Drive
Chambersburg, PA 17202

Phone: 812.855.8817
Phone: 800.842.6796
Email: iupress@indiana.edu
Indiv: (user I.D.)@indiana.edu

Orders: 800.648.3013
Fax: 812.855.8507
Email (vendors): pubsupport@
ingramcontent.com
Email (individuals): iuporder@indiana.edu

Canadian Representative:
Lexa Publishers' Representative

UK/European Representative:
Combined Academic Publishers

Website and Social Media:
Web: iupress.indiana.edu
Blog: iupress.typepad.com/blog
Twitter: @iupress
Facebook: www.facebook.com/iupress
YouTube: www.youtube.com/iupress
Pinterest: www. pinterest.com/iupforeign/

Staff
Director, Indiana University Press and Digital Publishing: Gary Dunham (email: dunhamg)
Acquisitions Editorial: Dee Mortensen, Editorial Director (African studies, Judaism and Judaica, philosophy, and religious studies) (email: mortense)
  Acquisition Editors: Jennika Baines (global and international studies) (email: bainesj); Janice Frisch (music, film and media, folklore) (email: frischj); Ashley Runyon (trade and regional) (email: asrunyon); Peggy Solic (Well House Books) (email: pegsolic)
  Acquisition Assistants: Allison Chaplin (email: abchapli); Ashante Thomas (email: ashtom); Anna Francis (email: ancfranc)
Operations: Michael Regoli, Director of Publishing Operations (email: regoli)
  Lead Project Manager/Editor: David Miller (email: Dm60)
  Project Managers: Nancy Lightfoot (email: nlightfo); Darja Malcolm-Clarke (email: dmalcolm); Rachel Rosolina (email: rrosolin)
  Senior Artists and Book Designers: Pam Rude (email: psrude); Jennifer Witzke (email: jwitzke)
  Online Publishing Manager: Dan Pyle (email: dapyle)
  Journals Production Manager: Sherondra Thedford (email: sherthed)

Production Manager: Laura Hohman (email: lhohman)
Publishing Services Coordinator: Tony Brewer (email: tbrewer)
Production Assistant: Rachel Kindler (email: rkindler)
Marketing and Sales: Dave Hulsey, Associate Director and Marketing and Sales Director (email: hulseyd)
Trade Marketing and Publicity Manager: Michelle Sybert (email: msybert)
Scholarly Marketing and Publicity Manager: Julie Davis (email: julmsmit)
Electronic Marketing Manager: Chantel Stavick (email: cstavick)
Publicity Coordinator: Theresa Halter (email: thalter)
Sales and Marketing Assistant: Rhonda Van Der Dussen (email: rdussen)
Rights and Permissions Manager: Stephen Williams (email: smw9)
Business and Operations: Michael Noth, Fiscal Officer (email: mnoth)
Human Resources Officer: Jennifer Chaffin (email: jlchaffi)
Staff Accountant: Brent Starr (email: brstarr)
Assistant Business Manager for Network Systems and Order Processing: Janie Pearson (email: cjfender)
Assistant Business Manager for Accounts Receivable & Customer Service: Kim Bower (email: kchilder)

Number of Press Staff: 29

Regular Member

Established: 1950	Admitted to the Association: 1952
Title output 2017: 180	Title output 2018: 152
Titles currently in print: 3,600	Journals published: 47

Editorial Program
African studies; anthropology; ethnomusicology; film and media studies; folklore; international studies; Irish studies; Jewish and Holocaust studies; Middle East studies; military history; music; paleontology; philosophy; public health; railroad history; religion; Russian and East European studies; science; women's and gender studies.
Journals: *Africa Today; ACPR: African Conflict and Peacebuilding Review; Aleph: Historical Studies in Science & Judaism; Anthropology of East Europe Review; Antisemitism Studies; Black Camera; Black Diaspora Review; Chiricu; e-Service Journal; Ethics & the Environment; Film History; The Global South; Hindsight: The Journal of Optometry History; Historical Performance; History & Memory; Indiana Journal of Global Legal Studies; Indiana Magazine of History; Indiana Theory Review; International Journal of Designs for Learning; Israel Studies; Jewish Social Studies; Journal of Feminist Studies in Religion; JFR: Journal of Folklore Research; Journal of Islam and Muslim Studies; Journal of Modern Literature; Journal of the Ottoman and Turkish Studies Association; Journal of the Scholarship of Teaching and Learning; Journal of the Student Personnel Association at Indiana University; Journal of Teaching and Learning with Technology; Journal of World Philosophies; Mande Studies; The Medieval Review; Museum Anthropology Review; Nashim: A Journal of Jewish Women's & Gender Issues; Pakistan Journal of Historical Studies; Philanthropy and Education; PMER: Philosophy of Music Education Review; Physical Disabilities: Education and Related Services; Prooftexts: A Journal of Jewish Literary History; Recreation, Parks, and Tourism in Public Health; Research in African Literatures; Spectrum: The Journal of Black Men; Transactions; Transition; Victorian Studies; The World Is Our Home*
Book series: African Expressive Cultures; African Systems of Thought; American Philosophy; Counterpoints: Music and Education; Digital Game Studies; Excavations at Ancient Halieis; Excavations at Franchthi Cave, Greece; Global African Voices; Global Research Studies; The Helen and Martin Schwartz Lectures in Jewish Studies; Indiana Repertoire Guides; Indiana Series in Middle East Studies; Indiana Series in the Philosophy of Religion; Indiana Series in Sephardi and Mizrahi Studies; Indiana Studies in Biblical Literature; Indiana-Michigan Series in Russian and East European Studies; Jewish Literature and Culture; Life of the Past; Material Vernaculars; The Modern Jewish Experience; Music and the Early Modern Imagination; Music, Nature, Place;

Musical Meaning and Interpretation; New Anthropologies of Europe; New Directions in National Cinema; Philanthropic and Nonprofit Studies; Polis Center Series on Religion and Urban Culture; Profiles in Popular Music; Public Cultures of the Middle East and North Africa; Publications of the Early Music Institute; Railroads Past and Present; Readings in African Studies; Religion in North America; Russian Music Studies; Scholarship of Teaching and Learning; Selections from the Writings of Charles S. Peirce; Spatial Humanities; Special Publications of the Folklore Institute, Indiana University; Studies in Antisemitism; Studies in Continental Thought; Tracking Globalization; Twentieth-Century Battles; The Variorum Edition of the Poetry of John Donne; World Philosophies; Writings of Charles S. Peirce: A Chronological Edition; The Year's Work: Studies in Fan Culture and Cultural Theory
Imprints: Well House Books; Prestyge Books

International Food Policy Research Institute (IFPRI)

1201 Eye St. NW
Washington DC 20005

Orders:
Email: ifpri-info@cgiar.org

Phone: 202.862.5600
Fax: 202.862.5606
Email: ifpri@cgiar.org

Website and Social Media:
Website: www.ifpri.org
Facebook: www.facebook.com/Ifpri.org/
Twitter: @IFPRI

Staff
Director, Communications and Public Affairs: Rajul Pandya-Lorch (202.862.8185; email; r.pandyalorch@cgiar.org)
Editorial Services Manager: Pamela Stedman-Edwards (202.862.4616; email: p.stedman-edwards@cgiar.org)
Translations Manager and Secretariat, IFPRI Publications Review Committee: Corinne De Gracia-Garber (202.862.8194; email: c.garber@cgiar.org)
Books Project Manager: John Whitehead (202.627.4343; email: j.whitehead@cgiar.org)
Manager, Visual Design and Production: Jamed Falik (202.862.4676; email: j.falik@cgiar.org)
Publications Manager: Michael Go (202.862.6475; email: m.go@cgiar.org)

Number of Press Staff: 6

Regular Member
Established: 1976
Title output: 2017: 8
Titles currently in print: 39

Admitted to the Association: 2018
Title output 2018: 5

Editorial Program
IFPRI publishes in the following disciplines: Food policy, agricultural economics, development economics, markets, business and trade, the environment and climate change, nutrition, and development and governance.

INSTAP Academic Press

2133 Arch St.
Suite 301
Philadelphia, PA 19103

Phone: 215.568.8041
Email: instappress@hotmail.com
Website: www.instappress.com

Orders:
Casemate Academic
Phone: 610.853.9131
www.oxbowbooks.com/dbbc/

UK Representative:
Oxbow Books
Tel. +44 (0)1865 241249
Website: www.oxbowbooks.com/oxbow/

Staff
Director: Susan Ferrence (215.568.8041; email: sferrence@instappress.com)

Number of Press Staff: 6

Introductory Member
Established: 2001
Title output 2017: 5
Titles currently in print: 70

Admitted to the Association: 2015
Title output 2018: 4

Editorial Program
The Institute for Aegean Prehistory (INSTAP) was founded in 1982 to support projects relevant to the history of the Aegean world from the Paleolithic to the 8th century B.C. In 2001, INSTAP Academic Press was started to help publish projects dealing with the subject of Aegean Prehistory. The Press is a scholarly publisher specializing in the publication of primary source material from archaeological excavations as well as individual studies dealing with material from the prehistoric periods. All publications are in English.
Book series: Prehistory Monographs, INSTAP Archaeological Excavation Manuals

University of Iowa Press

Editorial Office:
119 West Park Road
100 Kuhl House
Iowa City, IA 52242-1000

Phone: 319.335.2000
Fax: 319.335.2055
Email: (user I.D.)@uiowa.edu

Website and Social Media:
Website: www.uiowapress.org
Blog: buroakblog.blogspot.com/
Facebook: www.facebook.com/UIowaPress
Twitter: @UIowaPress

Order Fulfillment:
University of Iowa Press
c/o Chicago Distribution Center
11030 South Langley Avenue
Chicago, IL 60628
Phone: 800.621.2736
Fax: 800.621.8476

UK/European Representative:
Eurospan

Staff
Director: Jim McCoy (319.335.2013; email: james-mccoy)
    Assistant to the Director: TBA
    Rights and Permissions: Suzanne Glemot (319.384.2008; email: UIPress-Permissions)
Acquisitions Editors: Ranjit Arab (natural history, regional history, anthropology/archaeology, fan studies, food studies, performance studies) (319.384.1910; email: ranjit-arab@uiowa.edu); Jim McCoy (poetry, short fiction, general trade, literary nonfiction, literary criticism)
    Editorial Assistant: Meredith Stabel (319.335.2022; email: meredith-stabel)
Managing Editor: Susan Hill Newton (319.335.2011; email: susan-hillnewton)

Design and Production: Karen Copp, Associate Director and Design and Production Manager (319.335.2014; email: karen-copp)
Marketing: Allison Thomas Means, Marketing Manager (319.335.3440; email: allison-means)

Regular Member

Established: 1969

Admitted to the Association: 1982

Title output 2017: 36

Title output 2018: 37

Titles currently in print: 760

Number of Press Staff: 8

Editorial Program

American literary criticism and history, women's studies, contemporary American literature; memoirs; short fiction (award winners only); poetry (award winners and invited submissions only); creative nonfiction; regional studies; regional natural history; theatre history and criticism; American studies; food studies; fan studies; public humanities; veteran's affairs.

Book series: Bur Oak Books and Bur Oak Guides; Contemporary North American Poetry; Iowa Poetry Prize; Iowa Prize in Literary Nonfiction; Iowa Short Fiction Award and John Simmons Short Fiction Award; Iowa and the Midwest Experience; Iowa Whitman Series; Kuhl House Poets; Muse Books; New American Canon; Sightline Books: The Iowa Series in Literary Nonfiction; Studies in Theatre History and Culture; Writers in Their Own Time

Johns Hopkins University Press

2715 N. Charles Street
Baltimore, MD 21218-4363

Phone: 410.516.6900
Fax: 410.516.6998/6968
Email: (user I.D.)@press.jhu.edu

Website and Social Media:
Website: www.press.jhu.edu
Blog: jhupressblog.com
Facebook: www.facebook.com/
    JohnsHopkinsUniversityPress
Twitter: @JHUPress
YouTube: JHUPress
Pinterest: www.pinterest.com/jhupress/
SoundCloud: www.soundcloud.com/jhupress

Distribution Center:
C/O Maple Logistics Solutions
Lebanon Distribution Center
704 Legionaire Drive
Fredericksburg, PA 17026

Orders and Customer Service:
Phone: 800.537.5487 (HFS)
Phone: 800.548.1784 (Journals)
Phone: 410.516.6989 (MUSE)

UK Representative:
Oxford Publicity Partnership Ltd

UK Distribution
John Wiley & Sons Limited

Staff

Director: Barbara Kline Pope (410.516.6971; email: bkp)
Assistant to the Director: Marla Kanefsky (410.516.6971; email: mbk)
Associate Director, JHU Press & Senior Director Finance & Administration: Erik Smist
    (410.516.6941; email: eas)
Rights and Permissions Manager: Kelly Rogers (410.516.6063; email: klr)
Office and Facilities Coordinator: Nora Reedy (410.516.7035; email: ncr)
Chief Information Officer: TBA
    Acting Manager, IT: Stacey Armstead (410.516.6979; email: sla)
Acquisitions Editorial: Gregory M. Britton, Editorial Director (higher education) (410.516.6919;
    email: gb)
    Senior Editors: Laura Davulis (American history/Contemporary Affairs) (410.516.6917; email:
    lbd); Tiffany Gasbarrini (life sciences) (410.516.6999; email: tg); Matthew McAdam (history of
    STEM, Bioethics, Medical Humanities) (410.516.6903; email: mxm)

Editors: Robin Coleman (public health and health policy) (410.516.6997; email: rwg); Joe Rusko (health and wellness) (410.516.6904; email: jr); Catherine Goldstead (Literary studies & ancient studies) (410.516.7353; email: cg)
Project MUSE: Wendy J. Queen, Director (410.516.3845; email: wjq)
Director of Publisher Relations & Content Development: Kelley A. Squazzo, (410.516.6877; email: kas)
Associate Director, Finance & Operations, Project MUSE: Nicole Kendzejeski (410.516.6969; email: nak)
Director, Marketing and Sales: Melanie B. Schaffner (410.516.3846; email: mbs)
Manager, International Sales: Ann Snoeyenbos (410.516.6992; email: aps)
Sales Manager: Douglas Storm (217.823.0286; email: das)
Customer Service Coordinator: Lora Czarnowsky (410.516.2890; email: llc)
Business Solutions Analyst: Elizabeth R. Windsor (410.516.6510; email: brw)
Manuscript Editorial: Juliana M. McCarthy, Managing Editor (410.516.6912; email: jmm)
Senior Production Editors: Andre M. Barnett (410.516.6995; email: amb); Deborah L. Bors (410.516.6914; email: dlb); Kimberly F. Johnson (410.516.6915; email: kfj)
Production Editor: Hilary S. Jacqmin (410.516.6901; email: hsj)
Associate Production Editor: Kyle Howard Kretzer (410.516.6897; email: khk)
Assistant Production Editor: Robert Brown (410.516.6901; email: rmb)
Design and Production: John Cronin, Design & Production Manager (410.516.6922; email: jgc)
Art Director: Martha Sewall (410.516.6921; email: mds)
Senior Book Designer: Glen Burris (410.516.6924; email: gmb)
Production Controller, Electronic Media: Jennifer Paulson (410.516.7872; email: jcp)
Marketing: Cathleen Esposito, Marketing & Sales Director (410.516.6931; email: ce)
Sales Manager: TBA (410.516.6936)
Sales & Metadata Specialist: Devon Renwick (410.516.6951; email: dbr)
Marketing & Sales Coordinator: Catherine Bergeron (410.516.6934; email cab)
Associate Marketing Director: Claire McCabe Tamberino (410.516.6935; email: cmt)
Publicity Manager: Kathryn Marguy (410.516.4162; email: krm)
Publicist: Jack Holmes (410.516.6928; email: jmh)
Publicist: Emma All (410.516.6902; email: ea)
Digital Promotions Coordinator: Kristina Lykke (410.516.6972; email: kkl)
Journals: William Breichner, Publisher (410.516.6985; email: wmb)
Journals Fulfillment Systems Project Manager: Matt Brook (410.516.6899; email: mb)
Director, Sales and Marketing: Lisa Klose (410.516.6689; email: llk)
Journals Production Manager: Carol Hamblen (410.516.6986; email: crh)
Journals Operations Manager: Shannon Fortner, (410.516.6038; email: stf)
Journals Subscription Manager: Robert White Goodman (410.516.6964; email: rwg)
Journals Assistant Subscription Manager: Kathleen Young (410.516.6944; email: kmy)
Manager, Public Relations & Advertising: Brian Shea (410.516.7096; email: bjs)
Business: Tony Jacobson, Accounting Manager (410.516.6974; email: tlj)
Budget Manager: Steve Wolter (410.516.6886; email: sew)
Fulfillment: Davida G. Breier, Manager, Fulfillment Operations (410.516.6961; email: dgb)
Customer Service Supervisor, Fulfillment Operations: Terrence J. Melvin (410.516.4449; email: tjm)
Customer Service Coordinator: Alicia C. Catlos (410.516.4441; email: acc)
Credit & Collections: Christopher Walsh, Accounts Receivable Coordinator (410.516.3854; email: cdw)

Number of Press Staff: 123

Regular Member

Established: 1878	Admitted to the Association: 1937
Title output 2017: 135	Title output 2018: 163
Titles currently in print: 3,411	Journals published: 91

Editorial Program

History (American, ancient, history of science, technology, and medicine); humanities (literary and cultural studies, ancient studies); medicine and health (consumer health, public health); science (biology, physics, and natural history); mathematics; higher education; reference books; bioethics and medical humanities.

The Press through Hopkins Fulfillment Service (*HFS, hfs.jhu.edu* and *HFSBooks.com*) handles book order processing and distribution for: Catholic University of America Press, Center for Talented Youth, Family Development Press, Georgetown University Press, Johns Hopkins University Press, University Press of Kentucky, Maryland Historical Society, Northeastern University Press, University of Massachusetts Press, University of New Orleans Press, University of South Carolina Press, University of Washington Press, University of New Orleans Press, and Wesleyan University Press.

The Press, in cooperation with participating publishers, manages Project MUSE© (muse.jhu. edu). Project MUSE provides electronic subscription access to full-text content from 670 periodicals and 50,000 books published by more than 260 not-for-profit scholarly publishers in the humanities and the social sciences.

Other digital publishing initiatives include electronic versions of *The Complete Prose of T. S. Eliot: The Critical Edition; The Early Republic; The Johns Hopkins Guide to Literary Theory and Criticism; The Papers of Dwight David Eisenhower; the Encyclopedia of American Studies;* and the *World Shakespeare Bibliography*

Journals: *African American Review; American Imago; American Jewish History; American Journal of Mathematics; American Journal of Philology; American Quarterly; Arethusa; Arizona Quarterly Book History; ariel; Bookbird; Asian Perspective; The Bulletin of the Center for Children's Books; The Bulletin of Historical Society; Bulletin of the History of Medicine; Callaloo; The CEA Critic; Children's Literature; Children's Literature Association Quarterly; Classical World; College Literature: Configurations; Dante Studies; diacritics; Dickens Quarterly; Eighteenth-Century Studies; Encyclopedia of American Studies; The Emily Dickinson Journal; ELH: English Literary History; Feminist Formations; German Studies Review; The Henry James Review; The Hopkins Review; Hispania; Human Rights Quarterly; Journal of Asian American Studies; Journal of Chinese Religions, Journal of College Student Development; Journal of Colonialism and Colonial History; Journal of Democracy; Journal of Early Christian Studies; Journal of Health Care for the Poor and Underserved; Journal of Late Antiquity Journal of Modern Greek Studies; Journal of the History of Childhood and Youth; Journal of the History of Philosophy; Journal of Women's History; Kennedy Institute of Ethics Journal; Late Imperial China; L'Esprit Créateur; Leviathan; Library Trends; The Lion and the Unicorn; Literature and Medicine; MLN; Modern Fiction Studies; Modernism/Modernity; Narrative Inquiry in Bioethics and Digital Philology; New Literary History; Partial Answers: Journal of Literature and the History of Ideas; Perspectives in Biology & Medicine; Philosophy and Literature; Philosophy, Psychiatry, and Psychology; Poe Studies; portal: Libraries and the Academy; Postmodern Culture; Reviews in American History; Progress In Community Health Partnerships: Research, Education, and Action; Reviews in Higher Education; SAIS Review; SEL: Studies in English Literature; Sewanee Review; Shakespeare Bulletin; South Central Review; Spiritus: A Journal of Christian Spirituality; Social Research; Studies in American Fiction; Studies in the Novel ,Technology & Culture; Substance; Theatre Journal; Theatre Topics; Theory and Event; The Faulkner Journal, The Wallace Stevens Journal; Transactions of the American Philological Association; Twentieth-Century China; Victorian Periodical Review; Victorian Review; World Shakespeare Bibliography Online*

The Press also handles subscription fulfillment Penn State University Press, The Ohio State University Press, The University Press of Florida, Catholic University of America Press, and Georgetown University Press.

Book series, joint imprints, and/or copublishing programs: The Complete Poetry of Percy Bysshe Shelley; Documentary History of the First Federal Congress; Johns Hopkins: Poetry and Fiction; The Johns Hopkins Studies in the History of Technology; The Papers of Frederick Law Olmsted; The Papers of Thomas A. Edison; New Series in NASA History; Critical University Studies; Tech.EDU, Higher Ed Leadership Essentials

University Press of Kansas

2502 Westbrooke Circle
Lawrence, KS 66045-4444

Phone: 785.864.4154
Fax: 785.864.4586
Email: upress@ku.edu

Website and Social Media:
Website: www.kansaspress.ku.edu
Facebook: www.facebook.com/kansaspress
Blog: www.universitypressblog.dept.ku.edu/
Twitter: @Kansas_Press
YouTube: www.youtube.com/channel/UCaQrdXflKJRGp0Dr7S6E_cg
Instagram: www.instagram.com/kansas_press/

Warehouse Address:
2445 Westbrooke Circle
Lawrence, KS 66045-4440
Phone: 785.864.4156

Orders:
Phone: 785.864.4155
Email: upkorders@ku.edu

UK/European Representative:
Eurospan

Canadian Representative:
Scholarly Book Services

Staff
Director: Conrad Roberts (785.864.9158; email: ceroberts@ku.edu)
Administrative Assistant/Permissions Coordinator: Andrea Laws (785.864.9125; email: alaws09@ku.edu)
Editor-in-Chief: Joyce Harrison (military history and intelligence studies) (785.864.9162; email: joyce@ku.edu)
Acquisitions Editors: David Congdon (political science, law, presidential studies, US political history, American political thought) (785.864.6059; email: dcongdon@ku.edu); Kim Hogeland (American Studies, environmental history, western history, Native American studies, regional studies) (785.864.9161; email: khogeland@ku.edu)
Managing Editor: Kelly Chrisman Jacques (785.864.9186; email: kjchrism@ku.edu)
Production Editor: Larisa Martin (785.864.9169; email: lmartin@ku.edu)
Assistant Production Editor: Colin Tripp (785.864.9123; email: ctripp@ku.edu)
Marketing and Sales Director Michael Kehoe (785.864.9165; email: mkehoe@ku.edu)
Publicity Manager: Derek Helms (785.864.9170; email: dhelms@ku.edu)
Direct Mail & Exhibits Manager: Debra Diehl (785.864.9166; email: ddiehl@ku.edu)
Art Director & Webmaster: Karl Janssen (785.864.9164; email: kjanssen@ku.edu)
Marketing Assistant: Suzanne Galle (785.864.9167; email: sgalle@ku.edu)
Customer Service Coordinator: Katy Willson (785.864.9159; email: kwillson@ku.edu)
Warehouse Manager: Ralph Machado (785.864.4156; email: upkwhse@ku.edu)

Number of Press Staff: 15

Regular Member
Established: 1946
Title output 2017: 70
Titles currently in print: 1,876

Admitted to the Association: 1946
Title output 2018: 49

Editorial Program
American history; military and intelligence studies; western history; Native American studies; American government and public policy; presidential studies; constitutional and legal studies; environmental studies; American studies and popular culture; Kansas, the Great Plains, and the Midwest. The Press does not consider fiction, poetry, or festschriften for publication.
Book series, joint imprints, and/or copublishing programs: American Political Thought; American Presidential Elections; American Presidency; Civil Military Relations; Congressional Leaders; Constitutional Thinking; CultureAmerica; Environment and Society; Kansas Nature Guides; Landmark Law Cases and American Society; Modern First Ladies; Modern War Studies; Rethinking Careers, Rethinking Academia; Studies in Government and Public Policy; US Army War College Guides to Civil War Battles

The Kent State University Press

Street Address:
1118 University Library
1125 Risman Drive
Kent, OH 44242-0001

Mailing Address:
1118 University Library
PO Box 5190
Kent, OH 44242-0001

Phone: 330.672.7913
Fax: 330.672.3104
Email: (user I.D.)@kent.edu

Orders:
Phone: 800.247.6553
Fax: 419.281.6883

Website and Social Media:
Website: www.kentstateuniversitypress.com
Facebook: www.facebook.com/kentstateuniversitypress
Twitter: @KentStateUPress

UK/European Representative:
Eurospan

Canadian Representative:
Scholarly Book Services

Staff

Director: Susan Wadsworth-Booth (330.672.8099; email: swadswo2)
Acquiring Editor: Will Underwood (330.672.8094; email: wunderwo)
Managing Editor: Mary D. Young (330.672.8101; email: mdyoung)
Assistant Editor: Kat Saunders (330.672.8096; email: ksaunde5)
Design and Production Manager: Christine A. Brooks (330.672.8092; email: cbrooks)
Marketing and Sales Manager: Richard Fugini (330.672.8097; email: rfugini)
Marketing Associate and Designer: Darryl M. Crosby (330.672.8091; email: dcrosby)

Number of Press Staff: 7

Regular Member

Established: 1965
Title output 2017: 25
Titles currently in print: 720

Admitted to the Association: 1970
Title output 2018: 26
Journals published: 2

Editorial Program

History: American Civil War era; true crime; sports; Ohio/Midwestern studies; fashion/costume; material culture. Literature: US (to ca. 1970); regional/Midwestern; British (Inklings). Regional literary nonfiction; poetry only through Wick Poetry Center; no fiction other than in Literature and Medicine series.
Journals: *Civil War History*; *Ohio History*
Book series: American Abolitionism and Antislavery; The Civil War Era in the South; Civil War in the North; Civil War Soldiers and Strategies; Classic Sports; Costume Society of America; Interpreting American History; Literature and Medicine; Reading Hemingway; Teaching Hemingway; Translation Studies; True Crime History; Wick Poetry Prize
Imprints: Black Squirrel Books

The University Press of Kentucky

663 South Limestone Street
Lexington, KY 40508-4008

Phone: 859.257.7919
Fax: 859.323.1873
Email: (user I.D.)@uky.edu

<u>Website and Social Media:</u>
Website: www.kentuckypress.com
Blog: kentuckypress.wordpress.com
Facebook: www.facebook.com/
  KentuckyPress
Twitter: @KentuckyPress
YouTube: YouTube.com/univpressofky

<u>Warehouse Address:</u>
Maple Press Lebanon Distribution Center
704 Legionaire Drive
Fredericksburg, PA 17026

<u>Orders:</u>
c/o Hopkins Fulfillment Services
PO Box 50370
Baltimore, MD 21211
Phone: 800.537.5487 or 410.516.6956
Fax: 410.516.6998
Email: hfscustserv@ press.jhu.edu

<u>UK/European Representative:</u>
Oxbow Books

<u>Canadian Representative:</u>
Brunswick Books

Staff
Director: Leila W. Salisbury (859.257.8432; email: lsalisbury)
Assistant to the Director: Tasha Huber (859.257.7919; email: tasha.huber)
Senior Acquisitions Editors: Anne Dean Dotson (African American studies, American and southern history, American studies, Appalachian studies, film studies, general interest and scholarly books about Kentucky and the region, popular culture) (859.257.8434; email: adwatk0); Melissa Hammer (American history, Asian studies, foreign policy and diplomatic history, international studies, military history, political science, political theory, public policy, public health) (859.257.8150; email: melissa.hammer)
Acquisitions Editor: Patrick O'Dowd (agrarian studies, ecology and conservation, fiction and poetry, general interest and scholarly books about Kentucky and the region, nature and environmental history) (859.257.9492; email: patrick.odowd)
Acquisitions Assistant: Natalie O'Neal (859.257.8445; email: natalie.oneal)
Managing Editor: David Cobb (859.257.4252; email: dlcobb2)
Senior Editing Supervisor: Ila McEntire (859.257.8433; email: ila.mcentire)
Project Editor: Sarah Olson (859.257.8435; email: sarah.olson)
Production and Service Center Manager: Patty Weber (email: TBA)
Assistant Production Manager: Pat Gonzales (859.257.4669; email: pat.gonzales)
Book Designer: Hayward Wilkirson (859.257.8439; email: hayward.wilkirson)
Director of Marketing and Sales: Stephanie Williams (859.257.4249; email: stephanie.williams)
Publicity and Rights Manager: Mack McCormick (859.257.5200; email: permissions)
Direct Promotions and Exhibits Manager: Katie Cross Gibson (859.257.2817; email: krcr222)
Marketing Assistant: Jackie Wilson (859.257.6855; email: jacqueline.wilson)
Business Operations Manager: Teresa Collins (859.257.8405; email: teresa.collins)
Administrative Assistant: Robert Brandon (859.257.8400; email: rbrandon)
Information Technology Manager: Tim Elam (859.257.8761; email: timothy.elam)
Number of Press Staff: 18.5

Regular Member
Established: 1943
Title output 2017: 69
Titles currently in print: 1,977

Admitted to the Association: 1947
Title output 2018: 64

Editorial Program
Scholarly books in the fields of American and Southern history; military history; film studies; African American studies; international studies; folklore and material culture; popular culture; Asian studies, serious nonfiction of general interest. Regionally, the Press maintains an interest in Kentucky and the Ohio Valley, Appalachia, and the upper South. Submissions of fiction and poetry

are only accepted during an annual review period.
Book series: American Warriors; Asia in the New Millennium; Aviation & Air Power; Battles and Campaigns; Civil Rights and the Struggle for Black Equality in the Twentieth Century; Culture of the Land: A Series in the New Agrarianism; Foreign Military Studies: New Directions in Southern History; Place Matters: New Directions in Appalachian and Regional Studies; Religion in the South; Screen Classics; Studies in Conflict, Diplomacy, and Peace; Topics in Kentucky History; University Press of Kentucky New Poetry & Prose Series; Understanding and Improving Health for Minority and Disadvantaged Populations
Imprints: South Limestone, Andarta Books, Fireside Industries

Leuven University Press/Universitaire Pers Leuven

Minderbroedersstraat 4 - bus 5602
B-3000 Leuven
Belgium

Phone: +32 16 32 53 45
Fax: +32 16 32 53 52
Email: info@lup.be
Indiv. (user I.D.)@lup.be

Website and Social Media:
Website: www.lup.be
Facebook: www.facebook.com/pages/
  Leuven-University-Press/130250583714129
Twitter: @LeuvenUP
LinkedIn: leuven-university-press

UK and European Orders:
NBN International

US Representative:
Cornell University Press
Sage House
512 East State Street
Ithaca, NY 14850
Phone: 607.277.2338
Email: cupressinfo@cornell.edu

US Orders:
Longleaf Services
customerservice@longleafservices.org

Staff
Director and Acquisitions Editorial: Veerle De Laet (+32.16.32.81.26; email: veerle.delaet)
Acquisitions Editorial: Mirjam Truwant (+32.16.32.31.27; email: mirjam.truwant)
Manuscript Editorial: Beatrice Van Eeghem (+32.16.32.53.40; email: beatrice.vaneeghem)
Production: Patricia di Costanzo (+32.16.32.53.53; email: patricia.dicostanzo)
Marketing: Annemie Vandezande (+32.16.32.53.51; email: annemie.vandezande)
Customer Service and Order Processing: Margreet Meijer (+32.16.32.53.50; email: margreet.meijer)

Number of Press Staff: 7

Regular Member
Established: 1971
Title output 2017: 41
Titles currently in print: 1,977

Admitted to the Association: 2005
Title output 2018: 37
Journals published: 5

Editorial Program
Scholarly publications, books and journals, in the Humanities and Social Sciences with a special focus on music, art & theory, media & visual culture, text & literature, history & archaeology, philosophy & religion, society & gender & diversity, and law & economics.
Journals: *DiGeSt. Journal of Diversity and Gender Studies; HEROM, Journal on Hellenistic and Roman Material Culture; Music Theory and Analysis; Nieuwe Tijdingen. Over vroegmoderne geschiedenis; Transdisicplinary Insights*
Book series: Ancient and Medieval Philosophy - Series 1: Ancient and Medieval Philosophy - Series 2: Henrici de Gandavo Opera Omnia; Ancient and Medieval Philosophy - Series 3: Francisci de Marchia Opera Philosophica et Theologica; Avisos de Flandes; Bibliotheca Latinitatis Novae; CeMIS Migration and Intercultural Studies; Current Issues in Islam; Orpheus Institute Series;

Dynamics of Religious Reform; Egyptian Prehistory Monographs; Historisch Denken; Figures de l'Inconscient; Figures of the Unconscious; ICAG Studies; Jean François Lyotard Writings on Contemporary Art and Artists; Kadoc-Artes; Kadoc-Studies on Religion, Culture and Society; Lieven Gevaert Series; Mediaevalia Lovaniensia-Series 1/Studia; Plutarchea Hypomnemata; Sagalassos; Society, Crime & Criminal Justice; Studia Paedagogica; Studies in Archaeological Sciences; Studies in European Comics and Graphic Novels; Studies in Musical Form; Supplementa Humanistica Lovaniensia; Translation, Interpreting and Transfer
Imprints: Lipsius Leuven

Lever Press

Robert Frost Library, Amherst College
61 Quadrangle Drive
Amherst, MA 01002

Phone: 413.542.5709
Fax: 413.542.2662

Website and Social Media:
Website: www.leverpress.org/
Twitter: @Lever_Press

Staff
Director: Mark Edington (413.542.5709; email: medington@leverpress.org)
Editor-in-Chief: Beth Bouloukos (413.542.5519; email: bbouloukos@leverpress.org)
Social Media Marketing Manager: Leann Wilson (email: lwilson@leverpress.org)

Introductory Member
Established: 2016   Admitted to the Association: 2018
Title output 2017: 0   Title output 2018: 1

Editorial Program
Lever Press is a publisher of pathbreaking scholarship. Supported by a consortium of liberal arts institutions focused on, and renowned for, excellence in both research and teaching, we have founded our press on three essential commitments:
- To be a digitally native press;
- To be a peer-reviewed, open access press that charges no fees to either authors or their institutions; and
- To be a press aligned with the ethos and mission of liberal arts colleges.

Liverpool University Press

4 Cambridge Street
Liverpool L69 7ZU, UK

US Orders:
Oxford University Press
Phone: 800.445.9714

Phone: +44 151.7942233
Email: lup@liv.ac.uk
Indiv: (user I.D.)@liv.ac.uk

UK Representative:
Turpin Distribution

Website and Social Media:
Website: www.liverpooluniversitypress.co.uk
Twitter: @LivUniPress

Staff
Managing Director: Anthony Cond (+44.151.7942237; email: a.cond)
Editorial Director: Alison Welsby (+44.151.7942231; email: a.welsby)
Head of Production: Patrick Brereton, (+44.151.7943133; email: p.brereton)
Head of Journals: Clare Hooper (+44.151.7943135; email: c.hooper)
Finance Director: Justine Greig (+44.151.7942232; email: j.greig)
Head of Sales: Jennie Collinson (email: j.collinson)
Books Marketing Manager: Heather Gallagher (email: h.c.gallagher)

Number of Press Staff: 20

Regular Member
Established: 1899
Title output 2017: 100
Titles currently in print: 3,533

Admitted to the Association: 2013
Title output 2018: 100
Journals published: 32

Editorial Program
Scholarly books in ancient, medieval, Irish, slavery and labour history. The modern languages, notably French and Francophone and Hispanic and Lusophone Studies. Science Fiction criticism, contemporary poetry criticism and sculpture. Occasional Liverpool trade titles, building on the city's significance in global migration and popular culture.
Journals: *Australian Journal of French Studies; British Journal of Canadian Studies; Bulletin of Hispanic Studies; Byron Journal; Catalan Review; Comma, Contemporary French Civilization; Essays in Romanticism; European Journal of Language Policy; Extrapolation; Francosphères; Historical Studies in Industrial Relations; Hunter Gatherer Research International Development Planning Review; Journal of Literary and Cultural Disability Studies; Labour History Review; Modern Believing; Music, Sound, and the Moving Image; Québec Studies; Romani Studies; Science Fiction Film and Television; Sculpture Journal; Town Planning Review; Labor History; Transactions of the Historic Society of Lancashire and Cheshire; The Indexer; Archives; Modern Languages Open*
Book series: Contemporary French and Francophone Cultures; Contemporary Hispanic and Lusophone Cultures; Exeter Medieval Texts and Studies; Liverpool Science Fiction Texts and Studies; Reappraisals in Irish History; Liverpool English Texts and Studies; Liverpool Studies in International Slavery; Migrations and Identities; Public Sculpture of Britain; Poetry &....; Postcolonialism Across the Disciplines; Studies in Labour History; Translated Texts for Historians; Writers and their Work; Oxford University Studies in the Enlightenment
Imprints: Liverpool University Press; Clemson University Press; Littman Library of Jewish Civilization; Voltaire Foundation / Oxford University Studies in the Enlightenment; Writers and their Work

Louisiana State University Press

328 Johnston Hall
Louisiana State University
Baton Rouge, LA 70803

Phone: 225.578.6294
Email: (user I.D.)@lsu.edu

Website and Social Media:
Website: www.lsupress.org
Blog: blog.lsupress.org
Facebook: www.facebook.com/LSUPRESS
Twitter: @lsupress

Warehouse, Orders and Cust. Service:
Longleaf Services
116 S. Boundary St
Chapel Hill, NC 27514-3808

Phone: 800.848.6224
Fax: 800.272.6817
Email: customerservice@longleafservices.
org

Canadian Distributor:
Scholarly Book Services

Staff
Interim Director: Laura Gleason (225.578.6469; email: lgleasn)
Assistant to the Director, Subrights and Permissions: Erica Bossier (email: ebossie)
Acquisitions Editorial: Rand Dotson, Editor-in-Chief (southern history, southern roots music and Atlantic World history) (225.578.6412; email: pdotso1); Margaret Lovecraft (Louisiana and regional general interest, environmental studies, landscape architecture) (225.578.6319; email: lovecraft); James Long (literary studies, media studies, fiction, foodways, poetry) (225.578.6433; email: jlong12); Jennifer Keegan (fan studies, Caribbean history, contemporary social justice/civil rights issues in the South) (225.578.6453; email: jenniferkeegan)
Manuscript Editorial: Catherine Kadair, Senior Editor (email: clkadair)
Design and Production: Laura Gleason, Associate Director and Production Manager (225.578.6469; email: lgleasn)
  Assistant Production Manager: Amanda Scallan (email: amandas)
Marketing: James Wilson, Marketing Manager (225.578.8282; email: jwilson4)
  Assistant Marketing Manager/Exhibits and Advertising Coordinator: Kate Barton (email: kbart04)
Financial Operations Manager: Rebekah Brown (225.578.6415; email: rbrown1)
Subsidiary Rights: McIntosh & Otis, Inc., 353 Lexington Ave., New York, NY 10016 (212.687.7400)
The Southern Review
Fiction and Nonfiction Editor: Sacha Idell (225.578.5159; email: sacha)
Prose Editor: Jessica Faust (225.578.0896; email: jfaust1)

Number of Press Staff: 20

Regular Member
Established: 1935
Title output 2017: 64
Titles currently in print: 2,198

Admitted to the Association: unknown
Title output 2018: 63

Editorial Program
Humanities and social sciences, with special emphasis on Southern history and literature; regional studies; environmental studies; poetry; Louisiana roots music, and foodways.
Book series, joint imprints and/or copublishing programs: Antislavery, Abolition, and the Atlantic World; Conflicting Worlds; Making the Modern South; Southern Biography; Southern Literary Studies; Southern Messenger Poets; Barataria Poetry; Yellow Shoe Fiction; Natural World of the Gulf South; Reading the American Landscape; The Southern Table; distribute books for Pleiades Press.

Manchester University Press

Oxford Road
Manchester, M13 9NR
United Kingdom
Telephone: +44 (0)161 275 2310
Email: mup@manchester.ac.uk

Website and Social Media:
Website: www.manchesteruniversitypress.co.uk
Blog: www.manchesteruniversitypress.co.uk/articles
Twitter: @ManchesterUP, @MUPJournals, @GothicMUP, @MedievalSources
Facebook: www.facebook.com/ManchesterUniversityPress
Instagram: www.instagram.com/manchester_university_press

Distribution
Worldwide (excluding The Americas)
NBN International

The Americas
Oxford University Press
Phone: 919.677.0977

UK Representative
Yale University Press

US Representative
Oxford University Press

European Representative
Andrew Durnell

Ireland
Robert Towers

Australia and New Zealand
Footprint Books Pty Ltd

Asian Representative
Publisher's International Marketing Ltd

The Middle East
Ward International (Book Export) Ltd

India
The White Partnership

Staff
Chief Executive: Simon Ross (email: sross@manchester.ac.uk)
Editorial Director and Senior Commissioning Editor: Emma Brennan (history, art history and design) (email: emma.brennan@manchester.ac.uk)
　　Senior Commissioning Editor: Matthew Frost (literature, theatre and film) (email: matthew.j.frost@manchester.ac.uk)
　　Senior Commissioning Editor: Tony Mason (politics and economics) (email: anthony.r.mason@manchester.ac.uk)
　　Senior Commissioning Editor: Tom Dark (social sciences) (email: thomas.dark@manchester.ac.uk)
　　Journals Manager/Senior Commissioning Editor: Meredith Carroll (archeology) (email: meredith.carroll@manchester.ac.uk)
　　Contracts Coordinator: Deborah Smith (email: deborah.m.smith@manchester.ac.uk)
　　Assistant Editors: Paul Clarke (email: paul.m.clarke@manchester.ac.uk); Robert Byron (email: robert.byron@manchester.ac.uk); Alun Richards (email: alun.richards@manchester.ac.uk)
Head of Sales: Shelly Turner (email: shelly.turner@manchester.ac.uk)
Head of Marketing: Chris Hart (email: chris.hart@manchester.ac.uk)
　　Rights and Distribution Coordinator: Marilyn Cresswell (email: m.cresswell@manchester.ac.uk)
　　Sales and Marketing Coordinator: Bethan Hirst (email: bethan.hirst@manchester.ac.uk)
　　Sales and Marketing Executive: Rebecca Mortimer (email: rebecca.mortimer@manchester.ac.uk)
　　Sales Assistant/Export Sales: Melanie Richards (email: melanie.richards@manchester.ac.uk)
Production and Operations Director: John Normansell (email: john.normansell@manchester.ac.uk)
　　Production Editors: Danielle Shepherd (email: danielle.shepherd@manchester.ac.uk); Elizabeth Beck (email: elizabeth.beck@manchester.ac.uk)
　　Production Manager: David Appleyard (email: david.appleyard@manchester.ac.uk)
　　Managing Production Editor: Lianne Slavin (email: lianne.slavin@manchester.ac.uk)
Head of Finance: Sarah Roper (email: sarah.roper@manchester.ac.uk)
　　Accounts Controller: Claudette Johnson (email: claudette.johnson@manchester.ac.uk)

Publishing Support Assistant: Olivia Rye (email: olivia.rye@manchester.ac.uk)

Number of Press Staff: 30

Regular Member

Established: 1904	Admitted to the Association: 2013
Title output 2016: 170	Title output 2017: 179
Titles currently in print: 2,194	Journals published: 7

Editorial Program
History; art history; critical theory, cultural studies; literature and theatre; film and media; architecture; medieval studies; social science; international relations; philosophy, sociology; politics; economics
Journals: *Bulletin of the John Rylands Library; Film Studies; Gothic Studies; Human Remains and Violence: An Interdisciplinary Journal; James Baldwin Review; Journal of Humanitarian Affairs; Redescriptions*

The University of Manitoba Press

Street Address:
301 St. John's College
92 Dysart Road
University of Manitoba
Winnipeg Manitoba R3T 2M5
Canada

Phone: 204.474.9495
Fax: 204.474.7556
Email: uofmpress@umanitoba.ca

Canadian Orders:
University of Toronto Press
Phone: 800.565.9523
Email: utpbooks@utpress.utoronto.ca

US Orders:
Until February 28, 2019:
Michigan State University Press
c/o Chicago Distribution Center
Phone: 800.621.2736

As of March 1, 2019:
Longleaf Services, Inc.
orders@longleafservices.org
Phone: 800.848.6224 or 919.966.7449
Fax: 800.272.6817 or 919.962.2704

Website and Social Media:
Website: uofmpress.ca
Blog: uofmpress.ca/blog
Facebook: www.facebook.com/UofMPress
Twitter: @umanitobapress

UK and European Orders:
Eurospan Group
Email: eurospan@turpindistribution.com

Canadian Representative:
Ampersand and Company (Trade)
Brunswick Books (Academic)

Staff
Director and Editor: David Carr (204.474.9242; email: carr@umanitoba.ca)
Managing Editor: Glenn Bergen (204.474.7338; email: D.Bergen@umanitoba.ca)
Acquisitions Editor: Jill McConkey (204.474.8840; email: jill.mcconkey@umanitoba.ca)
Marketing: David Larsen, Sales and Marketing Supervisor (204.474.9998; email: david.larsen@umanitoba.ca)
Promotions and Publicity Coordinator: Ariel Gordon (204.474.8048; email: gordojd@umanitoba.ca)

Number of Press Staff: 6

Regular Member
Established: 1967
Title output 2017: 14
Titles currently in print: 182

Admitted to the Association: 2011
Title output 2018: 14

Editorial Program
Native studies; Native history; Canadian history; the Arctic and the North; ethnic and immigration studies; Aboriginal languages; Canadian literary studies, especially Aboriginal literature; political studies; environmental studies; regional trade titles.
Book series: Contemporary Studies on the North; Critical Studies in Aboriginal History (formerly Manitoba Studies in Native History); First Voices, First Texts (Aboriginal literary reprints); Studies in Immigration and Culture: Human Rights and Social Justice; Publications of the Algonquian Text Society

Marine Corps University Press

2044 Broadway
Quantico, VA 22134

Phone: 703.432.4880
Email: MCU_Press@usmcu.edu

Orders:
MCU Press
Phone: 703.432.4880
Email: MCU_Press@usmcu.edu

Website and Social Media:
Website: www.usmcu.edu/mcupress
Facebook: MC UPress
Twitter: @MC_UPress

Staff
Senior Editor/E&D Branch Chief: Angela Anderson (703.432.4880; email: angela.anderson@usmcu.edu)
Managing Editor: Jason Gosnell (email: jason.gosnell@usmcu.edu)
Managing Editor (*Marine Corps History Magazine*): Stephani Miller (email: stephani.miller@usmcu.edu)
Designers: Rob Kocher (email: robert.kocher@usmcu.edu); Young-hee Krouse (email: younghee.krouse@usmcu.edu)
Circulation Assistant: Jeff Moravetz (email: jeffrey.moravetz@usmcu.edu)

Number of Press Staff: 10

Introductory Member
Established: 2008
Title output 2017: 6
Titles currently in print: 45

Admitted to the Association: 2016
Title output 2018: 10
Journals published: 2

Editorial Program
Marine Corps University Press (MCUP) recognizes the importance of an open dialogue between scholars, policy makers, analysts, and military leaders and of crossing civilian-military boundaries to advance knowledge and solve problems. To that end, MCUP launched the *Marine Corps University Journal (MCU Journal)* in 2010 to provide a forum for interdisciplinary discussion of national security and international relations issues and how they impact the Department of Defense, the Department of the Navy, and the U.S. Marine Corps directly and indirectly. Though the press focuses on military topics, it does not accept biographies or historical fiction.
Journals: *MCU Journal* and *Marine Corps History*
Imprints: MCU Press and History Division

Marquette University Press

1415 West Wisconsin Avenue
Box 3141
Milwaukee, WI 53201-3141

<u>Warehouse Address:</u>
30 Amberwood Parkway
Ashland, OH 44805

Phone: 414.288.1564
Fax: 414.288.7813
Email: (user I.D.)@marquette.edu

<u>Orders and Customer Service:</u>
Phone: 800.266.5564; 419.281.1802
Fax: 419.281.6883

<u>Website and Social Media:</u>
Website: marquette.edu/mupress
Facebook: www.facebook.com/MarquetteUPress
Twitter: @MarquetteUPress

<u>UK/European Distributor:</u>
Eurospan

<u>Canadian Representative:</u>
Scholarly Book Services

Staff
Director: James South (414.288.1564; email: james.south)
Business, Marketing, Production: Maureen Kondrick (414.288.1564; email: maureen.kondrick)
Journals: James South
Journals Marketing: Pamela K. Swope (800.444.2419; email: pkswope@pdcnet.org)

Number of Press Staff: 3

Regular Member
Established: 1916
Title output 2017: 12
Titles currently in print: 450

Admitted to the Association 1998
Title output 2018: 5
Journals published: 1

Editorial Program
Philosophy; theology; history; urban studies; journalism; regional studies; and mediæval history.
Journal: *Philosophy & Theology*
Book series: Aquinas Lecture; Marquette Studies in Philosophy; Mediæval Philosophical Texts in Translation; Marquette Studies in Theology; Père Marquette Lecture; Reformation Texts with Translation: Biblical Studies, Women in the Reformation, Late Reformation; Klement Lecture (Civil War); Urban Studies Series; Diederich Studies in Media and Communication

University of Massachusetts Press

East Experiment Station
671 North Pleasant Street
Amherst, MA 01003

Phone: 413.545.2217
Fax: 413.545.1226
Email: (user I.D.)@umpress.umass.edu
(unless otherwise indicated)

Website and Social Media:
Website: www.umass.edu/umpress
Facebook: www.facebook.com/umasspress
Twitter: @umasspress
Blog: umasspress.wordpress.com

Canadian Representative:
Scholarly Book Services

Boston Office:
Brian Halley
UMass Boston
100 Morrissey Boulevard
Boston, MA 02125

Orders:
c/o Hopkins Fulfillment Services
PO Box 50370
Baltimore, MD 21211
Phone: 800.537.5487
Fax: 410.516.6998
Email: hfscustserv@press.jhu.edu

UK/European Distributor:
Eurospan

Staff
Director: Mary V. Dougherty (413.545.4990; email: mvd)
Executive Editor: Matt Becker (413.545.4989; email: mbecker)
Senior Editor (Boston): Brian Halley (617.287.5610; email: brian.halley@umb.edu)
Editorial, Design, and Production Manager: Sally Nichols (413.545.4997; email: snichols)
Production Editor: Rachael DeShano (413.545.4998; email: rdeshano)
Production & Design Assistant: Deste Roosa (413.545.4991)
Marketing Manager: Courtney Andree (413.545.4987; email: cjandree)
Business Manager: Yvonne Crevier (413.545.4994; email: ycrevier)

Number of Press Staff: 8

Regular Member
Established: 1963
Title output 2017: 40
Titles currently in print: 1,200

Admitted to the Association: 1966
Title output 2018: 40

Editorial Program
Scholarly books and serious nonfiction, with special interests in African American studies; American history; American studies; biography; childhood and youth studies; disability studies; educational studies; environmental studies; gender and sexuality studies; history of the book; history of New England; journalism and media studies; literary and cultural studies; Native American studies; public history; science and technology studies; transnational studies; and urban studies.
Imprints: Bright Leaf: Books that Illuminate
Book series, joint imprints and/or copublishing programs: African American Intellectual History; American Popular Music; The Amherst Series in Law, Jurisprudence, and Social Thought; AWP Award Series in Short Fiction (Grace Paley Prize); Childhoods: Interdisciplinary Perspectives on Children and Youth; Culture and Politics in the Cold War and Beyond; Environmental History of the Northeast; Juniper Prizes (poetry and fiction); Library of American Landscape History (Designing the American Park); Massachusetts Studies in Early Modern Culture; Native Americans of the Northeast; Public History in Historical Perspective; Science/Technology/Culture; Studies in Print Culture and the History of the Book; Veterans
Imprints: Bright Leaf: Books that Illuminate

McGill-Queen's University Press

Montreal Office:
1010 Sherbrooke Street West
Suite 1720
Montreal, QC H3A 2R7
Canada

Phone: 514.398.3750
Fax: 514.398.4333
Email: mqup@mcgill.ca
Indiv: (user I.D.)@mcgill.ca

Website and Social Media:
Website: www.mqup.ca/
Blog: www.mqup.ca/blog/
Facebook: www.facebook.com/McGillQueensUP
Twitter: @McGillQueensUP
YouTube: www.youtube.com/user/McGillQueens
Tumblr: mqup.tumblr.com/

Canadian Distributor:
University of Toronto Press
5201 Dufferin Street
Toronto, ON M3H 5T8
Canada
Phone: 1.800.565.9523
Fax: 1.800.221.9985
Email: utpbooks@utpress.utoronto.ca

UK/European Distributor:
Marston Book Services Ltd

Kingston Office:
Douglas Library Building
93 University Avenue
Kingston, ON K7L 5C4
Canada

Phone: 613.533.2155
Email: mqup@queensu.ca

US Distributor:
Chicago Distribution Center
11030 South Langley Avenue
Chicago, IL 60628
USA
Phone: 800.621.2736
Fax: 800.621.8476
Email: orders@press.uchicago.edu

Staff

Executive Director: Philip J. Cercone (Montreal, 514.398.3750; email: philip.cercone)
Finance and Business Manager: Carmen Dumitrescu (514.398.5336; email: carmen.dumitrescu)
Rights and Special Projects Manager: Natalie Blachere (514.398.2121; email: natalie.blachere)
Information Systems Administrator: Alex Stoica (514.398.4419; email: alex.stoica)
Publishing Administrator: Paloma Friedman (514.398.2911; email: paloma.friedman)
Accounts Payable: Carmie Vacca (514.398.5792; email: carmie.vacca)
   Accounting Clerk (Receivables): Tricia Henry (514.398.1825; email: tricia.henry)
Editor-in-Chief: Jonathan Crago (514.398.7480; email: jonathan.crago)
   Senior Editor: Kyla Madden (514.398.2056; email: kyla.madden)
   Editors: Mark Abley (514.398.6652; email: mark.abley); Jacqueline Mason (514.398.2250; email: jacqueline.mason); Khadija Coxon (613.533.2155; email: khadija.coxon@queensu.ca); Richard Ratzlaff (647.580.9333; email: richard.ratzlaff@queensu.ca); Richard Baggaley (+44.1295.720025; email: richard.baggaley.mqup@mcgill.ca)
   Editorial Assistants: Joanne Pisano (514.398.1823; email: joanne.pisano); Finn Purcell (514.398.3279; email: finn.purcell)
Managing Editor: Ryan Van Huijstee (514.398.3922; email: ryan.vanhuijstee)
   Assistant Managing Editor: Kathleen Fraser (514.398.2068; email: kathleen.c.fraser)
Production Manager: Elena Goranescu (514.398.7395; email: elena.goranescu)
   Assistant Production Manager: Rob Mackie (514.398.1342; email: robert.mackie)
   Production Assistant: Andrew Pinchefsky (514.398.6996; email: andrew.pinchefsky)
Marketing Director and Associate Director: Erin Rolfs (514.398.6306; email: erinrolfs.mqup)
   Sales Manager: Linda Iarrera (514.398.5165; email: linda.iarrera)

Educational Sales Administrator: Roy Ward (514.398.7177; email: roy.ward)
Direct Mail & Exhibits Coordinator: Filomena Falocco (514.398.2912; email: filomena.falocco)
Online Marketing and Data Manager: Shannon Wood (514.398.6166; email: shannon.wood)
Marketing Assistant: Jennifer Roberts (514.398.2914; email: marketing.mqup)
Publicist: Jacqueline Davis (514.398.2555; email: jacqueline.davis)

Number of Press Staff: 27

Regular Member
Established: 1969 as a joint press
Admitted to the Association: 1963 (as McGill University Press)
Title output 2017: 142   Title output 2018: 152
Titles currently in print: c. 3,810

Editorial Program
Scholarly books and well-researched studies of general interest in the humanities and social sciences, including anthropology, especially North American native peoples; architecture; Arctic and northern studies; art history; biography; Canadian studies; Canadian literature; classics; communication and media studies; cultural studies; demography; economics; education; environmental studies; ethnic studies; European studies; film studies; folklore and material culture; gender studies; geography; health and society; history; history of medicine; history of science; Irish and Gaelic studies; law; linguistics; literary criticism; medieval and renaissance studies; military studies; music history and theory; native studies; philosophy; poetry; photography; political economy; political science; public administration; public affairs; public health; Quebec studies; religious studies; Slavic and Eastern European studies; sociology; theatre; urban studies; and women's studies.

Book series: Advancing Studies in Religion; Art of the State; Arts Insights; Canada Among Nations; Canada: The State of the Federation; Canadian Association of Geographers Series in Canadian Geography; Canadian Public Administration; Carleton Library; Central Problems of Philosophy; Central Works of Philosophy; Centre for Editing Early Canadian Texts; CHORA: Intervals in the Philosophy of Architecture Comparative Charting of Social Change; Continental European Philosophy; Critical Perspectives on Public Affairs; Culture of Cities; Democracy, Diversity, and Citizen Engagement; Fields of Governance: Policy-Making in Canadian Municipalities; Fontanus Monograph; Footprints; Foreign Policy, Security, and Strategic Studies; Fundamentals of Philosophy; Global Dialogue on Federalism; Global Dialogue on Federalism Booklet; Governance and Public Management; Harbinger Poetry; How Ottawa Spends; Hugh MacLennan Poetry; Human Dimensions in Foreign Policy, Military Studies, and Security Studies; Innovation, Science, Environment; International Social Survey Programme; Library of Political Leadership; McGill-Queen's French Atlantic Worlds Series; McGill-Queen's Native and Northern; McGill-Queen's Refugee and Forced Migration Studies; McGill-Queen's Studies in Ethnic History; McGill-Queen's Studies in Gender, Sexuality, and Social Justice in the Global South; McGill-Queen's Studies in the History of Ideas; McGill-Queen's Studies in the History of Religion; McGill-Queen's/Associated Medical Services Studies in the History of Medicine, Health, and Society; McGill-Queen's/Beaverbrook Canadian Foundation Studies in Art History; McGill-Queen's Rural, Wildland, Resource Studies; McGill-Queen's Studies in Urban Governance; Migration and Diversity: Comparative Issues and International Comparisons; Nordic Voices; Outspoken; Philosophy Now; Philosophy and Science; Public Policy; Queen's Policy Studies; Rethinking Canada in the World; Rupert's Land Record Society; Social Union; States, People, and the History of Social Change; Studies in Christianity and Judaism; Studies in Nationalism and Ethnic Conflict; Studies on the History of Quebec/Études d'histoire du Québec; Thematic Issues in Federalism; Understanding Movements in Modern Thought; War and European Society, Women's Experience

Medieval Institute Publications

Street Address:
100 E Walwood Hall
Western Michigan University
Kalamazoo, MI 49008-5432

Mailing Address:
Western Michigan University
1903 W. Michigan Ave.
Kalamazoo, MI 49008-5432, USA

Phone: 269.387.8755
Fax: 269.387.8750

Website and Social Media:
Website: wmich.edu/medievalpublications
Twitter: @ MIP_MedPub

Backlist, Journals, and TEAMS Orders:
ISD
70 Enterprise Drive, Suite 2
Bristol, CT 06010, USA

Frontlist Orders USA/CA (via De Gruyter):
TriLiteral, LLC
100 Maple Ridge Drive
Cumberland, RI 02864, USA

Frontlist Orders Rest of World
(via De Gruyter):
HGV / Servicecenter Fachverlage
Holzwiesenstr. 2
72127 Kusterdingen, GERMANY

Staff
Acting Editor-in-Chief: Theresa M. Whitaker (email: theresa.m.whitaker@wmich.edu)
Finance and Assistant Managing Editor: Marjorie Harrington (email:
   marjorie.harrington@wmich.edu)
Program Coordinator with De Gruyter: Elisabeth Kempf (email: elisabeth.kempf@degruyter.com)

Number of Press Staff: 2

Regular Member
Established: 1978

Admitted to the Association: 2011
(Intro. Member)
Admitted to the Association: 2015
(Assoc. Member)

Titles currently in print: 267

Journals published: 2

Editorial Program
Publications in archeology, art history, dance, drama, history, literature, music, philosophy, and theology of the European Middle Ages and early modern period.
Book series: Christianities Before Modernity; Early Drama, Art, and Music; Festschriften, Occasional Papers, and Lectures; History and Cultures of Food, 1300-1800; Late Tudor and Stuart Drama: Gender, Performance, and Material Culture; Ludic Cultures, 1100-1700; Monastic Life; Monsters, Prodigies, and Demons: Medieval and Early Modern Constructions of Alterity; New Queer Medievalisms; The Northern Medieval World; Research in Medieval and Early Modern Culture; Publications of the Richard Rawlinson Center; Studies in Iconography: Themes and Variations; Studies in Medieval and Early Modern Culture; TEAMS Commentary Series; TEAMS Documents of Practice; TEAMS German Texts in Bilingual Editions; TEAMS Middle English Texts Series; TEAMS Secular Commentary Series; TEAMS Varia
Journals: *Medieval Prosopography; Studies in Iconography*

Mercer University Press

1501 Mercer University Drive
Macon, GA 31207

Phone: 478.301.2880
Fax: 478.301.2585
Email: (user I.D.)@mercer.edu

Orders:
Phone: 866.895.1472
Email: mupressorders@mercer.edu

Website and Social Media:
Website: www.mupress.org
Blog: merceruniversitypress.wordpress.com/
Facebook: www.facebook.com/MercerUniversityPress
Twitter: @mupress

Staff
Director and Acquisitions: Marc A. Jolley (email: jolley_ma)
Production: Marsha Luttrell, Publishing Assistant (email: luttrell_mm)
Marketing: Mary Beth Kosowski, Director of Marketing and Sales (email: kosowski_mb)
Business: Regenia (Jenny) Toole, Business Office (email: toole_rw)
Customer Service: Heather Comer (email: Comer_hm)

Number of Press Staff: 5.5

Regular Member
Established: 1979
Title output 2017: 33
Titles currently in print: 500+

Admitted to the Association: 2000
Title output 2018: 34

Editorial Program
Regional trade titles and serious works of nonfiction in history, particularly in the history of the United States (with an emphasis on the American South), the history of religion, and the history of literature; Southern regional studies; literature and literary criticism; Southern literary fiction; poetry; African American studies; political science; natural history.
Book series: Baptists; Civil War Georgia; the International Kierkegaard Commentary; Mercer Classics in Biblical Studies; the Mercer Commentary on the Bible; the Melungeons; Mercer Paul Tillich Series; Mercer Flannery O'Connor Series; Music and the American South; Sports and Religion; Voices of the African Diaspora.
Book Awards: The Ferrol Sams Award for Fiction; The Adrienne Bond Award for Poetry; The Will D. Campbell Award for Creative Nonfiction

University of Michigan Press

839 Greene Street
Ann Arbor, MI 48104-3209

Phone: 734.764.4388
Fax: 734.615.1540
Email: um.press@umich.edu
Indiv: (user I.D.)@umich.edu

Orders:
University of Michigan Press
c/o Chicago Distribution Center
11030 S. Langley Avenue
Chicago, IL 60628
Phone: 800.621.2736, 773.702.7000
Fax: 800.621.8476, 773.702.7212

Website and Social Media:
Website: www.press.umich.edu
Blog: blog.press.umich.edu
Facebook: www.facebook.com/pages/University-of-Michigan-Press/37383103953
Twitter: @UofMPress
YouTube: youtube.com/umichpress

UK and European Representative:
Eurospan

Staff
Director: Charles Watkinson (734.936.0452; email: watkinc)
Senior Administrative Assistant: Chris Butchart-Bailey (734.763.7751; email: chrisbu)
Acquisitions Editorial:
Editorial Director: Mary Francis (music, media studies, digital scholarship, digitalculturebooks.
   org) (734.763.4134; email: mfranci)
   Editors: Ellen Bauerle (classical studies, medieval studies, African studies) (734.615.6479;
   email: bauerle); LeAnn Fields (theater and performance studies) (734.647.2463; email: lfields);
   Elizabeth Demers (political science, international studies) (734.763.6419; email: esdemers); Sara
   Jo Cohen (American studies); Scott Ham (regional) (734.764.4387; email: scottom); Christopher
   Dreyer (Asian studies, German studies) (734.647.2463; email: mikage)
   Editorial Associates: Susan Cronin (734.936.2841; email: sjcronin); Danielle Coty (734.763.4134;
   email: dcoty); Anna Pohlod (734.763.1664; email: apohlod)
English as a Second Language: Kelly Sippell, ELT Manager and Executive Acquisitions Editor
   (734.764.4447; email: ksippell)
Assistant Marketing Manager: Jason Contrucci (734.936.0459; email: contrucc)
Publishing Production:
   Director of Publishing Production: Jillian Downey (734.615.8114; email: jilliand)
   Managing Editor: Marcia LaBrenz (734.647.4480; email: mlabrenz)
   Production Editors: Mary Hashman (734.936.0461; email: mhashman); Kevin Rennells
   (734.763.1526; email: rennells)
   Senior Designer: Paula Newcomb (734.763.6417; email: newcombp)
   Designer: Heidi Dailey (734.764.4128; email: hdailey)
Publishing Services:
   Director of Publishing Services: Jason Colman (734.647.6017; email: taftman)
   Senior Digital Production Coordinators: Patrick Goussy (email: pgoussy); Amanda Karby (email:
   akarby)
   Digital Publishing Coordinator: Lauren Stachew (email: lstachew)
   Journals Coordinator: Sean Guynes-Vishniac (email: gyunes)
Sales and Marketing:
   Director of Sales and Marketing: Lanell White (734.936.0388; email: lejames)
   Publication Sales Manager: Shaun Manning (734.763.0163; email: shaunman)
   Publicity and Promotions Coordinator: Sam Killian (734.763.0163; email: killians)
Publishing Technology:
   Publishing Technology Group Director: Jeremy Morse (734.615.5739; email: jgmorse)
   Project Manager: Melissa Baker-Young (734.764.6802; email: mbakeryo)
   Front End Developer & UI Designer: Jonathan McGlone (734.763.4260; email: jmcglone)

Business and Administration:
Director, Business and Admin: Gabriela Beres (734.936.2227; email: gsberes)
    Accounts Payable: Linda Rowley (734.647.9083; email: lrowley)
    Systems Administrator: James Vanderwill (734.936.3636; email: jvanderw)
    Intellectual Property Coordinator: Bryan Birchmeier (734.764.4330; email: bryanbir)

Number of Press Staff: 28

Regular Member

Established: 1930	Admitted to the Association: 1963
Title output 2017: 104	Title output 2018: 101
Titles currently in print: 5,740	

Editorial Program

Scholarly and trade works in political science; performing arts (theater, performance studies, music, media studies); classics; American Studies (disability studies, gender studies, race and ethnicity, class studies); Michigan and Great Lakes; African studies; Asian studies; German studies; English language teaching textbooks.

The Press distributes works for Michigan's Center for Chinese Studies, Center for Japanese Studies, the Center for South and Southeast Asian Studies; the American Academy in Rome; the American Society of Papyrologists; and the University of Michigan Museum of Anthropological Archaeology.

Book series: African Perspectives; Analytical Perspectives on Politics; The CAWP Series in Gender and American Politics; Class: Culture; Contemporary Political and Social Issues; Configurations: Critical Studies of World Politics; Corporealities: Discourses of Disability; Critical Performances; Digital Rhetoric Collaborative; Great Lakes Environment; International Series on the Research of Learning and Instruction of Writing; Jazz Perspectives; Kelsey Museum Studies; Landmark Video Games; Law and Society in the Ancient World; Law, Meaning, and Violence; Legislative Politics and Policy Making; The Memoirs of the American Academy in Rome; Michigan Classical Commentaries; Michigan Modern Dramatists; Michigan Papyri; Michigan Series in English for Academic and Professional Purposes; The Michigan Series on Teaching Multilingual Writers; Michigan Studies in International Political Economy; Michigan Studies in Political Analysis; New Comparative Politics; The New Media World; The Papers and Monographs of the American Academy in Rome; Perspectives on Contemporary Korea; Poets on Poetry; The Politics of Race and Ethnicity; Social History, Popular Culture, and Politics in Germany; Societas: Historical Studies in Classical Culture; Theater: Theory/Text/Performance; Thomas Spencer Jerome Lectures; Tracking Pop; Triangulations: Lesbian/Gay/Queer/Theater/Drama/Performance

Michigan State University Press

1405 South Harrison Road, Suite 25
East Lansing, MI 48823-5245

Phone: 517.355.9543
Director's Office Fax: 517.353.6766
Email: msupress@msu.edu
Indiv: (user I.D.)@msu.edu

Orders:
Chicago Distribution Center
11030 S. Langley Ave.
Chicago, IL 60628
Phone: 800.621.2736; (Int'l) 773.702.7000
Fax: 800.621.8476; (Int'l) 773.702.7212

Website and Social Media:
Website: msupress.org
Facebook: facebook.com/MSUPress
Twitter: @msupress

Staff
Director: Gabriel Dotto (European history; cultural history/humanities; urban studies, transportation history & architectural history) (517.884.6900; email: dotto)
Editor-in-Chief: Catherine Cocks (US history, African studies, anthropology, criminal justice, contemporary social issues) (517.884.6909; email: camcat)

Senior Acquisitions Editor: Julie L. Loehr (Great Lakes studies and regional history; environmental and natural sciences; agricultural sciences; ethnohistory) (517.884.6905; email: loehr)
Acquisitions Assistant: Terika Hernandez (517.884.6001; email: herna376)
Coordinating Editor, College of Arts & Letters projects: Kurt Milberger (517.884.7907; email: milberg2)
Managing Editor: Kristine Blakeslee (517.884.6912; email: blakes17)
Project Editor: Anastasia Wraight (517.884.6911; email: wraighta)
Marketing & Sales Manager: Julie Reaume (517.884.6920; email: reaumej)
Promotions Editor: Elise Jajuga (517.884.6918; email: jajugael)
Website Coordinator: Dawn Martin (517.884.6919; email: marti778)
Journals Manager: Natalie Eidenier (517.884.6915; email: eidenie1)
Business Manager: Julie Wrzesinski (517.884.6922; email: wrzesin2)

Number of Press Staff: 12

Regular Member
Established: 1947

Title output 2017: 44
Titles currently in print: 714

Admitted to the Association: 1992
(Previous membership, 1951-1972)
Title output 2018: 39
Journals published: 10

Editorial Program
Scholarly books and general nonfiction with areas of special interest in African studies; African American studies; anthropology; American Indian studies; Armenian studies; criminal justice; environmental science and natural history; Great Lakes studies; history; immigration studies; Latino/a studies; politics and the global economy; mimetic theory; sociology; US history; urban studies; women's studies.

The Press distributes publications for Broad Art Museum; Ecovision; the Michigan State University Museum; Ruth Mott Foundation.

Journals: *Contagion: Journal of Violence, Mimesis, and Culture; CR: The New Centennial Review; Fourth Genre: Explorations In Nonfiction; French Colonial History; Journal for the Study of Radicalism; Journal of West African History; Northeast African Studies; QED: A Journal in GLBTQ Worldmaking; Real Analysis Exchange; Rhetoric & Public Affairs*

Book series: African History and Culture Series; African Humanities and the Arts Series; Algonquian Series; American Food in History Series; American Indian Studies Series (related imprint: Makwa Enewed); The Animal Turn Series; Arab Literature and Language Series; Armenian Series; Breakthroughs in Mimetic Theory Series; Environmental Research Series; Discovering the Peoples of Michigan Series; Latinos in the United States Series; Rhetoric and Public Affairs Series; Rhetorical History of the United States Series; Ruth Simms Hamilton African Diaspora Series; Studies in Violence, Mimesis, and Culture Series; Transformations in Higher Education: The Scholarship of Engagement Series

Imprints: Greenstone Books

Minnesota Historical Society Press

345 Kellogg Blvd. West
Saint Paul, MN 55102

Phone: 651.259.3200
Fax: 651.297.1345
Email: (user I.D.)@mnhs.org

Orders:
Ingram Publisher Services
www.ingramcontent.com
One Ingram Boulevard
La Vergne, TN 37086
Phone: 615.793.5000

Website and Social Media:
Websites: www.mnhspress.org; www.mnopedia.org
www.mnhs.org/market/mhspress/minnesotahistory/
E-Marketing: edelweiss.abovethetreeline.com/HomePage.aspx?pubOrgID=MINN
Blog: discussions.mnhs.org/10000books/
Facebook: www.facebook.com/Minnesota-Historical-Society-Press-44328618980/
Twitter: @mnhspress, @mnopedia

UK/European Distributor:
Lightning Source International

Canadian Distributor:
Scholarly Book Services

Staff
Director: Josh Leventhal (651.259.3218; email: josh.leventhal)
Acquisitions: Josh Leventhal, Ann Regan, Shannon Pennefeather
Editor-in-Chief, Rights and Permissions: Ann Regan (651.259.3206; email: ann.regan)
Managing Editor: Shannon Pennefeather (651.259.3212; email: shannon.pennefeather)
Design and Production: Dan Leary (651.259.3209; email: daniel.leary)
Sales and Marketing Director: Mary Poggione (651.259.3204; email: mary.poggione)
Publicity and Promotions: Alison Aten (651.259.3203; email: alison.aten)
Sales Manager: Serenity Shanklin (651.259.3202; email: serenity.shanklin)
Minnesota History Journal: Laura Weber (651.259.3207; email: laura.weber)
MNopedia (online Minnesota encyclopedia) Editor: Linda Cameron (651.259.3216;
email: linda.cameron)

Number of Press Staff: 12

Affiliate Member
Established: 1851
Title output 2017: 16
Titles currently in print: 500+

Admitted to the Association: 2001
Title output 2018: 18
Journals published: 1

Editorial Program
The Minnesota Historical Society Press is a leading publisher of the history and culture of Minnesota and the Upper Midwest. The Press advances research, supports education, serves the local community, and expands the reputation of the Minnesota Historical Society through the publication of books and digital works, the *Minnesota History* journal, and the free, digital encyclopedia, *MNopedia*.
Journal: *Minnesota History*
Digital: *MNopedia*, an Encyclopedia of Minnesota
Book series: Minnesota Byways; Native Voices; People of Minnesota; Northern Plate
Imprints: MNHS Press; Borealis Books

University of Minnesota Press

111 Third Avenue South
Suite 290
Minneapolis, MN 55401-2552

Phone: 612.301.1990
Fax: 612.301.1980
Email: (user I.D.)@umn.edu

Orders:
University of Minnesota Press
Chicago Distribution Center
11030 South Langley Avenue
Chicago, IL 60628
Phone: 800.621.2736; 773.568.1550
Fax: 800.621.8476; 773.660.2235

Website and Social Media:
Website: www.upress.umn.edu
Blog: www.uminnpressblog.com
Facebook: www.facebook.com/pages/Minneapolis-MN/
    University-of-Minnesota-Press/40070783448
Twitter: @UMinnPress
Youtube: www.youtube.com/user/UMinnPress
Tumblr: uminnpress.tumblr.com
Instagram: @uminnpress

UK Distributor:
Marston Book Services Ltd

UK Representative:
Combined Academic Publishers

Staff
Director: Douglas Armato (612.301.1989; email: armat001)
    Associate Director and Test Division Manager: Beverly Kaemmer (612.301.1956;
    email: kaemm002)
    Rights and Permissions: Jeff Moen (612.301.1995; email: moenx017)
    Outreach and Development: Eric Lundgren (612.301.1991; email: lundg030)
Acquisitions Editorial: Jason Weidemann, Editorial Director (geography, sociology, anthropology)
    (612.301.1992; email: weide007)
    Senior Editors: Pieter Martin (architecture, art and visual studies, political science, urban
    studies) (612.301.1993; email: marti190); Danielle Kasprzak (literary and cultural studies, cin-
    ema, media) (612.301.0122; email: kasp0079); Erik Anderson (regional, Scandinavian studies)
    (612.301.1996; email: and00900)
Managing Editor: Laura Westlund (612.301.1985; email: westl003)
    Assistant Managing Editor: Michael Stoffel (612.301.1994; email: stoff004)
Design and Production Manager: Daniel Ochsner (612.301.1981; email: ochsn013)
    Assistant Design and Production Manager: Rachel Moeller (612.301.1984; email: moel0067)
    Manifold Digital Projects Editor: Terence Smyre (612.301.0073; email: smyre)
Marketing: Emily Hamilton, Assistant Director of the Book Division (612.301.1936; email: eph)
    Sales Manager: Matt Smiley (612.301.1931; email: mwsmiley)
    Publicist: Heather Skinner (612.301.1932; email: skinn077)
    Direct Mail and Web Marketing Manager: Maggie Sattler (612.301.1934; email: sattl014)
Business: Susan Doerr, Assistant Director, Digital Publishing and Operations (612.301.1987; email:
    doer0012)
Journals: Susan Doerr (Business); Jason Weidemann (Acquisitions)
IT Systems: John Henderson (612.301.1955; email: hende291)

Number of Press Staff: 32

Regular Member
Established: 1925
Title output 2017: 119
Titles currently in print: 3,518

Admitted to the Association: 1937
Title output 2018: 113
Journals published: 12

Editorial Program
Literary and cultural studies; social and political theory; cinema and media studies; art and visual studies; digital culture; feminist studies; gay and lesbian studies; anthropology; architecture; geography; international relations; Native American studies; personality assessment, clinical psychology and psychiatry; philosophy; and Upper Midwest studies.
Journals: *Buildings & Landscapes; Critical Ethnic Studies; Cultural Critique; Environment, Space, Place; Future Anterior; Journal of American Indian Education; Mechademia; The Moving Image; Native and Indigenous Studies Journal; Preservation Education & Research; Verge; Wicazo Sa Review*
Book series, joint imprints, and/or copublishing programs: Borderlines; Contradictions; Critical American Studies; Cultural Studies of the Americas; difference incorporated; Electronic Mediations; Fesler-Lampert Minnesota Heritage Book Series; First Peoples: New Directions in Indigenous Studies; Forerunners: Ideas First; Globalization and Community; Indigenous Americas; Minnesota Studies in the Philosophy of Science; MMPI-2 Monographs; MMPI-A Monographs; Muslim International; Posthumanities; Public Worlds; Quadrant; Social Movements, Protest, and Contention; Theory and History of Literature; Univocal

University Press of Mississippi

3825 Ridgewood Road
Jackson, MS 39211-6492

Phone: 601.432.6205
Fax: 601.432.6217
Email: press@mississippi.edu
Indiv: (user I.D)@mississippi.edu

Website and Social Media:
Website: www.upress.state.ms.us
Blog: upmississippi.blogspot.com
Facebook: www.facebook.com/UPMiss
Twitter: @upmiss
Instagram: instagram.com/upmississippi
Snapchat: @upmississippi
Tumblr: upm.tumblr.com
YouTube: University Press of Mississippi

Warehouse Address:
Maple Logistics Solutions
Lebanon Distribution Center
704 Legionaire Drive
Fredericksburg, PA 17026

Orders:
Phone: 800.737.7788; 601.432.6205

Canadian Representative:
Scholarly Book Services

UK Representative:
Eurospan

Staff
Director: Craig W. Gill (601.432.6205; email: cgill) (film studies, music, ethnomusicology, regional trade)
Assistant to the Director: Emily Bandy (601.432.6206; email: ebandy)
Rights and Permissions Manager/Administrative Assistant: Cynthia Foster (601.432.6205; email: cfoster)
Acquisitions Editorial:
Senior Acquisitions Editor: Katie Keene (601.432.6459; email: kkeene) (folklore, literature, children's literature studies, television studies, women's, gender, and sexuality studies)
Acquisitions Editor: Vijay Shah (601.432.6102; email: vshah) (history, Caribbean studies, American studies, African American studies, ethnic studies, comics studies)
Editorial Assistants: Mary Heath (601.432.6459; email: mheath); Lisa McMurtray (601.432.6272; email: lmcmurtray)
Electronic Publishing:
Marketing Assistant and Digital Publishing Coordinator: Jordan Nettles (601.432.6274; email: jnettles)
Manuscript Editorial:
Project Manager: Shane Gong Stewart (601.432.6249; email: sgong)

Project Editor: Valerie Jones (601.432.6554; email: vjones)
Associate Project Editor: Kristi Ezernack (601.432.6249; email: kezernack)
Design and Production:
Production and Design Manager: Todd Lape (601.432.6558; email: tlape)
Senior Book Designer: Pete Halverson (601.432.6559; email: phalverson)
Book Designer: Jennifer Mixon (601.432.6557; email: jmixon)
Marketing and Sales:
Associate Director/Marketing Director: Steve Yates (601.432.6695; email: syates)
Data Services and Course Adoptions Manager: Kathy Burgess (601.432.6105; email: kburgess)
Electronic, Exhibits, and Direct-to-Consumer Sales Manager: Kristin Kirkpatrick (601.432.6795; email: kkirkpatrick)
Publicity and Promotions Manager: Courtney McCreary (601.432.6424; email: cmccreary)
Marketing Assistant and Digital Publishing Coordinator: Jordan Nettles (601.432.6274; email: jnettles)
Business: Tonia Lonie, Business Manager (601.432.6551; email: tlonie)
Customer Service and Order Supervisor: Sandy Alexander (601.432.6704; email: salexander)

Number of Press Staff: 20

Regular Member
Established: 1970
Title output 2017: 137
Titles currently in print: 1,616

Admitted to the Association: 1976
Title output 2018: 145

Editorial Program
Scholarly and trade titles in African American studies; African Diaspora studies; American studies, literature, history, and culture; art and architecture; Caribbean studies; children's literature studies, comics studies; ethnic studies; folklore; film studies; media studies; memoir; music; ethnomusicology; natural sciences; photography; popular culture; regional studies; serious nonfiction of general interest; Southern studies; sports; women's, gender, and sexuality studies; other liberal arts.
Book series: African Diaspora Material Culture; American Made Music; America's Third Coast; Caribbean Studies; Chancellor Porter L. Fortune Symposium in Southern History; Children's Literature Association; Civil Rights in Mississippi; Conversations with Comics Artists; Conversations with Filmmakers; Critical Approaches to Comics Artists; Critical Approaches on Eudora Welty; Faulkner and Yoknapatawpha; Folklore Studies in a Multicultural World; Great Comic Artists; Heritage of Mississippi; Hollywood Legends; Literary Conversations; Margaret Walker Alexander Series in African American Studies; Race, Rhetoric, and Media; Television Conversations; University of Mississippi Museum and Historic Houses; Willie Morris Books in Memoir and Biography

University of Missouri Press

113 Heinkel Bldg.
201 S. 7th Street
Columbia, MO 65211-1344

Phone: 573.882.7641
Fax: 573.884.4498
Email: upress@missouri.edu
Indiv: (user ID)@missouri.edu

<u>Website and Social Media:</u>
Website: upress.missouri.edu
Blog: umissouripress.blogspot.com/
Facebook: University of Missouri Press
Twitter: @umissouripress

<u>Europe, Middle East & Africa Representative:</u>
Eurospan

<u>Orders:</u>
University of Missouri Press
c/o Chicago Distribution Center
11030 South Langley Avenue
Chicago, IL 60628-3830
Phone: 800.621.2736
Fax: 800.621.8476
Email: orders@press.uchicago.edu

<u>Canadian Representative:</u>
Scholarly Book Services

<u>Asia & the Pacific Representative:</u>
East-West Export Books

Staff
Director: David Rosenbaum (email: rosenbaumd)
Editor-in-Chief: Andrew Davidson (573.882.9997; email: davidsonaj)
Acquisitions Editor: Gary Kass (573.823.0813; email: kassg)
Associate Acquisitions Editor: Mary Conley (602.430.7802; email: conleyms)
Editorial, Production, and Design Coordinator: Drew Griffith (573.882.3044; email: griffithd)
Marketing and Sales Manager: Robin Rennison (573.882.9672; rennisonr)
Marketing Coordinator: Deanna Davis (573.882.3000; email: davisdea)
Marketing Assistant: Megan Casey (573.882.8735; email: caseymg)
Business Managers: Tracy Tritschler (573.882.9459; email: tritschlert)

Number of Press Staff: 9

Regular Member
Established: 1958
Title output 2017: 34
Title currently in print: 1,151

Admitted to the Association: 1960
Title output 2018: 33

Editorial Program
American history and culture, including intellectual history, military history, and biography; African American studies; Native American studies; sports; women's studies; American and British literary criticism; history and practice of journalism; political science; bioethics, and regional studies and the natural history of Missouri and the Midwest.
Book series: Advances in Organizational Psychodynamics; American Military Experience; Journalism in Perspective; Mark Twain and His Circle; Shades of Blue and Gray; Sports in American Culture; Studies in Constitutional Democracy

The MIT Press

1 Rogers Street
Cambridge, MA 02142-1315
Phone: 617.253.5646 (main)
Fax: 617.258.6779
Email: (user I.D.)@mit.edu

Journals:
Phone: 800.207.8354 (US/Can)
Phone: 617.253.2864 (main)
Fax: 617.258.6779
Email: journals-cs@mit.edu

Website and Social Media:
Website: mitpress.mit.edu
Blog: mitpress.mit.edu/blog
Facebook: www.facebook.com/mitpress
Twitter: @mitpress
YouTube: mitpress
Instagram: mitpress
Tumblr: mitpress
LinkedIn: the-mit-press
Medium: @mitpress

Book Orders/Customer Service:
Phone: 800.405.1619 (US/Can);
401.531.2800 (International)
Fax: 800.406.9145 (US/Can);
401.531.2801 (International)
Email: mitpress-orders@mit.edu

London Office:
The MIT Press, Ltd.
Suite 2, 1 Duchess Street
London, W1W 6AN, UK
United Kingdom
Phone: +44 (20) 7306 0603
Fax: +44 (20) 7306 0604
Email: info@mitpress.org.uk

Staff

Director: Amy Brand (617.253.4078; email: amybrand)
Assistant to the Director: Nicholas Green (617.253.5255; email: njgreen)
Community Resource and Development Associate: Kate Silverman Wilson (617.258.0564; email: kswilson)
Director of Finance and Operations: Brent Oberlin (617.253.5250; email: brento)
Controller: Charles Hale (617.258.0577; email: chale)
Senior Financial/Royalty Accountant: Janice Miller (617.253.3917; email: millerj)
Director for Strategic Initiatives: Terry Ehling (617.258.0583; email: ehling)
Web Product Manager: Ellen Cross (617.253.0583; email: ecross)
Senior Project Lead, Journals: Kelly McDougall (617.715.2820; email: kmcdouga)
Assistant Project Lead: Alexa Masi (617.253.6908; email: amasi)
Director of Business Development: Bill Smith (617.253.0629; email: smithwmj)
Manager of International & Institutional Sales & Marketing: Jessica Lawrence-Hurt (617.258.0582; email: jclh)
Subsidiary Rights Manager: Pam Quick (617.253.0080; quik)
Permissions Associate: Hannah Gotwals (617.258.0591; gotwals)
Editorial Director: Gita Manaktala (information science) (617.253.3172; email: manak)
   Editors: Matthew Browne (life sciences, neuropsychiatry, global health) (email: brownem); Susan Buckley (education and learning) (617.253.0763; email: susanb); Beth Clevenger (environmental studies, urbanism, food studies) (617.253.4113; email: eclev); Roger Conover (art, architecture, visual culture) (617.253.1677; email: conover); Victoria Hindley (design and visual culture) (617.253.3842; email: vhindley); Katie Helke (science, technology & society) (617.253.0974; email: helkekat); Justin Kehoe (communications) (617.253.3933; email: jkehoe); Philip Laughlin (cognitive science, philosophy, bioethics) (617.252.1636; email: laughlin); Marie Lee (computer science) (617.253.1588; email: marielee); Marc Lowenthal (linguistics, Boston Review, Semiotext(e), Zone Books) (617.258.0579; email: lowentha); Jermey Matthews (physical sciences, mathematics, engineering) (617.715.2048; email: jnamatt); Robert Prior (life sciences, neuroscience, engineering systems) (617.253.1584; email: prior); Doug Sery (new media, game studies, digital humanities, HCI) (617.253.5187; email: dsery); Marianne Stepanian (textbook strategy and development manager) (617.624.6682; email: mstep); Emily Taber (economics,

business, finance) (617.253.1585; email: etaber)
Managing Editor: Michael Sims (617.253.2080; email: msims)
 Associate Managing Editors: Judy Feldmann (617.258.0601; email: jmfeldma); Deborah Cantor-Adams (617.253.7887; email: dcantor)
Design Manager: Yasuyo Iguchi (617.253.8034; email: iguchi)
Production Manager: Janet Rossi (617.253.2882; email: janett)
 Assistant Production Manager: Jim Mitchell (617.253.5649; email: mitchelj)
 Marketing and Promotions: Katie Hope, Director of Marketing and Author Relations (617.258.0603; email: khope)
 Advertising and Digital Marketing Manager: Amanda Markell (617.253.3516; email: amarkell)
 Associate Publicist: David Ryman (617.253.5643; email: dryman)
 Catalog Manager & Copywriter: Susan Clark (617.258.6810; email: sclark)
 Executive Publicist and Communications Manager: Jessica Pellien (617.253.5646; email: pellien)
 Exhibits Manager: Kate Hensley (617.258.5764; email: khensley)
 Institutional Marketing Associate: Ling Zhu (617.452.3741; email: lingzhu)
 Manager for Institutional Marketing: Amy Harris (617.258.0595; email: aeharris)
 Marketing Associate for Professional Books and Journals: Beth Moore (617.253.2887; email: eemore)
 Publicist: Molly Grote (617.715.2997; email: mgrote)
 Publicist: Nicholas DiSabatino (617.253.2079; email: ndisabat)
 Publicity and Marketing Associate: Kyle Gipson (617.253.3383; email: kgipson)
 Publicity Associate: Heather Goss (617.253.6150; email: hgoss@mit.edu)
 Textbook Manager: Michelle Pullano (617.253.3620; email: mpullano)
 Sales Manager: David Goldberg (617.253.8838; email: davidgol)
 Sales Coordinator: Christopher Eyer (617.258.0584; email: cweyer)
Journals Director: Nick Lindsay (617.258.0594; email: nlindsay)
 Administrative Assistant: Rose O'Connell (617.253.3431; email: oconnell)
 Customer Service Manager: Abbie Hiscox (617.452.3765; email: hiscox)
 Customer Service Representative: John French Williamson (617.253.3332; email: jfrenchw)
 Financial/Administrative Assistant: Jane Powers (617.258.0592; email: jhpowers)
 Fulfillment System Assistant: Christie Lyons (617.528.6863; email: lyonsc)
 Order Fulfillment Assistant: Annalise Keeler (617.253.3428; email: annalise)
 PubPub Community Manager: Catherine Ahearn (617.715.5412; email: cahearn)
 Journals Editorial & Production Manager: Rachel Besen (617.258.0585; email: rbesen)
 Journals Production Coordinators: Ann Olson (617.258.0596; email: aolson); Levi Rubeck (617.258.0587; email: lrubeck)
 Senior Production Coordinator: Dan Bouchard (617.258.0588; email: bouchard)
 Senior Production Editor: Eric Witz (617.258.0586; email: ewitz)
 Data Services Manager: M. F. Gydus (617.258.0618; email: mfgydus)
Warehouse: Robert O'Handley, Director of Operations (email: bob.ohandley@triliteral.org)
Customer Service Manager: Cathy Morrone (800.405.1619; email: cathy.morrone@triliteral.org)

Number of Press Staff: 106

Regular Member

Established: 1961	Admitted to the Association: 1961
Title output 2017: 374	Title output 2018: 325
Titles currently in print: 5,342	Journals published: 36

Editorial Program
Architecture; artificial intelligence; bioethics; biology; business; cognitive sciences; communication; computer science; contemporary art; design; earth sciences; economics; education; engineering; environmental and urban studies; finance; game studies; information sciences; life sciences; linguistics; management; mathematics; natural history; new media studies; neuroscience; philosophy; physical sciences; performing arts; photography; political science; psychology; regional/MIT titles; science, technology, and society (STS); visual and cultural studies.
Co-publishing and distribution programs: Afterall Books; Alphabet City; Boston Review Books; Goldsmiths Press; MITxPress; Perspecta; SA+P Press; Semiotext(e); Strange Attractor Press; Whitechapel Documents of Contemporary Art; Zone Books

Journals: *African Arts; American Journal of Health Economics; Artificial Life; ARTMargins; Asian Development Review; Asian Economic Papers; Computational Linguistics; Computational Psychiatry; Computer Music Journal; Daedalus; Design Issues; Education Finance and Policy; Evolutionary Computation; Global Environmental Politics; Grey Room; Innovations; International Security; JoDS: Journal of Design and Science; Journal of Cognitive Neuroscience; Journal of Cold War Studies; The Journal of Interdisciplinary History; Leonardo; Leonardo Music Journal; Linguistic Inquiry; Nautilus; Network Neuroscience; Neural Computation; The New England Quarterly; October; Open Mind: Discoveries in Cognitive Science; PAJ: A Journal of Performance and Art; Perspectives on Science; Presence: The Review of Economics and Statistics; TDR: The Drama Review; Thresholds*
Book series: Acting with Technology; Adaptive Computation and Machine Learning; Afterall: One Work; Alvin Hansen Symposium Series on Public Policy; American Academy Studies in Global Security; American and Comparative Environmental Policy; Annotating Art's Histories; Arne Ryde Memorial Lectures; Basic Bioethics; BCSIA Studies in International Security; Boston Review Books; Bradford Books; Cairoli Lectures; Cellular and Molecular Neuroscience; Centre for European Policy Studies (CEPS); CESifo Book; CESifo Seminar; Cognitive Neuroscience; Computational Molecular Biology; Computational Neuroscience; Cooperative Information Systems; Current Studies in Linguistics; Dahlem Workshop Reports; Design Thinking, Design Theory Developmental Cognitive Neuroscience; Dibner Institute Studies in the History of Science and Technology; Digital Communication; Digital Libraries & Electronic Publishing; Documentary Sources in Contemporary Art; Documents Books; Documents of Contemporary Art; Earth System Governance; Economic Learning and Social Evolution; Electronic Culture; Engineering Studies; Engineering Systems; Essential Knowledge; Food, Health, and the Environment; Gaston Eyskens Lectures; George Santayana: Definitive Works; Global Environmental Accord: Strategies for Sustainability and Institutional Innovation; History and Foundation of Information Science; History of Computing; Information Revolution and Global Politics; Information Policy; Infrastructures; Inside Technology; Intelligent Robotics and Autonomous Agents; International Security Readers; Issues in Clinical and Cognitive Neuropsychology; Issues in the Biology of Language & Cognition; Jean Nicod Series; John D. & Catherine T. MacArthur Foundation Series on Digital Media and Learning; Lemelson Center Studies in Invention and Innovation; Leonardo Books; Life and Mind; Linguistic Inquiry Monographs; Lionel Robbins Lectures; Munich Lectures; Neural Information Processing; October Books; October Files; Ohlin Lectures; Perspecta: The Yale Architecture Journal; Philosophical Psychopathology: Disorders in Mind; Platform Studies; Playful Thinking; Politics, Science, and the Environment; Representation and Mind; Scientific and Engineering Computation; Semiotext(e); Short Circuits; Simplicity: Design, Technology, Business, Life; Social Neuroscience; Software Studies; Special Issues of Physica D; Structural Mechanics; Strüngmann Forum Reports; Studies in Contemporary German Social Thought; Studies in Neuropsychology & Neurolinguistics; Sustainable Metropolitan Communities Books; Tax Policy and the Economy; Technologies of Lived Abstraction; Topics in Contemporary Philosophy; Transformations: Studies in the History of Science and Technology; Urban and Industrial Environments; Vienna Series in Theoretical Biology; Walras-Pareto Lectures; Wicksell Lectures; Work Books; Writing Architecture; Writing Art; Yrjo Jahnsson Lectures Series; Zeuthen Lecture Series
Idea Commons: ARTECA; MIT CogNet

Modern Language Association of America

85 Broad Street, Suite 500
New York, NY 10004-2434

Phone: 646.576.5000
Fax: 646.458.0030
Email: info@mla.org
Indiv: firstinitiallastname@mla.org

Book Orders:
Phone: 646.576.5161
Fax: 646.576.5160
Email: bookorders@mla.org

Website and Social Media:
Website: www.mla.org
Blog: commons.mla.org
Twitter: @MLAnews, @MLAstyle
Facebook: www.facebook.com/modernlanguageassociation/
YouTube: www.youtube.com/channel/UCleB07C9Cj_KDToGMe7GEGQ

Staff
Executive Director: Paula M. Krebs (646.576.5102)
Director of Scholarly Communication: Angela Gibson (646.576.5016)
Senior Acquisitions Editor: James C. Hatch (646.576.5044)
Acquisitions Editor: Jaime Cleland
Coordinator of Permissions: Marcia E. Reid (646.576.5042)
Head of Book Publications: Erika Suffern (646.576.5134)
Head of Periodical Publications: Sara Pastel (646.576.5031)
Project Manager, Digital Initiatives: Anne Donlon (646.576.5041)
Head of Print Production: Judith Altreuter (646.576.5010)
Head of Online Production: Tom Lewek (646.576.5033)
Head of Marketing and Sales: Kathleen Hansen (646.576.5018)

Regular Member
Established: 1883
Title output 2017: 8
Titles currently in print: 328

Admitted to the Association: 1992
Title output 2018: 15
Journals published: 6

Editorial Program
Scholarly, pedagogical, and professional books on language and literature.
Journals: ADE and ADFL Bulletins; MLA International Bibliography; MLA Newsletter; PMLA; Profession
Book series: Approaches to Teaching World Literature; New Variorum Edition of Shakespeare; Options for Teaching; Teaching Languages, Literatures, and Cultures; Texts and Translations; World Literatures Reimagined

The Museum of Modern Art

11 West 53rd Street
New York, NY 10019

Phone: 212.708.9512
Fax: 212.333.6575 or 212.708.9779
Email: moma_publications@moma.org
Indiv: firstname_lastname@moma.org

Orders:
Individuals: 800.447.6662
www.store.moma.org
Trade: 212.627.9484/www.artbook.com

Website and Social Media:
Website: www.moma.org
Facebook: www.facebook.com/MuseumofModernArt
Twitter: @MuseumModernArt
Instagram: @TheMuseumofModernArt
YouTube: www.youtube.com/MoMAvideos
Tumblr: moma.tumblr.com

UK Representative:
Thames & Hudson

Canadian Representative:
ARTBOOK | D.A.P.

Staff
Publisher: Christopher Hudson (212.708.9445)
Department Coordinator: Sophie Golub (212.708.9512)
Editorial Director: Don McMahon (212.708.9448)
Editor: Emily Hall (212.708.9511)
Editor: Rebecca Roberts (212.708.9883)
Assistant Editor: Maria Marchenkova (212.708.9418)
Assistant Editor: Dawn Chan (212.708.9693)
Assistant Editor: Alex Garner (212.708.9456)
Rights Coordinator: Naomi Falk (212.708.9741)
Production Director: Marc Sapir (212.708.9745)
Production Manager: Matthew Pimm (212.708.9742)
Senior Designer: Amanda Washburn (212.708.6572)
Marketing and Production Senior Coordinator: Hannah Kim (212.708.9449)
Associate Business Manager: Bryan Stauss (212.708.9743)

Number of Press Staff: 14

Regular Member
Established: 1929
Title output 2017: 16
Titles currently in print: 370

Admitted to the Association: 2008
Title output 2018: 20

Editorial Program
Modern and contemporary art, including painting, sculpture, drawings, prints and illustrated books, photography, film, media and performance, architecture and design
Book series: MoMA Artist Series; MoMA Design Series; MoMA Primary Documents; Studies in Modern Art

The National Academies Press

500 Fifth Street, N.W.
Washington, DC 20001

Bookstore phone: 202.334.2612
Fax: 202.334.2793
Email: (user I.D.)@nas.edu

Website and Social Media:
Website: www.nap.edu
Facebook: www.facebook.com/NationalAcademies
Twitter: @theNASEM

Orders (US and Canada):
Phone: 800.624.6242; 202.334.3313
Fax: 202.334.2451
Email: zjones@nas.edu

UK Distributor:
Marston Book Services

Staff
Acting Executive Director: Alphonse MacDonald (202.334.3625; email amacdonald)
Managing Editor: Rachel Marcus (202.334.2275; email: rmarcus)
Production Manager: Dorothy Lewis (202.334.2409; email: dlewis)
Marketing & Sales Manager: Barbara Murphy (202.334.1902; email: bmurphy)
Business Manager: Rachel Levy (202.334.3329; email: rlevy)
Customer Service Manager: Zina Jones (202.334.3116; email: zjones)

Number of Press Staff: 25

Regular Member
Established: 1864
Title output 2017: 175
Titles currently in print: 7,196

Admitted to the Association: 1988
Title output 2018: 203

Editorial Program
Primarily scholarly, policy-oriented titles in agricultural sciences; behavioral and social sciences; biology; chemistry; computer sciences; earth sciences; economics; education; energy; engineering; environmental issues; industry; international issues; materials science; medicine; natural resources; nutrition; physical sciences; public policy issues; statistics; transportation; and urban and rural development.
Imprints: National Academies Press; Joseph Henry Press

National Gallery of Art

Street Address:
Sixth Street and Constitution Avenue NW
Washington, DC

Phone: 202.842.6200
Fax: 202.408.8530
Email: (firstinitial-lastname)@nga.gov

Website and Social Media:
Website: www.nga.gov
Facebook: www.facebook.com/NationalGalleryofArt
Twitter: @ngadc

Mailing Address:
2000B South Club Drive
Landover, MD 20785

Online shop:
shop.nga.gov

Customer Service/Order Fulfillment:
800.697.9350

Staff
Editor-in-Chief: Emiko K. Usui (202.842.6205; email: e-usui)
Deputy Publisher and Production Manager: Chris Vogel (202.842.6209; email: c-vogel)
Managing Editor for the Permanent Collection: Emily Zoss (202.842.6208; email: e-zoss)
Managing Editor of CASVA Publications: Cynthia Ware (202.842.6204; email: c-ware)

Senior Editor: Julie Warnement (202.842.6136; email: j-warnement)
Associate Senior Editor: John Strand (202.842.6613; email: j-strand)
Editor: Caroline Weaver (202.842.6032; email: c-weaver); Lisa Wainwright (202.842.6669; email:
   l-wainwright)
Design Manager: Wendy Schleicher (202.789.4601; email: w-schleicher)
Designers: Brad Ireland (202.789.3082; email: b-ireland); Rio DeNaro (202.842.6697; email:
   r-denaro)
Print and Digital Production Associate: John Long (202.842.6423; email: j-long)
Production Assistant: Mariah Shay (202.842.6758; email: m-shay)
Permissions Coordinator: Sara Sanders-Buell (202.842.6719; email: s-sanders-buell)
Rothko Research Associate: Laili Nasr (202.842.6779; email: l-nasr)
Associate Curator, Mark Rothko Catalogue Raisonné: Adam Greenhalgh (202.842.6323; email:
   a-greenhalgh)

Number of Press Staff: 18

Regular Member
Established: 1941   Admitted to the Association: 1992
Title output 2017: 10   Title output 2018: 8
Titles currently in print: 48 print
(125 backlist in PDF Library)

Editorial Program
The National Gallery publishes exhibition catalogues on all subjects and permanent collection
catalogues (including Western art of the early Renaissance through the contemporary era);
National Gallery of Art Online Editions; a symposium series; Studies in the History of Art, in conjunction with the Center for Advanced Study in the Visual Arts; educational online programs and
catalogues; exhibition brochures and wall texts; online features for permanent collection and special exhibitions; scholarly and popular publications based on objects in the museum's collections;
scholarly publications on conservation; educational materials and guides for use by the public
and by teachers and schools; and the calendar of events, film and music programs, bulletins, and
all Gallery collateral. Unsolicited manuscripts are not invited.

Naval Institute Press

291 Wood Road   Orders:
Annapolis MD 21402-5034   Phone: 800.233.8764

Phone: 410.268.6110
Fax: 410.295.1084/5
Email: firstinitiallastname@usni.org

Website and Social Media:
Website: www.nip.org
Facebook: www.facebook.com/NavalInstitute
Twitter: @USNIBooks

UK/European Representatives: Canadian Representatives:
Eurospan Group   Scholarly Book Service

Staff
Director: Richard A. Russell (410.295.1031)
Editorial Director: Paul Merzlak (410.295.1072)
   Gordon England Chair of Professional Naval Literature: Thomas J. Cutler (410.295.1038)
   Senior Acquisitions Editor/Subsidiary Rights Manager: Susan Todd Brook (410.295.1037)

Senior Acquisitions Editor for Professional Development Content: Jim Dolbow (410.295.1034)
Senior Acquisitions Editor: Paul Kingsbury (410.295.1051)
Acquisitions Editor: Glenn Griffith (410.295.1067)
Assistant Acquisitions Editor/Editorial Lead, Graphic Novels: Gary Thompson (410.295.1030)
Assistant Editor and Digital Assets Coordinator: Taylor Skord (410.295.1096)
Managing Editor: Susan Corrado (410.295.1032)
Senior Production Editor: Emily Bakely (410.295.1020)
Production Editor: Rachel Crawford (410.295.1040)
Managing Editor for Digital Content and Production: Kelly Oaks (410.295.1079)
Director of Sales and Marketing: Claire Noble (410.295.1039)
Sales Manager: Robin Noonan (410.295.1046)
Publicity Manager: Jacqline Barnes (410.295.1028)
Marketing Manager: Meagan Szekley (410.295.1033)
Oral History Program, U.S. Naval Institute
Director: Richard A. Russell (410.295.1031)
Manager: Eric Mills (410.295.1063)
Journals, U.S. Naval Institute:
Proceedings, Editor-in-Chief: Bill Hamblet (410.295.1043)
Naval History, Editor-in-Chief: Richard Latture (410.295.1076)
Publisher, U.S. Naval Institute: Vice Adm. Peter H. Daly, U.S. Navy (Ret.) (410.295.1094)
Chief Financial Officer, U.S. Naval Institute: Chip Wallen (410.295.1707)

Number of Press Staff: 17

Regular Member

Established: 1898	Admitted to the Association: 1949
Title output 2017: 85	Title output 2018: 80
Titles currently in print: 1,100	Journals published: 2

Editorial Program
General military subjects; military biography; naval history and literature; naval and military reference; navigation; military law; naval science; sea power; shipbuilding; professional guides; nautical arts and lore; technical guides; veterans affairs; fiction.
Journals: *Naval History; Proceedings*
Book series: Bluejacket Books (paperback); Blue and Gold Professional Library; Leatherneck Classics; New Perspectives on Maritime History and Nautical Archaeology; Scarlet & Gold Professional Library; Studies in Naval History and Seapower
Imprints: Dead Reckoning (graphic novels)

University of Nebraska Press

1111 Lincoln Mall
Lincoln, NE 68588-0630

Phone: 402.472.3581
Fax 402.472.6214
Email: pressmail@unl.edu
Email: (user I.D.)@unl.edu

Website and Social Media:
Website: www.nebraskapress.unl.edu;
 bisonbooks.com;
 potomacbooksinc.com
Blog: unpblog.com
Facebook: www.facebook.com/NebraskaPress
www.facebook.com/JewishPublicationSociety
www.facebook.com/PotomacBooks
Twitter: @UnivNebPress @PotomacBooks @JewishPub
Pinterest: UnivNebPress
Instagram: instagram.com/univnebpress

Orders:
University of Nebraska Press
Longleaf Services
116 S. Boundary Street
Chapel Hill, NC 27514-3808
Phone: 800.848.6224
Fax: 800.272.6817
Email:
customerservice@longleafservices.org

UK Distributor:
Combined Academic Publishers
Potomac: Casemate UK Ltd

Canadian Distributor:
Codasat Canada Ltd.

Asia/Pacific Distributor:
Eurospan

Staff

Director: Donna A. Shear (402.472.2861; email: dshear2)
Assistant Director for Business/CFO: Tera Beermann (402.472.0011; email: tbeermann2)
Rights and Permissions: Leif Milliken (402.472.7702; email: lmilliken2)
Editor-in-Chief: Alisa Plant (European and world history, regional trade) (402.472.4311; email: aplant2)
 Senior Editors: Bridget Barry (U.S. and world history, geography, environmental studies) (402.472.0645; email: bbarry2); Matthew Bokovoy (Native American and Indigenous studies, borderlands history) (402.472.4452; email: mbokovoy2); Rob Taylor (sports, spaceflight) (402.472.0325; email: rtaylor6)
 Editors: Alicia Christensen (American studies, cultural criticism, creative works) (402.472.0317; email: achristensen6)
 Potomac Books Editor: Tom Swanson (402.472.5945; email: tswanson3)
 Associate Editors: Courtney Ochsner (402.472.4282; email: cochsner2); Heather Stauffer (402.472.5821; email: unp-hstauffer)
 Assistant Editor: Emily Wendell (402.472.5940; email: ewendell2)
 Editorial Assistant: Abby Stryker (402.472.5937; email astryker2)
 JPS Acquisitions: Rabbi Barry L. Schwartz (bschwartz@jps.org); Joy Weinberg (jweinberg@jps.org)
Editorial, Design, and Production: Ann Baker, Manager, EDP (402.472.0095; email: abaker2)
 Project Editors: Joeth Zucco (402.472.0199; email: jzucco2); Sara Springsteen (402.472.4008; email: sspringsteen1); Elizabeth Zaleski (402.472.3638; email: ezaleski2); Margaret Mattern (402.472.3473; email: mmattern2)
 EDP Editorial Assistant: Abigail Goodwin (402.472.7712; email: agoodwin2)
 Assistant Production Manager: Alison Rold (402.472.7706; email: arold1)
 Book Production Associate: Terry Boldan (402.472.0890; email: tboldan2)
 Designers: Andrea Shahan (402.472.7718; email: ashahan1); Roger Buchholz (402.472.7713;

email: rbuchholz1); Nathan Putens (402.472.5943; email: nputens2)
Production Designer: Lindsey Auten (402.472.7716; email: lauten2)
Compositors: Mikala Kolander (402.472.1505; email: mkolandar2); Erin Cuddy (402.472.0318; email: ecuddy2)
Marketing and Sales: Manager: Mark Heineke (402.472.7946; email: mheineke2)
    Sales Coordinator: Rob Buchanan (402.472.0160; email: rbuchanan1)
    Publicity Manager: Rosemary Sekora (402.427.7710; email: rsekora)
    Publicists: Jackson Adams (402.472.3632; email: jadams30); Anna Weir (402.472.5938; email: aweir)
    Direct Mail Manager: Tish Fobben (402.472.4627; email: pfobben2)
    Advertising and Exhibits Coordinator: Amy Lage (402.472.2759; email: alage2)
    Electronic Marketing Coordinator: Erica Corwin (402.472.9313; email: ecorwin1)
    Marketing Designer: Kate Fiedler (402.472.5949; email: kfiedler3)
Journals: Management & Publishing Solutions: Manjit Kaur, Manager (402.472.7703; email: mkaur2)
    Marketing and Fulfillment Manager: Joyce Gettman (402.472.8330; email: jgettman2)
    Marketing Associate: Haley Mendlik (402.472.3581; email: hmendlik2)
    Fulfillment Coordinator: Odessa Anderson (402.472.8536; email: oanderson2)
    Project Supervisor: Joel Puchalla (402.472.3572; email: jpuchalla4)
    Project Coordinator: Aimee Allard (402.472.2292; email: aimee.allard)
    Graphic Designer/Compositor: Lacey Losh (402.472.5028; email: llosh2)
Business Services:
    Senior Accountant and Analyst: Mark Francis (402.472.5804; email: mfrancis2)
    Royalty Accountant & Accounts Receivable: Odessa Anderson (402.472.8536; email: oanderson2)
    Accounts Payable: Claire Schwinck (402.472.7711; email: cschwinck2)
    Business Assistant: Barbara Townsend (402.472.3581; email: btownsend2)
    Digital Assets and IT: Jana Faust, Manager (402.472.0171; email: jfaust2)
    Coordinator: Grey Castro (402.472.3663; email: gcastro3)

Number of Press Staff: 48

Regular Member
Established: 1941   Admitted to the Association: Unknown
Title output 2017: 142   Title output 2018: 160
Titles currently in print: 3,450   Journals published: 30

Editorial Program
Native American and Indigenous studies; American and European history; Western Americana; Latin America; sports; anthropology; geography; environmental studies; American studies; cultural criticism; creative works. JPS imprint: bible, bible commentary, Jewish history and culture. Potomac imprint: biography and memoir, Civil War history, military studies, world and national affairs.
    The Press distributes for the American Foreign Service, the Buros Institute of Mental Measurement, Confederated Salish Tribes, Salish Kootenai College Press, the Society for American Baseball Research, and Whale & Star Press.
Journals: *American Indian Quarterly; Anthropological Linguistics; Collaborative Anthropologies; Frontiers: A Journal of Women's Studies; Great Plains Quarterly; Great Plains Research; Hotel Amerika; Journal of Austrian Studies; Journal of Black Sexuality and Relationships; Journal of Literature and Trauma Studies; Journal of Sports Media; Legacy: A Journal of American Women Writers; Middle West Review; Native South; NINE: A Journal of Baseball History & Culture; Nineteenth-Century French Studies; Nouvelles Etudes Francophones; Resilience: A Journal of the Environmental Humanities; Storyworlds: A Journal of Narrative Studies; Studies in American Indian Literatures; Studies in American Naturalism; symplokē: A Journal for the Intermingling of Literary, Cultural, and Theoretical Scholarship; The Gettysburg Magazine; The Undecidable Unconscious: A Journal of Deconstruction and Psychoanalysis; Western American Literature; Women and Music: A Journal of Gender and Culture*; and *Women in German Yearbook: Feminist Studies in German Literature and Culture*

Imprints: Bison Books; JPS (The Jewish Publication Society); Potomac Books
Book series: African Poetry; American Indian Lives; American Lives; American Transnationalism; Anthropology of Contemporary North America; At Table; Bison Frontiers of Imagination; Boas Papers Documentary Edition; Borderlands and Transnational Studies; Cather Studies; Comprehensive History of the Holocaust; Complete Letters of Henry James; Critical Studies in the History of Anthropology; Cultural Geographies + Rewriting the Earth; Discover the Great Plains; Early American Places; Early Modern Cultural Studies; Ethnohistories of the Americas; Expanding Frontiers; Flyover Fiction; France Overseas; Frontiers of Narrative; Great Campaigns of the Civil War; Historical Archaeology of the American West; Histories of Anthropology Annual; History of the American West; Indians of the Southeast; Indigenous Education; Indigenous Films; Journals of the Lewis and Clark Expedition; Law in the American West; The Mexican Experience; Native Literatures of the Americas; Native Storiers; New Hispanisms; New Visions in Native American and Indigenous Studies; Our Sustainable Future; Outdoor Lives; Outward Odyssey; Papers of William F. "Buffalo Bill" Cody; Polar Studies; Politics and Governments of the American States; Postwestern Horizons; Prairie Schooner Book Prize in Fiction; Prairie Schooner Book Prize in Poetry; Provocations; Race and Ethnicity in the American West; Recovering Languages and Literacies of the Americas; Sports, Media, and Society; Studies in Antisemitism; Studies in the Anthropology of North American Indians; Studies in the Native Languages of the Americas; Studies in Pacific Worlds; Studies in War, Society, and the Military; Ted Kooser Contemporary Poetry; This Hallowed Ground: Guides to Civil War Battlefields; Willa Cather Scholarly Edition; Women and Gender in the Early Modern World; Women in the West
JPS series: Celebrating the Jewish Year; Folktales of the Jews; Jewish Choices, Jewish Voices; JPS Anthologies of Jewish Thought; JPS Bible Commentary; JPS Guides; JPS Scholar of Distinction; JPS Torah Commentary; The Rubin JPS Miqra-ot Gedolot: The Commentators' Bible
Imprints: Backwaters Press; Bison Books; JPS (The Jewish Publication Society); Potomac Books

University of Nevada Press

Continuing Education Building,
Mail Stop 0166
Reno, NV 89557-0166

Phone: 775.682.7389
Email: (user I.D.)@unpress.nevada.edu

Order Fulfillment:
Chicago Distribution Center
11030 South Langley Ave.
Chicago, IL 60628
Phone: 800.621.2736
Fax: 800.621.8476

Website and Social Media:
Website: www.unpress.nevada.edu
Facebook: www.facebook.com/universitynevadapress

Canadian Representative:
Scholarly Book Services

UK Representative:
Eurospan

Staff
Director: TBA (775.682.7389)
Acquisitions Editor: TBA
Marketing & Sales Manager: Sara Hendricksen (775.682.7395; email: shendricksen)
Marketing and Editorial Assistant: Iris Saltus (775.682.7394; email: isaltus)
Editorial, Design & Production Manager: Alrica Goldstein (775.682.7390; email: alricag)
Business Manager: JoAnne Banducci (775.682.7387; email: jbanducci)

Number of Press Staff: 5

Regular Member
Established: 1961
Title output 2017: 22
Titles currently in print: 415

Admitted to the Association: 1982
Title output 2018: 21

Editorial Program
Scholarly and general interest books about the history, literature, anthropology, archaeology, and natural history of the American West, Nevada, and the Great Basin. Additional interests include books dealing with the Basque peoples of Europe and the Americas; Native American Studies; mining; environmental studies; and gaming and gambling.
Book series: America's National Parks; Basque Studies; Cultural Ecologies of Food in the 21st Century; Gambling Studies; Migration, Demography, & Environmental Change: Global Challenges; Mining and Society; The Urban West; Waterscapes: History, Cultures, and Controversies; Wilbur S. Shepperson Series in Nevada History

University of New Mexico Press

Mailing Address:
MSCO5 3185
1 University of New Mexico
Albuquerque NM 87131-0001

Street Address:
1717 Roma NE
NE Albuquerque NM 87106-4509

Phone: 505.277.3495
Fax: 505.277.3343
Email: unmpress@unm.edu
Indiv: (user I.D.)@unm.edu
(unless otherwise indicated)

Warehouse, Orders, and Customer Service:
Longleaf Services
116 S. Boundary St.
Chapel Hill NC 27514-3803

Phone: 800.848.6224
Fax: 800.272.6817
Email: customerservice@longleafservices.
com

Website and Social Media:
Website: www.unmpress.com
Facebook: www.facebook.com/pages
/University-of-New-Mexico-Press/109620976711
Twitter: @UNMPress

UK/European Representative:
Eurospan

Canadian Representative:
Codasat Canada

Staff
Director: Stephen Hull (505.277.3280; email: sphull)
Rights and Permissions: Stacy Lunsford (505.277.3495; email: slunsford1)
Executive Editor: Clark Whitehorn (406.422.6771; email: clarkw) (anthropology, archaeology, Chicano/a studies, history, Latin American studies, Native studies, natural history)
Senior Acquisitions Editor: Elise McHugh (505.277.3327; email: elisemc) (American literature and criticism, poetry, fiction, art, photography)
Editorial, Design and Production: James Ayers (505.277.3324; email: ayers)
Editor: Alexandra Hoff (505.277.3436; email: aewhoff)
Assistant Acquisitions Editor/e-book Production Coordinator: Sonia Dickey (505.277.2153; email: soniad)
Senior Book Designer: Felicia Cedillos (505.277.2293; email: fcedillo)
Marketing & Sales Manager: Katherine White (505.277.3294; email: kwhite03)
Publicist: Adelia Humme (505.277.3291; email: ahumme)
Marketing Associate: Bryce Emley (505.277.3289; email: bemely)
Associate Director for Business Operations: Richard Schuetz (505.277.3284; email: rschuetz)
Accounting: Tiffany Rawls (505.272.7774; email: trawls)
Distributor Liaison: Susan Coatney (505.272.770; email susanc)
IT Support Manager: Darrell Banward (505.277.0978; email: dbanward)

Number of Press Staff: 20

Regular Member

Established: 1929
Title output 2017: 64
Titles currently in print: 1,080

Admitted to the Association: 1937
Title output 2018: 54

Editorial Program

Scholarly books, fiction, poetry, and literary nonfiction, with special interests in social and cultural anthropology; archaeology of the Americas; art, architecture, and photography; Chicano/a studies; frontier history; legal studies, especially water issues; American literature; Latin American studies; Native studies; and books that deal with important aspects of Southwest or Rocky Mountain states, including natural history and land grant studies

Book series, joint imprints, and/or copublishing programs: Barbara Guth Worlds of Wonder Science Series for Young Readers; Diálogos Series; Latin America in the World – The World in Latin America; Histories of the American Frontier; Mary Burritt Christiansen Poetry Series; Pasó por Aquí Series on the Nuevomexicano Literary Heritage; Recencies Series on Twentieth-Century American Poetics; Archaeologies of Landscapes in the Americas Series; Cambio Series on Business, Economics, and Society in Latin America; Querencias Series on Transnational Culture of the U.S./Mexico Borderlands; Contextos Series on Latino/a Contemporary Issues; Religions of the Americas; School for Advanced Research Copublications; River Teeth Literary Nonfiction Prize; Southwest Adventure

Imprints: UNM Press

UNSW Press Ltd

Street Address:
University of New South Wales
Randwick Campus
22-32 King Street
Randwick, NSW 2031, Australia

Mailing Address:
University of New South Wales
Sydney NSW 2052, Australia

Phone: +61 2 8936 1400
Email: enquiries@newsouthpublishing.com

Orders:
TL Distribution
15-23 Helles Ave
Moorebank NSW 2170
Australia

Website and Social Media:
Website: www.unswpress.com
www.newsouthbooks.com.au
Blog: www.newsouthpublishing.com
Facebook: www.facebook.com/
NewSouth-Books-Australia-131239900263716/
Twitter: @newsouthbook
Instagram: instagram.com/newsouthbooks/

Phone: +61 2 8778 9999
Email: orders@tldistribution.com.au
www.bookshop.unsw.edu.au/

USA & Canada Representative:
Independent Publishers Group
814 North Franklin Street
Chicago, IL 60610
Email: frontdesk@ipgbook.com

UK Representative:
Eurospan

Staff

Director: Kathy Bail (+61 2 8936 1417; email: kathy.bail@unswpress.com.au)
Chief Financial Officer: David Bridge (+61 2 8936 1412; email: d.bridge@unsw.edu.au)
NewSouth Books (sales & marketing) Director: Nella Soeterboek (+61 2 8936 1427; email: nella.s@newsouthbooks.com.au)

Publisher: Phillipa McGuinness (+61 2 8936 1418; email: p.mcguinness@newsouthpublishing.com.au)
Publisher: Elspeth Menzies (+61 2 8936 1419; email: e.menzies@newsouthpublishing.com.au)
Editors: Sophia Oravecz (email: sophia.oravecz@newsouthpublishing.com.au); Paul O'Beirne (email: p.obeirne@newsouthpublishing.com.au); Emma Hutchinson (email: e.hutchinson@newsouthpublishing.com.au)
National Sales Manager: Jane Kembrey (+61 2 8936 1409; email: jane.kembrey@newsouthbooks.com.au)
Digital & Production Manager: Rosie Marson (+61 2 8936 1428; email: r.marson@newsouthbooks.com.au)
Retail Director: Mark Halliday (+61 2 9385 6655; email: mark@bookshop.unsw.edu.au)
Information Systems: Brett Haydon (+61 2 8936 1438; email: brett.haydon@unswpress.com.au)

Number of Press Staff: 40

Regular Member
Established: 1962
Title output 2017: 46
Titles currently in print: 500

Admitted to the Association: 2015
Title output 2018: 50

Editorial Program
Literary and illustrated non-fiction across two imprints—NewSouth (trade) and UNSW Press (scholarly and specialist). We publish thought-provoking, well-written books in areas such as history, particularly the history of Australia (with an emphasis on Indigenous history and culture), military history, political science, natural history, environmental studies, popular science and medicine, art, architecture and biography. Select titles are published in partnership with organizations such as the Australian War Memorial, the State Library of NSW and the State Library of Victoria, as well as state galleries and museums. Our books prompt debate and tackle social, political, and scientific issues.

New York University Press

838 Broadway, 3rd Floor
New York, NY 10003-4812

Phone: 212.998.2575
Fax: 212.995.3833
Email: orders@nyupress.edu
Indiv: firstname.lastname@nyu.edu

Website and Social Media:
Website: www.nyupress.org
Blog: www.fromthesquare.org
Facebook: www.facebook.com/fromthesquare
Twitter: @NYUpress
YouTube: www.youtube.com/user/NYUPressOnline
Tumblr: nyupress.tumblr.com

Orders and Customer Service:
Phone: 855.802.8236

Distributor:
Ingram Publishing Services (IPS)
One Ingram Blvd.
La Vergne, TN 37086
Website: ipage.ingramcontent.com
Phone 855.8028236
Email: ips@ingramcontent.com

UK/European Representative:
Combined Academic Publishers

Staff
Director: Ellen Chodosh (212.998.2573)
Subsidiary Rights Administrator: TBA
Acquisitions Editorial: Eric Zinner, Associate Director and Editor-in-Chief (cultural and media studies, literary studies, American studies, twentieth-century American history) (212.998.2544)
Executive Editor: Ilene Kalish (sociology, criminology, politics) (212.998.2556)
Editor: Clara Platter (American history, military history, law) (212.998.2570)
Senior Editor: Jennifer Hammer (religion, Jewish studies, psychology, anthropology) (212.998.2491)
Editorial Director, Library of Arabic Literature: Chip Rossetti (212.998.2433)
Assistant Editor, Library of Arabic Literature: Lucie Taylor (212.998.2575)

Associate Editor: Alicia Nadkarni (film and media studies) (212.998.2426)
Assistant Editor: Sonia Tsuruoka (212.992.9013)
Editorial Assistant: Dolma Ombadykow (212.998.6832)
Digital Scholarly Publishing Specialist: Jonathan Greenberg (212.992.9984)
Editing, Design and Production Director: Martin Coleman (212.998.2572)
  Production and Design Manager: Charles Hames (212.998.2628)
  Assistant Production Manager: Adam Bohannan (212.998.2578)
  Production Editor: Alexia Traganas (212.992.9998)
  Editing and Production Specialist: Edith Alston (212.992.7303)
Marketing and Sales: Mary Beth Jarrad, Marketing and Sales Director (212.998.2588)
  Publicity Manager: Betsy Steve (212.992.9991)
  Marketing Manager: Sarah Bode (212.998.2591)
  Publicity Associate: Sydney Garcia (212.998.2571)
  Publicist and Subsidiary Rights Administrator: TBA
  Marketing Assistant: Amy Klopfenstein (212.998.4252)
Business: Joanne Ferenczi, Business and Finance Director (212.998.2569)
  Accounts Payable and Royalties Coordinator: Ayeida de Freitas (212.998.2524)
  Senior Operations Supervisor: Kevin Cooper (212.998.2546)

Number of Press Staff: 27

Regular Member
Established: 1916
Title output 2017: 140
Titles currently in print: 3,073

Admitted to the Association: 1937
Title output 2018: 113

Editorial Program
American history; law; sociology; Asian American studies; African American studies; Latino/a studies, political science; criminology; psychology; gender studies; cultural and literary studies; media, film, and communications; urban studies; Jewish studies; anthropology; religion; environmental studies; New York regional interest.

NYU Press is the exclusive North American distributor for Monthly Review Press, Wits University Press, and University of Regina Press, and the world-wide distributor for New Village Press.
Book series: Alternative Criminology; America and the Long Nineteenth Century; American History and Culture; Biopolitics; American Literatures Initiative; Children and Youth in America; Citizenship and Migration in the Americas; Clay Sanskrit Library; Critical Cultural Communications; Cultural Front; Culture, Labor, History; Early American Places; Families, Law, and Society; Gender and Political Violence; The History of Disability; Intersections: Transdisciplinary Perspectives on Genders and Sexualities; Library of Arabic Literature; Modern and Contemporary Catholicism; Nation of Newcomers; New and Alternative Religions; New Perspectives on Crime, Deviance, and Law; NOMOS; North American Religions; NYU Series in Social & Cultural Analysis; Postmillennial Pop; Psychology and Crime; Psychology of Law; Qualitative Studies in Psychology; Religion and Social Transformation; Religion, Race, and Ethnicity; Re-imagining North American Religions; Qualitative Studies in Psychology; Qualitative Studies in Religion; Sexual Cultures
Imprints: Washington Mews Books. Books of regional and cultural interest

The University of North Carolina Press

116 South Boundary Street
Chapel Hill, NC 27514-3808

Phone: 919.966.3561
Email: uncpress@unc.edu
Indiv: first name.last name@uncpress.org

Longleaf Services:
Phone: 800.848.6224
Fax: 800.272.6817
Email:
customerservice@longleafservices.org
Website: longleafservices.org

Website and Social Media:
Website: www.uncpress.org
Blog: uncpressblog.com
Facebook: www.facebook.com/UNCPress
Twitter: @uncpressblog
YouTube: www.youtube.com/user/UNCPress

UK/European Representative:
Eurospan

Canadian Representative:
Scholarly Book Services

Staff
Director: John Sherer (919.962.3748)
Executive Assistant: Laura Gribbin (919.962.0358)
Director of Development: Joanna Ruth Marsland (919.962.0924)
Director of Office of Scholarly Publishing Services: John McLeod (919.962.8419)
Acquisitions Editorial:
  Editorial Director: Mark Simpson-Vos (American studies, Native American and Indigenous stud-
  ies, Civil War and military history, music, regional trade) (919.962.0535)
  Executive Editors: Charles Grench (history) (919.962.0481); Elaine Maisner (religious studies,
  Latin American and Caribbean studies, cooking and foodways, regional trade) (919.962.0810)
  Senior Editor: Brandon Proia (history, current affairs, African American studies, environmental
  history) (919.962.0482)
  Editor: Lucas Church (regional trade, Southern studies, literary studies, sociology, health and
  medicine) (919.962.0536)
  Associate Editor: Jessica Newman (gender and sexuality studies) (919.962.4200)
  Acquisitions Manager: Cate Hodorowicz (919.962.9515)
  Acquisitions Assistants: Dylan White (919.962.0538); Andrew Winters
Manuscript Editorial:
  Managing Editor: Mary Caviness (919.962.0545)
  Assistant Managing Editors: Jay Mazzocchi (919.962.0546); Stephanie Wenzel (919.962.0366)
  Editor: Ian Oakes (919.962.0549)
Design and Production:
  Director of Design and Production: Kim Bryant (919.962.0571)
  Senior Designer: Jamison Cockerham (919.843.8021)
  Senior Designer & Reprints Manager: Rebecca Evans (919.962.0575)
  Production Manager: Michelle Wallen (919.962.0577)
  Production Associate: Madge Duffy (919.962.0569)
  Digital Assets Coordinator: Marjorie Fowler (919.962.0471)
Marketing:
  Assistant Director & Senior Director of Marketing & Digital Business Development: Dino
  Battista (919.962.0579)
  Sales Manager: Susan Garrett (919.962.0475)
  Director of Publicity: Gina Mahalek (919.962.0581)
  Publicist: Alison Shay (919.962.0585)
  Digital Initiatives and Database Director: Ellen Bush (919.962.0582)
  Exhibits Manager & Awards Coordinator: Ann Bingham (919.962.0594)
  Marketing Designer: Joanne Thomas (919.962.0590)
  Marketing Assistant: Anna Faison (919.843.7897)

Journals:
  Journals Manager: Suzi Waters (919.962.4201)
  Journals & OSPS Production Coordinator: Sam Dalzell (919.962.0572)
Business:
  Associate Director & CFO: Robbie Dircks (919.962.1400)
  Controller: Jami Clay (919.962.4203)
  Accounts Payable Manager & Accounting Assistant: Deborah Strickland (919.962.4204)
  Accounting Associate: Dylan Stroupe (919.962.0530)
  Human Resources Manager: Adele Sommerville (919.966.2908)
Information Systems:
  Information Technology Manager: Tom Franklin (919.962.4196)
  Desktop Support Specialist & Systems Administrator: Josef Kalna (919.962.0486)
Longleaf Services:
  Executive Director: Clay Farr (919.962.0540); email: clay.farr@longleafservices.org)
  Operations Manager: BJ Smith (919.962.1230; email: BJ.smith@ longleafservices.org)
  Editorial, Design, & Production Manager: Lisa Stallings (919.962.0544; email: lisa.stallings@ longleafservices.org)
  Client Sales and Marketing Manager: Jen Slajus (919.962.0369; email: jen.slajus@longleafservices.org)
  EDP Associate: Ihsan Taylor (919.962.9569; email: ihsan.taylor@longleafservices.org)
  Customer Service Manager: Beth Wiedenheft (919.962.1231; email: beth.Wiedenheft@longleafservices.org)
  Credit Manager: Terry Miles (919.962.1263; email: terry.miles@longleafservices.org)
  Finance Associate: Amanda Doboszenski (919.445.8767; email: amanda.doboszenski@longleafservices.org)

Number of Press Staff: 42

Regular Member
Established: 1922   Admitted to the Association: 1937
Title output 2017: 123   Title output 2018: 118
Titles currently in print: 4,500   Journals published: 11

Editorial Program
African American studies; American and European history; American literature; American studies; ancient history and classics; business and entrepreneurship; cooking and foodways; craft and craft history; diplomatic history; gender and sexuality; geography; Latin American studies; legal history; military history; Native American and Indigenous studies; nature and environmental studies; politics; popular culture; public policy; regional trade and North Caroliniana; religious studies; social medicine; sociology; southern studies; Women's studies. Submissions are not invited in fiction, poetry, or drama.
Journals: *Appalachian Heritage; The Comparatist; Early American Literature; The High School Journal; The Latin Americanist; Journal of Best Practices in Health Professions Diversity; Journal of the Civil War Era; North Carolina Literary Review; south: a scholarly journal; Southeastern Geographer; Southern Cultures; Studies in Philology*
Special series: Civil War America; Critical Indigeneities; David J. Weber Series in the New Borderlands History; Documentary Arts and Culture; Envisioning Cuba; Ethnographies of Religion; Flows, Migrations, and Exchanges; Gender and American Culture; Islamic Civilization and Muslim Networks; The John Hope Franklin Series in African American History and Culture; Justice, Power, and Politics; Latin America in Translation/en Traducción/em Traducão; The New Cold War History; New Directions in Southern Studies; The Steven and Janice Brose Lectures in the Civil War Era; Studies in Social Medicine; Studies in the History of Greece and Rome; Studies in United States Culture
Joint imprints: Omohundro Institute of Early American History and Culture, sponsored by the College of William and Mary
Distributed publishers: Editorial A Contracorriente; North Carolina Office of Archives and His-

tory; North Carolina State Extension; Reacting Consortium Press; University of North Carolina Department of Romance Studies; UNC School of Government

University of North Texas Press

1155 Union Circle #311336
Denton, TX 76203

Orders:
Phone: 800.826.8911

Phone: 940.565.2142
Fax: 940.565.4590
Email: firstname.lastname@unt.edu

UK Representative:
Eurospan

Canadian Representative:
Scholarly Book Services

Website and Social Media:
Website: untpress.unt.edu
Facebook: www.facebook.com/UniversityOfNorthTexasPress
Twitter: @untpress
Pinterest: NorthTexasPress

Staff
Director: Ronald Chrisman
Assistant to the Director: Denise Crosswhite
Assistant Director/Managing Editor: Karen DeVinney
Marketing Manager: Elizabeth Whitby

Number of Press Staff: 4

Regular Member
Established: 1988
Title output 2017: 24
Titles currently in print: 520

Admitted to the Association: 2003
Title output 2018: 24
Journals published: 3

Editorial Program
Humanities and social sciences, with special emphasis on Texas history and culture, military history, western history, music, criminal justice, folklore, multicultural topics, nature writing, natural and environmental history, culinary history, and women's studies. Submissions in poetry and fiction are invited only through the Vassar Miller and Katherine Anne Porter Prize competition.
Journals: *Journal of Schenkerian Studies; Military History of the West; Theoria*
Book series: A. C. Greene; Al Filo: Mexican American Studies; American Military Studies; Frances B. Vick; Great American Cooking; Katherine Anne Porter Prize in Short Fiction; North Texas Crime and Criminal Justice; North Texas Lives of Musicians; North Texas Military Biography and Memoir; Philosophy and the Environment; Practical Guide; Publications of the Texas Folklore Society; Southwestern Nature Writing Series; Temple Big Thicket; Texas Local; Vassar Miller Prize in Poetry; War and the Southwest; Western Life

Northern Illinois University Press

2280 Bethany Road
DeKalb, IL 60115

Phone: 815.753.1075
Fax: 815.753.1845
Email: (user I.D.)@niu.edu

Website and Social Media:
Website: www.niupress.niu.edu
www.switchgrass.niu.edu
Facebook: www.facebook.com/NIUPress
www.facebook.com/SwitchgrassBooks
Twitter: @NIUPress

UK Distributor:
John Wiley Distribution Center

Orders:
Chicago Distribution Center
11030 S. Langley Ave.
Chicago, IL 60628
Phone: 800.621.2736
Fax: 800.621.8476
Email: orders@press.uchicago.edu

Staff
Interim co-Directors: Amy Farranto (email: afarranto); Nathan Holmes (815.753.9908; email: nholmes1)
Assistant to the Director: Pat Yenerich (815.753.1075; email: pyenerich)
Acquisitions Editor: Amy Farranto (email: afarranto) (Russian studies, European history, religion, philosophy, political science, U.S. Civil War, midwestern regional studies, Southeast Asian studies, and fiction)
Managing Editor: Nathan Holmes (815.753.9908; email: nholmes1)
Production Manager: Yuni Dorr (815.753.9906; email: ydorr)

Regular Member
Established: 1965
Title output 2017: 20
Titles currently in print: 539

Admitted to the Association: 1972
Title output 2018: NR

Editorial Program
U.S. Civil War; European history; Russian studies; religion; philosophy; political science; Southeast Asian studies; regional studies on Chicago and the Midwest; Midwest literary fiction.
Book series: Early American Places; Orthodox Christian Studies; Russian Studies, Southeast Asian Studies
Imprint: Switchgrass Books

Northwestern University Press

629 Noyes Street
Evanston, IL 60208-4210

Phone: 847.491.2046
Fax: 847.491.8150
Email: nupress@northwestern.edu
Indiv: (user I.D.)@northwestern.edu

Orders:
Northwestern University Press
Chicago Distribution Center
11030 South Langley Avenue
Chicago, IL 60628
Phone: 800.621.2736; 773.568.1550
Fax: 800.621.8476; 773.660.2235

Website and Social Media:
Website: www.nupress.northwestern.edu
Facebook: www.facebook.com/pages/Northwestern-University-Press/116644703843
Instagram: instagram.com/nupress
Tumblr: northwesternup.tumblr.com
Blog: incidentalnoyes.com
Twitter: @NorthwesternUP

UK Distributor:
Eurospan

Canadian Distributor:
Scholarly Book Service

Staff
Director: Jane Bunker (847.491.8111; email: j-bunker)
Editor-in-Chief: Gianna Mosser (847.467.1279; email: g-barbera)
Acquisitions Editor: Trevor Perri (847.491.7384; email: trevor.perri)
Acquisitions Coordinator: Patrick Samuel (847.491.8113; email: Patrick.samuel)
Managing Editor and Manager of Design and Production: Anne Gendler (847.491.3844; email: a-gendler)
Special Projects Editor: Nathan MacBrien (847.467.7362; email: nathan.macbrien)
Creative Director: Marianne Jankowski (847.467.5368; email: ma-jankowski)
Production Manager: Morris (Dino) Robinson (847.467.3392; email: morris-robinson)
Director of Marketing and Sales: JD Wilson (847.467.0319; email: jdwilson)
Sales and Community Outreach Manager and Poetry Editor: Parneshia Jones (847.491.7420; email: p-jones3)
Marketing Manager: Greta Bennion (847.491.5315; email g-bennion)
Digital Content and Systems Coordinator: Emily Dalton (847.467.2434; email: emily.dalton)
Business Manager: TBA (847.491.8310)
Intellectual Property Specialist: Liz Hamilton (847.491.2458; email: emhamilton)
Number of Press Staff: 15

Regular Member
Established: 1959
Title output 2017: 70
Titles currently in print: 1,901

Admitted to the Association: 1988
Title output 2018: 70

Editorial Program
The Press publishes in African-American studies; Chicago regional; comparative literature; critical ethnic studies; critical theory; fiction; German studies; history; Jewish studies; literary criticism; literature in translation; philosophy; poetry; Slavic studies; theater and performance studies; trade nonfiction; women's studies.
Distributed presses: Lake Forest College Press; Tia Chucha Press
Book series: Critical Insurgencies; Diaeresis; Flashpoints; Jewish Lives; the Northwestern-Newberry Edition of the Writings of Herman Melville; Performance Works; Rereading Ancient Philosophy; Rethinking the Early Modern; Second to None: Chicago Stories; Studies in Phenomenology and Existential Philosophy; Studies in Russian Literature and Theory
Literary Competitions: Cave Canem Northwestern University Press Poetry Prize; Drinking Gourd Chapbook Poetry Prize; Global Humanities Translation Prize
Imprints: Curbstone; Marlboro; TriQuarterly; Hydra

University of Notre Dame Press

310 Flanner Hall
Notre Dame, IN 46556

Phone: 574.631.6346
Fax: 574.631.8148
Email: undpress@nd.edu
Indiv: (user I.D.)@nd.edu

Orders:
University of Notre Dame Press
Longleaf Services
116 South Boundary St.
Chapel Hill, NC 27514
Phone: 800.848.6224 ext. 1
Fax: 800.272.6817

Website and Social Media:
Website: www.undpress.nd.edu
Facebook: www.facebook.com/UNDpress/
YouTube: www.youtube.com/user/UofNotreDamePress
Pinterest: pinterest.com/undpress

UK/European Representative:
Eurospan

Staff
Director: Steve Wrinn (574.631.3265; email: swrinn)
Editor-in-Chief: Eli Bortz (574.631.4912; email ebortz)
    Acquisitions Editor: Stephen Little (574.631.4906; email: slittle2)
    Executive Assistant: Robyn Karkiewicz (574.631.4913; email: karkiewicz.2)
Managing Editor: Matthew Dowd (574.631.4914; email: mdowd1)
    Manuscript Editor: Elizabeth Sain (574.631.4911; email: sain.6)
Design and Production Manager: Wendy McMillen (574.631.4907; email: mcmillen.3)
    Digital Assets Manager: Jennifer Bernal (574.631.3266; email: bernal.7)
Marketing Manager: Kathryn Pitts (574.631.3267; email: pitts.5)
    Marketing and Promotions Assistant: Susan Berger (574.631.4905; email: susan.m.berger)
Business Manager/IT Program Manager: Paul Ashenfelter (574.631.7415; email: pashenfe)

Number of Press Staff: 11

Regular Member
Established: 1949
Title output 2017: 43
Titles currently in print: 1,000

Admitted to the Association: 1959
Title output 2018: 55

Editorial Program
Religion; theology; philosophy; ethics; political science; medieval and early modern studies; classics; Catholic studies; business ethics; American history; European history; European Studies, Latin American studies; religion and literature; Irish studies; history and philosophy of science; international relations; literary criticism; peace studies; patristics; political science, political theory. Submissions are not invited in the hard sciences, mathematics, psychology, or novel-length fiction.
Book series: Andrés Montoya Poetry Prize; The African American Intellectual Heritage; Catholic Ideas for a Secular World; Catholic Social Tradition; Christianity and Judaism in Antiquity; The Collected Works of Jacques Maritain; Contemporary European Politics and Society; The Conway Lectures in Medieval Studies; Critical Problems in History; Ernest Sandeen Prize in Poetry; Kellogg Institute Series on Democracy and Development; From the Joan B. Kroc Institute for International Peace Studies/Kroc Institute Series on Religion, Conflict, and Peacebuilding; John W. Houck Notre Dame Series in Business Ethics; Latino Perspectives; Liturgical Studies; Michael Psellos in Translation; Notre Dame Conferences in Medieval Studies; Notre Dame Review Book Prize; Notre Dame Studies in Ethics and Culture; Notre Dame Studies in Medical Ethics; Notre Dame Texts in Medieval Culture; Poetics of Orality and Literacy; Reading the Scriptures; ReFormations: Medieval and Early Modern; The Review of Politics Series; Richard Sullivan Prize in Short Fiction; Studies in Judaism and Christianity; Studies in Science and the Humanities

from the Reilly Center for Science, Technology, and Values; Studies in Spirituality and Theology; Thresholds in Philosophy and Theology; The Yusko Ward-Phillips Lectures in English Language and Literature; The William and Katherine Devers Series in Dante and Medieval Italian Literature; The Works of Cardinal Newman: Birmingham Oratory Millennium Edition.

Ohio University Press

Alden Library, Suite 101
30 Park Place
Athens, OH 45701-2979

Phone: 740.593.1154
Fax: 740.593.4536
Email: (user I.D.)@ohio.edu

Orders:
Ohio University Press
Chicago Distribution Center
11030 South Langley Avenue
Chicago, IL 60628
Phone: 800.621.2736
Fax: 800.621.8476

Website and Social Media:
Website: www.ohioswallow.com
Facebook: www.facebook.com/OhioUniversityPress
Twitter: @OhioUnivPress

UK/European Representative:
Combined Academic Publishers

Staff
Interim Director: Beth Pratt (740.593.1162; email: prattb)
Acquisitions and Permissions Administrator: Sally Welch (740.593.1154; email: welchs)
Acquisitions Editor: Ricky S. Huard (740.593.1157; email: huard)
Managing Editor: Nancy Basmajian (740.593.1161; email: basmajia)
Production Manager: Beth Pratt (740.593.1162; email: prattb)
Sales Manager: Jeff Kallet (740.593.1158; email: kallet)
Marketing Systems and Design: Sebastian Biot (email: biot)
Promotions and Exhibits Manager: Samara Rafert (740.593.1158; email: rafert)
Publicity Assistant: Maryann Gunderson (email: gundersm)
Business Manager: Omar Aziz (740.593.1156; email: azizo)
Business Office Assistant: Sandra Dixon (740.593.1155; email: dixons3)

Number of Press Staff: 10

Regular Member
Established: 1964
Title output 2017: 47
Titles currently in print: 1,450

Admitted to the Association: 1966
Title output 2018: 51

Editorial Program
Book series: Africa in World History; Biographies for Young Readers; Cambridge Centre of African Studies Series; The Civil War in the Great Interior; The Collected Letters of George Gissing; The Collected Works of William Howard Taft; The Complete Works of Robert Browning; Eastern African Studies; Hollis Summers Poetry Prize; Indian Ocean Studies Series; Modern African Writing; New African Histories; New Approaches to Midwestern Studies; Ohio Bicentennial Series; Ohio Quilt Series; Ohio Short Histories of Africa; The Papers of Clarence Mitchell, Jr.; Perspectives on the History of Congress 1789 – 1877 and Perspectives on the Art and Architectural History of the United States Capitol (for the US Capitol Historical Society); Perspectives on Global Health; Polish and Polish-American Studies Series; Research in International Studies: Southeast Asia, Africa, Latin America, and Global and Comparative Studies Series; Studies in Conflict, Justice, and Social Change; Series in Continental Thought; Series in Ecology and History; Series in Appalachian Studies; Series in Victorian Studies; Series on Law, Society, and Politics in the Midwest; War and Society in North America; Western African Studies; White Coat Pocket Guide Series
Imprints: Ohio University; Swallow Press

Ohio State University Press

180 Pressey Hall
1070 Carmack Road
Columbus, OH 43210

Phone: 614.292.6376
Fax: 614.292.2065
Email: info@ouspress.org
Indiv. (user I.D.)@osupress.org

Orders:
Ohio State University Press
Chicago Distribution Center
11030 South Langley Avenue
Phone: 800.621.2736
Fax: 800.621.8476

Website and Social Media:
Website: ohiostatepress.org
Twitter: @ohiostatepress
Facebook: www.facebook.com/ohiostatepress

Staff
Director: Tony Sanfilippo (614.292.7818; email: sanfilippo.16@osu.edu) (acquires regional & trade)
Editor-in-Chief: Kristen Elias Rowley (614.292.8256; email: eliasrowley.1@osu.edu) (American studies, race and ethnic studies, Latino studies, gender & sexuality studies, rhetoric, creative nonfiction, fiction, and poetry)
Acquisitions Editors: Ana Jimenez-Moreno (literary and cultural studies) (614.514.5815; email: jimenez-moreno.1@osu.edu); Tara Cyphers (Rhetoric & communication, gender & sexuality studies) (614.292.6198; email: tara)
Managing Editor: Tara Cyphers (614.292.6198; email: tara)
Editorial Assistant: Kristina Wheeler (614.688.3481; email: kristina)
Production Manager: Juliet Williams (614.292.3686; email: juliet)
Production Assistant: Debra Jul (614.292.0999; email: debra)
Marketing Manager: Laurie Avery (614.292.1462; email: laurie.avery)
Marketing Assistant: Meredith Nini (614.292.6824; email: meredith)
Journals Manager: Emily Taylor (614.292.1407; email: emily)
Business Manager: Kathy Edwards (614.292.3692; email: kathy)

Number of Press Staff: 15

Regular Member
Established: 1957

Title output 2017: 49
Titles currently in print: 673

Admitted to the Association: 2014
(prior membership: 1961-2007)
Title output 2018: 44
Journals published: 6

Editorial Program
Scholarly books in the humanities and literary studies, with lists in American and African American studies, gender and sexuality studies, Latinx and Chicano studies, rhetoric and communication, comic studies, Victorian studies, narrative theory, classics, medieval studies, creative works, regional and linguistics.
Journals: *Adoption & Culture; American Periodicals; Inks: The Journal of the Comics Studies Society; Narrative; North American Journal of Celtic Studies; Victorians: A Journal of Culture and Literature*
Book series: 21st Century Essays; Abnormativities: Queer/Gender/Embodiment; Black Performance and Cultural Criticism; Classical Memories/Modern Identities; Cognitive Approaches to Culture; Formations: Adoption, Kinship, and Culture; Global Latin/o Americas; Interventions: New Studies in Medieval Culture; Intersectional Rhetorics; The Journal Charles B. Wheeler Poetry Prize; The Journal Non/Fiction Prize; LatinoGraphix: The Ohio State Latin/o Comics Series; Literature, Religion and Postsecular Studies; Machete; New Directions in Rhetoric and Materiality; New Suns: Race Gender and Sexuality in the Speculative; Race and Mediated Cultures; Studies in Comics and Cartoons; Studies in Victorian Life and Literature; Theory and Interpretation of Narrative; Transoceanic Studies; Victorian Critical Interventions
Imprints: Trillium, Mad Creek

University of Oklahoma Press

Street/Mailing Address:
2800 Venture Drive
Norman, OK 73069

Order Fulfillment:
Longleaf Services, Inc.
116 South Boundary Street
Chapel Hill, ND 27514-3808

Phone: 405.325.2000
Fax: 405.325.4000
Email: (user I.D.)@ou.edu

Phone: 800.848.6224, ext. 1; 919-966-7449
Fax: 800.272.6817; 919.962.2704

Website and Social Media:
Website: www.oupress.com
Facebook: www.facebook.com/oupress
Twitter: @OUPress

UK Representative:
Bay Foreign Language Books

Canadian Representative:
Scholarly Book Services

Staff
Director: B. Byron Price (405.325.5666; email: b_byron_price)
Editorial: Adam C. Kane, Editor-in-Chief (405.325.7991; email: adam.kane)
   Acquisitions Editors: Kent Calder (Texas regional studies, contemporary American West, Borderlands) (405.325.5820; email: kent.calder); Alessandra Jacobi Tamulevich (native studies: North, Central, and South America, classical studies) (817.538.9802; email: jacobi); Adam C. Kane (military history, American West, environmental history) (405.325.7991; email: adam.kane; Kathleen Kelly (women's history, California & Southwest, race and culture in the American West, literature) (405.325.1216; email: kathleenkelly); Charles E. (Chuck) Rankin (American West, Mormon studies, Borderlands) (405.209.9833; email: cerankin)
Manuscript Editing: Steven Baker, Managing Editor (405.325.1325; email: steven.b.baker)
   Assistant Managing Editor: Stephanie Evans (405.325.4922; email: s.evans)
   Associate Editor: Emily Schuster (405.325.3786; email: ejerman)
Production: Tony Roberts, Production Manager (405.325.3186; email: tonyroberts)
   Production Coordinator: Anna Maria Rodriguez (405.325.3876; email: annamaria)
   Electronic Publishing Manager: Brent Greyson (405.325.3202; email: bgreyson)
Marketing and Sales: Dale Bennie, Associate Director, Sales and Marketing Manager (405.325.3207; email: dbennie)
   Publicity Manager: Katherine Baker (405.325.3200)
Business: Dale Bennie, Associate Director, Business Manager (405.325.3207; email: dbennie)
   Accounting: Amy Liu (405.325.2356; email: xliu)
   Accounts Receivable and Royalties: Diane Cannon (405.325.2326; email: dcannon)
   Customer Service: Kathy Benson (405.325.2287; email: pressscs)
Rights and Permissions: Shannon Gering (405.325.3182; email: segering)

Regular Member
Established: 1928
Title output 2017: 101
Titles currently in print: 1,984

Admitted to the Association: 1937
Title output 2018: 93

Number of Press Staff: 18

Editorial Program
Scholarly and general interest books, general nonfiction, and some fiction with special interests in the American West, Art and Photography, Classical Studies, Environmental History, Indigenous Studies (North, Central, and South America), Military History, Natural History, Political Science, Popular Music, and Regional Studies.
Book series: American Exploration and Travel Series; American Indian Law and Policy Series; American Indian Literature and Critical Studies Series; American Popular Music Series; American Trails Series (A.H. CLARK); Animal Natural History Series; Before Gold; Campaigns and

Commanders; Charles M. Russell Center Series on Art and Photography of the American West; Chicana and Chicano Visions of the Américas Series; Chinese Literature Today; Civilization of the American Indian Series; Congressional Studies Series; Early California Commentaries (A.H. CLARK); Environment in Modern North America, Frontier Military Series (A.H. CLARK); Hidden Springs of Custeriana (A.H. CLARK); International and Security Affairs Series; Julian J. Rothbaum Distinguished Lecture Series; Kingdom in the West (A.H. CLARK); New Directions in Native American Studies; Oklahoma Series in Classical Culture; Oklahoma Western Biographies; Political Violence in North America, Public Lands History; Race and Culture in the American West; Spain in the West Series (A.H. CLARK); Studies in American Constitutional Heritage; Variorum Chaucer; Ways of War, The Western Frontier Library; Western Frontiersmen Series (A.H. CLARK); Western Lands and Waters (A.H. CLARK); Western Legacies Series; The William F. Cody Series on the History and Culture of the American West
Imprints: The Arthur H. Clark Company

Oregon State University Press

121 The Valley Library
Corvallis, OR 97331-4501

Phone: 541.737.3166
Fax: 541.737.3170
Email: osu.press@oregonstate.edu
Indiv: (user I.D.)@oregonstate.edu

<u>Website and Social Media:</u>
Website: osupress.oregonstate.edu
Blog: www.osupress.oregonstate.edu/blog
Facebook: www.facebook.com/OregonStateUniversityPress
Twitter: @osupress
YouTube: OregonStateUPress
Instagram: osupress

<u>European, African, & Middle Eastern Dist.:</u>
Eurospan Group

<u>Order Fulfillment & Distribution:</u>
Chicago Distribution Center
11030 S. Langley Ave.
Chicago, IL 60628
Phone: 800.621.2736
Fax: 800.621.8476

<u>Canadian Distributor:</u>
University of British Columbia Press

Staff
Director: Faye A. Chadwell (541.737.8528; email: faye.chadwell)
Associate Director: Tom Booth (503.796.0547; email: thomas.booth)
Acquisitions Editor: Mary Elizabeth Braun (541.737.3873; email: mary.braun)
Editorial, Design, and Production Manager: Micki Reaman (541.737.4620; email: micki.reaman)
Marketing Manager: Marty Brown (541.737.3866; email: marty.brown)

Number of Press Staff: 5

Regular Member
Established: 1961
Title output 2017: 17
Titles currently in print: 304

Admitted to the Association: 1991
Title output 2018: 19

Editorial Program
The Oregon State University Press publishes scholarly and general interest books in the environmental humanities; forestry; natural resource management; environmental and natural history; Native American and Indigenous studies; and the history, culture, and arts of the Pacific Northwest.

Book series: First Peoples: New Directions in Indigenous Studies; Horning Visiting Scholars Publication Series; Northwest Reprints; Women and Politics in the Pacific Northwest.

Otago University Press

Street Address:
Level One
398 Cumberland Street
Dunedin, New Zealand 9016

Mailing Address:
Box 56
Dunedin, New Zealand 9016

Phone: 64.3.479.4194
Email: university.press@otago.ac.nz
Indiv: (first name.last name)@otago.ac.nz

Website and Social Media:
Website: www.otago.ac.nz/press/index.html
Facebook: www.facebook.com/OtagoUniversityPress
Twitter: @OtagoUniPress

Orders (NZ):
Nationwide Book Distributors
Phone: 64.3.312.1603
Email: books@nationwidebooks.co.nz

UK Representative:
Gazelle Book Services

US and Canadian Representative:
Independent Publishers Group (IPG)
814 N. Franklin Street
Chicago, IL 60610
Phone 800.888.4741

Staff
Publisher: Rachel Scott (64.3.479.4194)
Editorial/Permissions: Imogen Coxhead (64 3 479 4155)
Design and Production: Fiona Moffat, Production Manager (64.3.479.5851)
Marketing & Publicity: Victor Billot (64.3.479.9094)
Accounts: Arvin Lazaro (64.3.479.4194)
Sales reps: Archetype Book Agents (neilb@archetype.co.nz)

Number of Press Staff: 5

Regular Member
Established: 1958
Title output 2017: 20
Titles currently in print: 222

Admitted to the Association 2016
Title output 2018: 21
Journals published: 1

Editorial Program
Non-fiction books on New Zealand and the Pacific, including history and regional history (southern New Zealand); natural history; Māori and Pacific studies; biography and memoir; arts, culture and literary studies; poetry.
Journal: *Landfall: Aotearoa New Zealand Arts & Letters*

University of Ottawa Press | Les Presses de l'Université d'Ottawa

542 King Edward Avenue
Ottawa, ON K1N 6N5 Canada

Phone: 613.562.5246
Fax: 613.562.5247
Email: puo-uop@uottawa.ca

Website and Social Media:
Website: www.press.uottawa.ca
Facebook: www.facebook.com/uOttawaPress
Twitter: @uOttawaPress
Fax: 800.361.8088; 450.434.4135

US Orders (English and French titles):
Ingram Academic Services
Ingram Content Group
Customer Service
210 American Drive
Jackson, TN 38301
Phone: 800.343.4499
Fax: 800.351.5073
Email: academicorders@ingramcontent.com

Rest of World
Ingram

France (French titles):
Distribution du Nouveau Monde
Website: www.librairieduquebec.fr

Belgium, Netherlands, Luxembourg (French titles):
Patrimoine Diffusion Sprl
Avenue Milcamps 119
1030 Bruxelles
Belgique

Canadian Orders (English titles):
University of Toronto Press
Phone: 800.565.9523; 416.667.7791
Fax: 800.221.9985; 416.667.7832
Email: utpbooks@utpress.utoronto.ca

Canadian Orders (French titles):
Prologue Inc.
1650 Lionel-Bertrand Boulevard
Boisbriand, Quebec J7H 1N7 Canada
Phone: 800.363.2864; 450.434.0306
Email: prologue@prologue.ca

UK and European Orders (English titles):
Marston Book Services

Switzerland (French titles):
Servidis SA
Website: www.servidis.ch

Staff
Director: Lara Mainville (613.562.5663; email: lara.mainville@uottawa.ca)
Acquisitions Editor: Caroline Boudreau (613.562.5800 ext. 3065; email: acquisitions@uottawa.ca) (leave until May 2019); Veronica Omana (interim)
  Managing Editor: Elizabeth Schwaiger (613.562.5800 ext. 3064; email: eschwaig@uottawa.ca)
Digital Content Manager: Mireille Piché (613.562.5800 ext. 2854; email: mireille.piche@uottawa.ca)
Marketing, Distribution, and Administration: Sonia Rheault (613.562.5246; email: srheault@uottawa.ca)

Number of Press Staff: 6

Regular Member
Established: 1936
Title output 2017: 30
Titles currently in print: 552

Admitted to the Association: 2005
Title output 2018: 26
Journals published: 4

Editorial Program
North America's oldest French-language and only fully bilingual university press developed a publishing program in the social sciences and humanities that promotes critical and ethical thinking, first-class research, intellectual integrity, social responsibility, and innovation. UOP fully supports the open access movement and is committed to the open dissemination of scholarship and research insofar as it is financially viable. Titles are published in print and ebook formats.

UOP's mission is 1) To enrich intellectual and cultural life through the publication and dissemination of scholarly works; 2) To extend the reach and influence of the University of Ottawa and associate its name with excellence in research and knowledge creation. In order to fulfill its mission, UOP looks to its rich academic heritage to publish compelling books that engage with today's issues. UOP series are structured along three axes:

Francophonie & Canadian Studies: Amérique française, Archives des lettres canadiennes; Canadian Literature Collection; Canadian Studies; Mercury Series; Reappraisals: Canadian Writers; Perspectives on Translation; and Literary Translation

Politics, Public Policy and Globalization: International Development and Globalization; Law, Technology and Media; and Politics and Public Policy; and

Contemporary Society: Visual Arts; Education; Contemporary Issues; Criminology; Philosophica; Religion and Society; Health and Society; and Cultural Transfers.

A fourth axis, Praxis, is perpendicular to these. It comprises textbooks as well as our new 101 Collection designed to provide brief introductions to topics of interest to today's readers.

Imprints: Canadian Museum of History Harvest House

Oxford University Press, Inc.

Editorial Offices:
198 Madison Avenue
New York, NY 10016
Phone: 212.726.6000
Fax: 212.726.6440
Email: firstname.lastname@oup.com

Website and Social Media:
Website: www.oup.com/us
Blogs: blog.oup.com blog.oxforddictionaries.com/
Twitter: @OUPAcademic

Customer Service:
Orders/Prices: 800.451.7556
Inquiries: 800.445.9714
ELT: 800.542.2442
Journals: 800.852.7323
Fax: 919.677.1303

Distribution Center &
Journals Marketing Office:
2001 Evans Road
Cary, NC 27513
Phone: 919.677.0977
Dist. Fax: 919.677.8877
Journals Fax: 919.677.1714

Oxford University Press (UK):
Great Clarendon Street
Oxford OX2 6DP
United Kingdom
Phone: +44 1865 556767
Fax: +44 1865 556646

Staff
President: Niko Pfund
   Chief of Staff to the President: Haley Anderson
   Director of Finance, Academic: Charles Scobie
   Vice President, Legal, and General Counsel, Global Academic: Barbara Cohen
   Vice President and Publisher, Higher Education Group: John Challice
   Publisher, Reference and Online: Damon Zucca

Publisher, Trade, Academic and Journals: Niko Pfund
President, Dictionaries Division: Casper Grathwohl
Director, Global Business Development and Rights, Academic & US Divisions:
Casper Grathwohl
Vice President, Global Marketing and Digital Strategy: Colleen Scollans
Vice President, Human Resources: Rosann Ashe
Vice President, Operations: Laurea Salvatore
Trade and Academic
Publisher: Niko Pfund
Editor-in-Chief, History and Religion: Theodore Calderara
Editor-in-Chief, Social Sciences: David McBride
Editor-in-Chief, Humanities: Suzanne Ryan
Editorial: Tim Bent (trade, history and politics); Theodore Calderara (history, religion); Angela Chnapko (politics); James Cook (sociology, criminology); Alexandra Dauler (world history, business history, history of science); Susan Ferber (history); Norm Hirschy (dance, film and media studies, music); Sarah Humphreville (science and technology studies); Donald Kraus (Bibles); Jeremy Lewis (earth science, life sciences, physics); David McBride (politics); Peter Ohlin (bioethics, philosophy); David Pervin (economics, finance, business and management); Lucy Randall (bioethics, philosophy); Cynthia Read (religion); Suzanne Ryan (music); Hallie Stebbins (linguistics); Nancy Toff (Very Short Introductions, history); Steve Wiggins (biblical studies); Stefan Vranka (ancient history, archaeology, classics)
Law
Publisher: John Louth
Editors: Jamie Berezin (legal theory, constitutional and administrative law, scholarly corporate law, legal history, law and public policy); Blake Ratcliff (international law, national security law, human rights law); Alex Flach (intellectual property law, law and technology, antitrust law, EU law)
Medical
Publishing Director, Clinical Medicine: Sean Pidgeon
Associate Editorial Director: Craig Panner (neurology, clinical neuroscience)
Senior Editors: Andrea Knobloch (psychiatry, anesthesia, critical care, pain medicine); Chad Zimmerman (public health/epidemiology, infectious disease)
Editor: Marta Moldvai (palliative care, emergency medicine)
Psychology/Social Work Division
Vice President/Editorial Director of Brain & Behavioral Sciences: Joan Bossert (neuropsychology, cognitive neuroscience, cognitive psychology)
Senior Editors: Dana Bliss (social work); Abby Gross (social psychology, positive psychology, industrial & organizational psychology, developmental psychology, educational psychology); Sarah Harrington (clinical psychology, forensic psychology, school psychology)
Reference
Publisher: Damon Zucca
Editor-in-Chief: Ada Brunstein (psychology, neuroscience, public health)
Senior Editors: Molly Balikov (economics, business, political science, social science); Alodie Larson (Oxford/Grove Art); Robert Repino (African studies, African American studies, Chinese studies, Latinx studies, religion); Anna-Lise Santella (Oxford/Grove Music); Anthony Wahl (communication, criminology, sociology)
Editors: Timothy Allen (anthropology, education, law, social work); Louis Gulino (history); Sarah Kain (earth and physical sciences); Benjamin Leonard (archaeology, classics, history, philosophy)
Dictionaries
President: Casper Grathwohl
Dictionaries Editorial: Katherine Martin (Head of US Dictionaries); Jessie Fry (Senior Associate Editor)
Higher Education
Publisher: John Challice

Editorial: Petra Recter (director of content & digital strategy); Dean Scudder (president of Sinauer); Robert Miller (philosophy, religion); Richard Carlin (art, music); Jennifer Carpenter (politics, economics, finance and business); Sherith Pankratz (sociology, anthropology, archaeology); Steve Helba (English, criminology and criminal justice); Jane Potter (psychology); Jason Noe (life sciences, chemistry); Sydney Carroll (psychology, neuroscience); Dan Sayre (earth and environmental sciences, engineering and computer science); Keith Chasse (communication and journalism); Charles Cavaliere (history and classics)
National Sales Manager: Bill Marting

Content Operations
Head of Content Operations: Deborah Shor
  Production Manager: Lisa Grzan
  Demand Planning Manager: Brenda Tamayo
  Business Development and Rights
  Director, Global Business Development and Rights: Casper Grathwohl
  US Director of Business Development: Zachary Haynes

Marketing
Chief Marketing Officer: Colleen Scollans
  Director of Product Marketing: Kim Craven
  Head of Trade Marketing: Erin Meehan
  Director of Customer Engagement and Audience Development: Rose Pintaudi-Jones
  Head of Publicity and Social Media: Sarah Russo
  Head of Institutional Marketing: Tricia Hudson
  Associate Director of Marketing Technology and Change: Erin Ganley
  Digital Strategy: Jessica Chesnutt

Sales
Senior Director of Institutional Sales, Americas: Rebecca Seger
  Director of Global Library Reseller Accounts: Lisa Nachtigall
  Senior Manager, Global Customer Training and Implementation: Ryan Warden
  Director of Consortia Sales: Keith Allen
  Institutional Sales Manager: Jeff Shoup
  Institutional Sales Support Manager: Lesa Owen
  Sales Data & Program Manager: Jessica Barbour
  Director of Corporate Sales: Amy Luchsinger

Human Resources
Director, Human Resources, Academic: Rosann Ashe

Operations (New York)
Office Services Facility Manager, NY: Lorraine Betancourt

Finance
Director of Finance, Academic: Charles Scobie
  Director of Finance: Scott Grande
  Director of Accounting: Dottie Warlick
  Head of Commercial Support, Research & Reference: Andrew Knippenberg
  Financial Controller: Lindsay Barnes

English Language Teaching—New York
Content Director, Adult ELT: Stephanie Karras
US Head of Sales and Marketing: Adriana Acosta

Journals
Publishing Director: Alison Denby
  US Director, Corporate Sales: Amy Luchsinger
  Editorial Director, Journals Policy: David Crotty
  Editorial Director of Science & Medicine: Deborah Dixon
  Editorial Director Humanities and Social Sciences: Rhodri Jackson
  Executive Publishers: Laura Bannon (humanities and social sciences); Ashley Petrylak (science and medicine); Chris Reid (science and medicine); Patricia Thomas (humanities and social sciences)
  Senior Publishers: Julia McDonnell (science and medicine); Rachel Safer (science and medicine); Fiona Williams (science and medicine)
  Publishers: Sarah Andrus (science and medicine); Michael Blong (humanities and social

sciences); Phyllis Cohen (humanities and social sciences); Anna Hernandez-French (science and medicine); Sara McNamara (science and medicine); Matt Turney (science and medicine)
Distribution Center (North Carolina)
Assistant Director, Freight/ Facilities/Procurement/Receiving: James Torrence
  Director of Accounting Services: Dottie Warlick
  Director of Customer Service: Cheryl Ammons-Longtin
  Director of Warehouse Operations: Todd Hayes
Technology
Technology Director, Academic: Casper Grathwohl
IT Operations Manager: Martin Bodek

Number of Press Staff: 650

Regular Member

Established: 1896	Admitted to the Association: 1950
Title output 2017: 1,500	Title output 2018: 1,500
Titles currently in print: 27,500	Journals published: (US only): 145

Editorial Program
Scholarly monographs; general nonfiction; Bibles; college textbooks; medical books; music; reference books; journals; children's books; English language teaching. Submissions are not invited in the area of fiction or autobiography.
Journals published in the US from 2017: *Aesthetic Surgery Journal; Aesthetic Surgery Journal Open Forum; American Entomologist; American Historical Review; American Journal of Agricultural Economics; American Journal of Clinical Pathology; American Journal of Epidemiology; American Journal of Health-System Pharmacy; American Journal of Hypertension; American Journal of Legal History; American Literary History; Animal Frontiers; Annals of Behavioral Medicine; Annals of the Entomological Society of America; Applied Economic Perspectives & Policy; Archives of Clinical Neuropsychology; Arthropod Management Tests; Biology of Reproduction; The Auk: Ornithological Advances; BioScience; The British Journal of Social Work; Cerebral Cortex; Children & Schools; Christian Bioethics; Clinical Infectious Diseases; Communication Theory; Communication, Culture & Critique; Condor: Ornithological Applications; Critical Values; Crohn's & Colitis 360; Diplomatic History; Diseases of the Esophagus; Endocrine Reviews; Endocrinology; Environmental Entomology; Environmental History; Epidemiologic Reviews; Evolution, Medicine, and Public Health; Foreign Policy Analysis; Forest Science; The Gerontologist; GigaScience; Global Summitry; Health & Social Work; Health Education Research; Holocaust and Genocide Studies; Human Communication Research; ILAR Journal; Inflammatory Bowel Diseases; Innovation in Aging; Insect Systematics and Diversity; International Journal of Neuropsychopharmacology; International Journal of Public Opinion Research; International Political Sociology; International Studies Perspectives; International Studies Quarterly; International Studies Review; ISLE: Interdisciplinary Studies in Literature and Environment; JNCI: Journal of the National Cancer Institute; Journal of American History; Journal of Analytical Toxicology; Journal of Animal Science; The Journal of Applied Poultry Research; Journal of Breast Imaging; Journal of Chromatographic Science; Journal of Church and State; The Journal of Clinical Endocrinology & Metabolism; Journal of Communication; Journal of Computer-Mediated Communication; Journal of Consumer Research; Journal of Deaf Studies and Deaf Education; Journal of Economic Entomology; Journal of Financial Econometrics; Journal of Forestry; Journal of Global Security Studies; Journal of Heredity; The Journal of Infectious Diseases; Journal of Insect Science; Journal of Integrated Pest Management; Journal of Mammalogy; Journal of Medical Entomology; Journal of Medicine and Philosophy; Journal of Music Therapy; Journal of Neuropathology and Experimental Neurology; Journal of Pediatric Psychology; Journal of Public Administration Research and Theory; Journal of Social History; Journal of Survey Statistics and Methodology; Journal of the American Academy of Religion; Journal of the Canadian Association of Gastroenterology; Journal of the Endocrine Society; Journal of the History of Medicine and Allied Sciences; Journal of the National Cancer Institute; Journal of the National Cancer Institute Monographs; Journal of the Pediatric Infectious Diseases Society; Journal of World Energy Law & Business; Journals of Geron-*

tology Series A: Biomedical Sciences and Medical Sciences; Journals of Gerontology – Series B: Psychological Sciences and Social Sciences; Laboratory Medicine; Literary Imagination; Mammalian Species; Medical Mycology; Military Medicine; Modern Judaism: A Journal of Jewish Ideas and Experience; Monist; Multi-Ethnic Literature of the United States; Music Theory Spectrum; Music Therapy Perspectives; The Musical Quarterly; Neurosurgery; Nicotine and Tobacco Research; Nutrition Reviews; Open Forum Infectious Diseases; Opera Quarterly; Operative Neurosurgery; The Oral History Review; Paediatrics & Child Health; Pain Medicine; Perspectives on Public Management and Governance; Physical Therapy; Poultry Science; Public Opinion Quarterly; Public Policy & Aging Report; Publius; Quarterly Journal of Economics; The Review of Asset Pricing Studies; The Review of Corporate Finance Studies; Review of Environmental Economics & Policy; The Review of Financial Studies; Schizophrenia Bulletin; Shakespeare Quarterly; SLEEP; Social Forces; Social Problems; Social Work; Social Work Research; Sociology of Religion: A Quarterly Review; Systematic Biology; Toxicological Sciences; Translational Animal Science; Translational Behavioral Medicine; Western Historical Quarterly; Work, Aging, and Retirement; The World Bank Economic Review; The World Bank Research Observer
Imprints: Sinauer Associates

University of Pennsylvania Press

3905 Spruce Street
Philadelphia, PA 19104-4112

Phone: 215.898.6261
Fax: 215.898.0404
Email: (user I.D.)@upenn.edu

Orders:
Ingram Publisher Services (IPS)
14 Ingram Blvd.
La Vergne TN 37086
Website: ipage.ingramcontent.com
Phone: 866.400.5351
Email (inquiries only):
ips@ingramcontent.com

Website and Social Media:
Website: www.pennpress.org
Blog: pennpress.typepad.com
Facebook: www.facebook.com/PennPress
Twitter: @PennPress

UK/European Distributor:
Combined Academic Publishers

Canadian Representative:
Canadian Manda Group

Staff
Director: Eric Halpern (215.898.1672; email: ehalpern)
Assistant to the Director and Rights Administrator: Kim Leichner (215.898.6263; email: kleic)
Acquisitions: Peter Agree, Editor-in-Chief (human rights, policy and politics, anthropology) (215.573.3816; email: agree)
   Senior Editors: Jerome E. Singerman (literary criticism and cultural studies; ancient, medieval, and Renaissance studies; landscape architecture; Jewish studies) (215.898.1681; email: singerma); Robert Lockhart (American history, regional books) (215.898.1677; email: rlockhar)
   Consulting Editors: Deborah Blake (ancient studies) (44.7867.540881; email: dcblake.pennpress@virginmedia.com); Damon Linker (current affairs, digital shorts) (610.613.4546; email: linkerpennpress@gmail.com)
Manuscript Editing and Production: Elizabeth Glover, Editing & Production Manager (215.898.1675; email: gloverel)
   Assistant Production Manager: William Boehm (215.573.4059; email: boehmwj)
   Managing Editors: Lily Palladino (215.898.1678; email: lilypall); Erica Ginsburg (215.898.1679; email: eginsbur); Noreen O'Connor (215.898.1709; email: nmoconno)
   Production Coordinator: Susan Staggs (215.898.1676; email: sstaggs)
   Art Director: John Hubbard (215.573.6118; email: wmj)
Marketing: Laura Waldron, Marketing Director (215.898.1673; email: lwaldron)
   Publicity & Public Relations Manager: Gigi Lamm (215.898.1674; email: glamm)
   Electronic Marketing Coordinator: Peter Valelly (215.898.8678; email: pvalelly)
   Direct Mail & Advertising Manager: Tracy Kellmer (215.898.9184; email: tkellmer)

Journals: Paul Chase, Operations Manager (215.573.1295; email: paulbc)
Editing and Production Coordinator: Emily Stevens (215.898.7588; email: emilyste)
Journals Assistant: Syra Ortiz-Blaines (215.573.4585; email: syra)
Business: Joseph Guttman, Business Manager (215.898.1670; email: josephgg)
Financial Coordinator: Kathy Ranalli (215.898.1682; email: ranalli)
Administrative Assistant: Barbara Nolan (215.898.1671; email: custserv@pobox.upenn.edu)

Number of Press Staff: 27

Regular Member

Established: 1890	Admitted to the Association: 1967
Title output 2017: 137	Title output 2018: 129
Titles currently in print: 3,262	Journals published: 20

Editorial Program
Scholarly and semipopular nonfiction, with special interests in American history and culture; ancient, medieval, and early modern studies; human rights; urban studies, politics and public policy; Jewish studies; anthropology; landscape architecture; and Pennsylvania regional studies.
Journals: *Capitalism and History; Change Over Time; Dissent; Early American Studies; The Eighteenth-Century: Theory and Interpretation; French Forum; Hispanic Review; Humanity; Huntington Library Quarterly; Jewish Quarterly Review; Journal for Early Modern Cultural Studies; Journal of the Early Republic; Journal of Ecumenical Studies; Journal of the History of Ideas; J19: The Journal of Nineteenth-Century Americanists; Magic, Ritual, and Witchcraft; Manuscript Studies; Pennsylvania Magazine of History and Biography; Revista Hispanica Moderna.*
Book series: American Business, Politics, and Society; American Governance; American in the Nineteenth Century; Arts and Intellectual Life in Modern America; Contemporary Ethnography; City in the 21st Century; Democracy, Citizenship, and Constitutionalism; Divinations; Early American Studies; Early Modern Americas; Empire and After; Encounters with Asia; Ethnography of Political Violence; Hagley Perspectives on Business and Culture; Intellectual History of the Modern Age; Jewish Culture and Contexts; Material Texts; The Middle Ages; Penn Studies in Landscape Architecture; Pennsylvania Studies in Human Rights; Politics and Culture in Modern America
Copublishing programs: Ceramics Handbooks
Imprint: University of Pennsylvania Museum of Archaeology and Anthropology

Pennsylvania State University Press

820 North University Drive	Orders:
USB-1, Suite C	Phone: 800.326.9180
University Park, PA 16802-1003	Fax: 877.778.2665

Phone: 814.865.1327
Fax: 814.863.1408
Email: (user I.D.)@psu.edu

Website and Social Media:
Website: www.psupress.org
Twitter: @PSUPress
Facebook: www.facebook.com/psupress

UK Representative:	Canadian Distributor:
The Oxford Publicity Partnership	University of Toronto Press

Staff
Director: Patrick H. Alexander (814.867.2209; email: pha3)
Assistant to the Director: Teresa Craig (814.867.5443; email: tac6)

Acquisitions Editorial: Kendra Boileau, Editor-in-Chief (814.867.2220; email: klb60)
Executive Editor, Art History and Humanities: Eleanor Goodman (814.867.2212; email: ehg11)
Acquisitions Editors: Kathryn Yahner (814.865.1327; email: kby3); Ryan Peterson (814.867.2216; email: rzp290
Editorial Assistants: Hannah Hebert (814.865.1328; email: hnh1); Alex Vose (814.865.1592; email: hav4)
Editorial, Design, and Production: Jennifer Norton, Associate Director, EDP Manager (814.863.8061; email: jsn4)
Managing Editor: Laura Reed-Morrisson (814.865.1606; email: lxr168)
Senior Designer: Regina Starace (814.867.2215; email: ras35)
Production Coordinator and Data Administrator: Brian Beer (814.867.2210; email: bxb110)
Production Editor: Alex Ramos (email: ajr586)
Production Assistant: Jon Gottshall (814.867.2213; email: jeg31)
Marketing/Sales: Brendan Coyne, Sales and Marketing Director (814.863.5994; email: bcc5228)
Advertising and Direct Mail Manager: Heather Smith (814.863.0524; email: hms7)
Publicity Manager: Cate Fricke (814.865.1329; email: crf16)
Sales and Exhibits Manager: TBA
Rights and Permissions Manager: TBA
Marketing and Sales Coordinator: Janice North (814.867.2831; email: jrn61)
Journals Manager: Diana Pesek (814.867.2223; email: dlp28)
Production Coordinator: Julie Lambert (814.863.5992; email: jas1035)
Managing Editor: Astrid Meyer (814.863.3830; email: aum38)
Marketing Manager: Kathryn Luu (857.997.0952; email: kel274)
Production Assistants: Jessica Karp (814.867.2211; email: jxk82); Rachel Ginder (814.863.1307; email: rlg5195)
Business Office/Order Fulfillment: TBA, Financial Manager (814.863.5993)
Financial Coordinator: Susan Peters (814.863.6771; email: sgp16)
Shipping Clerk: Dave Buchan (814.863.5496; email: dcb11)
Information Systems Manager: Ed Spicer (814.865.1327; email: res122)

Number of Press Staff: 29

Regular Member

Established: 1956   Admitted to the Association: 1960
Title output 2017: 56   Title output 2018: 78
Titles currently in print: 3,000   Journals published: 67

Editorial Program
Scholarly books in the humanities and social sciences, with current emphasis on animal studies; architecture; art history; American, European, and Latin American history; communication studies and rhetoric; graphic medicine; interdisciplinary literary studies; medieval studies; occultism and esoterism; religion. Submissions are not invited in fiction, poetry, or drama.
Journals: *ab-Original: Journal of Indigenous Studies and First Nations' and First Peoples' Cultures; The Author Miller Journal; Bulletin for Biblical Research; Bustan: The Middle East Book Review; Calíope: Journal for the Society for Renaissance and Baroque Hispanic Poetry; The Chaucer Review; Comedia Performance; Comparative Literature Studies; Cormac McCarthy Journal; Critical Philosophy of Race; Dickens Study Annual; Ecumenica:Performance and Religion; The Edgar Allan Poe Review; The Edith Wharton Review; The Eugene O'Neill Review; The F. Scott Fitzgerald Review; George Eliot-George Henry Lewes Studies: Gestalt Review; The Good Society; The Harold Pinter Review; Interdisciplinary Literature Studies; International Journal of Persian Literature; Journal of Africana Religions; Journal of Asia-Pacific Pop Culture; Journal of Assessment and Institutional Effectiveness; Journal of Austrian-American History; The Journal of Ayn Rand Studies; Journal of Development Perspectives; Journal of Eastern Mediterranean Archaeology and Heritage Studies; Journal of General Education; Journal of Information Policy; Journal of Jewish Ethics; Journal of Medieval Religious Cultures; Journal of Modern Periodical Studies; Journal of Moravian History; Journal of Natural Resources Policy Research; Journal of Nietzsche Studies; Journal of the Pennsylvania Academy of Science; Journal for the Study of Paul and His Letters; Journal of Posthuman Studies; Journal of Speculative Philosophy; Journal of Theological Interpretation; Journal of World Christian-*

ity; *Korean Language in America; Libraries: Culture, History, and Society; Langston Hughes Review; Milton Studies; The Mark Twain Annual; Mediterranean Studies; Nathaniel Hawthorne Review; Pacific Coast Philology; Pennsylvania History; Philosophy and Rhetoric; Preternature; Reception: Texts, Readers, Audiences, History; Resources for American Literary Study; SHAW: The Journal of Bernard Shaw Studies; Soundings; Steinbeck Review; Studies in American Humor; Studies in American Jewish Literature; Style; Transformations: The Journal of Inclusive Pedagogy; Transportation Journal; Utopian Studies; Wesley and Methodist Studies; William Carlos Williams Review*
Book series: Africana Religions; Animalibus: Of Animals and Cultures; AnthropoScene: The SLSA Book Series; Buildings, Landscapes, and Societies; Edinburgh Edition of Thomas Reid; Dimyonot: Jews and the Cultural Imagination; The Frick Collection Studies in the History of Art Collecting in America; Graphic Medicine; Iberian Encounter and Exchange, 475–1755; Inventing Christianity; Latin American Originals; Magic in History; Magic in History Sourcebooks; The Max Kade Research Institute Series: Germans beyond Europe; Medieval and Renaissance Literary Studies; Penn State Series in Critical Theory; Penn State Series in the History of the Book; Pietist, Moravian, and Anabaptist Studies; RSA Series in Transdisciplinary Rhetoric; Refiguring Modernism; Religion Around; Rhetoric and Democratic Deliberation; Signifying (on) Scriptures; World Christianity
Imprints: Keystone Books; Eisenbrauns

University of Pittsburgh Press

7500 Thomas Boulevard
Pittsburgh, PA 15260
info@upress.pitt.edu
Phone: 412.383.2456
Fax: 412.383.2466
Email: (user I.D.)@upress.pitt.edu

Order Fulfillment:
University of Pittsburgh Press
Chicago Distribution Center
11030 South Langley Avenue
Chicago, IL 60628
Phone: 773.568.1550; 800.621.2736
Fax: 773.660.2235

Website and Social Media:
Website: www.upress.pitt.edu
Facebook: www.facebook.com/pages/University-of-Pittsburgh-Press/319974668123448
Facebook (Poetry): www.facebook.com/pittpoetry.series
Twitter: @UPittPress
Twitter (Poetry): @PittPoetry
Instagram: www.instagram.com/upittpress/

UK Representative:
Eurospan

Canadian Representative:
Scholarly Book Services

Staff
Director: Peter Kracht (email: pkracht)
Editorial Director: Sandy Crooms (email: scrooms)
Senior Acquisitions Editors: Joshua Shanholtzer (email: jshanholtzer); Abby Collier (email: acollier)
Director of Editorial and Production: Alex Wolfe (email: awolfe)
Design and Production Manager: Joel Coggins (email: jcoggins)
Managing Editor: Amy Sherman (email: asherman)
Production Editor: Melissa Dias-Mandoly (email: mdiasmandoly)
Marketing and Sales Director: John Fagan (email: jfagan)
Publicist: Maria Sticco (email: msticco)
Social Media Coordinator: Chloe Wertz (email: cwertz)
Director of Operations: David Baumann (email: dbaumann)
Operations Administrator: Eileen O'Malley (email: eomalley)
Subsidiary Rights Manager: Margie Bachman (email: mbachman)

Number of Press Staff: 14

Regular Member

Established: 1936   Admitted to the Association: 1937
Title output 2017: 69   Title output 2018: 67
Titles currently in print: 1,407

Editorial Program
Scholarly, general interest, reference, text, and trade books in all disciplines within the humanities and social sciences, with an emphasis on: Latin America; the history and philosophy of science, technology, and medicine; the history of architecture and the built environment; Central and Eastern Europe, Russia, and Central Asia; urban studies; environmental studies; African American studies; composition and literacy studies; Pittsburgh and western Pennsylvania; and poetry. We take a particular interest in books that cross over more than one discipline or topical area published by the Press. Submissions are not invited in the hard sciences, original fiction, festschriften, or memoirs.

Book series: Central Eurasia in Context; Composition, Literacy, and Culture; Correspondence of John Tyndall; Cuban Studies; Culture, Politics, and the Built Environment; Histories and Ecologies of Health; History of the Urban Environment; Illuminations: Cultural Formations of the Americas; Intersections: Histories of Environment, Science and Technology; Latinx and Latin American Profiles; Pitt Latin American Series; Pitt Poetry Series; Russian and East European Studies; Science and Culture in the Nineteenth Century.

Book Awards: Drue Heinz Literature Prize; Agnes Lynch Starrett Poetry Prize; Donald Hall Prize for Poetry; Cave Canem Poetry Prize

Princeton University Press

Executive Offices:
41 William Street
Princeton, NJ 08540-5237

Phone: 609.258.4900
Fax: 609.258.6305
Email:
firstname_lastname@press.princeton.edu

Website and Social Media:
Website: press.princeton.edu
Blog: blog.press.princeton.edu
Facebook:@PrincetonUniversityPress
Twitter: @PrincetonUPress
Instagram: @PrincetonUPress
Youtube: www.youtube.com/user/PUPress
Vimeo: www.vimeo.com/princetonuniversitypress
Tumblr: pupdesign.tumblr.com
Linkedin: linkedin.com/company/princeton-university-press
Google+: princetonuniversitypress

European Office:
6 Oxford St.
Woodstock, Oxfordshire
OX20 1TR
United Kingdom
Phone: +44 1993 814500
Fax: +44 1993 814504
Email:
firstname_lastname@press.princeton.edu

Order Fulfillment (US and Canada):
Ingram Content Group LLC
One Ingram Blvd.
La Vergne, TN 37086
Phone: 800.400.5351
Email: ips@ingramcontent.com

UK/European Sales Representation:
The University Press Group Ltd.
California | Columbia | MITP | Princeton
New Era Estate, Oldlands Way,
Bognor Regis
West Sussex P022 9NQ
Phone: +44 1243 842165
United Kingdom
Fax: +44 1243 842167

China Office: Princeton Asia (Beijing) Consulting Co. Ltd.
Unit 2602, NUO Centre, 2A Jiangtai Rd., Chao yang Distr.
Beijing, People's Republic of China, 100016
Phone: +86 10 8457 8802
Email: firstname_lastname@press.princeton.edu

Staff
Director: Christie Henry (609.258.8704)
Chief of Staff: Lyndsey Claro (609.258.0183)
Associate Director and CFO: Scot Kuehm (609.258.8602)
Director of Human Resources: Kate Danser (609.258.9387)
Director of Publishing Operations: Cathy Felgar
Director of Strategic Partnerships: Marla Dirks (609.258.8144)
Global Development and Rights: Brigitta van Rheinberg, Associate Director/Director of Global
     Development (609.258.4935)
Director of Rights, Contracts and Permissions: Ines ter Horst
International Rights Manager: Rebecca Bengoechea (+44 1993 814 509)
Director of Contracts: Shaquona Crews (609.258.5799)
Permissions Manager: Lisa Black (609.258.2195)
Digital and Audio Publisher: Kimberley Williams (+44 1993 814509)
China Office: Lingxi Li, Chief Representative (86 181 8661 2519)
Acquisitions Editorial:
     Humanities: Eric Crahan, Editorial Director (609.258.4922); Michelle Komie, Publisher (art,
     architecture) (609.258.4569); Anne Savarese, Executive Editor (literature) (609.258.4937); Ben
     Tate, Editor (humanities) (+44 1993 814502); Rob Tempio, Senior Publisher (philosophy, ancient

world, political theory)
Sciences: Alison Kalett, Editorial Director (609.258.1739); Ingrid Gnerlich, Publisher, Sciences in Europe (+.44.1517.096972); Robert Kirk, Executive Editor and Publisher (Field Guides and Natural History) (609.258.4884); Vickie Kearn, Executive Editor (mathematics) (609.258.2321); Susannah Shoemaker, Associate Editor (mathematics) (609.258.8969); Hallie Stebbins, Editor (neuroscience and computer science) (609.258.1739); Jessica Yao, Associate Editor (physical sciences) (609.258.9116)
Social Sciences: Sarah Caro, Editorial Director (+44.1993 804501); Fred Appel, Executive Editor (anthropology, religion) (609.258.2484); Peter Dougherty, Editor At Large (economic history, education) (609.258.6778); Joe Jackson, Senior Editor (economics) (609.258.9428); Meagan Levinson, Senior Editor (sociology, psychology) (609.248.4908); Hannah Paul, Associate Editor (economics, political science) (+44 1993 814 901)
Editorial Manager: Samantha Nader (609.258.2336)
Manuscript Editorial: Neil Litt, Assistant Director/Director of Editing, Design, and Production (609.258.5066)
Managing Editor: Elizabeth Byrd (609.258.2589)
Associate Managing Editors: Terri O'Prey (609.258.7963); Karen Fortgang (609.258.1410)
Manager of Digital Production: Ken Reed (609.258.2485)
Assistant Manager of Digital Production: Eileen Reilly (609.258.2719)
Production Manager: Jacqueline Poirier (609.258.4929)
Creative Media Lab: Maria Lindenfeldar, Creative Director (609.258.7557)
Assistant Creative Director: Donna Liese (609.258.4924)
Marketing: TBA, Director of Marketing (609.258.4896)
Associate Director of Marketing: Leslie Nangle (609.258.5881)
Director of Sales: Tim Wilkins (609.258.4898)
Associate Director of Sales and Marketing: Laurie Schlesinger (609.258.4898)
International Sales Director: Andrew Brewer
Social Media, Content, and Partnerships Manager: Debra Liese (609.258.4283)
Director of Exhibits: Melissa Burton (609.258.4915)
Senior Text Promotion Manager: Julie Haenisch (609.258.6856)
Publicity: Caroline Priday, Global Publicity Director and Head of European Office (+44 1993 814503)
Assistant Director of Publicity: Julia Haav (609.258.2831)
Assistant Director of Publicity: Julia Hall (+44 1993 814 900)
Associate Controller: Debbie Greco (609.882.0550)
Director of Finance Operations: Jim Jordan (609.258.2486)
Information Systems: Dennis Langlois, Chief Information Officer (609.258.7782)
Director of Web Technology and Services: Ann Ambrose (609.258.7749)

Number of Press Staff: 146

Regular Member
Established: 1905
Title output 2017: 331
Titles currently in print: 8,491

Admitted to the Association: 1937
Title output 2018: 327

Editorial Program
Humanities: American, European, World, Asian, Slavic, and Jewish history; ancient world; classics; architecture and art history; philosophy; poetry; literature; religion
Reference: humanities; social sciences; and science
Science: astrophysics; biology; computer and information science; earth sciences; history of knowledge and science; mathematics; natural history; neuroscience; ornithology; physical sciences
Social Science: anthropology; economics; education; finance; law; political science; political theory; psychology; sociology

University of Puerto Rico Press

Street Address:
Jardín Botánico Norte Carr.
#1 Km. 12.0 Río
Piedras, San Juan PR 00927

Mailing Address:
PO Box 23322
U.P.R. Station
San Juan, PR 00931-3322

Phone: 787.758.8345
Email: info@laeditorialupr.com

Website and Social Media:
Website: www.laeditorialupr.com
Facebook: www.facebook.com/editorialupr/

Staff
Director: Neeltje van Marissing (email: neeltje.vanmarissing@upr.edu)
Editor: Rosa V. Otero
Sales: José Burgos (email: jburgos@upr.edu)
Marketing and Promotion: Ruth Morales (email: ruth.morales2@upr.edu)
Exhibits and Special Projects: José Burgos (email: jburgos@upr.edu), Ruth Morales (email: ruth.
    morales2@upr.edu)
Shipping, Receiving and Inventory: Carlos Santiago (email: carlos.santiago36@upr.edu)
Warehouse: Ángel Ortiz
Journals Marketing: Ruth Morales

Regular Member
Established:1943   Admitted to the Association: 1971
Title output 2017: NR   Title output 2018: NR
Titles currently in print: 989   Journals published: 1

Editorial Program
Scholarly studies on Puerto Rico, the Caribbean and Latin America; philosophy; history; architecture; law; social sciences; health; women's studies; economics; literary theory and criticism;
creative poetry and prose; literary anthologies; nature studies; flora; fauna; ecosystems; children's
books; reference; other general interest publications.
Journals: *Revista La Torre* (the humanities). In distribution: *Revista de Estudios Hispánicos* (Spanish language studies); and *Historia y Sociedad* (Puerto Rican and Caribbean history); *Diálogos*
(philosophy)
Book series: literary anthologies; philosophy; creative literature; scholarly nonfiction; nature
Imprints: Antología Personal (Selections by renowned hispanic writers); Clásicos no tan clásicos
(Faithful re-edition of works written between 1890 and 1930 with annotations by 21st century
scholars); Books on Puerto Rican Cooking; Colección Eugenio María de Hostos (complete
works); San Pedrito (children's books); Colección Nueve Pececitos (young readers); Cuentos de
un mundo perdido (middle school readers)

Purdue University Press

Stewart Center
504 West State Street
West Lafayette, IN 47907-2058

Phone: 765.494.2038
Fax: 765.496.2442
Email: pupress@purdue.edu
Indiv: (user I.D.)@purdue.edu

Orders:
Purdue University Press
PO Box 388
Ashland, OH 44805
Phone: 800.247.6553
Fax: 419.281.6883
Email: orders@btpubservices.com

Website and Social Media:
Website: www.press.purdue.edu;
Facebook: www.facebook.com/purduepress
Twitter: @purduepress

European Distributor:
Eurospan

Canadian Distributor:
Baker & Taylor Publishing Services

Staff
Director: Justin Race (765.494.8251; email: racej)
Editorial, Design, and Production Manager: Katherine Purple (765.494.6259; email: kpurple)
Sales and Marketing Manager: Bryan Shaffer (765.494.8428; email: bshaffer)
Graphic Designer: Chris Brannan (765.494.6430; email: cbrannan)
Marketing and Outreach Specialist: Matthew Mudd (765.494.2578; email: mudd5)
Senior Production Editor: Kelley Kimm (765.494.8024; email: kkimm)
Administrative Assistant: Becki Corbin (765.494.8144; email: rlcorbin)
Editorial Assistant: Liza Hagerman (765.494.4943; email: lhagerma)
Digital Repository Specialist: Marcy Wilhelm-South (765.494.6311; email: wilhelms)
Scholarly Publishing Specialist: Nina Collins (765.494.8511; email: nkcollin)

Number of Press Staff: 10

Regular Member
Established: 1960
Title output 2017: 22
Titles currently in print: 543

Admitted to the Association: 1993
Title output 2018: 21
Journals published: 20

Editorial Program
Dedicated to the dissemination of scholarly and professional information aligned with the strengths of its parent institution, the Press provides quality resources in technology and engineering, library and information science, public policy, aeronautics and astronautics, Indiana history, agriculture, health and human sciences, veterinary studies, European history, Jewish studies, and global languages and literatures.

Journals (Purdue University Press): *CLCWeb: Comparative Literature and Culture; Education and Culture: The Journal of the John Dewey Society; First Opinions—Second Reactions; The Interdisciplinary Journal of Problem-Based Learning; Journal of Aviation Technology and Engineering; Journal of Pre-College Engineering Education Research; Journal of Problem Solving; Phillip Roth Studies; Shofar: An Interdisciplinary Journal of Jewish Studies; Studies in Jewish Civilization*

Journals (Scholarly Publishing Services): *Journal of Applied Farm Economics; Artl@s Bulletin; CLARITAS: Journal of Dialogue and Culture; Data Curation Profiles Directory; IMPACT Profile Directory; Journal of Human Performance in Extreme Environments; People and Animals: The International Journal of Research and Practice; Purdue Journal of Service-Learning and Inter*national *Engagement; Journal of Purdue Undergraduate Research; Journal of Southeast Asian American Education and Advancemen*t

Book series: Central European Studies; Comparative Cultural Studies; New Directions in the Human-Animal Bond; Purdue Handbooks in Building Construction; Purdue Studies in Aeronautics and Astronautics; Purdue Studies in Romance Literatures; Purdue Information Literacy Handbooks; and Charleston Insights in Library, Archival, and Information Sciences with Against the Grain Press.

RAND Corporation

Street Address:
1776 Main Street
Santa Monica, CA 90407

Mailing Address:
PO Box 2138
Santa Monica, CA 90407-2138

Phone: 310.393.0411
Fax: 310.451.7026

Website and Social Media:
Website: www.rand.org/publications
Facebook: www.facebook.com/RANDCorporation
Twitter: @RANDCorporation
YouTube: www.youtube.com/user/TheRANDCorporation
Blog: www.rand.org/blog.html

Customer Service:
Phone: 877.584.8642
Fax: 412.802.4981
Email: order@rand.org

US Distributor:
National Book Network
Phone: 800.462.6420 or 717.794.3800
Fax: 800.338.4550

UK/European Distributor:
NBN International

Staff
Director: Paul Murphy (ext. 7806; email: murphy@rand.org)
Business Manager, OEA: Laura Shaw (ext. 6722; email: lshaw@rand.org)
Managing Editor: Erin-Elizabeth Johnson (ext. 5450; email: ejohnson@rand.org)
Production Manager: K. Todd Duft (ext. 7868: email: duft@rand.org)
Computing Manager: Edward Finkelstein (ext. 7417; email: edwardf@rand.org)

Number of Press Staff: 5

Regular Member
Established: 1948
Title output 2017: 425
Titles currently in print: 21,900

Admitted to the Association: 2000
Title output 2018: 396
Journals published: 2

Editorial Program
The RAND Corporation is a research organization that develops solutions to public policy challenges to help make communities throughout the world safer and more secure, healthier and more prosperous. RAND is nonprofit, nonpartisan, and committed to the public interest. Publication topics include policy issues such as education; environment and energy; health care; immigration, labor, and population; international affairs; national security; public safety and justice; science and technology; and terrorism and homeland security. Unsolicited manuscripts are not accepted.
Journals: *RAND Health Quarterly; RAND Journal of Economics*

University of Regina Press

Street/Courier Address:
246 – 2 Research Drive
Regina Research Park
Regina, SK S4S 7J7
Canada

Mailing Address:
University of Regina Press
University of Regina
3737 Wascana Parkway
Regina, SK S4S 0A2 Canada

Phone: 306.585.4758
Fax: 306.585.4699
Email: uofrpress@uregina.ca
Indiv.: (User I.D.)@uregina.ca

Orders (U.S.)
Ingram Publisher Services
Account No. S210
Phone: 800.565.9523
Fax: 800.838.1149
Email: utpbooks@utpress.utoronto.ca

Website and Social Media:
Website: www.uofrpress.ca
Facebook: facebook.com/uofrpress
Twitter: @UofRPress
Instagram: @UofR_Press
YouTube: www.youtube.com/user/CPRCPRESS (U of R Press TV)

UK Representative:
Gazelle Academic

Staff
Director: Bruce Walsh (306.585.4795; email: bruce.walsh)
Acquisitions Editorial (scholarly): Karen Clark, Acquisitions Editor (306.585.4664; email: karen.clark)
Acquisitions Editorial (trade): Sean Prpick, Editor (306.585.4789; email: sean.prpick)
Manuscript Editorial: Donna Grant, Senior Editor (306.585.4787; email: donna.grant)
Design and Production: Duncan Campbell, Art Director (306.585.4326; email: duncan.campbell)
Sales and Marketing Manager: Morgan Tunzelmann (306.337.3325; email: morgan.tunzelmann)
Publicist: Melissa Shirley (587.389.9510; email: melissa.shirley)
Office Manager: Wendy Whitebear (306.585.4758; email: wendy.whitebear)

Introductory Member
Established: 2014 (predecessor Canadian Plains Research Centre Press)
Admitted to the Association: 2014
Title output 2017: 19   Title output 2018: NR
Titles currently in print: 31 (192 with CPRC Press backlist)

Editorial Program
Scholarly and trade books on Indigenous Studies, the environment, Canadian Studies, American Studies, biography, gender studies, gay and lesbian studies, the arts, public affairs, anthropology, sociology, and more (see the subject area listings for further details).
Book series: First Nations Language Readers; The Regina Collection; Oskana Poetry & Poetics; The Exquisite Corpse; Digestions; The Henry and Mary Bibb Series of Black Canadian Studies

RIT Press

90 Lomb Memorial Drive
Rochester, NY 14623-5604

Phone: 585.475.6766
Fax: 585.475.4090
Email: lmdwml@rit.edu

<u>Website and Social Media:</u>
Website: ritpress.rit.edu
Facebook: www.facebook.com/pages/RIT-Press/172326337130?ref=hl
Twitter: @RITPress
Instagram: @ritpress
Pinterest: ritpress

<u>Orders:</u>
Phone: 585.475.6766

<u>UK and Asian Distributor:</u>
Boydell & Brewer, Ltd.

Staff
Director: Bruce A. Austin (585.475.2879; email: baagll@rit.edu)
Managing Editor: Molly Q. Cort (585.475.4088; email: mqcwml@rit.edu)
Business Manager: Laura DiPonzio Heise (585.475.5819; email: lmdwml@rit.edu)
Design & Marketing Specialist: Marnie Soom (585.475.4089; email: mxswml@rit.edu)

Number of Press Staff: 4

Regular Member
Established: 2001

Title output 2017: 5
Titles currently in print: 100

Admitted to the Association: 2009
(intro. member)
Admitted to the Association: 2014
(full member)
Title output 2018: 10
Journals published: 1

Editorial Program
RIT Press is the scholarly book publishing enterprise at Rochester Institute of Technology. RIT Press is dedicated to the innovative use of new publishing technology while upholding high standards in content quality, publication design, and print/digital production. The Press publishes specialized titles for niche academic audiences, trade editions for mass-market audiences, and occasional limited edition books with unique aesthetic standards. Established in 2001 as RIT Cary Graphic Arts Press, the Press initially focused on publishing titles documenting graphic communication processes, printing history, and bookmaking. As its editorial policies evolved, the Press broadened its reach to include content supporting all academic disciplines offered at RIT.
Book series: Graphic Design Archives Chapbook; Philosophy and the Future; Popular Culture Series (Comics Monograph Series); Printing Industry Series; Sports Studies
Journal: *HAYDN* an online journal of the Haydn Society of North America, peer-reviewed, bi-annual digital-only publication of musicological research.

The University of Rochester Press

668 Mount Hope Avenue
Rochester NY 14620-2731

Phone: 585.275.0419
Fax: 585.271.8778

Orders:
Phone: 585.275.0419
Email: boydell@boydellusa.net

Website and Social Media:
Website: www.urpress.com
Facebook: www.facebook.com/boydellandbrewer
Twitter: @boydellbrewer
Pinterest: boydellbrewer
Instagram: boydellandbrewer

UK Representative:
Boydell & Brewer, Ltd.

Canadian Representative:
Scholarly Book Services

Staff
Editorial Director/Acquisitions: Sonia Kane (585.273.5778; email: sonia.kane@rochester.edu)
Managing Editor/Manuscript Editorial: Julia Cook (585.273.4356; email: cook@boydellusa.net)
Editorial Assistant: Jaqueline Heinzelmann (585.273.4429; email: heinzelmann@boydellusa.net)
Production Manager: Sue Smith (585.273.2817; email: smith@boydellusa.net)
Production Editor: Tracey Engel (585.273.2818; email: engel@boydellusa.net)
International Sales & Marketing Director: Michael Richards (+ 44 (0)1394 610; email: mrichards@boydell.co.uk)
Marketing Manager: Katie Kumler (585.273.0391; email: kumler@boydellusa.net)
Marketing Executive: Rosemary Shojaie (585.273.5779; email: shojaie@boydellusa.net)
Global Marketing Executive: Gretchen Hitt (585.273.5787; email: hitt@boydellusa.net)
Marketing Assistant: Jennifer Shannon (585.273.2959; email: shannon@boydellusa.net)
Accounts Assistant: Olga Reshota (585.273.5780; email: reshota@boydellusa.net)
Website Coordinator: Jessica Aston (+44 (0)1394 610606; email: jaston@boydell.co.uk.net)
Customer Service: Kate Stein (610.853.9131; email: kate.stein@casematepublishers.com)

Regular Member
Established: 1989

Admitted to the Association: 2008
(intro. member)
Admitted to the Association: 2011
(full member)

Title output 2017: 24
Titles currently in print: 682

Title output 2018: 28

Editorial Program
Musicology and music theory; ethnomusicology; African and diaspora studies with an emphasis on political and economic history; the history of medicine in the US and internationally; early modern European history; East and Central European studies; gender and race in nineteenth and twentieth century America; political theory and philosophy; film; Latin American studies; eighteenth-century studies.

Book series: Changing Perspectives on Early Modern Europe; Eastman Studies in Music; Eastman/Rochester Studies in Ethnomusicology; Gender and Race in American History; Rochester Studies in African History and the Diaspora; Rochester Studies in East and Central Europe; Rochester Studies in Medical History; Rochester Studies in Medieval Political Thought

Imprints: Meliora Press (books related to the University of Rochester)

The Rockefeller University Press

950 Third Avenue, 2nd Floor
New York, NY 10022-2705

Phone: 212.327.7938
Fax: 212.319.1080
Email: (user I.D.)@rockefeller.edu

Website and Social Media:
Websites: www.rupress.org, jcb.rupress.org, jem.rupress.org, jgp.rupress.org
Facebook: www.facebook.com/RockefellerUniversityPress,
www.facebook.com/JCellBiol, www.facebook.com/JExpMed, www.facebook.com/JGenPhysio
Twitter: @RockUPress, @JCellBiol, @JExpMed, @JGenPhysiol
YouTube: www.youtube.com/user/JGenPhysiol, www.youtube.com/user/RockefellerUnivPress
Instagram: www.instagram.com/rockefeller_university_press
LinkedIn: www.linkedin.com/company/rockefeller-university-press/

Staff
Executive Director: Susan L. King (212.327.8881; email: sking01)
Assistant Finance Director: Laura Bisberg (212.327.8590; email: lbisberg)
Office Administrator: Sati Motieram (212.327.8583; email: motierd)
Manuscript Editorial: Rebecca Alvania, Executive Editor, *The Journal of Cell Biology*, Director of
    Editorial Development, Rockefeller University Press (212.327.8011; email: ralvania); Teodoro Pul-
    virenti, Executive Editor, *The Journal of Experimental Medicine* (212.327.8361; email: tpulvirent);
    Meighan Schreiber, Managing Editor, *The Journal of General Physiology* (212.327.8615)
Advertising: Lorna Petersen, Sales Director (212.327.8880; email: petersl)
Journals: Robert O'Donnell, Director of Publishing Technologies (212.327.8545; email: odonner)
Business: Laura Bisberg, Assistant Finance Director (212.327.8590; email: lbisberg)
    Business Development Director: Gregory Malar (212.327.7948; email: malarg)
Communications and Marketing Director: Rory Williams (212.327.8603; email:
    rwilliams02)

Number of Press Staff: 32

Affiliate Member
Established: 1958   Admitted to the Association: 1982
Title output 2017: 0   Title output 2018: 0
Titles currently in print: 40   Journals published: 3

Editorial Program
The Rockefeller University Press publishes three biomedical research journals. *The Journal of Cell Biology* provides a rigorous forum for publication of topics across the complete spectrum of cell biology. *The Journal of Experimental Medicine* publishes papers providing novel conceptual insight into immunology, cancer biology, vascular biology, microbial pathogenesis, neuroscience, and stem cell biology. Articles in *The Journal of General Physiology* elucidate important biological, chemical, or physical mechanisms of broad physiological significance.
Life Science Alliance is a new global, open-access, peer-reviewed journal jointly published by three leading science organizations (EMBO Press, Rockefeller University Press and Cold Spring Harbor Laboratory Press), which have formed a non-profit alliance committed to rapid, fair, and transparent publication of papers of high value to the community across the full spectrum of the life sciences and biomedicine.

Russell Sage Foundation

112 East 64th Street
New York, NY 10065

Phone: 212.750.6000
Fax: 212.371.4761
Email: pubs@rsage.org
Indiv: firstname@rsage.org

<u>Website and Social Media:</u>
Website: www.russellsage.org/publications/bookstore
Blog: www.russellsage.org/blog
Facebook: www.facebook.com/russellsagefoundation
Twitter: @RussellSageFdn
RSS feed: www.russellsage.org/rss.xml
YouTube: www.youtube.com/user/RussellSageFdn

<u>Orders:</u>
Russell Sage Foundation
Chicago Distribution Center
11030 Langley Avenue
Chicago, IL 60628

Phone: 773.702.7010
Fax: 800.621.8476

Staff
Director of Publications: Suzanne Nichols (212.750.6026)
Publications Assistant: Thalia Bloom (212.750.6038)
Director of Communications: David A. Haproff (212.750.6037)
Assistant Book Marketing Manager and Web Programmer: Bruce Thongsack (212.750.6021)
Web Editor and Staff Writer: Jennifer Pan (212.750.2024)
Production Manager: Marcelo Agudo (212.750.6034)
Exhibits/Permissions: Thalia Bloom (212.750.6038)
Foundation President: Sheldon Danziger

Number of Press Staff: 3.5

Regular Member
Established: 1907
Title output 2017: 8
Titles currently in print: 55

Admitted to the Association: 1989
Title output 2018: 7
Journals published: 1

Editorial Program
Scholarly books on current research and policy issues in the social sciences. Recent research programs sponsored by the Russell Sage Foundation include the future of work, sustainable employment, current US immigration, the analysis of the US Census, cultural contact, the social dimensions of inequality, carework, political representation, and behavioral economics. The foundation no longer enters into copublishing agreements.
Journal: *RSF: The Russell Sage Foundation Journal of the Social Sciences / www.rsfjournal.org*

Rutgers University Press

106 Somerset Street, 3rd Floor
New Brunswick, NJ 08901

Phone: 848.445.7762
Fax: 732.745.4935
Email: (user I.D.)@press.rutgers.edu

Orders:
c/o Chicago Distribution Center
11030 S Langley Ave, Chicago, IL 60628
Phone: 773.702.7010
Fax: 800.621.8476

Website and Social Media:
Website: www.rutgersuniversitypress.org
Facebook: www.facebook.com/RutgersUPress/
Twitter: @RutgersUPress
Pinterest: rutgersuniv0180
Instagram: rutgersupress

UK/European/Asian Representative:
Eurospan

Canadian Representative:
Scholarly Book Services

Staff

Director: Micah Kleit (848.445.7784; email: micah.kleit)
Assistant to the Director/Permissions and Subsidiary Rights Manager/E-book Coordinator:
Elisabeth Maselli (848.445.7785; email: esm102)
Acquisitions Editorial: Kimberly Guinta, Editorial Director (anthropology, Caribbean studies, and
women's studies) (848.445.7786; email: kimberly.guinta)
Executive Editors: Peter Mickulas (regional studies, health, sociology, environment, and crimi-
nology) (848.445.7752; email: mickulas); Nicole Solano (American studies, humanities, Latino
studies, popular culture, film, and media) (848.445.7752; email: nicole.solano); Lisa Banning
(Asian American studies, human rights, new media, higher education) (848.445.7791; email:
lmb333)
Assistant Editor: Elisabeth Maselli (Jewish studies) (848.445.7785; email: esm102)
Editorial Assistant: Jasper Chang (848.445.7791; email: jasper.chang)
Production: Jennifer Blanc-Tal, Production and Art Director (848.445.7761; email: jfb131)
Production Editors: Daryl Brower (848.445.7764; email: djb147); Alissa Zarro (848.445.7756;
email: ajz45); Vincent Nordhaus (848.445.7797; email: vincent.nordhaus)
Marketing: Jeremy Grainger, Sales and Marketing Director (848.445.7781; email: jeremy.grainger)
Publicity Director: Courtney Brach (848.445.7775; email: clb103)
Senior Promotion Manager/Webmaster: Brice Hammack (848.445.7765; email: bhammack)
Marketing Manager: Victoria Verhowsky (848.445.7782; email: victoria.verhowsky)
Business: David Flum, Finance Director (848.445.7763; email: dflum)
Business Assistant: Bryan Martinez (email: bmart10)
IT Manager: Penny Burke (848.445.7788; email: pborden)

Number of Press Staff: 18

Regular Member
Established: 1936
Title output 2017: 120
Titles currently in print: 2,915

Admitted to the Association: 1937
Title output 2018: 130

Editorial Program
American Literatures Initiative; American studies; anthropology; Asian American studies; African
American studies; Caribbean studies; childhood and family studies; criminology; film and media;
food studies; higher education studies; history of science and technology; human rights; Jewish
studies; Latino/a studies; popular culture; public policy; regional studies; religious studies; sociology; women's studies
Book series: The American Campus; Asian American Studies Today; Behind the Silver Screen;

Comics Culture; Critical Caribbean Studies; Critical Issues in Crime and Society; Critical Issues in Health and Medicine; Critical Issues In Sport and Society; Families in Focus; Genocide, Political Violence, Human Rights; Global Perspectives on Aging; Jewish Cultures of the World; Junctures: Case Studies in Women's Leadership; Key Words In Jewish Studies; Latinidad: Transnational Cultures in the United States, Nature, Society, and Culture; New Directions in International Studies; The Politics of Marriage and Gender: Global Issues in Shifting Local Contexts;; Quick Takes: Movies and Popular Culture; Rivergate Regionals Collection; Rutgers Series in Childhood Studies; Techniques of the Moving Image; Violence Against Women and Children; War Culture
Joint imprints and co-publishing programs: Co-publishing with Bucknell University Press and caboose

Saint Joseph's University Press

5600 City Avenue
Philadelphia, PA 19131-1395

Phone: 610.660.3402
Fax: 610.660.3412
Email: sjupress@sju.edu
Indiv: (user I.D.)@sju.edu

Orders:
Phone: 610.660.3402
Email: orders@sjupress

Website and Social Media:
Website: www.sjupress.com

Staff
Director: Carmen Robert Croce (610.660.3402; email: ccroce)
Editorial Director: Joseph F. Chorpenning (610.660.1214; email: jchorpen)

Introductory Member
Established: 1997
Title output 2017: 4
Titles currently in print: 78

Admitted to the Association: 2011
Title output 2018: 4

Editorial Program
Jesuit studies (with an emphasis on history and the visual arts), regional studies (Philadelphia and environs)
Book series: Early Modern Catholicism and the Visual Arts (1500-French Revolution)

SBL Press

The Society of Biblical Literature
The Luce Center
825 Houston Mill Road, Suite 350
Atlanta, GA 30329

Phone: 404.727.3100
Fax: 404.727.3101
Email: SBLPressM@sbl-site.org
Indiv: SBLPressP@sbl-site.org

Orders:
Phone: 877.725.3334
Fax: 802.864.7626
Email: sblpressorders@aidcvt.com

Journal Subscriptions and Membership:
Phone: 866.727.9955
Fax: 404.727.2419
Email: sblservices@sbl-site.org

Website and Social Media:
Website: www.sbl-site.org/publications
Twitter: @SBLsite
Blog: sblhs2.com

Staff
Executive Director: John F. Kutsko (404.727.3038; email: john.kutsko@sbl-site.org)
Director, SBL Press: Bob Buller (970.669.9900; email: bob.buller@sbl-site.org)

Production Manager: Nicole Tilford (404.727.2327; email: nicole.tilford@sbl-site.org)
Serials Manager: Jonathan Potter (404.727.0807; email: jonathan.potter@sbl-site.org)
Publishing Marketing Manager: Kathie Klein (404.727.2325; email: kathie.klein@sbl-site.org)
Sales Manager: Heather McMurray (404.727.3096; email: heather.mcmurray@sbl-site.org)
Manager of Membership & Subscriptions: Navar Steed (404.727.9494; email: navar.steed@sbl-site.org)

Number of Press Staff: 5

Regular Member

Established: 1880

Title output 2017: 47

Titles currently in print: 827

Admitted to the Association: 2003

Title output 2018: 33

Journals published: 2

Editorial Program
The Society of Biblical Literature publishes works in biblical and religious studies through SBL Press. Monographic publications include major reference works; commentaries; text editions and translations; collections of essays; revised doctoral dissertations; tools for teaching and research fields; archaeological, sociological, and historical studies; volumes that use archaeological and historical data to illuminate Israelite religion or the culture of biblical peoples; scholarly works on the history, culture, and literature of early Judaism; scholarly works on various aspects of the Masorah; scholarly congress proceedings; critical texts of the Greek Fathers including evaluations of data; philological tools; studies employing the methods and perspectives of linguistics, folklore studies, literary criticism, structuralism, social anthropology, and postmodern studies; studies of the Septuagint including textual criticism, manuscript witnesses and other versions, as well as its literature, historical milieu, and thought; studies related to the Jewish apocryphal and pseudepigraphical works of the Hellenistic period, and the subsequent development of this literature in Judaism and early Christianity; studies in biblical literature and/or its cultural environment; text-critical works related to the Hebrew Bible/Old Testament and New Testament, including investigations of methodology, studies of individual manuscripts, critical texts of a selected book or passage, or examination of more general textual themes; translations of ancient Near Eastern texts; translations of ancient texts from the Greco-Roman world; translations of early Jewish and Christian texts from the Islamic world; and studies in the history of interpretation and reception history of biblical traditions. SBL Press also publishes *The SBL Handbook of Style*, now in its second edition.

SBL Press is the exclusive North American distributor for Sheffield Phoenix Press's backlist titles (UK) and the sole producer and distributor of volumes in the Brown Judaic Studies series (Brown University) and the History of Bible Translations series (NIDA). SBL Press also distributes the Manuscripts of the Greek New Testament Series by Reuben Swanson.

Journals: *Journal of Biblical Literature; Review of Biblical Literature*

Special series: Ancient Israel and Its Literature; Ancient Near East Monographs; Archaeology and Biblical Studies; the Bible and Its Interpretation; the Bible and its Reception; the Bible and Women; Biblical Encyclopedia; Biblical Scholarship in North America; Commentary on the Septuagint; Early Christianity and Its Literature; Early Judaism and Its Literature; Emory Studies in Early Christianity; Global Perspectives on Biblical Scholarship; the Hebrew Bible: A Critical Edition; History of Biblical Studies; International Voices in Biblical Studies; The New Testament in the Greek Fathers; Resources for Biblical Study; Rhetoric of Religious Antiquity; Semeia Studies; Septuagint and Cognate Studies; Studia Philonica Annual and Monographs; Text-Critical Studies; Wisdom Literature from the Ancient World; Writings from the Ancient World; Writings from the Ancient World Supplements; Writings from the Greco-Roman World; Writings from the Greco-Roman World Supplements; Writings from the Islamic World

Joint imprints and co-publishing programs: *HarperCollins Study Bible* (NRSV); *HarperCollins Bible Dictionary*, revised edition; *HarperCollins Bible Commentary*, revised edition, and *Harper's Bible Pronunciation Guide* with HarperCollins; *The Greek New Testament: SBL Edition*, with Logos Bible Software; Ancient Near East Monographs/Monografías Sobre el Antiguo Cercano Oriente, co-published with the Centro de Estudios de Historia del Antiguo Oriente (Argentina); *A User's*

Guide to the Nestle-Aland 28 Greek New Testament, with the Deutsche Bibelgesellschaft; and *A New Approach to Textual Criticism: An Introduction to the Coherence-Based Genealogical Method* with DBG.

Online books: SBL Press, along with six participating partners, provides PDF files of academic books for free download to individuals and libraries in underresourced areas of the globe. Through software that recognizes the IP address of the web visitor, persons from countries whose GDP is considerably less than the average GDP of the US and the EU are given access to the files. The program, as of late 2012, includes almost 350 titles. In addition, SBL Press also publishes two open-access book series: Ancient Near East Monographs, and International Voices in Biblical Studies.

EBooks: SBL Press has entered the e-book market and partners with Bibliovault to make titles available in multiple formats. We also use Amazon Print Replica to make Kindle-compliant e-books available through Amazon.

The University of South Carolina Press

1600 Hampton Street
5th Floor
Columbia, SC 29208-3400
Baltimore, MD 21211

Phone: 803.777.5245
Fax: 803.777.0160
Email: (user I.D.)@mailbox.sc.edu

US Orders:
Hopkins Fulfillment Service
PO Box 50370
Phone: 800.537.5487
Fax: 410.516.6998
Email: hfscustserv@press.jhu.edu

Website and Social Media:
Website: www.sc.edu/uscpress
Facebook: www.facebook.com/USC.Press
Twitter: @USCPress

UK/European Distributor:
Eurospan

Canadian Distributor:
Scholarly Book Services

Staff
Director: Richard Brown (803.777.2243; email: brownri)
Publishing Assistant/Permissions: Vicki Bates (803.777.5245; email: batesvc)
Acquisitions Editors: Ehren Foley (Southern History, African American Studies, Civil Rights, regional) (803.777.9055; email: foleyk@email.sc.edu); Richard Brown (regional, trade, literary studies, rhetoric)
Acquisitions Assistant: Carol Powers (803.777.4859; powers4)
Managing Editor: Bill Adams(803.777.5075; email: adamswb)
Design and Production Manager: Pat Callahan, Design and Production Manager (803.777.2449; email: mpcallah)
Design and Production Assistant/Digital Publishing: Ashley Mathias (803.777.2238; email: samathi)
Marketing and Sales Director: Suzanne Axland (803.777.2021; email: axland)
Promotions Manager: Carolyn Martin (803.777.5029; email: clmartin)
Publicity Manager: MacKenzie Collier (803.777.5231; email: colliemf)
Business Manager: Vicki Leach (803.777.4848; email: sewellv)

Number of Press Staff: 11

Regular Member
Established: 1944
Title output 2017: 52
Titles currently in print: 1,400

Admitted to the Association: 1948
Title output 2018: 55

Editorial Program
Scholarly works in the humanities and social sciences, and general interest and trade titles, particularly those of importance to the region and the state. Core subjects include southern history, African American studies, civil rights; literature and literary studies; and rhetoric/communication.
Book series: AccessAble Books; The Belle W. Baruch Library in Marine Science; The Carolina Lowcountry and the Atlantic World; Chief Justiceships of the United States Supreme Court; The Papers of John C. Calhoun; The Papers of Henry Laurens; The Papers of Howard Thurman; South Carolina Encyclopedia Guides; South Carolina Poetry Book Prize; Southern Classics; Southern Revivals; Studies in Comparative Religion; Studies in Maritime History; Studies in Rhetoric/Communication; Studies on Personalities of the New Testament; Studies on Personalities of the Old Testament; Understanding Contemporary American Literature; Understanding Contemporary British Literature; Understanding Modern European and Latin American Literature; Women's Diaries and Letters of the South.
Distributed Books: McKissick Museum
Imprints: Story River Books, Young Palmetto Books

South Dakota Historical Society Press

South Dakota Historical Society Press
900 Governors Drive
Pierre, SD 57501

Orders
Phone: 605.773.6009
Email: orders@sdhspress.com

Phone: 605.773.6009
Fax: 605.773.6041
Email: info@sdhspress.com
Indiv.: (firstname.lastname)@state.sd.us

Website and Social Media:
Website and blog: www.sdhspress.com
Pioneer Girl Project website: www.pioneergirlproject.org
Facebook: www.facebook.com/SDHSPress/
Twitter: @sdhspress

International (outside of North America) Representative:
Eurospan

Sales Representative:
Miller Book Trade Marketing
Email: bruce@millertrade.com

Staff
Director/Acquisitions: Nancy Tystad Koupal (605.773.4371; email: nancy.koupal)
Managing Editor of *South Dakota History*: Jeanne Ode (605.773.6008; email: Jeanne.ode)
Marketing Director/Rights and Permissions: Jennifer McIntyre (605.773.8161; email: jennifer.mcintyre)
Accounting Assistant/Order Fulfilment: Judy Uecker (605.773.6009; email: judy.uecker)

Number of Press Staff: 4

Affiliate Member
Established: 1997
Title output 2017: 5
Titles currently in print: 70

Admitted to the Association: 2017
Title output 2018: 6
Journals published: 1

Southern Illinois University Press

1915 University Press Drive
SIUC Mail Code 6806
Southern Illinois University
Carbondale, IL 62901-6806

Fax: 618.453.1221
Email: (user I.D.)@siu.edu

<u>Website and Social Media:</u>
Website: www.siupress.com
Facebook: www.facebook.com/siupress
Twitter: @SIUPress

<u>UK/European Distributor:</u>
Eurospan

<u>Orders:</u>
Southern Illinois University Press
c/o Chicago Distribution Center
11030 South Langley Avenue
Chicago, IL 60628-3830

Phone: 800.621.2736
Fax: 800.621.8476
Email: custserv@press.uchicago.edu
EDI; PUBNET at 202-5280

<u>Canadian Representative:</u>
Scholarly Book Services

Staff
Interim Co-Directors: Angela Moore-Swafford, Amy Etcheson
Business Manager, Rights and Permissions and Interim Co-Director: Angela Moore-Swafford (618.453.6617; email: angmoore) (rights email: rights)
Accounts Payable: Judy Verdich (618.453.3786; email: jverdich)
Executive Editor: Sylvia Frank Rodrigue American History women's studies, true crime) (508.297.2162; email: sylvia@sylverlining.com)
Acquisitions Editor: Kristine Priddy (composition, criminology, poetry, rhetoric, theater) (618.453.6631; email: mkpriddy)
Acquisitions Assistant: Jennifer Egan (618.453.6633; email: siupressacquisitions)
Editing, Design, and Production Manager/Book Designer: Linda Buhman (618.453.6612; email: ljbuhman)
Project Editor: Wayne Larsen (618.453.6628; email: wlarsen)
Marketing and Sales Manager and Interim Co-Director: Amy Etcheson (618.453.6623; email: aetcheson)
IT Specialist: Jerry Richardson (618.453.6624; email: jerryric)

Number of Press Staff: 7.5

Regular Member
Established: 1956
Title output 2017: 33
Titles currently in print: 1,200

Admitted to the Association: 1980
Title output 2018: 31

Editorial Program
Scholarly books, primarily in the humanities and social sciences. Particular strengths are theatre and stagecraft; regional and Civil War history; rhetoric and composition; aviation; contemporary poetry. Submissions in fiction and festschriften are not invited.
Book series: Civil War Campaigns in the West; The Collected Works of John Dewey; The Concise Lincoln Library; The Crab Orchard Series in Poetry; The Elmer H. Johnson and Carol Holmes

Johnson Series in Criminology; Engaging the Civil War; The Illustrated Flora of Illinois; Landmarks in Rhetoric and Public Address; Looking for Lincoln in Illinois; The Papers of Ulysses S. Grant; Perspectives on Crime and Justice; Rhetoric in the Modern Era; Shawnee Books; Shawnee Classics; Studies in Rhetorics and Feminisms; Theater in the Americas; World of Ulysses S. Grant; Writing Research, Pedagogy, and Policy.

Stanford University Press

500 Broadway
Redwood City, CA 94063

Phone: 650.723.9434
Fax: 650.725.3457
Email: (user I.D.)@stanford.edu

Order Fulfillment (US and Canada):
Ingram Academic Services
One Ingram Blvd
La Vergne, TN 37086
Phone: 866.400.5351
Email: ips@ingramcontent.com

Website and Social Media:
Website: www.sup.org
Blog: stanfordpress.typepad.com
Facebook: www.facebook.com/stanforduniversitypress
Twitter: @stanfordpress

European/Asia Pacific Representative:
Combined Academic Publishers Ltd

Staff

Director: Alan Harvey (650.723.6375; email: aharvey)
Acquisitions: Kate Wahl, Publishing Director and Editor-in-Chief (Middle East studies) (650.498.9420; email: kwahl)
  Executive Editor: Emily-Jane Cohen (philosophy, religion, literature) (650.725.7717; email: beatrice)
  Senior Editors: Steve Catalano (business, economics) (650.724.7079; email: catalan); Michelle Lipinski (anthropology, law) (650.736.4641; email: mlipinsk)
  Acquisition Editors: Margo Irvin (history, Jewish studies) (650.498.9023; email: mcirvin); Marcela Maxfield (sociology, Asian studies) (650.498.3396; email: mmaxfiel); Friederike Sundaram (digital projects) (650.721.5616; email: fsundaram)
  Associate Editor: Faith Wilson Stein (650.497.4991; email: fwstein)
  Assistant Editors: Leah Pennywark (650.498.9420; email: lpennyw); Nora Spiegel (650.724.7080; email: nspiegel)
  Editorial Assistant: Sunna Juhn (650.736.0597; email: sjuhn)
Editorial, Design, and Production: Patricia Myers, EDP Director (650.724.5365; email: pmyers)
  Senior Production Editor: Emily Smith (650.736.0686; email: emilys)
  Production Editors: Gigi Mark (650.724.9990; email: vmark); Anne Fuzellier Jain (650.736.0719; email: anne7); Jessica Ling (650.725.0828; email: jessling)
  Digital Production Associate: Jasmine Mulliken (email: jmullike)
  Art Director: Rob Ehle (650.723.1132; email: ehle)
  Senior Designer: Kevin Kane (650.723.6808; email: kbk)
  Production Manager: Mike Sagara (650.725.0839; email: msagara)
  Production Coordinator: Vicki Vandeventer (650.725.0836; email: vickiv)
Sales and Marketing: Stephanie Adams, Marketing Manager (650.736.1782; email: sadams3)
  Sales and Exhibits Manager: Kate Templar (650.725.0820; email: ktemplar)
  Publicist: Ryan Furtkamp (650.724.4211; email: furtkamp)
  Digital Media Specialist: Kendra Schynert (650.497.3033; email: kschyner)
  Marketing Specialist: Meilina Dalit (650.725.0823; email: mdalit)
  Marketing Assistants: Abigail Schott-Rosenfield (650.736.1781; email: aschott); Maxwell Shanley

(650.724.9280; email: mshanley)
Business: Jean Kim, Director of Finance and Operations (650.725.0838; email: jean.h.kim)
Royalties/Accounts Receivable: Su-Mei Lee (650.725.0837; email: sumeilee)
Accounts Payable: Aurelia Hernandez (650.724.8697; email: aureliah)
Systems: Chris Cosner, IT Manager (650.724.7276; email: ccosner)
Desktop Support Administrator: Meide Guo (650.723.9598; email: meideguo)

Regular Member
Established: 1892
Title output 2017: 119
Titles currently in print: 3,500

Admitted to the Association: 1937
Title output 2018: 125

Editorial Program
Anthropology, Asian Studies, Business, Economics, History, International Relations, Jewish Studies, Latin American Studies, Law, Literature, Middle East Studies, Philosophy, Politics, Religion, Security Studies, Sociology.
Book series: Anthropology of Policy; Asian America; Asian Security; Cold War International History Project; The Complete Works of Friedrich Nietzsche; Contemporary Issues in Asia and the Pacific; The Cultural Lives of Law; Cultural Memory in the Present; Emerging Frontiers in the Global Economy; Encountering Traditions; Global Competition Law and Economics; High Reliability and Crisis Management; Innovation and Technology in the World Economy; Jurists: Profiles in Legal Theory; Meridian: Crossing Aesthetics; Post*45; RaceReligion; Social Science History; Square One: First Order Questions in the Humanities; Stanford Business Classics; Stanford Nuclear Age Series; Stanford Series in Comparative Race and Ethnicity; Stanford Studies in Human Rights; Stanford Studies in Jewish History and Culture; Stanford Studies in Law and Politics; Stanford Studies in Middle Eastern and Islamic Societies and Cultures; Studies in Asian Security; Studies in Social Inequality; Studies in the Modern Presidency; Studies of the Weatherhead East Asian Institute; Studies of the Walter H. Shorenstein Asia-Pacific Research Center; Thinking Theory Now
Imprints: Redwood Press; Stanford Briefs; Stanford Business Books

State University of New York Press

Street Address:
10 North Pearl Street
Albany, NY 12207

Phone: 518.944.2800
Fax: 518.320.1592
Email: info@sunypress.edu
Indiv: firstname.lastname@sunypress.edu

Website and Social Media:
Website: www.sunypress.edu
Facebook: www.facebook.com/pages/
SUNY-Press/112308762113504
Twitter: @SUNYPress

Canadian Representative:
Lexa Publishers' Representatives

Mailing Address:
353 Broadway
State University Plaza
Albany, NY 12246-0001

Customer Service:
SUNY Press
PO Box 960
Herndon, VA 20172-0960
Phone: 703.661.1575
Toll free: 877.204.6073 (US only)
Fax: 703.996.1010
Toll free: 877.204.6074 (US only)
Email: suny@presswarehouse.com

UK/European Distributor:
NBN International

Staff
Co-Directors: Donna Dixon (518.944.2802); James Peltz (518.944.2815)
Executive Assistant to the Co-Directors: Janice Vunk (518.944.2821)
Receptionist: Diana Altobello (518.944.2804)
Acquisitions Editorial
Co-Director: James Peltz (518.944.2815) (Excelsior Editions, film studies, transpersonal psychology)

Senior Acquisitions Editors: Christopher Ahn (Asian studies, religious studies); Michael Rinella (518.944.2811) (African American politics and sociology, environmental studies, political science) Acquisitions Editors: Rebecca Colesworthy (518.944.2813) (education, Hispanic studies, queer studies, women's and gender studies); Andrew Kenyon (518.944.2808) (philosophy); Amanda Lanne-Camilli (518.944.2809) (New York State studies, native and indigenous studies, Italian American studies)
 Assistant Acquisitions Editor: Rafael Chaiken (518.944.2828) (Jewish studies)
Production
 Co-Director: Donna Dixon (518.944.2802) (journals)
 Senior Production Editors: Diane Ganeles (518.944.2825); Ryan Morris (518.944.2814); Eileen Nizer (518.944.2812)
 Production Editor: Jenn Bennett-Genthner (518.944.2801)
 Production and Composition Coordinator: Aimee Harrison (518.944.2816)
Marketing and Publicity
 Director of Marketing and Publicity: Fran Keneston (518.944.2807)
 Executive Promotions Manager: Anne Valentine (518.944.2820)
 Senior Promotions Manager: Michael Campochiaro (518.944.2827)
 Exhibits and Awards Manager: Michelle Alamillo (518.944.2824)
 Promotions Manager: Kate Seburyamo (518.944.2810)
Revenue and Business Operations
 Accounting Manager: Sharla Clute (518.944.2803)
 Sales and Digital Programs Assistant: Renee Jones (518.944.2806)
 Digital Programs Manager: Daniel McShane (518.944.2819)

Number of Press Staff: 23

Regular Member
Established: 1966
Title output 2017: 160
Titles currently in print: 6,086

Admitted to the Association: 1970
Title output 2018: 172
Journals published: 5

Editorial Program
Scholarly titles and serious works of general interest in many areas of the humanities and the social sciences, with special interest in African American studies; Asian studies; education; gender studies; Hispanic studies; native and indigenous studies; philosophy; political science; psychology; queer studies; religious studies; transpersonal psychology; and women's and gender studies.
 SUNY Press distributes books from the Albany Institute of History and Art, Codhill Press, Global Academic Publishing, Hudson River Valley National Heritage Area, Mount Ida Press, Muswell Hill Press, New Netherland Institute, Parks & Trails New York, Rockefeller Institute Press, Samuel Dorsky Museum and the Uncrowned Queens Institute.
Journals: *The Journal of Buddhist Philosophy; The Journal of Japanese Philosophy; Mediaevalia; Palimpsest; philoSOPHIA*
Imprints: Excelsior Editions

Syracuse University Press

621 Skytop Road, Suite 110
Syracuse, NY 13244-5290

Phone: 315.443.5534
Fax: 315.443.5545
Email: (user I.D.)@syr.edu

Website and Social Media:
Website: syracuseuniversitypress.syr.edu
Blog: syracusepress.wordpress.com/
Facebook: www.facebook.com/pages/
    Syracuse-University-Press/22430126190l
Twitter: @supress
YouTube: www.youtube.com/channel/UCOtUPRTWoHyQ9NL4QQlM32g
Pinterest: www.pinterest.com/supress/
Goodreads: www.goodreads.com/review/list/15207023

Warehouse:
Longleaf Publishers c/o
Ingram Publisher Services
1550 Heil Quaker Blvd
La Vergne, TN 37086

Orders:
Longleaf Services
Phone: 800.848.6224
Fax: 800.272.6817
Email: orders@longleafservices.org

Canadian Distributor:
Scholarly Book Services, Inc.

UK Distributor:
Eurospan

Staff
Director: Alice R. Pfeiffer (315.443.5535; email: arpfeiff)
    Office Coordinator: Mary Doyle (315.443.5541; email: mdoyle)
Acquisitions Editorial: Suzanne E. Guiod, Editor-in-Chief (315.443.5539; email: seguiod)
    Acquisitions Editors: Deborah Manion (315.443.5647; email: dmmanion)
    Assistant Editor: Kelly Balenske (315.443.5541; email: klbalens)
Editorial and Production Manager: Kay Steinmetz (315.443.9155; email: kasteinm)
    Senior Designers: Victoria Lane (315.443.5540; email: vmlane); Fred Wellner (315.443.5540; email: fawellne)
    Project Editor: Kaitlin Carruthers-Busser (315.443.5544; email: klcarrut)
Marketing: Lisa Kuerbis, Marketing Coordinator (315.443.5546; email: lkuerbis)
    Marketing Analyst: Mona Hamlin (315.443.5547; email: mhamlin)
    Design Specialist: Lynn Wilcox (315.443.1975; email: lphoppel)
Business: Karen Lockwood, Senior Business Manager (315.443.5536; email: kflockwo)
    Accounting Clerk: Bobbi Claps (315.443.5538; email: baclaps)

Number of Press Staff: 16

Regular Member
Established: 1943
Title output 2017: 51
Titles currently in print: 1,740

Admitted to the Association: 1946
Title output 2018: 40

Editorial Program
Scholarly books and works of general interest in the areas of Middle East, Irish, Jewish, New York State, women's, Native American, ethnic, disability studies; religion; television; popular culture; sports history; journalism; human and urban geography; politics; peace and conflict resolution; Arab American studies; and selected fiction.

The Press distributes books bearing the imprints of Adirondack Museum; Moshe Dayan Center for Middle Eastern and African Studies (Tel-Aviv University); New Netherlands Project; Arlen House; Sheep Meadow Press; Blackhall Publishing; Litteraria Pragensia; Ethnic Heritage Studies Center of Utica College; Syracuse University In Florence; Graduate School Press, Syracuse University; Syracuse University; and the Pucker Gallery, Boston.

Special series, joint imprints, and/or copublishing programs: The Adirondack Museum; The Albert Schweitzer Library; America in the Twentieth Century; Critical Arab-American Studies;

Contemporary Issues in the Middle East; Critical Perspectives on Disability; Gender, Culture, and Politics in the Middle East; Gender and Globalization; Irish Studies; Iroquois and Their Neighbors; Judaic Traditions in Literature, Music, and Art; Library of Modern Jewish Literature; Middle East Beyond Dominant Paradigms; Middle East Literature in Translation; Modern Intellectual and Political History of the Middle East; Modern Jewish History; New York State Studies; Religion and Politics; Sports and Entertainment; Syracuse Studies in Geography; Syracuse Studies in Peace and Conflict Resolution; Syracuse Unbound; Television and Popular Culture; Writing, Culture, and Community Practices.

TCU Press

Mailing Address:
TCU Box 298300
Fort Worth, TX 76129

Street Address:
3000 Sandage Ave.
Fort Worth, TX 76109

Phone: 817.257.7822
Fax: 817.257.5075

Orders:
Phone: 800.826.8911

Website and Social Media:
Website: www.prs.tcu.edu
Facebook: www.facebook.com/tcupress
Twitter: @TCUPress
Instagram: @tcupress
Tumblr: tcupress.tumblr.com

Staff
Director: Dan Williams (email: d.e.williamms@tcu.edu)
Editor: Kathy Walton (email: k.s.walton@tcu.edu)
Production Manager: Melinda Esco (email: m.esco@tcu.edu)
Marketing Coordinator: Rebecca Allen (email: rebecca.a.allen@tcu.edu)
Editorial Assistant: Molly Spain (email: molly.spain@tcu.edu)

Number of Press Staff: 5

Regular Member
Established: 1966
Title output 2017: 21
Titles currently in print: 440

Admitted to to the Association: 1982
Title output 2018: 17

Editorial Program
Humanities and social sciences, with special emphasis on local, Texas, and Southwestern history and literature; American studies, especially border studies; art and architecture; fiction; and poetry; also publishes, descant, the Fort Worth literary journal.
Book series: Chaparral Books for Young Readers; The Chisholm Trail Series; Literary Cities; The Texas Tradition Series; The Texas Biography Series; TCU Texas Poets Laureate

Teachers College Press

1234 Amsterdam Avenue
New York, NY 10027-6696

Phone: 212.678.3929
Fax: 212.678.4149
Email: (user I.D.)@tc.edu
(unless otherwise indicated)

Orders:
Teachers College Press
30 Amberwood Parkway
Ashland, OH 44805
Phone: 800.575.6566
Fax: 419.281.6883

Website and Social Media:
Website: www.tcpress.com
Facebook: www.facebook.com/TCPress
Twitter: @TCPress
Instagram: @tcpress

European Representative:
Eurospan

Canadian Representative:
University of Toronto Press

Staff

Director: Carole Pogrebin Saltz (212.678.3927; email: saltz)
  Assistant to the Director: Rachel Banks (212.678.3965; email: rb3397)
Acquisitions Editorial: Brian Ellerbeck, Executive Acquisitions Editor (administration, school change, leadership, policy, special and gifted education, multicultural education, teacher research, curriculum studies) (212.678.3908; email: ellerbeck)
  Senior Acquisitions Editor: Sarah Biondello (early childhood) (212.678.3928;email: biondello)
  Acquisitions Editor: Emily Spangler (language and literacy, technology and education) (212.678.3909; email: spangler)
  Consulting Senior Acquisitions Editor: Jean Ward (curriculum, professional development, literacy) (847.224.02785; email: ward)
  Assistant Acquisitions Editor: Caritza Berlioz (212.678.3905; email: cb3493)
Production: Michael Weinstein, Production Manager (212.678.3926; email: weinstein)
  Senior Production Editor: Karl Nyberg (212.678.3806; email: nyberg)
  Production Editors: Lori Tate (212.678.3907; email: tate); John Bylander (212.678.3914; email: bylander); Jennifer Baker (212.678.3902; email: baker)
  Production Assistants: Debra Jackson-Whyte (212.678.3926; email: jackson-whyte)
Marketing: Leyli Shayegan, Director, Sales and Marketing and Assistant Director (212.678.3475; email: shayegan)
  Business Development/Sales Manager: Sarah (Sally) Kling (212.678.7439; email: kling@tc.columbia.edu)
  Marketing Manager: Nancy Power (212.678.3915; email: power)
  Graphic Arts Manager: David Strauss (212.678.3982; email: strauss)
  Publicist: Joy Mizan (212.678.3963; email: jm4864)
  Outreach Coordinator: Michael McGann (212.678.3919; email: mcgann)
  Rights and Permissions Manager/Special Sales Coordinator: Christina Brianik (212.678.3827; email: brianik)
Business: Monica Carrera, Business Manager (212.678.3913; email: carrera)
  Business Assistant: Tim Osinowo (212.678.3917; email: osinowo)
  Secretary/Receptionist: Marcia Ruiz (212.678.3929; email: myr3)

Regular Member

Established: 1904
Title output 2017: 54
Titles currently in print: 998

Admitted to the Association: 1971
Title output 2018: 56

Editorial Program
Scholarly, professional, text, and trade books on education, education-related areas, and parenting. Multimedia instructional materials, tests, and evaluation materials for classroom use at all levels of education.

Specific areas of interest in education are: curriculum; early childhood; school administration and educational policy; counseling; mathematics; philosophy; psychology; language and literacy; multicultural education; science; sociology; special education; social justice; social studies; teacher education; cultural studies; technology and education; women and higher education.
Book series: Advances in Contemporary Educational Thought; Disability, Culture, and Equity; Early Childhood Education; Education and Psychology of the Gifted; International Perspectives on Education Reform; Language and Literacy; Multicultural Education; Practitioner Inquiry; Professional Ethics in Education; School : Questions; Teaching for Social Justice; Technology, Education—Connections (TEC)

Temple University Press

Mailing Address:
TASB
1852 N. 10th Street
Philadelphia, PA 19122

Phone: 215.926.2140
Fax: 215.926.2141
Email: firstname.lastname@temple.edu

Website and Social Media:
Website: www.temple.edu/tempress
Blog: templepress.wordpress.com
Facebook: www.facebook.com/pages/
   Temple-University-Press/21638877349
Twitter: @TempleUnivPress

UK Distributor:
Combined Academic Publishers

Street Address:
TASB
2450 West Hunting Park Avenue
Philadelphia, PA 19129

Orders:
Chicago Distribution Center
11030 South Langley Avenue
Chicago, IL 60628
Phone: 800.621.2736
Fax: 800.621.8476

Staff
Director: Mary Rose Muccie (215.926.2145)
Rights and Permissions: Ashley Petrucci (215.926. 3181)
Electronic Publishing Manager: Mary Rose Muccie (215.926.2145)
Editor-in-Chief: Aaron Javsicas (215.926.2159)
Editors: Sara Cohen (215.926.2146); Ryan Mulligan (215.926.2157)
Editorial Assistant: Ashley Petrucci (215.926. 3181)
Senior Production Editors: Joan Vidal (215.926.2148); Dave Wilson (215.926.2147)
Art Manager: Kate Nichols (215.926.2167)
Assistant Director and Director of Marketing: Ann-Marie Anderson (215.926.2143)
Advertising and Promotion Manager: Irene Imperio (215.926.2153)
Publicity Manager: Gary Kramer (215.926.2154)
Finance Manager: Karen Baker (215.926.2156)

Number of Press Staff: 12

Regular Member
Established: 1969
Title output 2017: 46
Titles currently in print: 1,265

Admitted to the Association: 1972
Title output 2018: 44
Journals published: 2

Editorial Program
African American studies; American studies; anthropology; Asian studies; Asian American studies; communication; criminology; disability studies; education; ethnicity and race; LGBTQIA studies; gender studies; geography; immigration; labor studies; Latin American studies; law and society; Philadelphia regional studies; political science and public policy; race and class studies, religion; sexuality studies; sociology; social justice; sports; urban studies; US and European history; women's studies.
Journals: *Commonwealth: A Journal of Pennsylvania Politics and Policy; Kalfou: A Journal of Comparative and Relational Ethnic Studies*
Book series: Animals and Ethics; Asian American History and Culture; Black Male Studies; Critical Race, Indigeneity, and Relationality; Global Youth; History and the Public; Insubordinate Spaces; Pennsylvania History; Politics, History, and Social Change; Religious Engagement in Democratic Politics; Sexuality Studies; Sporting; Studies in Latin American and Caribbean Music; Urban Life, Landscape, and Policy
Co-publishing program: Pennsylvania Historical Association

University of Tennessee Press

Mailing Address:
110 Conference Center
Knoxville, TN 37996-4108

Shipping Address:
600 Henley Street
Suite 110 Conference Center
Knoxville, TN 37902-2911

Phone: 865.974.3321
Fax: 865.974.3724
Email: custserv@utpress.org
Indiv: (user I.D.)@utk.edu

Orders:
Chicago Distribution Center
11030 South Langley Ave.
Chicago, IL 60628
Phone: 800.621.2736
Fax: 773.702.7212

Website and Social Media:
Website: utpress.org
Blog: utpress.org/utpressblog
Facebook page: www.facebook.com/pages/
    University-of-Tennessee-Press/80814711590?ref=ts
Twitter: @utennpress

Staff
Director: Scot Danforth (email: danforth)
Acquisitions Editorial: Thomas Wells (email: twells)
Editorial Assistant: Jon Boggs (email: jboggs6)
Production Coordinator: Stephanie Thompson (email: sthomp20)
Designer: Kelly Gray (email: kgray14)
Exhibits/Publicity Manager: Tom Post (email: tpost)
Marketing Assistant: Linsey Perry (email: lsims9)
Business Manager: Lisa Davis (email: ldavis49)
IT Manager: Jake Sumner (email: jsumner2)

Number of Press Staff: 9

Regular Member
Established: 1940
Title output 2017: 31
Titles currently in print: 932

Admitted to the Association: 1964
Title output 2018: 31

Editorial Program
American studies; Appalachian studies; African American studies; history; religion; folklore; vernacular architecture; historical archaeology; material culture; literature; and literary fiction. Submissions in poetry, textbooks, and translations are not invited.

Book series: America's Baptists; Appalachian Echoes; Charles K. Wolfe American Music Series; Correspondence of James K. Polk; Legacies of War, Outdoor Tennessee; The Papers of Andrew Jackson; Sport and Popular Culture; Tennessee Studies in Literature; Vernacular Architecture Studies; Voices of the Civil War; and The Western Theater in the Civil War

University of Texas Press

Street Address:
3001 Lake Austin Blvd
Stop E4800
Austin, TX 78703-4206

Mailing Address:
PO Box 7819
Austin, TX 78713-7819

Phone: 512.471.7233
Fax: 512.232.7178
Email: info@utpress.utexas.edu
Indiv: firstinitiallastname@utpress.utexas.edu

Orders:
Phone: 800.252.3206
Fax: 800.687.6046
Warehouse: 512.471.7656

Website and Social Media:
Website: www.utexaspress.com
Blog: utpressnews.blogspot.com/
Facebook: www.facebook.com/utexaspress
Twitter: @UTexasPress
Instagram: instagram.com/utexaspress
Pinterest: www.pinterest.com/utpress
YouTube: www.youtube.com/c/utexaspress
Tumblr: www.utexaspress.tumblr.com
Soundcloud: www.soundcloud.com/university-of-texas-press

Staff
Director: David Hamrick (512.232.7604)
Assistant to the Director: Allison Faust (512.232.7603)
International Rights Manager: Angelica Lopez-Torres (512.232.7605)
Rights and Permissions Coordinator: Peggy Gough (512.232.7624)
Assistant Director and Editor-in-Chief: Robert Devens (architecture, history, American studies, Texas) (512.232.7615)
 Senior Editors: Jim Burr (classics, Jewish studies, film and media studies, Middle Eastern studies) (512.232.7610); Kerry Webb (Latin American and pre-Columbian studies, Latin American history, Latinx studies) (512.232.7612)
 Sponsoring Editor: Casey Kittrell (anthropology, archaeology, nature and environment, food studies, music, Texas) (512.232.7616)
 Assistant Editor: Sarah McGavick (512.232.7608)
 Editorial Assistant: Andrew Hnatow (512.232.2589)
Managing Editor: Robert Kimzey (512.232.7614)
 Senior Manuscript Editor: Lynne Chapman (512.232.7607)
 Manuscript Editor: Bruce Bethell (512.232.7668)
Design and Production Manager: Dustin Kilgore (512.232.7640)
 Production Coordinator: Sarah Mueller (512.232.7627)
 Production Assistant: Cassandra Cisneros (512.232.7638)
Assistant Director and Marketing and Sales Manager: Gianna LaMorte (512.232.7647)
 Publicity and Communications Manager: Cameron Ludwick (512.232.7633)
 Digital Media Producer and Direct Promotions Manager: Bailey Morrison (512.471.1728)
 Advertising and Catalog Production Manager: Simon Renwick (512.232.7630)
 Exhibits Manager and Marketing Assistant: Demi Marshall (512.232.7637)
 Publicity and Promotions Assistant: Joel Pinckney (512.232.7634)
 Regional Sales Manager: Bob Barnett (502.345.6477)

Journals Manager: Christopher Farmer (512.232.7620)
Journals Production Editors: Karen Broyles (512.232.7622); Stacey Salling (512.232.7600)
Journals Circulation and Customer Service Coordinator: Elizabeth Locke (512.232.7621)
Chief Financial Manager: Allison Lambert (512.232.7646)
Royalty and HR Manager: Kristin Duvall (512.232.7648)
Accounts Payable Manager: Linda Ramirez (512.232.7649)
Accounts Receivable Manager: Jennifer Nuzzo (512.232.7602)
Orders and Customer Service Associates: Dawn Bishop (512.232.7652); Kate Shannon (512.232.7650)
Assistant Director and Information and Business Systems Manager: William Bishel (512.232.7609)
Digital Publishing and Reprints Manager: Sharon Casteel (512.232.7631)
Warehouse Supervisor: Paul Guerra (512.232.7657)
Warehouse Staff: David Guerrero (512.232.7655); Rey Renteria (512.232.7654); Ramon Zazueta (512.232.7656)

Number of Press Staff: 40

Regular Member

Established: 1950	Admitted to the Association: 1954
Title output 2017: 93	Title output 2018: 85
Titles currently in print: 2,886	Journals published: 13

Editorial Program

American studies, anthropology, archaeology, architecture, art, classics, film and media studies, photography, food studies and cookbooks, history, Jewish studies, Latin American and pre-Columbian studies, Latinx studies, Middle Eastern studies, music, nature and environment, and Texas and the Southwest.

The Press distributes publications for the Jack S. Blanton Museum of Art; Center for Mexican American Studies; Center for Middle Eastern Studies; Dolph Briscoe Center for American History; Harry Ransom Center; and Teresa Lozano Long Institute of Latin American Studies.

Journals: *Asian Music; Diálogo; Information and Culture; JCMS: Journal of Cinema and Media Studies; The Journal of the History of Sexuality; The Journal of Individual Psychology; Journal of Latin American Geography; Latin American Music Review; Studies in Latin American Popular Culture; Texas Studies in Literature and Language; The Textile Museum Journal; US Latina & Latino Oral History Journal; The Velvet Light Trap*

Book series: American Music; Border Hispanisms; Center for Creative Photography; Cities of the Etruscans; CMES (Center for Middle Eastern Studies) Modern Middle East Literatures In Translation; CMES Modern Middle East Series; CMES Emerging Voices from the Middle East; CMES Middle East Monograph Series; CMES Binah Yitzrit Foundation Series in Israel Studies; Exploring Jewish Arts and Culture (with Schusterman Center for Jewish Studies); Focus on American History (with Briscoe Center for American History); Handbook of Latin American Studies (with Library of Congress); Historia USA; The Katrina Bookshelf; Lateral Exchanges: Architecture, Urban Development, and Transnational Practices; The Oratory of Classical Greece; Terry and Jan Todd Series on Physical Culture And Sports; Texas Film and Media Studies; Texas Natural History Guides; World Comics and Graphic Nonfiction Series

Endowed book series: Ashley and Peter Larkin Series in Greek and Roman Culture; Bill and Alice Wright Photography Series; Brad and Michele Moore Roots Music Series; Bridwell Texas History Series; Charles N. Prothro Texana Series; Clifton and Shirley Caldwell Texas Heritage Series; The Corrie Herring Hooks Series; Ellen and Edward Randall Series; Jack and Doris Smothers Series in Texas History, Life, and Culture; Jamal and Rania Daniel Series in Contemporary History, Politics, Culture, and Religion of the Levant; Jess and Betty Jo Hay Series; Joe R. and Teresa Lozano Long Series in Latin American and Latino Art and Culture; Linda Schele Series in Maya and Pre-Columbian Studies; Louann Atkins Temple Women and Culture Series; M. Georgia Hegarty Dunkerley Contemporary Art Series; Mildred Wyatt-Wold Series in Ornithology; Peter T. Flawn Series in Natural Resources; Roger Fullington Series in Architecture; William and Bettye Nowlin Series in Art, History, and Culture of the Western Hemisphere

Imprints: Tower Books

Texas A&M University Press

Street Address:
John H. Lindsey Building, Lewis Street
College Station, TX 77843

Mailing Address:
4354 TAMU
College Station, TX 77843-4354

Phone: 979.845.1436
Fax: 979.847.8752
Email: upress@tamu.edu
Indiv: (user I.D.)@tamu.edu

Orders:
Phone: 800.826.8911
Fax: 888.617.2421
Email: bookorders@tamu.edu

Website and Social Media:
Website: www.tamupress.com
Facebook: www.facebook.com/tamupress
Twitter: @TAMUPress
Instagram: www.instagram.com/tamupress
YouTube: www.youtube.com/channel/UCFFpUgvj4qVlaQTf0r5-RxA

European Representative:
Eurospan

Staff

Edward R. Campbell '39 Press Director: Shannon Davies (979.458.3980; email: sdavies)
Acquisitions Editorial: Jay Dew, Editor-in-Chief (Texas, Western, and Southern history; military history; Texas women's history; environmental history; borderland studies; political history) (979.845.0759; email: jaydew)
Senior Editor: Thom Lemmons (physical anthropology; archaeology; nautical archaeology; sports; Texas art, music, and culture) (979.845.0758; email: thom.lemmons)
Acquisitions Editor: TBA (natural history and natural sciences; agriculture; gardening and horticulture; conservation and the environment)
Editorial Assistant: Emily Seyl (979.845.2521; email: emilyseyl@exchange.tamu.edu)
Manuscript Editorial: Katie Duelm, Managing Editor (979.458.3975; email: katie.duelm)
Associate Editor: Patricia Clabaugh (979.458.3979; email: pclabaugh)
Design/Production: Mary Ann Jacob, Design & Production Manager (979.845.3694; email: m-jacob)
Assistant Design and Production Manager: Cierra Bowers (979.458.3995; email: cbowers)
Design and Production Assistant: Kristie Lee (979.458.1331; email: K-lee)
Marketing: Gayla Christiansen, Marketing Manager (979.845.0148; email: gayla-c)
Publicity and Advertising Manager: Christine Brown (979.458.3982; email: christinebrown)
Promotional Design and Electronic Marketing Manager: Kyle Littlefield (979.458.3983; email: k-littlefield)
Marketing Communications and Exhibit Manager: Katelyn Knight (979.458.3984; email: k_knight)
Sales Manager: Kathryn Lloyd (979.458.3988; email: k-krol)
Financial Manager: Dianna Sells (979.845.0146; email: d-sells)
Business Operations Manager: Wynona McCormick (979.845.0136; email: wynona)
Order Fulfillment Supervisor: Genny Jennings (979.458.3991; email: genny.howard)
Warehouse Manager: Mike Martin (979.458.3986; email: mike.martin)
Assistant Warehouse Manager: Cliff O'Connell (979.458.3987; email: c-oconnell)

Number of Press Staff: 22

Regular Member
Established: 1974
Title output 2017: 60
Titles currently in print: 1,415

Admitted to the Association: 1977
Title output 2018: 48

Editorial Program

American, Western, and Southern history; Texas and the Southwest; borderlands; Texas women's history; military history; business history; environmental history; natural history; conservation; agriculture; natural resource science; veterinary medicine; consumer health; physical anthropology; archaeology; nautical archaeology; architecture; Texas music, art, and culture; political history. Submissions are not invited in poetry or fiction.

Book series: AgriLife Research and Extension Service Series; Brannen Series in Military Studies; Centennial Series of the Association of Former Students; Connecting the Greater West; Cox Books on Conservation Leadership; Dickson Series in Texas Music; Fay Series in Analytical Psychology; Gulf Coast Books; Harte Research Institute for Gulf of Mexico Studies; Integrative Natural History; Lindsey Series in the Arts and Humanities; Marine, Maritime, and Coastal Books; Merrick Natural Environment; Montague Business and Oil History; Moody Natural History; Moore Texas Art; Peoples and Cultures of Texas; Peopling of the Americas; Perspectives on South Texas; Presidential Rhetoric and Political Communication; Prothro Texas Photography; Rachal Foundation Series in Nautical Archaeology; Ranching Heritage Series; Red River Valley Books; River Books; Sam Rayburn Rural Life; Seventh Generation: Survival, Sustainability, Sustenance in a New Nature; Southwestern Studies in the Humanities; Spencer Series in the West and Southwest; Swaim-Paup-For an Spirit of Sports Series; The Texas Experience; University of Houston Mexican American Studies; Wardlaw Books; Williams-Ford Series in Military History; Williams Texas Life; Women in Texas History

Texas Review Press

Street Address:
SHSU Department of English
1901 University Ave, Ste. 152
Huntsville, TX 77341

Mailing Address:
SHSU Department of English
Box 2146
Huntsville, TX 77341-2146

Phone: 936.294.1992
Fax: 936.294.3070
Email: TexasReview@shsu.edu

US Orders
Texas A&M University Press
Orders: 800-826-8911
Email: bookorders@tamu.edu

Website and Social Media:
Website: www.texasreviewpress.org
Facebook: www.facebook.com/TexasReviewPress/
Twitter: @TxReviewPress
Instagram: @texasreviewpress

UK, Europe, Africa & the Middle East
Eurospan

Canada
Scholarly Book Services

Staff

Director: TBA
EDP Manager: Lisa Tremaine (936.294.1429; email: ltremaine@shsu.edu)
Acquiring Editor: J Bruce Fuller (936.294.1418; email: jbf026@shsu.edu)
Administrative Assistant: Claude Wooley (936.294.1992; email: cww006@shsu.edu)

Number of Press Staff: 2.5

Introductory Member

Established: 1979
Title output 2017: 18
Titles currently in print: 292

Admitted to the Association: 2017
Title output 2018: 184
Journals published: 2

Editorial Program

Texas Review Press publishes fiction, nonfiction, memoir, literary criticism, and poetry with a focus on regional works from Texas and the Deep South. We sponsor four annual competitions that invite submissions from around the world. These are the Robert Phillips Poetry Chapbook

Competition, The X.J. Kennedy Competition for a full-length poetry collection, the George Garrett Fiction Competition for novel or a collection of short stories, and the Clay Reynolds Novella Competition.
Journals: *The Texas Review, The Beacon*
Book series: The Southern Poetry Anthology and Best Creative Nonfiction of the South.

Texas Tech University Press

Street Address:
1120 Main Street
Second Floor
Lubbock, TX 79409-1037

Mailing Address:
Box 41037
Lubbock, TX 79409-1037

Phone: 806.742.2982
Fax: 806.742.2979
Email: firstname.lastname@ttu.edu

Website and Social Media:
Website: www.ttupress.org
Facebook: www.facebook.com/ TTUPress
Twitter: @TTUPress

Orders:
Grantham Building
608 North Knoxville Avenue #120
Lubbock, TX 79415
Phone: 800.832.4042;
International: 806.742.2982
Fax: 806.742.2979
International fax: 806.742.2979

UK and European Distributor:
Eurospan

Staff
Director: Brian L. Ott
Managing Director: Joanna Conrad
Marketing and Sales Director: John Brock

Number of Press Staff: 4.5

Regular Member
Established: 1971
Title output 2017: 10
Titles currently in print: 452

Admitted to the Association: 1987
Title output 2018: 8
Journals published: 2

Editorial Program
American legal studies; American Indian studies; history and culture of Texas and the American West, the Great Plains, and modern Southeast Asia during and after the Vietnam War; border studies; natural history and natural science; poetry (by invitation only); nonfiction for young readers; sport in the American West; American roots music; renewable energy studies; and environmental history
Journals: *Conradiana; Helios*
Book series: American Liberty and Justice; Grover E. Murray Studies in the American Southwest; Peace and Conflict Series; Plains Histories; Walt McDonald First-Book Series in Poetry; Voice in the American West; Women, Gender, and the West

University of Tokyo Press

4-5-29 Komaba, Meguro-ku
Tokyo 153-0041, Japan

US Representative:
Columbia University Press

Phone: +81.3.6407.1921, +81.3.6407.1904
Fax: +81.3.6407.1582, +81.3.6407.1991
Email: info@utp.or.jp

Staff
President: Makoto Gonokami
Chairman of the Board: Shunya Yoshimi
Managing Director: Takuya Kuroda (email: kuroda@utp.or.jp)
Editorial Director: Mika Komatsu
Marketing Director: Hiroki Hashimoto
Production Director: Hiroshi Takagi
International Liaisons Executive: Kensuke Goto (email: gauteau@utp.or.jp)

Number of Press Staff: 33

Regular Member

Established: 1951
Title output 2017: 124
Titles currently in print: 4,700

Admitted to the Association: 1970
Title output 2018: 113

Editorial Program

Titles published in Japanese reflect the research carried out at the university in the humanities, social sciences, and natural sciences. Continuing series are published in biology, earth sciences, sociology, economics, philosophy, and Japanese art and historical studies. Special projects include publication of textbooks and reprinting of historical source materials.

English-language publishing began in 1960; special strengths include Japanese and Asian studies (including art, history, economics, law, and sociology). English-language publications also include translations of historical and important literary works and diaries.

University of Toronto Press

Book Publishing
800 Bay Street, Mezzanine
Toronto, ON M5Y 3A9 Canada

Phone: 416.978.2239
Fax: 416.978.4738
Email: publishing@utorontopress.com

UTP Distribution:
5201 Dufferin Street
North York, ON M3H 5T8 Canada
Phone: 416.667.7791

Journals Division:
5201 Dufferin Street
North York, ON M3H 5T8 Canada

Phone: 416.667.7810
Fax: 416.667.7832; 800.221.9985
Email: journals@utpress.utoronto.ca

UTP Distribution US Warehouse:
2250 Military Road
Tonawanda, NY 14150
Phone: 716.693.2768

Websites and Social Media:
Publishing: www.utorontopress.com
Journals: www.utpjournals.press
Blog: utorontopress.com/ca/blog
Distribution: www.utpdistribution.com
Facebook: www.facebook.com/utpress; www.facebook.com/utpjournals
Twitter: @utpress; @utpjournals
Instagram: www.instagram.com/utpress/

UK Representative:
Oxford Publicity Partnership Ltd.
gary.hall@oppuk.co.uk

UK & European Distribution:
NBN International

Japan Distribution:
MHM Limited

Staff
Administration
Indiv. email: firstinitiallastname@utpress.utoronto.ca
  President, Publisher and CEO: John Yates (ext. 7750)
  Vice President, HR & Administration: Lindsay Whillans (ext. 7784)
  Vice President, Finance: Shawn O'Grady (416.667.7765)
  Vice President, Distribution & MIS: Hamish Cameron (416.667.7773)
Book Publishing
Indiv. email: firstinitiallastname@utorontopress.com
  Vice President, Book Publishing: Lynn Fisher (ext. 2243)
  Publishing Coordinator: Charley LaRose (ext. 2237)
  Rights Coordinator: Marilyn McCormack (ext. 2223)
  Permissions Coordinator: Vanessa Pickett (ext. 2252)
Acquisitions Editorial
  Manager, Humanities Acquisitions: Suzanne Rancourt (classics, medieval, renaissance studies, Erasmus) (ext. 2239)
  Manager, Social Sciences Acquisitions: Jennifer DiDomenico (business & economics) (ext. 2259)
  Acquisitions Editors: Len Husband (Cdn history, native studies, philosophy) (ext. 2238); Mark Thompson (film, literature, cultural studies, book history, communications) (ext. 2231); Stephen Shapiro (history, literature, semiotics) (ext. 2233); Daniel Quinlan (political science & law) (ext. 2254); Jodie Lewchuk (anthropology, geography, sociology, urban studies) (ext. 2251); Meg Patterson (social work, education, medicine & health) (ext. 2230); Stephen Jones (science & technology) (ext. 4227); Textbooks: Anne Brackenbury (anthropology, criminology, geography, indigenous studies, social work, sociology, women's and gender studies) (ext. 2887); Natalie Fingerhut (history, Medieval studies) (ext. 2884); Mat Buntin (politics, international development

studies, human rights, security studies, Latin American studies, environmental studies, business) (ext. 4235)
Manuscript Editorial & Production
    Managing Editor: Lisa Jemison (ext. 2226)
    Production Manager: Ani Deyirmenjian (ext. 2227)
Electronic Publishing
    Electronic Publishing Coordinator: Barry Meikle (ext. 2232)
Sales & Marketing
    Director, Sales and Marketing: Jane Kelly (ext. 2268)
    Sales Manager: Michelle Lobkowicz (4231)
    Marketing Manager, Humanities: Anna Del Col (ext. 4224)
    Marketing Manager, Social Sciences: Cheryl Noseworthy (ext. 2253)
    Publicist: Chris Reed (ext. 2248)
    Advertising, Journal Review Coordinator: Sebastian Frye (ext. 2247)
    Marketing Coordinator: Inae Heo (ext. 2250)
    Marketing Specialist: Breanna Muir (ext. 2257)
    Awards & Events Coordinator: Ankit Pahwa (ext. 2260)
    Data & Web Coordinator: Bob Currer (ext. 2249)
    Sales & Marketing Coordinator: Joanna Kincaide (ext. 2240)
Journals (5201 Dufferin St.) (416.667.7777)
Indiv. email: firstinitiallastname@utpress.utoronto.ca
    Director, Journals: Antonia Pop (416.667.7838)
    Production Manager, Journals: Katie Yantzi (ext. 7971)
    Circulation & Distribution Manager: Adele D'Ambrosio (ext. 7781)
    Marketing Manager: Vesna Micic (ext. 7849)
UTP Distribution Centre
Indiv email: firstinitiallastname@utpress.utoronto.ca
    Vice President, Distribution & MIS: Hamish Cameron (416.667.7773)
    Manager, Customer Service: Mary Dinardo (416.667.7860)
    Manager, Client Publisher Services: Bessie Luciano (416.667.7946)
    Credit Manager: Clive Williams (416.667.7774)

Number of Press Staff: 240

Regular Member

Established: 1901	Admitted to the Association: 1937
Title output 2017: 180	Title output 2018: 170
Titles currently in print: 4,500	Journals published: 43

Editorial Program
UTP publishes scholarly books, serious non-fiction, course books and books for business professionals with a particular focus on: business & economics; classical studies; medieval studies; renaissance studies; Slavic studies; environmental studies; Erasmian studies; Victorian studies; English literature; Canadian studies; North American Studies; Canadian literature; cultural studies; literary theory and criticism; modern languages and literatures; philosophy; political science; law and criminology; religion and theology; education; Canadian and international history; history of science and medicine; sociology; anthropology; gender studies; Indigenous studies; social work; geography; urban studies; and women's studies. Submissions are not invited in poetry or fiction. Our textbook publishing program provides an alternative to larger textbook publishers, both for instructors looking for a refreshing change from the standard course book offerings and for potential authors who value creative and editorial license as well as the personal attention provided by our editors. The possibilities for rethinking how texts can be used in the classroom, along with new formats for their delivery, are endless, and we looks to partner with instructors and scholars in this innovative endeavour.
Journals: *Anthropologica; Canadian Bulletin of Medical History; Canadian Historical Review; Canadian Journal of Criminology and Criminal Justice; Canadian Journal of Film Studies; Canadian Journal of History; Canadian Journal of Human Sexuality; Canadian Journal of Information and Library Sciences; Canadian Journal of Program Evaluation; Canadian Journal of Women and the Law; Canadian Liver Journal; Canadian Modern Language Review; Canadian Public Policy; Cana-*

dian Review of American Studies; Canadian Theatre Review; Cartographica; Diaspora: A Journal of Transnational Studies; Eighteenth-Century Fiction; Florilegium; Genocide Studies International; International Journal of Canadian Studies; IJFAB: International Journal of Feminist Approached to Bioethics; Journal of the Association of Medical Microbiology and Infectious Disease Canada (JAMMI); Journal of Canadian Studies; Journal of Comparative Family Studies; Journal of Education for Library and Information Science; Journal of Military, Veteran and Family Health; Journal of Religion and Popular Culture; Journal of Scholarly Publishing; Journal of Veterinary Medical Education; Lexicons of Early Modern English; Modern Drama; Mouseion; National Gallery of Canada Review; Physiotherapy Canada; Publications of the Champlain Society; Seminar; The Tocqueville Review; Toronto Journal of Theology; Ultimate Reality and Meaning; University of Toronto Law Journal; University of Toronto Quarterly; Yearbook of Comparative Literature
New series: The L.M. Montgomery Library; The Canadian Experience of War. Studies in Atlantic Canadian History; Political Development Comparative Perspectives; Latinoamericana
Book series Anthropological Horizons; Asian Canadian Studies; Benjamin Disraeli Letters; Business & Sustainability Series; Canadian Cinema; Canadian Social History Series; Collected Works of Bernard Lonergan; Collected Works of Erasmus; Collected Works of Northrop Frye; Cultural Spaces; Dictionary of Canadian Biography; Digital Futures; Erasmus Studies; European Union Studies; Frye Studies; Global Suburbanism; Innovation, Creativity, and Governance in Canadian City-Regions; IPAC Series in Public Management and Governance; Japan and Global Society; Joanne Goodman Lectures; The Kenneth Michael Tanenbaum Series in Jewish Studies; Lonergan Studies; Lorenzo DaPonte Italian Library; Medieval Academy Books; Medieval Academy Reprints for Teaching; New Studies in Phenomenology and Hermeneutics; Osgoode Society for Canadian Legal History; Phoenix Supplementary Volumes; Provincial and Territorial Health System Profiles; Renaissance Society of America Reprint Texts; Robson Classical Lectures; Selected Correspondence of Bernard Shaw; Studies in Book and Print Culture; Studies in Comparative Political Economy and Public Policy; Studies in Gender and History; The James Scarth Gale Library of Korean Literature; The Munk Series on Global Affairs; Themes in Canadian History; Toronto Anglo Saxon Series; Toronto Iberic; Toronto Italian Studies; Toronto Old Norse-Icelandic Series; Toronto Studies in Medieval Law; Toronto Studies in Philosophy; Toronto Studies in Semiotics and Communication; UCLA Clark Memorial Library Series; University of Toronto Romance Series; UTP Insights. Textbook Series: Teaching Culture: UTP Ethnographies for the Classroom Anthropological Insights; ethnoGRAPHIC (new approaches to pedagogy, ethnography meets graphic novel); Readings in Medieval Civilizations and Cultures; Companions to Medieval History; Rethinking the Middle Ages; CHA/UTP International Themes and Issues; Johnson-Shoyama Series on Public Policy.
Imprints: Rotman-UTP Publishing and New Jewish Press

Trinity University Press

Street Address:
One Trinity Place
Services
San Antonio, TX 78212

Phone: 210.999.8884
Fax: 210.999.8838
Email: books@trinity.edu

Distribution:
Publishers Group West/Ingram Publisher

In-House Orders:
10.999.8884 ext. 8553;
Email: bmcgrego@trinity.edu

Website and Social Media:
Website: tupress.org/
Facebook: www.facebook.com/trinityuniversitypress/
Twitter: @tupress

Staff:
Director: Tom Payton (ext. 8882; email: tpayton@trinity.edu)
Senior Acquisitions Editor: Marguerite Avery (ext. 7344; email: mavery@trinity.edu)
Managing Editor: Sarah Nawrocki (ext. 8881; email: snawrock@trinity.edu)
Marketing Manager: Burgin Streetman (ext. 8947; email: bstreetm@trinity.edu)
Business Manager: Lee Ann Sparks (ext. 8886; email: lsparks@trinity.edu)
Assistant Editor: Steffanie Mortis (ext. 8897; email: smortis@trinity.edu)
Sales Representative: Bridget McGregor (ext. 8553; email: bmcgrego@trinity.edu)

Number of Press Staff: 7

Regular Member
Established: 2002
Title output 2017: 12
Titles currently in print: 225

Admitted to the Association: 2018
Title output 2018: 12

Editorial Program
The press publishes books in these areas:
- Nature and the environment. Wide-ranging and world-changing titles that help us to understand humans' place and effects on the only world we've got.
- The Writer's World. Acclaimed anthologies in this series explore what it means to write elsewhere on the globe: open a book, open a world.
- Literary works. Narrative prose books taking creative approaches to topics that range in an unpredictable variety but at their heart share literary style and virtuosity.
- Regional books. Surprising stories, cultural narratives, and unique explorations that enhance our literacy about the places we live.
Architecture and landscape. Thoughtful and powerful examinations about our built and shaped urban and natural environments with an eye toward creating sustainable and beautiful spaces.

UCL Press

University College London (UCL)
Gower Street,
London, WC1E 6BT
UK
Phone: +44 (0) 20 7679 2000
email: uclpresspublishing@ucl.ac.uk

Orders (US and Canada):
Chicago Distribution Center
11030 South Langley Ave
Chicago, IL 60628 USA
Phone: 800.621.2736 (US & Canada)
Email: custserv@press.uchicago.edu

Website and Social Media:
Website: www.ucl.ac.uk/ucl-press
Facebook: www.facebook.com/uclpresspublishing
Twitter: @UCLpress
Instagram: @uclpress

UK and Rest of World:
NBN International

UK Representative:
Compass Academic

Staff
Head of Publishing: Lara Speicher (+44 (0) 203 54 9749; email: l.speicher@ucl.ac.uk)
Publishing Assistant: Paz Berlese (+44 (0) 203 549 5696; email: p.berlese@ucl.ac.uk)
Commissioning Editor: Dr. Chris Penfold, (+4(4 (0) 207 679 2612; email: c.penfold@ucl.ac.uk)
Production Manager: Jaimee Biggins (+44 (0) 203 549 5754; email: j.biggins@ucl.ac.uk)
Marketing and Distribution Manager: Alison Fox (+44 (0) 20 3108 7343; email:
    alison.fox@ucl.ac.uk)
Journals Manager: Ian Caswell (+44 (0) 203 549 5749; email: i.caswell@ucl.ac.uk)

Number of Press Staff: 7

Regular Member
Established: 2015
Title output 2017: 35
Titles currently in print: 97

Admitted to the Association: 2018
Title output 2018: 42
Journals published: 8

Editorial Program
Academic titles and serious works of nonfiction in anthropology, archaeology, area studies; built environment/architecture; economics; education; history; history of art; geography; academic law and jurisprudence; literary criticism; linguistics; media and communication studies; philosophy and political science; Sociology; sustainability and development studies and translation studies.
Journals: *Architecture_MPS; Europe and the World (A Law Review); International Journal of Social Pedagogy; Jewish Historical Studies; Journal of Bentham Studies; Radical Americas; The London Journal of Canadian Studies; The Journal of Sylvia Townsend Warner Society*
Book Series: Comparative Literature and Culture; Economic Exposures in Asia; FABRICATE; FRINGE; Global Dutch; Grammars of World and Minority. Languages; Housing – Critical Futures; Literature and Translation; Modern Americas; Spotlights, Why We Post

United States Institute of Peace Press

2301 Constitution Avenue, NW
Washington, DC 20037

Phone: 202.457.1700
Fax: 202.223.9320
Email: (user I.D)@usip.org

Website and Social Media:
Website: bookstore.usip.org
Facebook: United States Institute of Peace
Twitter: @USIP

Orders:
PO Box 605
Herndon, VA 20172
Phone: 800.868.8064; 703.661.1590
Fax: 703.661.1501
Email:
usipmail@presswarehouse.com

UK/European Distributor:
NBN International

Canadian Representative:
Renouf Books

Asia and the Pacific:
East-West Export Books (EWEB)

Staff
Director of Publishing Operations: Jake Harris (email: jharris)
Sales, Rights, and Marketing Specialist: Cecilia Stoute (email: cstoute)
Managing Editor: Richard Walker (email: rwalker)
Publication Production Specialist: Christopher Brown (email: cbrown)
Publications Assistant: Sarah Mink (email: smink)

Number of Press Staff: 6

Regular Member
Established: 1991
Title output 2017: 10
Titles currently in print: 210

Admitted to the Association: 1993
Title output 2018: 10

Editorial Program
The Press publishes books that are based on work supported by the Institute. Created by Congress in 1984, the Institute is an independent, nonpartisan institution that works to prevent, mitigate, and resolve violent international conflicts. The Institute's publications range across the spectrum of international relations, including conflict prevention, management, and resolution; diplomacy and negotiation; human rights; mediation and facilitation; foreign policy; gender; ethnopolitics; political science; and religion and ethics.
Book series: Academy Guides; Cross-Cultural Negotiation Series; Peacemaker's Toolkits

W. E. Upjohn Institute for Employment Research

300 South Westnedge Avenue
Kalamazoo, MI 49007-4686

Orders:
Phone: 888.227.8569

Phone: 269.343.4330
Fax: 269.343.7310
Email: publications@upjohn.org
Indiv: lastname@upjohn.org

Website and Social Media:
Website: www.upjohn.org
Repository: research.upjohn.org
Facebook: facebook.com/Upjohn.Institute
Twitter: @upjohninstitute

Staff
Director of Publications: Brad Hershbein (269.343.5541)
Assistant to the Director: Claire Black (269.343.5541)
Manager of Publications and Marketing: Richard Wyrwa (269.343.5541)
Editor: Ben Jones (269.343.5541)
Editor: Allison Colosky (269.343.5541)
Production Coordinator: Erika Jackson (269.343.5541)

Number of Press Staff: 6

Regular Member
Established: 1945
Title output 2017: 7
Titles currently in print: 2,229

Admitted to the Association: 1997
Title output 2018: 4

Editorial Program
Scholarly works on employment-related issues; labor economics; current issues in the social sciences, with an emphasis on public policy. Books are authored by resident research staff and other scholars in the academic and professional communities. The Institute also publishes working papers, policy papers, policy briefs, and technical reports authored by the resident research staff and grantees; a quarterly journal on the West Michigan economy, *Business Outlook for West Michigan*, and a quarterly newsletter, *Employment Research*.
Imprints: Upjohn Press

University of Utah Press

J. Willard Marriott Library, Suite 5400
295 South 1500 East, Suite 5400
Salt Lake City, UT 84112-0860

Fax: 801.581.3365
Indiv: (user I.D.)@utah.edu

Orders:
Chicago Distribution Center
11030 South Langley Ave
Chicago, IL 60628
Phone: 800.621.2736
Fax: 800.621.8476

Website and Social Media:
Website: www.UofUpress.com
Facebook: www.facebook.com/uofupress
Twitter: @UofUPress
Instagram: uofupress

UK/European Representative:
Eurospan University Press Group

Staff
Director: Glenda Cotter (801.585.0083; email: glenda.cotter)
Acquisitions: Reba Rauch (anthropology and archaeology, linguistics, natural history, regional guidebooks) (801.585.0081; email: reba.rauch); Tom Krause (American history; American West, Mormon studies, folklore, Middle East studies, religious studies, environment) (801.585.3203; email: tom.krause)
Managing Editor: Patrick Hadley (email: patrick.hadley)
Design & Production Manager: Jessica Booth (email: jessica.booth)
Sales and Marketing Manager: Hannah New (801.585.9786; email: hannah.new)
Business Manager, Rights and Permissions: Janalyn Guo (email: janalyn.guo)

Number of Press Staff: 7

Regular Member
Established: 1949
Title output 2017: 32
Titles currently in print: 52346

Admitted to the Association: 1979
Title output 2018: 29

Editorial Program
Anthropology and archaeology, linguistics, Mesoamerica, America Indian studies, creative nonfiction, environmental history, folklore, history of the North American West, Utah and Mormon studies, Middle East studies, natural history, nature writing, regional guidebooks, and general titles of regional interest.
Book series: Agha Shahid Ali Prize in Poetry; Foundations of Archaeological Inquiry; Don D. and Catherine S. Fowler Prize (Anthropology & Archaeology); The Juanita Brooks Prize in Mormon Studies; Perspectives on the Mormon Experience; Tanner Lectures on Human Values; Utah Series in Middle East Studies; University of Utah Anthropological Papers; The Wallace Stegner Prize in Environmental Humanities

Vanderbilt University Press

Street Address:
2014 Broadway
Suite 320
Nashville, TN 37203

Mailing Address:
VU Station B 351813
Nashville, TN 37235

Phone: 615.322.3585
Fax: 615.343.8823
Email: vupress@vanderbilt.edu
Indiv: firstname.lastname@vanderbilt.edu

Customer Service/Order Fulfillment:
Longleaf Services, Inc.
116 South Boundary Street
Chapel Hill, NC 27514-3808
Phone: 800.848.6224
Fax: 800.272.6817

Website and Social Media:
Website: www.vanderbiltuniversitypress.com
Facebook: www.facebook.com/pages/Vanderbilt-University-Press/46334873151
Twitter: @VanderbiltUP

Canadian Distributor:
Scholarly Book Services

UK/European Distributor:
Eurospan

Staff
Associate Provost for Academic Initiatives and Interim Director: Dawn Turton
Acquisitions Editor: Beth Kressel Itkin
Assistant Editor: Zach Gresham
Managing Editor: Joell Smith-Borne
Marketing Manager: Betsy Phillips
Marketing and New Media Associate: Jenna Phillips
Business Manager: Greta Thomas

Number of Press Staff: 7

Regular Member
Established: 1940
Title output 2017: 17
Titles currently in print: 345

Admitted to the Association: 1993
Title output 2018: 20

Editorial Program
Scholarly books and serious nonfiction in most areas of the humanities, the social sciences, health care, and higher education. Special interests include health care and social issues; cargiving and family policy; studies of race, class, gender, and sexuality; human rights and social justice; public policy; Hispanic and Latin American studies; African American studies; sociology and anthropology; and regional books.
Copublishing program: Country Music Foundation

The University of Virginia Press

Street Address:
Bemiss House
210 Sprigg Lane
Charlottesville, VA 22903-0608

Mailing Address:
PO Box 400318
Charlottesville, VA 22904-4318

Phone: 434.924.3468
Fax: 434.982.2655
Email: vapress@virginia.edu
Indiv: (user I.D.)@virginia.edu

Warehouse Address:
Longleaf Services, Inc
116 S. Boundary Street
Chapel Hill, NC 27514-3808
Telephone: 800-848-6224
Fax: 800-272-6817
orders@longleafservices.org

Website and Social Media:
Website: www.upress.virginia.edu
Facebook: www.facebook.com/uvapress
Twitter: @uvapress

UK/European Representative:
Eurospan

Canadian Representative:
Scholarly Book Services

Staff

Director: Mark H. Saunders (434.924.6064; email: msaunders)
Intellectual Property and Database Manager: Mary MacNeil (434.924.3468; email: mmm5w)
Acquisitions Editorial: Eric Brandt, Assistant Director and Editor-in-Chief (humanities)
    (434.982.3033; email: ebrandt)
    Editors: Richard K. Holway, Senior Executive Editor (history and social sciences) (434.924.7301;
    email: rkh2a); Boyd Zenner (architecture, environmental studies, ecocriticism, and regional)
    (434.924.1373; email: bz2v)
    Associate Editor: Angie Hogan (literary and cultural studies, history of science) (434.924.3361;
    email: arhogan)
    Acquisitions Assistant: Helen Chandler (434.924.4725; email: hc7kb)
    Electronic Imprint: Mark H. Saunders, Rotunda Manager (434.924.6064; email: mhs5u)
    Editorial and Technical Manager: David Sewell, Manager of Digital Initiatives, UVAP
    (434.924.9973; email: dsewell)
    Rotunda Marketing and Sales Manager: Jason Coleman (434.924.1450; email: jcoleman)
    Editorial and Technical Specialist: Patricia Searl (434.982.2310; email: pls4e)
Editorial: Ellen Satrom, Managing Editor (434.924.6065; email: egs6s)
    Assistant Managing Editor and Senior Editor (BUS/SAH Archipedia): Mark Mones
    (434.924.6066; email: emm4t)
    Project Editor: Morgan Myers (434.924.6067; email: jm3yg)
    Design and Production: Ellen Satrom, Editorial, Design, and Production Manager (434.924.6065;
    email: egs6s)
    Production Manager: Anne Hegeman, (434.924.3585; email: aeh7v)
    Senior Designer and Assistant Production Manager: Cecilia Sorochin (434.924.6069; email:
    scs6ak)
    Editorial, Design, and Production Coordinator: Nicolle Coggins (434.982.2704; email: ncoggins)
Marketing: Jason Coleman, Marketing & Sales Director (434.924.4150; email: jcoleman
    Publicity and Social Media Director: Emily Grandstaff (434.982.2932; email: egrandstaff)
    Marketing Associate: Emma Donovan (434.924.6070; email: efd4s)
Business Manager: Duncan Pickett (434.924.6068; email: fdp7e)
    Customer Service and Operations Manager: Brenda Fitzgerald (434.924.3469; email: bwf)

Number of Press Staff: 20

Regular Member

Established: 1963
Title output 2017: 62
Titles currently in print: 1,688

Admitted to the Association: 1964
Title output 2018: 50

Editorial Program
Scholarly and general trade publications in humanities and social sciences, with concentrations in American history; African American studies; Southern studies; political science; literary and cultural studies, with particular strengths in African and Caribbean studies; Enlightenment studies; Victorian studies; religious studies; architecture and landscape studies; environmental studies; animal studies; Virginiana.

The Press also publishes digital publications, primarily critical and documentary editions, and an architectural dictionary, through Rotunda. Documentary editions (ongoing): Selected Papers of John Jay; The Papers of Abraham Lincoln; The Papers of James Madison; The Diaries of Gouverneur Morris; The Eleanor Roosevelt Papers; The Papers of George Washington; The Papers of Andrew Jackson Digital Edition; The Dolly Madison Digital Edition; The Papers of Woodrow Wilson Digital Edition.

Book series: The American South; American Spirituality; Buildings of the United States; CARAF Books (Caribbean and African Literature translated from the French); The Carter G. Woodson Institute Series in Black Studies; Constitutionalism and Democracy; Contemplative Sciences; Cultural Frames, Framing Culture; Early American Histories; Jeffersonian America; Kapnick Lectures; The Malcolm Lester Phi Beta Kappa Lectures on Liberal Arts and Public Life; MidCentury: Architecture, Landscape, Urbanism, and Design; Miller Center Studies on the Presidency; A Nation Divided: Studies in the Civil War Era; New World Studies; The Page-Barbour and Richard Lecture Series; Peculiar Bodies: Stories and Histories; Race, Ethnicity, and Politics; Reconsiderations in Southern African History; Richard E. Myers Lecture Series; SAH/BUS City Guide; Studies in Early Modern German History; Studies in Pure Sociology; Studies in Religion and Culture; Traditions and Transformations in Tibetan Buddhism; Under the Sign of Nature: Explorations in Ecocriticism; Victorian Literature and Culture; Walker Cowen Memorial Prize in Eighteenth-Century Studies; Writing the Early Americas
Imprints: Darden Business School Imprint

University of Washington Press

Street Address:
4333 Brooklyn Avenue NE
Seattle, WA 98105

Mailing Address:
Campus Box 359570
Seattle, WA 98195

Phone: 206.543.4050
Fax: 206.543.3932
Email: (user I.D.)@uw.edu

Orders:
Hopkins Fulfillment Services
Phone: 800.537.5487 or 410.516.6956
Fax: 410.516.6998
Email: hfscustserv@press.jhu.edu

Website and Social Media:
Website: washington.edu/uwpress
Facebook: facebook.com/UniversityofWashingtonPress
Twitter: twitter.com/uwapress/
YouTube: youtube.com/uwashingtonpress/
Pinterest: pinterest.com/uwapress/
Instagram: instagram.com/uwpress/
Tumblr: uwpress.tumblr.com/

EU, Middle East, & Asia-Pacific Reps.
Combined Academic Publishers

Canadian Representative:
University of British Columbia Press

Staff
Administration:
  Director: Nicole Mitchell (206.685.9373; email: nfmm)
  Assistant to the Director: Rebecca Brinbury (206.221.3597; email: rbrinson)
  Grants and Digital Projects: Beth Fuget (206.616.0818; email: bfuget)
  Assistant Director of Advancement: Meredith Wisti (206.543.3056; email: wistim)
Acquisitions:
  Editor-in-Chief: Larin McLaughlin (critical ethnic studies; American studies; Asian American studies; women's, gender, and sexuality studies; Native and Indigenous studies; Asian American studies; visual culture) (206.221.4995; email: lmclaugh)
  Executive Editor: Lorri Hagman (Asian studies, cultural and environmental anthropology) (206.221.4989; email: lhagman)
  Senior Acquisitions Editor: Andrew Berzanskis (social justice, environmental history, general interest books about science, the environment, and the Pacific Northwest) (email: andrewlb)
  Associate Acquisitions Editor: Mike Baccam (Asian American studies, Western US history, critical ethnic studies) (206.897.1738; email: mbaccam),
  Editorial Assistant: Neecole Bostick (206.221.4940; email: neecoleb)
Editorial, Design, and Production:
  EDP Manager: Margaret Sullivan (206.221.4987; email: mksu)
  Senior Project Editor: Julie Van Pelt (206.685.9165; email: jvp)
  Production Manager and Coordinator: Shirley Woo (206.221.4993; email: surely2)
  Art Director: Katrina Noble (206.221.7004; email: krnoble)
Marketing and Sales:
  Director of Marketing and Sales: Michael Campbell (206.221.5889; email: moc3)
  Publicity Manager: M'Bilia Meekers (206.221.4994; email: mmeekers)
  Exhibits and Direct Mail Manager: Julie Fergus (206.543.4053; email: jaf88)
  Catalog and Metadata Manager: Kathleen Pike Jones (206.221.4986; email: kpike)
Finance and Operations:
  CFO: Rebecca Schrader (206.221.5892; email: recs)
  Contracts and Rights Manager: Neal Swain (206.221.4997; email: nmswain)
  Accounts Receivable: Linda Tom (206.543.4722; email: lindatom)
  Accounts Payable: Heidi Olson (206.543.2858; email: hoatar)

Number of Press Staff: 21.5

Regular Member
Established: 1920   Admitted to the Association: 1937
Title output 2017: 81   Title output 2018: 78
Titles currently in print: 1,276

Editorial Program
American studies; anthropology; art history and visual culture; Asian American studies; Asian studies; critical ethnic studies; environmental history; Jewish studies; Native American and Indigenous studies; nature and environment; Scandinavian studies; sustainable design; women's, gender and sexuality studies; and Western and Pacific Northwest history. The press also publishes a broad range of books about the Pacific Northwest for general readers, often in partnership with regional museums, cultural organizations, and local tribes.
Book series: Center for Korea Studies Publications; Classics of Asian American Literature (no editor); Classics of Chinese Thought; Critical Dialogues in Southeast Asian Studies; Culture, Place, and Nature: Studies in Anthropology and Environment; Decolonizing Feminisms: Antiracist and Transnational Praxis; Feminist Technosciences; Food, People, Planet; Gandharan Buddhist Texts; Gandharan Studies; Global Re-Visions; Global South Asia; Indigenous Confluences; Korean Studies of the Henry M. Jackson School of International Studies; Native Art of the Pacific Northwest: A Bill Holm Center Series; New Directions in Scandinavian Studies; Pacific Northwest Poetry Series; Samuel and Althea Stroum Lectures in Jewish Studies; Scott and Laurie Oki Series in Asian American Studies; Studies on Ethnic Groups in China; Sustainable Design Solutions from the Pacific Northwest; Weyerhaeuser Environmental Books
Publishing partners (world rights unless noted): Art Gallery of New South Wales; Fowler

Museum at UCLA; International Sculpture Center; LM Publishers; Lost Horse Press; Lynx House Press; Museum for African Art; National Gallery of Australia (North America); Power Institute of Fine Arts (North America); Silkworm Books (world outside Southeast Asia); UCLA Chicano Studies Research Center

Washington State University Press

Cooper Publications Building
2300 Grimes Way
PO Box 645910
Pullman, WA 99164-5910

Phone: 509.335.7880
Fax: 509.335.8568
Email: wsupress@wsu.edu
Indiv: (user I.D.)@wsu.edu

Orders:
Phone: 800.354.7360; 509.335.7880

Canadian Representatives:
Ingram Book Company
Baker & Taylor Books

Website and Social Media:
Website: wsupress.wsu.edu
Facebook: www.facebook.com/pages/
   Washington-State-University-Press/121327661093
YouTube: www.youtube.com/channel/UClaaQ895LjckK41nt7MmlzA

Staff
Director: Edward Sala (509.335.3518; email: sala)
Editor-in-Chief: Beth DeWeese (509.335.8821; email: beth.deweese)
Marketing Manager: Caryn Lawton (509.335.3518; email: lawton)
Order Fulfillment/Operations: Kerry Darnall (509.335.7880; email: kdarnall)
Permissions: Beth DeWeese (509.335.8821; email: beth.deweese)

Number of Press Staff: 3.2

Regular Member
Established: 1927
Title output 2017: 9
Titles currently in print: 162

Admitted to the Association: 1987
Title output 2018: 8
Journals published: 2

Editorial Program
Pacific Northwest; natural history; history, science, politics, and culture relating to the region; Western American history; ethnic studies; Native American studies; women's studies; and environmental issues.
   The Press distributes publications for the Oregon-California Trails Association, Oregon Writers Colony, Wenatchee Valley Museum and Cultural Center, WSU Museum of Art, WSU School of Hospitality Business Management, WSU Thomas S. Foley Institute, Washington State Historical Society, Anarene Books, and Yakt Publishing.
Journals: *Northwest Science*; *We Proceeded On*

Wayne State University Press

The Leonard N. Simons Bldg.
4809 Woodward Avenue
Detroit, MI 48201.1309

Orders:
Phone: 800.WSU.READ (978.7323)

Phone: 313.577.6126
Fax: 313.577.6131
Email: (user I.D.)@wayne.edu

Website and Social Media:
Website: wsupress.wayne.edu
Facebook: www.facebook.com/wsupress
Instagram: www.instagram.com/wsupress
Pinterest: www.pinterest.com/wsupress
Youtube: www.youtube.com/user/wsupress1
Tumblr: wsupress.tumblr.com
Twitter: @WSUPress

International Distributor:
East-West Export Books

Canadian Distributor:
Scholarly Book Services

UK/European Distributor:
Eurospan Group

Staff
Interim Director: Kathryn Wildfong (313.577.6070; email: k.wildfong)
Rights and Permissions: Ceylan Akturk (313.577.6130; email: ceylan.akturk)
Acquisitions Editorial: Annie Martin, Editor-in-Chief (313.577.8335; email: annie.martin)
    Acquisitions Editor: Marie Sweetman (313.577.4220; email: marie.sweetman)
Editorial, Design, and Production: Kristin Harpster, EDP Manager (313.577.4604; email: kmharpster)
    Assistant Editorial Manager and Reprints Manager: Carrie Downes Teefey (313.577.6123; email: carrie.downes)
    Senior Designer: Rachel Ross (313.577.4626; email: rachelsross)
Marketing/Sales: Emily Nowak, Marketing and Sales Manager (313.577.6128; email: enowak)
    Promotion and Direct Mail Manager: Kristina Stonehill (313.577.6127; email: kristina.stonehill)
    Advertising and Exhibits Manager: Jamie Jones (313.577.6054; email: jamie.jones2)
Journals: Tara Reeser, Journals Manager (313.577.4607; email: tara.reeser)
    Journals Marketing and Sales Coordinator: Julie Warheit (313.577.4603; email: julie.warheit)
Business: Andrew Kaufman, Business Manager (313.577.3671; email: akaufman)
    Fulfillment Manager: Theresa Martinelli (313.577.6126; email: theresa.martinelli)
    Accounts Receivable: DeLisa Fields (313.577.6257; email: delisafields)
    Warehouse Manager: Todd Richards (313.577.4619; email: aa5624)
    Shipping: Aaron Hearn (313.577.4609; email: eu7890)
IT: Bonnie Russell, Technical Project Manager (313.577.1283; email: bonnie.russell)

Number of Press Staff: 17.5

Regular Member
Established: 1941
Title output 2017: 44
Titles currently in print: 1,383

Admitted to the Association: 1956
Title output 2018: 34
Journals published: 11

Editorial Program
Scholarly books and serious nonfiction, with special interests in regional and local history, literature, and culture; African American studies; environmental studies; ethnic studies; fairy tales and folklore; film and media studies; gender studies; immigration studies; Jewish studies; queer studies; urban studies. Poetry, short fiction, and creative nonfiction by Michigan authors
Journals: *Antipodes; Criticism; Discourse; Fairy Tale Review; Framework; Human Biology; Jewish Film & New Media; Marvels and Tales; Merrill Palmer Quarterly; Narrative Culture; Storytelling, Self, Society*

Book series: Contemporary Approaches to Film and Media; Series in Fairy-Tale Studies; Great Lakes Books; Made in Michigan Writers Series; Queer Screens; Raphael Patai Series in Jewish Folklore and Anthropology; TV Milestones
Joint imprints, copublishing, and distribution programs: University of Alberta Press; Broadside/Lotus Press; Cranbrook Institute of Science; Ladyslipper Press
Imprints: Painted Turtle Books

Wesleyan University Press

Editorial Offices:
215 Long Lane
Middletown, CT 06459

Phone: 860.685.7711
Fax: 860.685.7712
Email: (user I.D.)@wesleyan.edu

Orders:
Hopkins Fulfillment Services
Phone: 800.537.5487 or 410.516.6956
Email: hfscustserv@press.jhu.edu

Website and Social Media:
Website: www.wesleyan.edu/wespress/
Facebook: www.facebook.com/pages/Middletown-CT/
  Wesleyan-University-Press/101994439844863
Twitter: @weslpress

UK/European Representative:
Eurospan

Canadian Representative:
University of British Columbia Press

Staff
Director/Editor-in-Chief: Suzanna Tamminen (860.685.7727; email: stamminen)
Marketing Manager: Jaclyn Wilson (860.685.7725; email: jwilson05)
Publicist: Stephanie Elliott Prieto (860.685.7723; email: selliott)

Number of Press Staff: 3

Regular Member
Established: 1957

Title output 2017: 28
Titles currently in print: 520

Admitted to the Association: 2001
(Former membership: 1966-1991)
Title output 2018: 24

Editorial Program
The current editorial program focuses on poetry, music, dance, science fiction studies, film/TV/media studies, regional studies, and American studies.
Book series: Wesleyan Poetry; Music/Culture; Early Classics of Science Fiction; Garnet Books

The University of the West Indies Press

7A Gibraltar Hall Road
Kingston 7
Jamaica, West Indies
Phone: 876.977.2659/702.4082
Fax: 876.977.2660
Email: uwipress@uwimona.edu.jm

US and Caribbean Orders:
Longleaf Services
116 South Boundary St.
Chapel Hill, NC 27514-3808
Phone: 800.848.6224
Fax: 800.272.6817

Website and Social Media:
Website: www.uwipress.com
Facebook: www.facebook.com/uwipress
YouTube: www.youtube.com/user/uwipress
Twitter: @UWIPRESS

UK/European Distributor:
Eurospan Group

Canadian Distributor:
Scholarly Book Services

Staff
Director: Dr. Joseph B. Powell (email: joseph.powell@uwimona.edu.jm)
Rights & Permissions/Finance Manager: Nadine D. Buckland (email: nadine.buckland@uwimona.edu.jm)
Marketing & Sales Manager: Donna Muirhead (email: donna.muirhead@uwimona.edu.jm)
Editorial & Production Project Manager: Shivaun Hearne (email: uwipress.edp@uwimona.edu.jm
Accountant: Jodie McBean Douglas (email: jodie.mcbean02@uwimona.edu.jm)

Number of Press Staff: 9

Regular Member
Established: 1992
Title output 2017: 16
Titles currently in print: 432

Admitted to the Association: 2005
Title output 2018: 18
Journals published: 3

Editorial Program
Scholarly books in the humanities and social sciences with an emphasis on Caribbean cultural studies, gender studies, history, literature, economics, education, environmental studies, sociology, political science, linguistics, legal studies, medical studies, psychology, media studies, and general interest.
Journals: *Journal of Caribbean History* (a peer-reviewed journal published by the University of the West Indies Press on behalf of the Departments of History and Archaeology of the University of the West Indies); *Caribbean Journal of Psychology* (a peer-reviewed journal published by the University of the West Indies Press on behalf of the University of the West Indies School for Graduate Studies and Research and the Departments of Sociology, Psychology and Social Work, University of the West Indies, Mona campus); *Journal of Law, Governance & Society* (a peer-reviewed journal published by the University of the West Indies Press on behalf of the Faculty of Law, The University of the West Indies).
Book series: Caribbean Biography Series
Imprints: University of the West Indies Press; Canoe Press

West Virginia University Press

Street Address:
Bicentennial House
1535 Mileground Road
Morgantown, WV 26506

Mailing Address:
PO Box 6295
Morgantown, WV 26506-6295

Phone: 304.293.8400
Fax: 304.293.6585

Website and Social Media:
Website: www.wvupress.com
Facebook: www.facebook.com/
westvirginiauniversitypress
Twitter: @wvupress

Order Fulfillment and Distribution:
Chicago Distribution Center
11030 South Langley Ave.
Chicago, IL 60628
Phone: 800.621.2736
Fax: 800.621.8476

UK Representative:
Eurospan

Staff
Director: Derek Krissoff (304.293.8403; email: derek.krissoff@mail.wvu.edu)
Marketing Manager/Fiction Editor: Abby Freeland (304.293.6188; email: abby.freeland@mail.wvu. edu)
Production Manager/Art Director: Than Saffel (304.293.6185; email: than.saffel@mail.wvu.edu)
Managing Editor: Sara Georgi (304.293.6186; email: sara.georgi@mail.wvu.edu)
Editor-at-Large: Elizabeth Catte (email: elizabeth.catte@gmail.com)
Office Manager: Floann Downey (304.293.8402; email: floann.downey@mail.wvu.edu)

Number of Press Staff: 9

Regular Member
Established: 1963
Title output 2017: 19
Titles currently in print: 206

Admitted to the Association: 2003
Title output 2018: 23
Journals published: 5

Editorial Program
Serious works of nonfiction in the humanities social sciences, with a particular emphasis on energy, environment, and resources; American history; Appalachian studies; and higher education. WVU Press also has a small but highly regarded program in fiction and creative nonfiction.
Journals: *Education and Treatment of Children; Essays in Medieval Studies; Tolkien Studies; Victorian Poetry; West Virginia History*
Book series: Histories of Capitalism and the Environment; Energy and Society; Radical Natures; In Place; Gender, Feminism, and Geography; Sounding Appalachia; Regenerations: African American Literature and Culture; Rural Studies; Teaching and Learning in Higher Education; West Virginia and Appalachia Series; Salvaging the Anthropocene

Wilfrid Laurier University Press

75 University Avenue West
Waterloo, ON N2L 3C5 Canada

Phone: 519.884.0710 ext. 6124
Fax: 519.725.1399
Email: press@wlu.ca
Indiv: (user I.D.)@ wlu.ca

Website and Social Media:
Website: www.wlupress.wlu.ca
Blog: nestor.wlu.ca/blog/
Facebook: www.facebook.com/wlupress
Twitter: @wlupress
Instagram: wlu.press

Canadian Distributor:
UTP Distribution

US Distributor:
Ingram Publisher Services

UK/European Distributor:
Gazelle Book Services Limited

Staff
Director: Lisa Quinn (ext. 2843; email: lquinn)
Senior Editor: Siobhan McMenemy (ext. 3782; email: smcmenemy)
Managing Editor: Rob Kohlmeier (ext. 6119; email: rkohlmeier)
Production Coordinator: Michael Bechthold (ext. 6122; email: mbechthold)
Digital Projects Coordinator: Murray Tong (ext. 3029; email: mtong)
Sales and Marketing Coordinator: Clare Hitchens (ext. 2665; email: chitchens)
Marketing Assistant: Marian Toledo-Candelaria (ext. 2894; email: mtoledocandelaria)f

Number of Press Staff: 7

Regular Member
Established: 1974
Title output 2017: 28
Titles currently in print: 765

Admitted to the Association: 1986
Title output 2018: 28

Editorial Program
Scholarly titles and comprehensively researched titles for general audiences in the humanities
and social sciences, including: Canadian art; Canadian literature; comic and graphic narrative
studies; cultural studies; environmental studies; family studies; film and media studies; gender
and women's studies; history; indigenous studies; life writing, including memoirs; literary criticism; literature in translation; military history; music; poetry; political philosophy; politics; regional
culture and history; religious studies; social work; sociology.
Book series and joint imprints: Canadian Command, Unit and Formation Histories; Canadian
Commentaries; Centre for Memory and Testimony Studies; Collected Works of Florence Nightin-
gale; Crossing Lines: International Comics and Graphic Narrative Studies; Cultural Studies; Early
Canadian Literature; Environmental Humanities; Film and Media Studies; Indigenous Studies;
Laurier Centre for Military, Strategic and Disarmament Studies; Laurier Poetry; Laurier Studies in
Political Philosophy; Life Writing; SickKids Community and Mental Health; Studies in Childhood
and Family in Canada; Toronto International Film Festival; TransCanadas; WCGS German Studies

The University of Wisconsin Press

1930 Monroe Street, 3rd Floor
Madison, WI 53711-2059

Phone: 608.263.1110
Fax: 608.263.1120
Email: uwiscpress@uwpress.wisc.edu
Indiv: (user I.D.)@wisc.edu
(unless otherwise indicated)

Orders:
Chicago Distribution Center
11030 South Langley Ave.
Chicago, IL 60628-3892
Phone: 800.621.2736; 773.702.7000
Fax: 800.621.8476; 773.702.7212

Website and Social Media:
Website: uwpress.wisc.edu
Blog: uwpress.wisc.edu/blog
Facebook: University of Wisconsin Press
Twitter: @UWiscPress
GoodReads: UW Press

UK Distributor:
Eurospan

Staff
Director: Dennis Lloyd (608.263.1101; email: dlloyd2)
Subsidiary Rights and Permissions Manager: Anne McKenna (608.263.1131; email: rights@uwpress.wisc.edu)
Editor-in-Chief: TBA
    Executive Editor: Gwen Walker (608.263.1123; email: gcwalker) (American history and politics, environmental studies, Irish history, human rights, Latin American studies, Russian/East European studies, Southeast Asian studies, regional Wisconsin history and natural history)
    Assistant Editor: Amber Rose (608.263.1134; email: ajrose2) (Classics, folklore)
    Acquisitions Assistants: Anna Muenchrath (608.263.1134; email: muenchrath); Paul Grant (608.263.1134; email: pgrant)
Managing Editor: Adam Mehring (608.263.0856; email: amehring)
    Senior Editor: Sheila McMahon (608.263.1133; email: samcmahon)
Production Manager: Terry Emmrich (608.263.0731; email: temmrich)
Art Director: Jennifer Conn (608.263.0732; email: jeconn)
    Senior Compositor: Scott Lenz (608.263.0794; email: sjlenz)
Marketing and Sales Manager: Casey LaVela (608.263.0814; email: casey.lavela)
Publicity Manager: Kaitlin Svabek (608.263.0734; email: svabek)
Journals Manager: Toni Gunnison (608.263.0667; email: toni.gunnison)
    Journals Production Manager: John Ferguson (608.263.0669; email: john.ferguson)
    Editorial Assistant: Chloe Lauer (608.263.0534; email: chloe.lauer)
    Journals Marketing Specialist: Claire Eder (608.262.7652; email: ceeder)
Business and Operations Manager: Ryan Pingel (608.263.1137; email: rpingel)
    Accountant: Pahnia Lee (608.890.4615; email: plee76)

Number of Press Staff: 19

Regular Member
Established: 1936
Title output 2017: 57
Titles currently in print: 2,128

Admitted to the Association: 1945
Title output 2018: 63
Journals published: 11

Editorial Program
Scholarly and general-interest works in African and African American studies; agriculture; American history and politics; Classics; environmental studies; fiction; folklore; film; foreign language

learning; human rights; Jewish studies; LGBT; Latin American studies; memoir and autobiography; modern European and Irish history; poetry; Russian and East European studies; Southeast Asian studies; and Wisconsin and the Upper Midwest

Journals: *African Economic History; Arctic Anthropology; Contemporary Literature; Ecological Restoration; Ghana Studies; Journal of Human Resources; Land Economics; Landscape Journal; Luso-Brazilian Review; Monatshefte; Native Plants Journal*

Book series: Africa and the Diaspora: History, Politics, Culture; Critical Human Rights; Folklore Studies in a Multicultural World; George L. Mosse Series in Modern European Cultural and Intellectual History; Harvey Goldberg Series for Understanding and Teaching History; History of Ireland and the Irish Diaspora; The History of Print and Digital Culture; Languages and Folklore of the Upper Midwest; Living Out: Gay and Lesbian Autobiographies; New Perspectives in Southeast Asian Studies; Publications of the Wisconsin Center for Pushkin Studies; Wisconsin Film Studies; Wisconsin Land and Life; Wisconsin Poetry Series; Wisconsin Studies in Autobiography; Wisconsin Studies in Classics; Women in Africa and the Diaspora

Imprints: Terrace Books, Popular Press

Wits University Press

Street Address:
Fifth Floor, University Corner
University of the Witwatersrand,
Jorissen Street, Braamfontein, Johannesburg.

Mailing Address:
Private Bag 3, Wits, 2050
Johannesburg
South Africa

Phone: +27 11 717 8700 / 1

Website and Social Media:
Website: www.witspress.co.za
Facebook: www.facebook.com/Wits-University-Press
Twitter: @WitsPress

Orders in Africa
Blue Weaver
Tel: + 27 21 701 4477
orders@blueweaver.co.za

Orders in UK, Europe, Middle East:
Eurospan

Orders in North and South America:
New York University Press
Email: nyupressinfo@nyu.edu
Website: witsuniversitypress.nyupress.org

Staff
Publisher: Veronica Klipp (+27 11 717 8704l; email: Veronica.klipp@wits.ac.za)
Administrator: Matselane Monggae (+ 27 11 717 8700; email:
    matselane.monggae@wits.ac.za)
Commissioning Editor: Roshan Cader (+27 11 717 8707; email: roshan.cader@wits.ac.za
Digital Publisher: Andrew Joseph (+27 11 717 8703; email: andrew.joseph@wits.ac.za)
Marketing Coordinator: Corina van der Spoel (+27 11 717 8705;
    email: corina.vanderspoel@wits.ac.za)
Production Editor: Kirsten Perkins (+27 11 7178706; email: Kirsten.perkins@wits.ac.za)

Number of Press Staff: 7

Regular Member
Established: 1922
Title output 2017: 24
Titles currently in print: 500

Admitted to the Association: 2016
Title output 2018: 24

Editorial Program
Wits University Press is strategically placed at the crossroads of African and global knowledge production and dissemination. We are committed to publishing well-researched, innovative books for both academic and general readers. Our areas of focus include art and heritage, popular science, history and politics, biography, literary studies, women's writing and select textbooks.

The Woodrow Wilson Center Press

Woodrow Wilson International Center for Scholars
One Woodrow Wilson Plaza
1300 Pennsylvania Avenue, N.W.
Washington, DC 20004-3027

Phone: 202.691.4042
Fax: 202.691.4001

Website and Social Media:
Website: www.wilsoncenter.org/press

Regular Member
Established: 1987
Title output 2017: NR
Titles currently in print: 174

Admitted to the Association: 1992
Title output 2018: NR

Editorial Program
Woodrow Wilson Center Press shares in the mission of the Wilson Center by publishing outstanding scholarly and public policy books for a worldwide readership. Written by the Center's worldwide network of scholars and its expert staff, our books concentrate on subjects of the Center's greatest strength, especially energy, security, environmental and social resilience, urban studies, U.S. foreign policy, cold war history, and area studies.

All the Press's books are copublished. Partners include Columbia University Press, Stanford University Press, Cornell University Press, Cambridge University Press, University of California Press, Johns Hopkins University Press, Indiana University Press, and University of Pennsylvania Press. The Cold War International History Project Series is copublished with Stanford.

Yale University Press

Street Address:
302 Temple Street
New Haven, CT 06511

Mailing Address:
PO Box 209040
New Haven, CT 06520-9040

Main: 203.432.0960
203.432.6129 (Reception)
203.432.0900 (Acquisitions Editorial)
203.432.4060 (Design/Production)
203.432.0961 (Marketing)
203.432.0163 (Publicity)
Email: (firstname.lastname)@yale.edu

Distribution/Customer Service:
Triliteral LLC
Customer Service Toll Free: 1.800.405.1619
Customer Service Fax 800.406.9145

Yale Press Fax Numbers:
203.432.6862 (Accounting)
203.432.0948 (Administration)
203.436.1064 (Acquisitions 1st Floor)
203.432.2394 (Acquisitions 2nd Floor)
203.432.8485 (Marketing 3rd Floor)
203.432.5455 (Promotion)
203.432.4061 (Design/Production)
401.658.4193 (Warehouse)

London Office:
47 Bedford Square
London WCIB 3DP
United Kingdom
Phone: +44-20 7079 4900
Fax: + 44-20 7079 4901
Email: firstname.lastname@yale.co.uk

Website and Social Media:
Website: www.yale.edu/yup/
Blog: yalepress.typepad.com/yalepresslog/
Facebook: www.facebook.com/yalepress
Twitter: @yalepress

Staff
Director: John E. Donatich (203.432.0933)
Sr. Executive Assistant to the Director: Danielle Di Bianco Caracas (203.432.4301)
Chief Operating Officer: Katherine Brown (203.432.8496)
Director of Legal Affairs: Pam Chambers (203.432.0936)
Contracts Associate: Kristy Leonard (203.432.0934)
Permissions and Ancillary Rights Manager: Donna Anstey (203.432.0932)
Acquisitions Editorial: Seth Ditchik, Editorial Director (economics) (203.432.0935); Jean E. Thomson Black, Senior Executive Editor (life sciences, physical sciences, environmental sciences, medicine) (203.432.7534); William Frucht, Executive Editor (law, political science international relations, and economics) (203.432.7571); Patricia Fidler, Art Publisher (art and architectural) (203.432.0927); Jennifer Banks, Executive Editor (religion, literature, classics, philosophy) (203.432.6807); Joseph Calamia, Sr. Editor (science & technology) (203.432.0904); Jaya Chatterjee, Editor (world history, geopolitics, and international relations); Heather Gold, Assistant Editor (religion) (203.432.8541); Katherine Boller, Senior Acquisitions Editor (art and architecture) (203.432.7217); Sarah Miller, Editor (language and literature) (203.432.0901); Adina Popescu Berk (American history) (203.432.9698)
Director of Editorial Design & Production: Jenya Weinreb (203.432.0914)
Manuscript Editorial: Dorothea Halliday, Managing Editor (203.432.4062)
    Assistant Managing Editor: Mary Pasti (203.432.0911)
    Editors: Dan Heaton (203.432.1017); Ann-Marie Imbornoni (203.432.0903); Phillip King (203.432.1015); Susan Laity (203.432.0922); Margaret Otzel (203.432.0918); Jeffrey Schier (203.432.4001); Heidi Downey (203.432.2390)
    Art Workshop: Kate Zanzucchi, Managing Editor (203.432.0916)
    Assistant Managing Editor: Heidi Downey (203.432.2390)
Production: Maureen Noonan, Associate Production Manager (203.432.4064)
    Reprint Controller: Orna Johnston (203.432.4060)
    Design and Production Manager Art Books: Mary Mayer (203.432.0925)
    Production Controller: Katherine Golden (203.436.8022)
    Senior Production Controller: Aldo Cupo (203.432.7484)
Design: Nancy Ovedovitz, Art Director (203.432.4067)
    Designers: Sonia Scanlon (203.432.4066); Mary Valencia (203.432.8092)
Sales: Jay Cosgrove, Sales Director (203.432.0968)
    General Sales Queries: (203.432.0966)
    Assistant Director, Sales: Stephen Cebik (203.432.2539)
    Marketing and Promotions Director: Heather D'Auria (203.432.8193)
    Publicity Director: Brenda King (203.432.0917)
    Publicists: Robert Pranzatelli (203.432.0972); Elizabeth Pelton (410.467.0989); Jennifer Doerr (203.432.0969); Roland Coffey (203.432.0964)
    General Publicity Inquiries: Publicity Assistant (203.432.0163)
    Online Marketing Manager: Michael Hoak (203.432.0961)
    Educational Marketing Manager: Debra Bozzi (203.432.0959)
    Academic Discipline Marketer: Karen Stickler (203.436.8467)
    Direct Mail Assistant: Lisa Scecina (203.432.0957)
    Exhibits/Advertising Manager: Ellen Freiler (203.432.0958)
    New Business and Product Manager: Sara Sapire (203.432.0965)
    Digital Product and Production Editor: John Carlson (203.436.9298)
Finance:
    Deputy Director of Finance: Timothy Haire (203.436.1924)
    Accounting Manager: Wendy DeNardis (203.432.0951)
    Publishing Accountant: Adnan Orucevic (203.432.0937)
    Senior Administrative Assistant: Stephanie Pierre (203.432.0952)
    Royalty Accountant: Kim Jones (203.432.0946)
    Database Analyst: Marc Benigni (203.432.8446)
    Inventory & Building Operations Manager: Jim Stritch (203.432.0939)

London Office:
Managing Director, London and Editorial Director (Humanities): Heather McCallum
Head of Marketing: David Brand
Foreign Rights Manager: Karen McTigue

Number of Press Staff: 79

Regular Member
Established: 1908
Title output 2017: 432
Titles currently in print: 6,589

Admitted to the Association: 1937
Title output 2018: 420

Editorial Program
Humanities, social sciences, natural sciences, physical sciences, medicine. Poetry is not accepted except for submissions to the Yale Series of Younger Poets contest, held annually. Festschriften and collections of previously published articles are not invited and very rarely accepted.
Book series: Agrarian Studies; Anchor Bible and Commentaries; Annals of Communism; The Annotated Shakespeare; Babylonian Collection; Bard Graduate Center; Carnegie Endowment for International Peace; The Castle Lectures in Ethics, Politics, and Economics; A Century Foundation Book; Complete Prose Works of John Milton; Complete Works of St. Thomas More; Council on Foreign Relations; Cowles Foundation; Culture and Civilization of China; Darden Innovation and Entrepreneurship; David Brion Davis Lectures; Democracy in America; The Diary of Joseph Farington; Dodge Lectures; Dura-Europos; Economic Census Studies; Economic Growth Center; Economic History; Elizabethan Club; English Monarchs; Faith and Globalization; George Elliot Letters; The Henry McBride Series in Modernism and Modernity; Henry Roe Cloud Series for American Indigenous Peoples and Modernity; History of the Soviet Gulag System; Horace Walpole Correspondence; Institute for Social and Policy Studies; Institute of Far Eastern Languages; Institution of Human Relations; Intellectual History of the West; Italian Literature and Culture; James Boswell; Jewish Lives; Lamar Series In Western History; Library of Medieval Philosophy; Neighborhoods of New York City; Margellos World Republic of Letters; New Directions In Narrative History; The New Republic; Oak Spring Garden Library; Okun; Open University; Page Lectures; The Papers of Benjamin Franklin; The Papers of Benjamin Latrobe; Papers of Frederick Douglass; Papers on Soviet & East European, Economic & Political Science; Paul Mellon Centre for Studies in British Art; Pelikan History of Art; Percy Letters; Petroleum Monographs; Pevsner Series: Buildings of England, Scotland, and Ireland; Phillips Andover Archaeology; Philosophy and Theory and Art; Poems of Alexander Pope; Posen Library of Jewish Culture and Civilization; Psychoanalytic Study of the Child; The Relations of Canada and the United States; Rethinking the Western Tradition; Russian Classics; Science in Progress; The Selected Papers of Charles Willson Peale and His Family; Silliman Lectures; Society and the Sexes; Stalin Archives; Storrs Lectures; Studies in Comparative Economics; Studies in Hermeneutics; Studies in Modern European Literature and Thought; Terry Lectures; Theoretical Perspectives in Archaeological History; Walpole Series in Eighteenth Century Studies; Why X Matters; The Works of Jonathan Edwards; The Works of Samuel Johnson; Yale Classical Monographs; Yale Classical Studies; Yale Contemporary Law Series; Yale Drama Series; Yale Edition of the Unpublished Works of Gloria Stein; Yale French Studies; Yale Guide to English Literature; Yale Health and Wellness; Yale Historical Publications; Yale Judaica; Yale Law Library Publications; Yale Law School Studies; Yale Library of Military History; Yale Liebniz; Yale Linguistics; Yale New Classics; Yale Publications in Religion; Yale Romantic Studies; Yale Series of Younger Poets; Yale Studies in Economics; Yale Studies in English; Yale Studies in History & Theory of Religious Education; Yale Studies in Political Science voloreh enimus.

ASSOCIATION PARTNERS

The Association's Partner Program was launched in 2008. For more details about the Partner Program, visit the Association's website The following companies enrolled as Partners in 2018

Baker & Taylor

2550 W Tyvola Road
Suite 300
Charlotte, NC 28217

Website and Social Media:
Website: www.baker-taylor.com
 Facebook: www.facebook.com/pages/Baker-Taylor/140688295944178
Twitter: @BakerandTaylor
YouTube: www.youtube.com/user/BakerandTaylorTV?feature=mhw5

Staff Contacts
VP Global Supply Chain Relations: Beth Reiser (908.541.7309;
   email: beth.reiser@baker-taylor.com)
Merchandising Manager, Academic & Higher Ed: Lorraine Ferry (908.541.7435;
   email: lorraine.ferry@baker-taylor.com)

Year enrolled as an Association Partner: 2012

Company Description
Baker & Taylor, a Follett company, is the premier worldwide distributor of digital and print books and entertainment products. We love books and leverage our unsurpassed distribution network to deliver rich content in multiple formats, anytime and anywhere, to readers worldwide. Baker & Taylor offers cutting-edge digital media services, a full range of publisher services, and innovative technology platforms to thousands of publishers, libraries and retailers globally

BAKER & TAYLOR PUBLISHER SERVICES

30 Amberwood Parkway
Ashland, OH 44805

Phone: 888.814.0208
Toll-free: 567.215.0030

Website and Social Media:
Website: www.btpubservices.com

Staff Contacts
Senior Vice President of Sales & Client Services: Mark Suchomel (email: Mark.Suchomel@baker-taylor.com)
Vice President of Business Development: Tony Proe (email: tproe@btpubservices.com)
Director of POD Publisher Services: Larisa Elt (email: lelt@btpubservices.com)

Year enrolled as an Association Partner: 2009

Company Description
Baker & Taylor Publisher Services partners with publishers to maximize sales and reduce risk in the domestic and international book trade, library, academic, retail, and wholesale specialty markets while providing exceptional economies of scale and service.

Books International

Fulfillment / Print / Digital

22883 Quicksilver Dr.
Dulles, VA 20166

Phone: 703.661.1500
Fax: 703.661.1501
Website: www.booksintl.com

Staff Contacts
Vice President: Vartan Ajamian (703.661.1519; email: vartan@booksintl.com)
Vice President, Print Sales: Bill Clockel (703.996.1025; email: bclockel@booksintl.com)
Director Business Development: Ellen Loerke (703.661.1512;
   email: eloerke@booksintl.com)
Chief Information Officer: Charles Thies (703.661.1514; email: charles@booksintl.com)

Year enrolled as an Association Partner: 2010

Company Description
Third party print, fulfillment and digital services. Complete fulfillment services including EDI, standing orders, collections, and royalties provided on publisher-branded databases. Internet access to data and reports. We provide on-site digital printing (color, b&w) for stock replenishment or print to order, as well as ONIX feeds, electronic title and digital asset management, and ebook sales and distribution.

De Gruyter

 **DE GRUYTER**

121 High Street
Boston, MA 02110

Website and Social Media:
Website: www.degruyter.com

Staff Contact
Vice President of Strategic Partnerships: Steve Fallon (email: steve.fallon@degruyter.com)

Year enrolled as an Association Partner: 2018

Company Description
The independent academic publisher De Gruyter can look back at a company history of over 260 years.

Today, the De Gruyter group publishes over 1,300 new titles each year in the humanities, social sciences, STM and law, more than 700 subscription based or Open Access journals, and a variety of digital products.

The company is headquartered in Berlin, with offices in Basel, Beijing, Boston, and Munich.

Firebrand Technologies

Where Publishers, Content, and Readers Meet

44 Merrimac Street
Newburyport, MA 01950

Phone: 978.465.7755

Website and Social Media:
Website: www.firebrandtech.com
Facebook: www.facebook.com/FirebrandTechnologies
Twitter: @firebrandtech

Staff Contacts
CEO and Chief Igniter: Fran Toolan (email: fran@firebrandtech.com)
Chief Community Officer: Robert Stevens (email: robert@firebrandtech.com)
Director of Sales and Education: Joshua Tallent (email: joshua@firebrandtech.com)

Year enrolled as an Association Partner: 2013

Company Description
Firebrand Technologies is dedicated to providing leading software and services to help publishers achieve success. Title Management Enterprise Software tracks titles from pre-acquisition through post-production, marketing, and sales. Eloquence on Demand is the industry gold standard for implementing ONIX and maximizing control of how data and content reach the marketplace.

ITHAKA
ARTSTOR / ITHAKA S·R / JSTOR / PORTICO
101 Greenwich Street, 18th floor
New York, NY 10006

Phone: 212.358.6400
Fax: 212.358.6499

Website and Social Media:
Website: ithaka.org
Twitter: @ITHAKA_org

Staff Contacts:
VP, Communications: Heidi McGregor (212.358.6400; email: heidi.mcgregor@ithaka.org)

Year enrolled as an Association Partner: 2012

Company Description
ITHAKA is a not-for-profit organization that works with the global higher educational community to advance and preserve knowledge and to improve teaching and learning through the use of digital technologies. ITHAKA has launched some of the most transformative and widely used services in higher education: Ithaka S+R, JSTOR, and Portico. Recently ITHAKA has enhanced its mission through a strategic alliance with Artstor, facilitating access to its services for researchers, teachers, and students worldwide.

KnKPublishing

89 Headquarters Plaza North
Suite 1478
Morristown, NJ 07043

Phone: +1 908 206 4599
Email: info@knk.com

Website and Social Media:
Website: www.knkpublishingsoftware.com

Staff Contacts
Chief Marketing Officer - Business Development Manager: David Hetherington (email: David. Hetherington@knk.com)
Marketing Manager: Oliver Holden (email: oliver.holden.knk.com)

Year enrolled as an Association Partner: 2018

Company Description
KnkPublishing combines classic business functions such as financial account, logistics, and the powerful CRM functionality of Microsoft Dynamics with industry specific functions for book, periodical, and specialist publishers

ProQuest

789 E Eisenhower Pk
Ann Arbor, Michigan 48106

Website and Social Media:
Website: www.proquest.com
Twitter: @ProQuestEbooks

Staff Contacts
Alliance Manager: Matthew Kull (650.475.8794; email: matthew.kull@proquest.com)

Year enrolled as an Association Partner: 2009

Company Description
ProQuest is committed to empowering researchers and librarians around the world. Through content, technologies, and deep expertise, our company drives better research outcomes for users and greater efficiency for the libraries and organizations that serve them.

Thomson-Shore

THOMSON-SHORE
Helping you put your best book forward®

7300 West Joy Road
Dexter, MI 48130

Phone: 734.426.3939
Toll Free: 844.575.8163
Fax: 800.706.4545
Email: info@tshore.com

<u>Website and Social Media:</u>
Website: www.thomsonshore.com
Facebook: www.facebook.com/ThomsonShore
Twitter: @ThomsonShore
Instagram: instagram/thomsonshore
LinkedIn: www.linkedin.com/company/thomson-shore-Inc-

Staff Contacts
University Press Market Sales Coordinator: Kelley Jones (734.426.6237; email: kelleyj@tshore.com)
VP of Sales & Marketing: Bob Durgy (734.726.0766; email: bdurgy@tshore.com)
President: Kevin Spall (734.426.3939; email: kevins@tshore.com)
Customer Service Representatives: Kelley Jones (734.426.6237; email: kelleyj@tshore.com); Carrie Gamblin (734.426.6229; email: carrieg@tshore.com); Julie McLean (734.426.6203; email: juliem@tshore.com); Dawn Rice (734.426.6299; email: dawnr@tshore.com)

Year enrolled as an Association Partner: 2008

Company Description
Thomson-Shore is an award-winning, employee-owned, full service book manufacturer offering high quality offset (soft and case bound), short run digital and consumer driven print-on-demand production options in both black and white and full color text. Thomson-Shore is also a full trade distribution company with fulfillment capabilities. For a complete list of the products and services we offer, visit us on the web at Thomsonshore.com.

Transforma Pvt Ltd

No. 310 - 312, II Floor, Ten Square Mall
Jawaharlal Nehru Road
Koyambedu, Chennai
India - 600 107

Tel. +91 44 40461222
USA Phone: 732.444.2565; 732.593.7540

Website and Social Media:
Website: www.transforma.in
Facebook: facebook.com/www.transforma.in
LinkedIn: www.linkedin.com/company/transforma-private-limited/

Staff Contacts
Managing Director: Krishnan Murali (email: murali@transforma.in; Mobile +91 9444360789)
Senior Vice President: Sankaran Mathrubutham (email: sankaran@transforma.in; Mobile +91 9980555586)
Vice President: Ganesh Koumar (email: ganeshkoumar@transforma.in)
Head of Technology: Jeyakumar D (email: jeyakumar@transforma.in)

Year enrolled as an Association Partner: 2018

Company Description
Transforma is content processing and data management company with reputation for integrity, quality, stability and excellence in management. It caters to STM, Academic and Educational as well as Professional, Scholarly and Open Access Publishers in USA, Europe, UK, and Japan.

Its core management has people with 20+ years' experience in the publishing services industry, also people who has held leadership positions at large international publishers.

The comprehensive service offerings of Transforma include editorial, peer review management, composition, proof reading, indexing and project management for books and journal apart from content transformation services. Transforma is ISO 9001:2015 Quality Management Systems and ISMS 27001: 2013 Information Security Management Systems certified company.

Transforma also specializes in LaTeX and helps convert content into XML/MathML, thus allowing your content to be indexed, retrieved, and reused in multiple formats over time. Additionally, they can integrate the end to end management of your publishing cycle using LaTeX as source: authoring – submission – reviewing – production – proofing.

Their proprietary XPERT WMS integrated with VEDAS, a feature rich, multi-function WYSIWYG Editor can be customized to your requirements.

Ubiquity Press

2120 University Avenue
Berkeley, CA 94704

Phone: (510) 473-2717

<u>Website and Social Media:</u>
Website: www.ubiquitypress.com
Twitter: @ubiquitypress

Staff Contacts
CEO: Brian Hole (email: brian.hole@ubiquitypress.com
Community Manager: Chealsye Bowley (email:chealsye.bowley@ubiquitypress.com)
Year enrolled as an Association Partner: 2017

<u>Company Description</u>
Ubiquity Press is both a publisher and a platform enabling sustainable open access publishing for
university presses and library publishing programs.

Virtusales Publishing Solutions

Third Floor, Sheridan House
112-116 Western Road
Brighton & Hove
BN3 1DD   UK

Phone: 212.461.3686
Fax: +44 8454584021
Email: info@virtusales.com

Website and Social Media:
Website: www.virtusales.com
Twitter: www.twitter.com/virtusales
LinkedIn: www.linkedin.com/company/virtusales-publishing-solutions/

Staff
Executive Vice President North America: Rodney Elder (email: rodney.elder@virtusales.com)
Projects Consultant: Tricia McCraney (email: tricia@virtusales.com)
Year enrolled as an Association Partner: 2013

Company Description
Virtusales is the creator of BiblioLIVE, the industry leading suite of publishing software. Virtusales is working with some of the world's leading academic, scholarly and trade publishers such as Harvard University Press, Princeton University Press, Pearson Education, Macmillan and Penguin Random House to streamline their workflows and bring efficiencies to their business processes. With web-based technology, a rapid release cycle and exceptional client support, BiblioLIVE enables publishers to adapt to industry trends and challenges, now and in the future.

Westchester Publishing Services

4 Old Newtown Road
Danbury, CT 06810

Phone: 203.791.0080

Website and Social Media:
Website: westchesterpublishingservices.com
Twitter: @WestchesterPub
LinkedIn: www.linkedin.com/company/10627500

Staff Contacts
Chief Revenue Officer: Tyler Carey (email: tyler.carey@westchesterpubsvcs.com)
Marketing and Conference Manager: Nicole Tomassi (email: nicole.tomassi@westchester-pubsvcs.com)
Key Accounts Manager: Bill Foley (email: bill.foley@westchesterpubsvcs.com)
Director, Editorial Services: Susan Baker (email: susan.baker@westchesterpubsvcs.com)
Director of Technology: Michael Jensen (email: Michael.jensen@westchesterpubsvcs.com)

Year enrolled as an Association Partner: 2015

Company Description
Westchester Publishing Services is a nearly fifty-year-old, U.S.-employee owned company focused on editorial, composition, and digital conversion services for book, journal, and white paper publishers. Our offerings include project management, copyediting, composition, art services, design, and ePub creation. Westchester is headquartered in the United States and has offices in India.

Wizdom

Taylor & Francis Group
2&4 Park Square, Milton Park
Abingdon, OX14 4RN UK

Phone: 0207-017-5000

Website and Social Media:
Website: www.wizdom.ai
Facebook: www.facebook.com/wizdomai
Twitter: @wizdomai

Staff Contacts
Marketing Executive: George Waters (email: george.waters@informa.com)

Year enrolled as an Association Partner: 2018

Company Description
Wizdom is a digital research services start-up launched out of the University of Oxford's software incubator, and acquired by the Taylor & Francis Group in 2017. Wizdom's mission is to accelerate research globally through intelligence that presents a comprehensive picture of the global research landscape.

With wizdom.ai, we empower researchers and institutions with comprehensive analytics to make fast paced, data driven decisions to improve the efficiency of their research process.

Wizdom uses artificial intelligence, machine learning and natural language processing to disambiguate, interconnect and analyze one of the largest datasets available on the scholarly landscape; processing data about $850 billion in research funding, 50 million researchers, 90 million publications and growing further every day.

International Sales Agents and Distributors

Artbook LLC & D.A.P. | Distributed Art Publishers, Inc.
75 Broad Street, Suite 630
New York, NY 10004 USA
Phone: 212.627.1999
Fax: 212.627.9484
Website: www.artbook.com

Asia Publishers Services Ltd.
Units B&D, 17th Flr Gee Chang
Hong Centre
65 Wong Chuk Hang Rd
Aberdeen, Hong Kong
Phone: 852.2553.9289
Fax: 852.2554.2912

Baker & Taylor International
1120 Route 22 East
Bridgewater, NJ 08807 USA
Phone: 800.775.1500; 908.541.7000
Email: btinfo@baker-taylor.com
Website: www.baker-taylor.com
international.cfm

Bay Foreign Language Books Ltd.
Unit 4, Kingsmead
Park Farm
Folkestone, Kent CT19 5EU United Kingdom
Fax: + 44 (0) 1233 721 272
Email: sales@baylanguagebooks.co.uk
Website: www.baylanguagebooks.co.uk

Boydell & Brewer, Ltd.
Bridge Farm Business Park
Top Street
Martlesham, Suffolk IP12 4RB United Kingdom
Phone: +44 (0) 1394 610600
Fax: +44 (0) 1394 610316
Website: www.boydellandbrewer.com

Brunswick Books
20 Maud St. Suite 303
Toronto, Ontario, M5V 2M5
Phone: 416.703.3598
Fax: 416.703.6561
Email: info@brunswickbooks.ca
Website: brunswickbooks.ca/

Casemate Academic (formerly the David Brown Book Company)
1950 Lawrence Road
Havertown, PA 19083 USA
Phone: 610.853.9131
Email: info@casemateacademic.com
Website: www.oxbowbooks.com/dbbc

Codasat Canada Ltd.
Phone: 604.228.9952
Email: info@codasat.com
Website: www.codasat.com

Combined Academic Publishers, Ltd.
Windsor House
Cornwall Road
Harrogate, North Yorkshire HG1 2PW United Kingdom
Phone: +44 (0) 1423 526350
Email: enquiries@combinedacademic.co.uk
Website: www.combinedacademic.co.uk

Compass Academic
Website: www.compassips.london

Distribution du Nouveau Monde
30, rue Gay Lussac
F-75005 Paris, France
Phone: +33 1 43 54 50 24
Fax: +33 1 43 54 39 15
Website: www.librairieduquebec.fr/distribution.html

East West Export Books
University of Hawaii Press
2840 Kolowalu Street
Honolulu, Hawaii 96822 USA
Phone: 888 UHPRESS (847.7377)
Fax: 800.650.7811
Email: eweb@hawaii.edu
Website: uhpress.wordpress.com/eweb/

Eurospan Group
3 Henrietta Street
Covent Garden
London WC2E 8LU United Kingdom
Email: info@eurospangroup.com
Website: www.eurospangroup.com

Footprint Books
4/8 Jubilee Avenue
Warriewood NSW 2102 Australia
Phone: +61 (0) 2 9997 3973
Fax: +61 (0) 2 9997 3185
Website: www.footprint.com.au

Gazelle Book Services, Ltd.
White Cross Mills
Hightown
Lancaster, Lancashire LA1 4XS
United Kingdom
Phone: +44 (0) 1524 528500
Fax: +44 (0) 1524 528510
Email: sales@gazellebookservices.co.uk
Website: www.gazellebookservices.co.uk

Georgetown Terminal Warehouses
34 Armstrong Avenue
Georgetown, ON L7G 4R9 Canada
Phone: 905.873.2750
Fax: 905.873.6170
Email: info@gtwcanada.com
Website: www.gtwcanada.com

Libro Co. Italia srl.
Via Borromeo, 48
50026 San Casciano V.P.
Firenze, Italy
Phone: +39 055 822.84.61
Fax: +39 055 822.84.62
Email: libroco@libroco.it
Website: www.libroco.it

Login Brothers Canada
300 Saulteaux Crescent
Winnipeg, MB R3J 3T2 Canada
Phone: 800.665.1148 or 204.837.2987
Website: www.lb.ca

Marston Book Services, Ltd.
160 Eastern Avenue
Milton Park
Oxfordshire OX14 4SB United Kingdom
Phone: +44 (0) 1235 465500
Fax: +44 (0) 1235 465509
Website: www.marston.co.uk

NBN International
10 Thornbury Road
Plymouth PL6 7PP United Kingdom
Phone: +44 (0) 1752 202301
Email: cservs@nbninternational.com
Website: distribution.nbni.co.uk

Orca Book Services
160 Eastern Ave
Milton Park
Abingdon OX14 4SB United Kingdom
Phone: +44 (0) 1235 465500
Email: tradeorders@orcabookservices.co.uk
Website: www.orcabookservices.co.uk

Oxbow Books
The Old Music Hall
106-108 Cowley Road
Oxford OX4 1JE United Kingdom
Phone: +44 (0) 1865 241249
Fax: +44 (0) 1865 794449
Website: www.oxbowbooks.com/oxbow

Oxford Publicity Partnership Ltd.
2 Lucas Bridge Business Park
Old Greens Norton Road
Towcester NN12 8AX United Kingdom
Phone: +44 (0) 1327 357770
Email: info@oppuk.co.uk
Website: www.oppuk.co.uk

Publishers Group UK
63-66 Hatton Garden
London EC1N 8LE United Kingdom
Phone: +44 (0) 207 405 1105
Fax: +44 (0) 207 242 3725
Email: info@pguk.co.uk
Website: www.pguk.co.uk

Renouf Publishing Co. Ltd.
22-1010 Polytek Street
Ottawa, ON K1J 9J1 Canada
Phone: 866.767.6766
Fax: 613.745.7660
Email: orders@renoufbooks.com
Website: www.renoufbooks.com

Roundhouse Group
Unit B
18 Marine Gardens
Brighton BN2 1AH United Kingdom
Phone: +44 (0) 1273 603 717
Fax: +44 (0) 1273 697 494
Email: sandy@roundhousegroup.co.uk
Website: www.roundhousegroup.co.uk

Scholarly Book Services Inc.
289 Bridgeland Avenue, Unit 105
Toronto, ON M6A 1Z6 Canada
Phone: 800.847.9736
Fax: 800.220.9895
Email: lstevens@sbookscan.com
Website: www.sbookscan.com

Servidis SA
Chemin des Chalets, 7
1279 Chavannes-de-Bogis, Switzerland
Phone: +41 22 960 95 10
Fax: +41 22 776 63 64
Website: www.servidis.ch

University of Toronto Press Distribution
5201 Dufferin St.
Toronto, ON M3H 5T8 Canada
Phone: 416.667.7791
Fax: 416.667.7832
Email: utpbooks@utpress.utoronto.ca
Website: www.utpress.utoronto.ca/UTP_Dis-
tribution/

Yale Representation Ltd
47 Bedford Square
London WC1B 3DP United Kingdom
Phone: +44 020 7079 4900
Email: yalerep@yaleup.co.uk
Website: www.yalerep.co.uk

THE ASSOCIATION

The Association of University Presses was established by a small group of university presses in 1937. In the subsequent years, the association has grown steadily. Today the Association consists of 147 member presses, ranging in size from those publishing a handful of titles each year to those publishing more than a thousand.

The Association is a nonprofit organization. Its sources of financing are limited to membership dues and to revenues derived from such activities as organizing national conferences and seminars, producing publishing-related books and catalogs, and operating cooperative marketing programs.

The Association's member presses provide much of the personnel that guide the association and carry out its work. A Board of Directors sets policy for the organization. Almost one hundred and fifty individuals serve on committees and task forces. Their activities reflect the diverse concerns of the membership, including keeping up with emerging technologies, production and analysis of industry statistics, maintaining copyright protections, professional development, marketing, and journals publishing.

The Association has office space in both New York City and Washington, DC. The executive director and a small professional staff manage member programs and coordinate the work of the board and committees.

Association members currently fall into three categories—regular, affiliate, and introductory. For a complete description of membership requirements, consult the "Guidelines on Admission to Membership and Maintenance of Membership," on page 230.

AUPresses Central Office

Association of University Presses
1412 Broadway, Suite 2135
New York, NY 10018

Phone: 212.989.1010
Email: info@aupresses.org

DC Office:
1775 Massachusetts Avenue, NW
Washington, DC 20036

Website and Social Media:
Website: www.aupresses.org
Facebook: www.facebook.com/universitypresses
Twitter: @aupresses

Staff
Executive Director: Peter Berkery (917.288.5594; email: pberkery@aupresses.org)
Research and Communications Director: Brenna McLaughlin (917.244.2051; email:
  bmclaughlin@aupresses.org)
Membership and Events Director: Susan Patton (917.244.1915; email: spatton@aupresses.org)
Business Manager Kim Miller (917.244.1264; email: kmiller@aupresses.org)
Communications Program Manager: Kate Kolendo (917.244.3859; email: kkolendo@aupresses.org
External Communications Manager: Annette Windhorn (917.244.1463: email:
  awindhorn@aupresses.org)
Program Coordinator: Angelica DeVoe (917.244.2665; email: adevoe@aupresses.org)

2018-2019 AUPresses Board of Directors

Jennifer Crewe, Columbia University Press, President (2018-2019)
Kathryn M. Conrad, University of Arizona Press, President-Elect (2018-2019)
Nicole Mitchell, University of Washington Press, Past-President (2018-2019)
Robbie Dircks, University of North Carolina Press Treasurer (2018–2019)
Jean Kim, Stanford University Press, Treasurer-Elect (2018-2019)
Gregory M. Britton, Johns Hopkins University Press (2017–2020)
Nadine D. Buckland, University of the West Indies Press (2018-2019)
Anthony Cond, Liverpool University Press (2018-2021)
John E. Donatich, Yale University Press (2016-2019)
Dennis Lloyd, University of Wisconsin Press (2017–2020)
Gita Manaktala, MIT Press (2017–2020)
Fredric W. Nachbaur, Fordham University Press (2018-2021)
Donna A. Shear, University of Nebraska Press (2018-2019)
Peter Berkery, Executive Director, AUPresses, *ex officio*

2018-2019 AUPresses Committees and Task Forces

The work of Committees and Task Forces, staffed by volunteer members, is essential to the Association. To learn more about the charges and projects of each, visit the Association"s Website.

Committees of the Board

Admissions and Standards
Lisa Bayer, Georgia, Chair
Anthony Cond, Liverpool
Mary V. Dougherty, Massachusetts
Fredric W. Nachbaur, Fordham
Dennis Lloyd, Wisconsin
Mark Simpson-Vos, North Carolina

Audit
Mike W. Bieker, Arkansas, Chair
Robbie Dircks, Johns Hopkins
Jean Kim, Stanford
Donna A. Shear, Nebraska

Nominating
Darrin Pratt, Colorado, Chair
Douglas Armato, Minnesota
Gregory M. Britton, Johns Hopkins
Ellen Chodosh, NYU
John E. Donatich, Yale
Nicole Mitchell, Washington

Committees of the Association

Acquisitions
Clark Whitehorn, New Mexico, Chair
Matthew Bokovoy, Nebraska
Beth Bouloukos, Amherst
Allyson Carter, Arizona
Brian Halley, Massachusetts
Kim Hogeland, Kansas
Deborah Gershenowitz, Cambridge
Michael J. McGandy, Cornell
Kristen Elias Rowley, Ohio State

Annual Meeting 2019
Mary Francis, Michigan, Chair
Walter Biggins, Georgia
Elizabeth Brown, Johns Hopkins
Jane Bunker, Northwestern
Jocelyn Dawson, Duke
Natalie Eidenier, Michigan State
Mark Heineke, Nebraska
Jamie Jones, Wayne State
Laurie Matheson, Illinois

Annual Meeting 2020
Laurie Matheson, Illinois, Chair

Book, Jacket, and Journal Show
Karen Copp, Iowa, Chair
Jessica Booth, Utah
Alan Brownoff, Alberta
Joel Coggins, Pittsburgh
Lisa Hamm, Columbia
Marianne Jankowski, Northwestern
Rachel Ross, Wayne State
Dan Ruccia, Duke
Isaac Tobin, Chicago

Business Systems
Brent Oberlin, MIT, Chair
Duane Anderson, Abilene Christian
Lynne Benedetto, Cornell
Davida G. Breier, Johns Hopkins
Alice Ennis, Illinois
Scot Kuehm, Princeton
Ryan Pingel, Wisconsin
Ioan Suciu, Georgetown

Digital Publishing
Lynn Fisher, Toronto, Chair
Michael Boudreau, Chicago
Darcy Cullen, British Columbia
Taylor Dietrich, Cambridge
Teresa A. Ehling, MIT
Kevin Hawkins, North Texas
Beth Kressel Itkin, Vanderbilt
Jeremy Morse, Michigan
Bonnie Russell, Wayne State
Clara Totten, Georgetown

Editorial, Design, and Production
Jillian Downey, Michigan, Co-Chair
Kristin Harpster, Wayne State,
   Co-Chair
Angela Anderson, Marine Corps
Taylor Dietrich, Cambridge
Kelly Finefrock-Creed, Alabama
Mary Lui, Toronto
Amanda Krause, Arizona
David Rosenbaum, Missouri

Faculty Outreach
Angela Gibson, MLA, Chair
Patrick H. Alexander, Penn State
Ann Baker, Nebraska
Seth Denbo, American Historical Association
Ilene Kalish, NYU
Julie R. Laut, Illinois
Gita Manaktala, MIT
Trevor Perri, Northwestern
Steve Wrinn, Notre Dame

IP and Copyright
Puja Telikicherla, Georgetown, Chair
Bryan Birchmeier, Michigan
Shaquona Crews, Princeton
Margie Guerra, NYU
Lisa Jemison, Toronto
Cathy Rimer-Surles, Duke
Kelly Rogers, Johns Hopkins
Jordan Stepp, Georgia
Stephen Williams, Indiana

Investment
Donna A. Shear, Nebraska, Chair
Mike W. Bieker, Arkansas
Robbie Dircks, North Carolina
Susan Doerr, Minnesota
Jean Kim, Stanford
Erik Smist, Johns Hopkins

Journals
Katie Smart, American Historical, Chair
Claire Eder, Wisconsin
Clare Hooper, Liverpool
Jessica Karp, Penn State
Joel Puchalla, Nebraska
Julie Warheit, Wayne State
Brian Shea, Johns Hopkins
Ann Snoeyenbos, Johns Hopkins
Emily Taylor, Ohio State

Library Relations
Beth Fuget, Washington, Co-Chair
Katherine Purple, Purdue, Co-Chair
Liz Hamilton, Northwestern
Geoffrey Little, Concordia
John McLeod, North Carolina
Abby Mogollón, Arizona
Elizabeth Scarpelli, Cincinnati

Marketing
Erin Rolfs, McGill-Queen's, Chair
Stephanie Adams, Stanford
Michelle Alamillo, SUNY
Jennie Collinson, Liverpool
Amy Harris, MIT
Casey LaVela, Wisconsin
Bailey Morrison, Texas
Kathryn Pitts, Notre Dame

Professional Development
Alison Shay, North Carolina, Chair
Rafael Chaiken, SUNY
Melissa Hammer, Kentucky
Lara Mainville, Ottawa
Christine Thorsteinsson, Harvard
Victoria Verhowsky, Rutgers

Task Forces

Equity, Inclusion, and Justice
Gita Manaktala, MIT, Co-Chair
Larin McLaughlin, Washington, Co-Chair
Ellen Bush, North Carolina
Susan Doerr, Minnesota
Gisela Fosado, Duke
Brian Halley, Massachusetts
Alexandria Leonard, Princeton
Jill Petty

Gender, Equity, and Cultures of Respect
Christie Henry, Princeton, Chair
Allyson Carter, Arizona
Lyndsey Claro, Princeton
Dawn Durante, Illinois
Gisela Fosado, Duke
Ana Jimenez-Moreno, Ohio State
Parneshia Jones, Northwestern
Levi Stahl, Chicago
Christian Winting, Columbia

Operating Statistics
Susan Doerr, Minnesota, Chair
Lynn Benedetto, Cornell
Nadine D. Buckland, West Indies
Chris Heiser, Chicago
Brent Oberlin, MIT
Darrin Pratt, Colorado
Kim Schmelzinger, MeanLine Publisher Services
Elizabeth R. Windsor, Project MUSE/Johns Hopkins
Steve Young, British Columbia

Research
Elizabeth R. Windsor, Project MUSE/John Hopkins, Chair
Anthony Cond, Liverpool
Toni Gunnison, Wisconsin
Mary Frances Gydus, MIT
Kimberly Lutz, ITHAKA S+R
Cason Lynley, Duke
Alphonse MacDonald, National Academies
Brigitte Shull, Cambridge
Rebecca Welzenbach, Michigan
Stephanie Williams, Kentuckyi *

University Press Week
Colleen Lanick, Harvard, Chair
Rosemary Brandt, Arizona
Joyce Harrison, Kansas
Chris Hart, Manchester
Catherine Hobbs, Columbia
Jessica Massabrook, Princeton
James Schneider, Princeton
Mark H. Saunders, Virginia
Laura Sell, Duke
Cameron Ludwick, Texas

By-Laws (As revised August 29, 2017)

ARTICLE I: PREAMBLE

This Corporation, existing under the Not-for-Profit Corporation Law of the State of New York, shall be known as the Association of University Presses, Inc. (hereinafter referred to as the "Association"). The Association expects members to recruit, employ, train, compensate, and promote their employees without regard to race, ethnic background, national origin, status as a veteran or handicapped individual, age, religion, gender, gender orientation, marital status, or sexual orientation.

ARTICLE II: PURPOSES

The purposes of the Association shall be:

a) To encourage dissemination of the fruits of research and to support university presses in their endeavor to make widely available the best of scholarly knowledge and the most important results of scholarly research;

b) To provide an organization through which the exchange of ideas and information relating to university presses and other non-profit publishers within the scholarly communications ecosystems may be facilitated;

c) To afford technical advice and assistance to learned bodies, scholarly associations, and institutions of higher learning; and

d) To do all things incidental to and in furtherance of the fore¬going purposes without extending the same.

ARTICLE III: MEMBERSHIP

The Association admits members in three categories: (1) regular membership, (2) affiliate membership, and (3) introductory membership.

Section 1: Regular Membership.

The regular membership of the Association shall consist of those members who were in good standing at the time of the incorporation of the Association in 1964, except those who have since resigned or whose membership has been otherwise terminated, and all other members who have since been admitted in accordance with the procedures set forth in Section 3 of this Article. Presses with associate member or international member status as of June 2016 (both of which have now been eliminated as membership categories) will be instated as regular members.

Section 2: Definition of a Press Eligible for Regular Membership.

A press eligible for regular membership is hereby defined as: (i) the nonprofit scholarly publishing arm of a university or college, or of a group of such institutions within a defined geographic region, or (ii) the scholarly publishing arm of a non-profit organization (as constituted under local law) that functions in a manner substantially similar to an entity described in clause (i) herein. A non-profit scholarly publisher eligible for membership as here defined must be an integral part of one or more such non-profit institutions, and should be so recognized in the manual of organization, catalog, website, or other official publication of at least one such parent institution. The organization and functions of the non-profit scholarly publisher described herein must lie within the prescription of its parent institution or institutions.

Section 3: Eligibility Criteria for Regular Membership.

Any non-profit scholarly publisher described in Section 2 of these Bylaws and satisfying the requirements set forth in the "Guidelines on Admission to Membership and Maintenance of Membership" (hereinafter, the "Guidelines") that are in force at the time of application shall be eligible for election to regular membership in the Association. A non-profit scholarly publisher shall be elected to membership by a majority vote of the membership on the recommendation of the Board of Directors at the Annual or a Special Meeting of the membership. Such action shall be taken by the Board only on the prior recommendation of the Committee on Admissions and Standards, which shall be responsible for determining that the applying non–profit scholarly publisher satisfies the minimum requirements for membership. Annual dues for regular members shall be set from time to time by the Board of Directors.

Section 4: Associate Membership.

This category of membership shall be closed to new applicants as of June 2016.

Section 5: Affiliate Membership.

The affiliate membership of the Association shall consist of those affiliate members who have been admitted since the time of the incorporation of the Association in 1964, in accordance with the procedures in force at the time of application.

Affiliate membership may be applied for by a non-profit scholarly publisher that meets some but not all of the criteria for regular membership. To qualify for affiliate membership in the Association, a non-profit scholarly publisher must submit the same application as applicants for regular member status, but only will need to meet a subset of the editorial, staffing and organizational requirements applicable to regular members, as that subset may be set forth from time to time in the Guidelines. Admission to affiliate membership shall be by a majority vote of the membership at an Annual or Special Meeting, a quorum being present, on the prior recommendation of the Committee on Admissions and Standards and the Board of Directors.

Affiliate members shall enjoy such rights and privileges as determined by the Board of Directors, but in no event shall their rights extend to: (i) service on the Board of Directors; (ii) vote in any business being con¬ducted by the Association, the Board of Directors, or the membership; (iii) receive without charge any compilation of member or other statistics undertaken by the Association from time to time; (iv) serve in any capacity on the Committees of the Board; or serve as chair of the Annual Meeting Program Committee. Any reference elsewhere in these By-Laws to a voting right, therefore, shall be read so as to exclude affiliate members. Annual dues for affiliate members shall be set from time to time by the Board.

As a condition of membership, an Association affiliate member shall include the term "affiliate" in any reference to its Association membership.

As a condition of membership, an Association affiliate member shall refrain from referring to itself as a "university press" unless it is recognized as such in the manual of organization, catalog, website, or other official publication of its parent institution.

Section 6: Introductory Membership.

Eligible for introductory membership are nonprofit scholarly publishers that intend to apply for Association membership in one of the other categories either during their introductory term or at the end of that term. Introductory members may not stay in that category for more than five years.

Candidates for introductory membership will be expected to provide evidence concerning the scholarly character of their publishing programs and information about present staffing, reporting relationships, editorial review processes, and also any changes or developments proposed in these areas, but they will not be expected to meet the requirements of regular or affiliate membership. Admission to introductory membership shall be made at the discretion of the Executive Director of the Association after favorable review by the Committee on Admissions & Standards upon receipt of an application that includes the requested information.

At any time during the introductory period introductory members may apply for regular or affiliate membership. After five years, introductory membership is automatically terminated.

Introductory members shall enjoy such rights and privileges as determined by the Board of Directors, but in no event shall their rights extend to: (i) service on the Board of Directors; (ii) vote in any business being con¬ducted by the Association, the Board of Directors, or the membership; (iii) receive without charge any compilation of member or other statistics undertaken by the Association from time to time; (iv) chair any Association committee (v) serve in any capacity on the Committees of the Board of the Association. Any reference elsewhere in the By-Laws to a voting right, therefore, shall be so read as to exclude introductory members. Annual dues for introductory members shall be set from time to time by the Board.

Section 7: Voting and Other Privileges.

Each regular member of the Association shall be entitled to one vote in such business as may come before the Association. Only regular members in good standing shall be entitled to vote, and only members in good standing shall be entitled to enjoy the other privileges of membership in the Association.

Section 8: Cancellation of Membership and Resignation.

An Association member, by its very nature, must be devoted to scholarly and educational ends; the failure of a member to pursue such ends as its fundamental business shall constitute grounds for canceling its membership in the Association. Any accusation of such a failure will be brought to the Committee on Admissions and Standards for a recommendation to the Board.

A membership may also be canceled for continued nonpayment of dues or for continued failure, after admission to membership, to meet the minimum requirements set forth in the Guidelines.

Cancellation of membership shall be effected, on recommendation of the Board of Directors, by a two-thirds vote of the members present and voting at the Annual Meeting or a Special Meeting, a quorum being present.

Any member may resign at any time if its current annual dues are paid, provided its resignation is confirmed in a written communi¬cation to the Executive Director and President of the Association from a responsible officer or group of officers of the parent institution or institutions.

Should a member in any class of membership resign after the due date of the annual dues payment and before the next annual dues payment date, the member is responsible for the payment of such dues at the time of resignation.

Section 9: Determination of Membership Category.

All Association members are expected to maintain their membership in the Association at the highest level of membership for which they qualify. Association members are expected to notify the Association promptly of any material change in circumstance which might impact the category in which they are eligible to maintain their membership.

ARTICLE IV: MEMBERSHIP MEETINGS

Section 1: The Annual Meeting.
The Annual Meeting of members shall be held at such time and place within or without the State of New York as may be designated by the Board of Directors after giving due weight to preferences ex¬pressed by members. Such meetings shall be held for the purpose of electing the Board of Directors, approving the annual budget, and transacting such other business as may be properly brought before the meeting. At each Annual Meeting of members, the Board of Directors shall cause to be presented to the membership a report verified by the President and the Treasurer, or by a majority of the Board, in accordance with the requirements of Section 519 of the New York Not-for-Profit Corporation Law.

Section 2: Special Meetings.
Special Meetings of the members shall be held at such time and place within or without the State of New York as may be designated by the Board of Directors. Such meetings may be called by (a) the Board of Directors; or (b) the Executive Committee; or (c) the President, the President-elect, or the Executive Director, acting on a request received in writing that states the purpose or purposes of the meeting and signed by 30 percent or more of the members of the Association.

Section 3: Notice of Meetings.
Notice of the purpose or purposes and of the time and place of every meeting of members of the Association shall be in writing and signed by the President, President-elect, or the Executive Director, and a copy thereof shall be delivered personally, by first class mail, by facsimile or by electronic mail not less than ten or more than fifty days before the meeting, to each member entitled to vote at such meeting. In the case of a special meeting, such notice shall also set forth the purpose or purposes of the meeting.

Section 4: Representation by Proxy.
A member may authorize a person or persons to act by proxy on all matters in which a member is entitled to participate by providing such authorization in writing, including by facsimile or electronic mail, to the person who will be the holder of the proxy, provided that any such authorization by electronic mail shall set forth information from which it can be reasonably determined that the authorization by electronic mail was authorized by the member. If it is determined that such authorization by electronic mail is valid, the inspectors or, if there are no inspectors, such other persons making that determination shall specify the nature of the information upon which they relied. No proxy shall be valid after the expiration of eleven months from the date thereof unless otherwise provided in the proxy. Every proxy shall be revocable at the pleasure of the member executing it.

Section 5: Quorum.
Except for a special election of Directors pursuant to Section 604 of the New York Not-for-Profit Corporation Law, the presence at a meeting in person or by proxy of a majority of the members entitled to vote thereat shall constitute a quorum for the transaction of any business, except that the members present may adjourn the meeting even if there is no quorum.

Section 6: Voting.
In the election of members of the Board of Directors and the election of Officers, a plurality of the votes cast at an Annual Meeting shall elect. Any other action requires a majority of votes cast except as otherwise specifically provided in these By-Laws. Any action required or permitted to be taken at a meeting of members may be taken without a meeting, without prior notice, if all of the members consent to the adoption of a resolution authorizing the action. Such consent may be written or electronic. If written, the consent must be executed by each member by signing such consent or causing his or her signature to be affixed to such consent by any reasonable means including, but not limited to, facsimile signature. If electronic, the transmission of the consent must be sent by electronic mail and must set forth, or be submitted with, information from which it can reasonably be determined that the transmission was authorized by the member. The resolution and consents thereto shall be filed with the minutes of the proceedings of the members.

ARTICLE V: DIRECTORS AND OFFICERS

Section 1: The Board of Directors.
The Association shall be managed by its Board of Directors, and, in this connection, the Board of Directors shall establish the policies of the Association while considering the wishes of the membership and the constituency of the Association (which constituency consists of the employees of the member presses), and shall evaluate the performance of the Executive Director. The Board of Directors shall meet at least three times each year, once in the fall and once in the winter, and in conjunction with the Annual Meeting of the membership of the Association. The Board of Directors shall consist of not fewer than nine or more than thirteen Directors, all of whom shall be at least nineteen years of age, at least two-thirds of whom shall be citizens of the United States, four of whom shall be the elected Officers of the Association as described in Section 3 (hereinafter, "Officers"). Directors other than Officers (hereinafter, "Directors-at-Large"), like Officers, must be on the staff of a member press, except that the Executive Director shall serve ex officio as a nonvoting member of the Board of Directors and the Executive Committee.

Section 2: Election Procedure and Term of Office.
Directors shall be elected by a plurality vote of the members present at the Annual Meeting. Candidates may be nominated by the Nominating Committee appointed by the President or from the floor. Officers shall be elected for a one-year term, except that the President shall remain on the Board of Directors for an additional year as Past-President. Directors-at-Large shall be elected for a three-year term. Directors shall not succeed themselves except that (a) Directors who are elected Officers shall continue as Directors as long as they remain Officers, and (b) the Treasurer shall remain on the Board for an additional year as a Director-at-Large. Each newly elected Director and Officer shall assume office at the close of the Annual Meeting at which the election is held. Any Director or Officer may resign by notifying the President, the President-elect, or the Executive Director. The resignation shall take effect at the time therein specified. Except as provided for in Article IX ("The Executive Director"), Directors shall not receive any compensation for serving as Directors. However, nothing herein shall be construed to prevent a Director from serving the Association in another capacity for which compensation may be received.

Section 3: Officers.
The elected Officers of the Association, each of whom must be on the staff of a member press, shall be a President, a President-elect, a Treasurer, and a Treasurer-elect, each to be elected for a one-year term by a plurality vote of the members present at the Annual Meeting. No employee of the Association may serve as President. Between Annual Meetings of members, a Special Meeting of members may elect, by a plurality vote of the members present, an Officer to complete the term of an Officer who has resigned or otherwise ceased to act as an Officer.

Section 4: Duties of Officers.
The President shall serve as presiding officer at all meetings of the membership and all meetings of the Board of Directors and the Executive Committee. The President, with the Executive Director, serves as spokesperson for the Association. At the Annual Meeting of members, the President and the President-elect shall provide a forum for the Association membership and constituency to discuss and assess the Association's program. The President-elect shall discharge the duties of the President in the President's absence, and shall succeed to the office of President in the event of a vacancy in that office, filling out the unexpired term as well as the term to which he or she subsequently may be elected President.

The Treasurer shall be custodian of the Association's funds, shall be responsible for the preparation of its financial records as the basis for an annual audit, and shall report at the Annual Meeting of members on the Association's financial condition. The Treasurer-elect shall discharge the duties of the Treasurer in the Treasurer's absence, and shall succeed to the office of Treasurer in the event of a vacancy in that office, filling out the unexpired term as well as the term to which he or she may be elected Treasurer.

Section 5: Removal from Office and Replacement.
Any Director or elected Officer may be removed from office at any time, for cause or without cause, by a majority vote of the membership or may be removed for cause by a majority vote of the Board, in either case acting at a meeting duly assembled, a quorum of not less than a majority being present. If one or more Director-at-Large vacancies should occur on the Board for any reason, the remaining members of the Board, although less than a quorum, may by majority vote elect a successor or successors to hold office until the next Annual Meeting of members at which the election of directors is in the regular order of business and until the election and qualification of a successor or successors.

Section 6: Board Meetings.
Meetings of the Board of Directors shall be held at such place within or without the State of New York as may from time to time be fixed by resolution of the Board, or as may be specified in the notice of the meeting. Notice of any meeting of the Board need not be given to any Director who submits a signed waiver of such notice. Special Meetings of the Board may be held at any time upon the call of the Executive Committee, the Executive Director, the President, or the President-elect.

Section 7: Board Quorum.
A majority of the members of the Board of Directors then acting, but in no event less than one-half of the entire board of Directors, acting at a meeting duly assembled, shall constitute a quorum for the transaction of business. If at any meeting of the Board there shall be less than a quorum present, a majority of those present may adjourn the meeting without further notice from time to time until a quorum shall have been obtained. The "entire Board of Directors" shall mean the total number of Directors entitled to vote that the Association would have if there were no vacancies.

Section 8: Board Voting.
Except as otherwise specified in these By-Laws, all decisions of the Board shall be by majority vote of the Directors in attendance, a quorum being present. Any Board action may be taken without a meeting if all members of the Board or committee thereof consent to the adoption of a resolution authorizing the action. Such consent may be written or electronic. If written, the consent must be executed by the director by signing such consent or causing his or her signature to be affixed to such consent by any reasonable means including, but not limited to, facsimile signature. If electronic, the transmission of the consent must be sent by electronic mail and must set forth, or be submitted with, information from which it can reasonably be determined that the transmission was authorized by the director. The resolution and consents thereto shall be filed with the minutes of the proceedings of the board or committee as applicable. The resolution and consents thereto shall be filed with the minutes of the proceedings of the Board. Any member of the Board or of any committee thereof may participate in a meeting of such Board or committee thereof by means of a conference telephone or similar communications equipment or by electronic video screen communication al¬lowing all persons participating in the meeting to hear each other at the same time. Participation by such means shall constitute presence in person at a meeting.

ARTICLE VI: EXECUTIVE COMMITTEE
The Executive Committee of the Board of Directors shall consist of the President, Past-President, President-elect, Treasurer, Treasurer-elect, and the Executive Director (ex officio, nonvoting). The Executive Committee shall advise and confer with the Executive Director, call Special Meetings of the Board of Directors as necessary, appoint committee members not otherwise appointed pursuant to these By-Laws, and unless otherwise delegated serve as the investment committee for the Association. The Executive Committee shall, if necessary, act for the full Board of Directors between meetings of the Board, but only in those matters not establishing policy or not requiring a vote of more than a majority of Directors in attendance. Neither the Executive Committee nor any other committee shall have the power to (a) submit to the members any action requiring the approval of the members, (b) amend, repeal or adopt By-Laws, (c) fill vacancies in the Board of Directors or in any committee of the Board, (d) fix the compensation of Directors for serving on the Board or on any Committee of the Board, or (e) amend or repeal any resolution of the Board which by its terms shall not be so amendable or repealable.

ARTICLE VII: COMMITTEES OF THE BOARD

The Board, by resolution adopted by a majority of the entire Board, may designate from among its members other Committees of the Board, each including three or more Directors. Such Committees of the Board, to the extent provided in a resolution, shall have the authority of the Board, except as limited by the Board of Directors or by law. The Committees of the Board (in addition to the Executive Committee) shall be the Committee on Admissions and Standards, the Committee on the Audit, and the Nominating Committee. The Committee on Admissions and Standards shall be constituted as provided in the Guidelines. Appointments to the Committee on the Annual Meeting Program and the Nominating Committee shall be made in accordance with Article VIII of these By-Laws.

ARTICLE VIII: OTHER COMMITTEES AND TASK FORCES

Other committees and task forces may be established by agreement of the Executive Director and the Board, to include a Committee on the Annual Meeting Program.
Such committees shall be advisory in nature and shall not have the authority to bind the Board of Directors or the Association. The President-elect shall appoint chairs of said committees (and the Committees of the Board) and such of their members as the Executive Committee may care to designate. The President-elect shall charge the said committees with such duties, including reporting duties, as he or she may deem appropriate. Task forces shall be established for a limited time to accomplish a specific goal. The President shall appoint chairs of task forces and provide their charges. Reports of Committees of the Board and all other committees and task forces shall be made to the Board of Directors, in writing or orally, as requested by the Executive Director.

ARTICLE IX: THE EXECUTIVE DIRECTOR

The Board of Directors may appoint at such times, and for such terms as it may prescribe, an Executive Director of the Association who shall report to the Board of Directors and who is responsible for implementing policy through fiscally sound programs; monitoring the work of committees and task forces; and managing the Central Office (such Central Office consisting of salaried employees hired by the Executive Director in order to carry out the business of the Association). The Executive Director shall prepare an operating plan and budget and shall participate in meetings of the Board of Directors and Executive Committee in an ex officio nonvoting capacity as appropriate. Under the authority of the Board of Directors, the Executive Director shall have responsibility for the execution of Association policy, for the furtherance of the Association's interests, and for the day-to-day operation of the Association's business and programs. The Executive Director or his or her designee shall act as secretary at all Board meetings, Executive Committee meetings, and Annual and Special Meetings of the Association, and shall prepare and distribute minutes of the same. The Executive Director shall serve as Corporate Secretary. The Executive Director's salary shall be fixed annually by the Board, or by the Executive Committee if the Board so decides.

ARTICLE X: DUES

The amount of the annual dues payment by members shall be voted each year at the Annual Meeting on recommendation of the Board of Directors. The fiscal year of the Association shall be April 1 to March 31. Dues shall be payable by September 30, at which time any member which has not paid its dues shall be subject to suspension at the Board's discretion. When a member is suspended for nonpayment of dues, the President of the Association shall so notify the director of the said member and the responsible officer or officers of its parent institution or group of institutions, and shall further advise them that if such member has not paid its dues by the end of the Association's fiscal year its membership shall be subject to cancellation.

ARTICLE XI: BOOKS AND RECORDS

The Association shall keep at its office within the State of New York correct and complete books and records of account; minutes of meetings of the members, of the Board of Directors, and of the Executive Committee; and an up-to-date list of the names and addresses of all members. These books and records may be in written form or in any other form capable of being converted to written form within a reasonable time.

ARTICLE XII: CHANGES IN BY-LAWS

Members may propose changes to these By-Laws by submitting the proposed change and its rationale to the Executive Director. S/He will arrange for the Board's review of any such proposal at the next appropriate Board Meeting. If the Board recommends Association approval of the proposed change, the change will be presented with at least thirty days advance notice to the membership at the next Annual Meeting or Special Meeting called for that purpose at which a quorum is present. A change to the By-Laws requires a two-thirds majority of all Members eligible to vote (in person or by proxy). Whenever there is a conflict between these By-Laws and the Guidelines, any Statement of Governance, or a resolution of the membership, Board of Directors, or Executive Committee, or any other document published by the Association, these By-Laws shall prevail.

In the event the Board recommends against approval of a proposed change, the member proposing the change may call a vote on the measure at the Annual Meeting or at a Special Meeting for that purpose, provided thirty days' notice is given and thirty percent of the Association's voting members sign a request that said proposal be voted upon. Requirements for adoption of the measure in such circumstance are as stated elsewhere in this Article.

Guidelines on Admission to Membership and Maintenance of Membership

As revised August 29, 2017
(Hereinafter, "Guidelines")

A. Preamble

The mission of the Association is to advance the essential role of a global community of publishers whose mission is to ensure academic excellence and cultivate knowledge.

The purposes of the Association are to encourage dissemination of the fruits of research and to support university presses and other non-profit scholarly publishers in their endeavor to make widely available scholarly knowledge and the most important results of scholarly research; to provide an organization through which the exchange of ideas relating to the functions of university presses and other non-profit scholarly publishers may be facilitated; to afford technical advice and assistance to learned bodies, scholarly associations, and institutions of higher learning; and to do all things incidental to and in furtherance of the foregoing purposes without extending the same.

B. Types of Membership

The Association admits members in three categories: (1) regular membership, (2) affiliate membership, and (3) introductory membership.

1. Regular Membership

Eligible for regular membership are: (i) the non-profit scholarly publishing arm of a university or college, or of a group of such institutions within a defined geographic region, or (ii) the scholarly publishing arm of a non-profit organization (as constituted under local law) that functions in a manner substantially similar to as an entity described in clause (i) herein, which satisfies the following criteria:

(a) Eligible university presses and other non-profit scholarly publishers must be an integral part of one or more such parent institutions, and should be so recognized in the manual of organization, catalogue, website, or other official publication of at least one such parent institution. The organization and functions of the university press or other non-profit scholarly publisher must lie within the prescription of its parent institution or institutions.

(b) Both of the following editorial criteria: (i) a committee or board of the scholars (or other officials of directly comparable rank and authority) of the parent institution or institutions shall be charged with certifying the scholarly quality of the publications that bear the institutional imprint; and, (ii) the peer review of their scholarly publications in a manner consistent with commonly understood notions of peer review among university presses, including such notions as they may be expressed in any written guidelines for best practice which the Association may from time to time issue or update.

(c) Publication of ten or more scholarly titles in a given twenty-four month period. Scholarly books, journals, and digital projects that include original scholarly content will all be counted to satisfy this requirement. The word "scholarly" is used here in the sense of original research of a character usually associated with the scholarly interests of a college, university or comparable research institution college. (Publications for which the press serves solely as a printer and/or distributor for other departments or divisions of the parent institution are not to be included in the aforementioned minimum scholarly publishing requirement.)

(d) An acceptable scholarly publishing program shall have the benefit of the service of not fewer than three full-time equivalent staff, of whom one shall have the functions of director. This official shall report, organizationally, to the president of the university or college, or to an officer at the vice-presidential or decanal level (i.e., an officer reporting either to the president or to the chief academic officer) having both academic and fiscal authority, or to the designated representative of a group of such institutions who shall have both kinds of authority, or to an individual of directly comparable rank and authority to one of the three proceeding classes of individuals.

Any university press or other non-profit scholarly publisher satisfying these requirements shall be eligible in principle for election to regular membership in the Association.

2. Affiliate Membership

Eligible for affiliate membership shall be university presses and other non-profit scholarly publishers who meet some but not all of the criteria for regular membership, and more specifically which satisfy at least the following criteria:

(a) The non-profit institutional affiliation required for regular membership.

(b) Either of the following editorial criteria: (i) the committee or review board criteria required for regular membership; or, (ii) the peer review of their scholarly publications in a manner consistent with commonly understood notions of peer review among university presses, including such notions as they may be expressed in any written guidelines for best practice which the Association may from time to time issue or update.

(c) Either of the following indicia of sustained commitment: (i) publication of five or more scholarly titles in a given twenty-four month period; or, (ii) the benefit of the service of at least one full-time equivalent staff.

3. Introductory Membership

Eligible for introductory membership are non-profit scholarly publishers that intend to apply for Association of University Presses membership in one of the other categories either during their introductory term or at the end of that term.

Candidates for introductory membership will be expected to provide evidence concerning the scholarly character of their publishing programs and information about present staffing, reporting relationships, review processes, and also any changes or developments proposed in these areas, but they will not be expected to meet the publication rate, staffing, or organizational requirements of full membership. Presses may not stay in the introductory category for more than five years.

At any time during the introductory period introductory members may apply for membership in the regular or affiliate category. If a press does not wish to continue as an introductory member for five years, it may resign from the Association after payment of its current annual dues. At the end of five years, the introductory membership is automatically terminated.

C. Application, Admission, and Cancellation

1. Application

All inquiries from prospective applicants for membership in the Association are to be directed to the Association's Executive Director, or such staff member as he or she may designate. The Executive Director, or his or her designee, shall advise the candidate of the substance of these Guidelines on Admission to Membership and Maintenance of Membership, and shall require as evidence of satisfactory compliance with the following materials for submission to the Committee on Admissions and Standards:

(a) One copy of each of 10 or more different scholarly titles published by the applicant and certified by its faculty editorial board or committee in the twenty-four months preceding the date on which the application for membership is filed, and full runs of the issues of any journals for the year or years in which a journal serves as one of the titles. If original digital publications are submitted, the applicant will provide access to committee members.

(b) A list of the peer reviewers (names and affiliations) for each of the books or original digital publications submitted as part of the application. Published reviews of the titles and information about scholarly awards received may be submitted as part of the application.

(c) Copies of the applicant press's catalogs for the past two years for each member of the Committee on Admissions and Standards.

(d) A complete list, by name and title, of the staff of the applicant press, to be prepared in that form in which such information is given for active members in the most recent edition of the Directory of the Association of American University Presses. For part-time staff the list should indicate the percentage of time each person devotes to the press.

(e) A statement from a senior administrative officer of the parent institution, or the designated representative of a group of institutions, outlining the immediate and long-term intentions and financial expectations of the institution or group of institutions for its press, and reflecting a realistic appreciation of the cost of supporting a serious program of scholarly publication.

(f) Copies of its financial operating statements for the two most recently completed fiscal years.

(g) Documentation demonstrating the non-profit status of the applicant and/or its parent institution.

With respect to the scholarship of published works, the Association will in general accept the certification of the press's own faculty board or committee and will not pass judgment on the scholarship of any individual work. However, the Committee on Admissions and Standards will take into account the observance by the press of commonly accepted standards of editorial review, ordinarily including at least one positive evaluation by a qualified scholar not affiliated with the author's own institution.

Applicants for regular membership shall be expected to adhere strictly to all submission requirements.

Applicants for affiliate membership shall be expected to adhere strictly to those submission requirements relevant to the eligibility criteria upon which they are basing their application for membership.

Applicants for introductory membership shall be expected to make a good faith effort to adhere to as many submission requirements as practicable.

2. Admission
Following the filing of a formal application for regular, affiliate, or introductory membership and notification by the Association's Executive Director to the applicant of its acceptance for consideration, the candidate press shall be regarded as having entered a period of probation, which will last for a period of time no longer than one year.
A press shall be elected to regular or affiliate membership by an affirmative vote of a majority of the Association's regular members at the Annual Meeting or a Special Meeting, a quorum being present, on the recommendation of the Board of Directors. Such action shall be taken by the Board only on the prior recommendation of the Committee on Admissions and Standards, which shall be responsible for determining that the applying press satisfies the minimum requirements for membership. Admission of a new member to the Association shall take effect immediately following approval by the members as described herein.

Admission to introductory membership shall be made at the discretion of the Executive Director after favorable review by the Committee on Admissions & Standards.

To maintain its active membership status, each member shall be required to submit each year to the Central Office of the Association, for publication in the annual Directory of members, both a roster of its current staff and an indication of the number of books, journals, and original digital publications that it has published in each of the two calendar years preceding and that have been certified as to scholarship by its editorial board or committee.

3. Cancellation
An Association of University Presses member, by its very nature, must be devoted to scholarly and educational ends; the failure of a press to pursue such ends as its fundamental business shall constitute grounds for canceling its membership in the Association. Any accusation of such a failure will be brought to the Committee on Admissions and Standards for a recommendation to the Board. Cancellation of membership shall be effected, on recommendation of the Board of Directors, by a two-thirds majority vote of the members present and voting at the Annual Meeting or a Special Meeting, a quorum being present.

It shall be the responsibility of the Executive Director, or his or her designee, to review each listing of an active member in each annual edition of the membership Directory, and to undertake action as follows when any member seems to have fallen below the qualifying criteria for membership: (a) to make an inquiry and, if current standards are not being met, offer the assistance and cooperation of the Association in bringing about satisfactory corrections to the member's deficiencies; (b) to advise the Committee on Admissions and Standards, and the Board when notification of an apparent delinquency has been sent and an offer of assistance made; (c) to inform the Committee on Admissions and Standards, and the Board of any response received from the member press following the offer of assistance.

Should the delinquent press fail to resolve its deficiencies within one year of the Executive Director's notice, the Committee on Admissions and Standards shall submit to the Board of Directors a full report of the situation, and recommend, for endorsement by the Board and transmission to the membership for ratification, that the membership of the delinquent press be terminated. Two years from the date of its expulsion, a press shall be entitled to apply for readmission through initiation of the application procedures herein prescribed.

D. The Committee on Admissions and Standards
The official agency for the administration of these Guidelines shall be the Committee on Admissions and Standards, which shall operate under authority delegated by the Board of Directors, and which shall consist of between four and six members, at least three of whom shall be members of the Board of Directors and at least two of whom shall be the director of a member press. The incoming President will appoint the chair of the committee from among members of the current committee with at least one year of service. The chairs shall each serve a term of one year as part of their three-year term on the committee and may not succeed themselves in office. Consistent with the requirements of the Association's Policies & procedures, and in consultation with the President and the Executive Director, the chair shall appoint the remaining committee members. Terms of the committee members normally will be three years. Committee members will not be eligible to serve more than two successive terms.

E. Amendments
Members may propose changes to these Guidelines by submitting the proposed change and its rationale to the Executive Director. S/He will arrange for the Board's review of any such proposal at the next appropriate Board Meeting. If the Board recommends Association approval of the proposed change, the change will be presented with at least thirty days advance notice to the membership at the next Annual Meeting or Special Meeting called for that purpose at which a quorum is present. A change to the Guidelines requires a majority of all Members eligible to vote (in person or by proxy). Whenever there is a conflict between the By-Laws and these Guidelines, any Statement of Governance, or a resolution of the membership, Board of Directors, or Executive Committee, or any other document published by the Association, the By-Laws shall prevail.

In the event the Board recommends against approval of a proposed change, the member proposing the change may call a vote on the measure at the Annual Meeting or at a Special Meeting for that purpose, provided thirty days' notice is given and thirty percent of the Association's voting members sign a request that said proposal be voted upon. Requirements for adoption of the measure in such circumstance are as stated elsewhere in this Article.

PERSONNEL INDEX

Catlos, Alicia C.	86	Cobra, Alison	44
Catte, Elizabeth	194	Cockerham, Jamison	127
Cavaliere, Charles	141	Cocks, Catherine	105
Caviness, Mary	127	Coffey, Roland	199
Cebik, Stephen	199	Coggins, Joel	146, 220
Cedillos, Felicia	123	Coggins, Nicolle	187
Cerbone, Will	67	Cohen, Barbara	139
Cercone, Philip J.	100	Cohen, Emily-Jane	164
Chadwell, Faye A.	136	Cohen, Phyllis	142
Chaffin, Jennifer	82	Cohen, Sara	170
Chaiken, Rafael	166, 221	Cohen, Sara Jo	104
Challice, John	139, 140	Cohn, Stephen A.	63
Chambers, Pam	199	Coleff, Patrick	64
Chan, Dawn	116	Colella, Alexa	79
Chan, Derick	41	Coleman, Jason	187
Chan, Tina	54	Coleman, Martin	126
Chandler, Helen	187	Coleman, Robin	86
Chaney, Margo	79	Colesworthy, Rebecca	166
Chang, Jasper	158	Colleps, Donovan Kūhiō	77
Chaplin, Allison	81	Collier, Abby	146
Chapman, Lynne	172	Collier, MacKenzie	161
Chase, Paul	144	Collins, Don P.	53
Chasse, Keith	141	Collins, Mike	59
Chatterjee, Jaya	199	Collins, Nina	151
Chen, Angela	46	Collins, Teresa	90
Chesnutt, Jessica	141	Collinson, Jennie	93, 221
Ching, Emma	77	Colman, Jason	104
Chnapko, Angela	140	Colosky, Allison	184
Chodosh, Ellen	125, 220	Comeau, Jennifer	78
Chorpenning, Joseph F.	159	Comer, Heather	103
Chrisman, Ronald	129	Cond, Anthony	93, 219, 220, 221
Christensen, Alicia	120	Congdon, David	88
Christiansen, Gayla	174	Conley, Mary	111
Christofides, Marika	78	Conn, Jennifer	196
Chu, Carol	40	Connell, Carol	25
Chun, Stephanie	77	Connelly, Rich	53
Church, Lucas	127	Conner, Bonnie	63
Ciaccio, Michele	74	Connery, Lisa	79
Cisneros, Cassandra	172	Connors, Logan J.	43
Clabaugh, Patricia	174	Conover, Roger	112
Claps, Bobbi	167	Conrad, Joanna	176
Clark, Jennifer	78	Conrad, Kathryn M.	35, 219
Clark, Karen	153	Contrucci, Jason	104
Clark, Rakia	40	Cook, James	140
Clark, Susan	113	Cook, Julia	155
Clarke, Paul	95	Cook, Rick	25
Claro, Lyndsey	148, 221	Cook, Tonya	60
Clay, Jami	128	Cooper, Kevin	126
Cleland, Jamie	115	Cooper, Pam	47
Clevenger, Beth	112	Copp, Karen	85, 220
Clingham, Greg	43	Corbin, Becki	151
Clockel, Bill	203	Corrado, Susan	119
Cloherty, Tyler	33	Cort, Molly Q.	154
Clute, Sharla	166	Cortés, Julián	34
Coates, Laraine	41	Corwin, Erica	121
Coatney, Susan	123	Cosgrove, Jay	199
Cobb, Caelyn	57	Cosner, Chris	165
Cobb, David	90	Cosseboom, Joel	76

Dixon, Sandra	133	Elliott, Maryse	33
Doboszenski, Amanda	128	Elliott, Steve	47
Doerr, Jennifer	199	Elt, Larisa	202
Doerr, Susan	108, 221	Emley, Bryce	123
Dolbow, Jim	119	Emmirch, Terry	196
Doll, Rachel	66	Engel, Carrie	42
Donatich, John	199, 219, 220	Engel, Tracey	155
Donlon, Anne	115	Engelhardt, James	78
Donovan, Emma	187	Ennis, Alice	79, 220
Dorr, Yuni	130	Esco, Melinda	168
Doskow, Sara	47	Esposito, Cathleen	86
Dotson, Anne Dean	90	Etcheson, Amy	163
Dotson, Rand	93	Eubanks, Debra	29
Dotto, Gabriel	105	Evans, Claire Lewis	25
Dougan, Jill	40	Evans, Justine	57
Dougherty, Mary V.	99, 220	Evans, Rebecca	127
Dougherty, Peter	149	Evans, Sally	70
Douglas, Jodie McBean	193	Evans, Stephanie	135
Dove, Lucia	33	Eyer, Christopher	113
Dowd, Matthew	132	Ezernack, Kristi	110
Downey, Floann	194	Fagan, John	146
Downey, Heidi	199	Fagan, Teresa	52
Downey, Jillian	104,, 220	Fahmy, Miriam	31
Doyle, Mary	167	Fairfield, Benjamin	77
Dreesen, Robert	47	Faison, Anna	127
Dreyer, Christopher	104	Falik, Jamed	83
Duelm, Katie	174	Falk, Naomi	116
Duff, Katharine	52	Fallon, Steve	204
Duffy, Madge	127	Falocco, Filomena	101
Duft, K. Todd	152	Famiano, David	45
Dumitrescu, Carmen	100	Farmer, Christopher	173
Dunbar, Christine	57	Farr, Clay	128
Duncan, Alanna	57	Farranto, Amy	130
Duncan, Michael	47	Fasciani, Susan	35
Dunham, Chantel	72	Faust, Allison	172
Dunham, Gary	81	Faust, Jana	121
Durante, Dawn	78, 221	Faust, Jessica	94
Durgy, Bob	209	Fehrenbacher, Micah	52
Durham, Cynthia	63	Feinsod, Denise	45, 46
Duvall, Kristin	173	Feldmann, Judy	113
Dyson, Elizabeth Branch	51	Felgar, Cathy	148
Eager, Leslie	64	Ferber, Susan	140
Eder, Claire	196, 221	Ferenczi, Joanne	126
Edington, Mark	31, 92	Fergus, Julie	189
Edwards, Kathy	134	Ferguson, John	196
Egan, Jennifer	163	Ferreira, Adriana	61
Ehle, Rob	164	Ferrence, Susan	84
Ehling, Terry	112	Ferry, Lorraine	201
Ehlingm Teresa A.	220	Fiana, William	42
Eidenier, Natalie	106, 220	Fidler, Patricia	199
Eisenstark, Stacy	45	Fiedler, Kate	121
El Barrase, Wala'a	80	Fields, DeLisa	191
El Manialawi, Basma	31	Fields, LeAnn	104
El-Elaimy, Tarek	31	Figueira, Sarah George	30
El-Hadi, Nadine	31	Fikes, Jason	23
Elam, Tim	90	Finefrock-Creed, Kelly	25, 220
Elder, Rodney	212	Fingerhut, Natalie	178
Ellerbeck, Brian	169	Finkelstein, Edward	152

Fisher, Jennie 79
Fisher, Lynn 178, 220
Fitzgerald, Brenda 187
Fiyak-Burkley, Michele 66
Flach, Alex 140
Fletcher-Jones, Nigel 31
Fletcher, Anna 65
Flores, Jessica 71
Flum, David 158
Fobben, Tish 121
Foley, Bill 213
Foley, Ehren 161
Fortgang, Karen 149
Fortner, Shannon 86
Fosado, Gisela 63, 221
Foster, Cynthia 109
Fowler, Marjorie 127
Fox, Alison 182
Francis, Anna 81
Francis, Mark 121
Francis, Mary 104, 220
Franklin, Tom 128
Fraser, Kathleen 100
Freed, Nate 43
Freeland, Abby 194
Freels, Amy 24
Freiler, Ellen 199
Fricke, Cate 145
Friedman, Paloma 100
Frisch, Janice 81
Frost, Matthew 95
Frucht, William 199
Fry, Jenni 52
Fry, Jessie 140
Frye, Sebastian 179
Fuget, Beth 189, 221
Fugini, Richard 89
Fuller, J. Bruce 175
Furney, Laura 56
Furtkamp, Ryan 164
Gabriele, Louis 58
Gaffney, Erika 33
Gaines, Kayla 66
Galante, Edward 48
Gallagher, Heather 93
Gallaway, Matt 47
Galle, Suzanne 88
Gamblin, Carrie 209
Gammon, Julie 24
Gan, Qi 54
Ganeles, Diane 166
Ganley, Erin 141
Garcia, Sydney 126
Gardiner, Sarah 53
Garner, Alex 116
Garrett, Susan 127
Garrison, Patrick 61
Gasbarrini, Tiffany 85

Gasso, Ale 66
Gast, Scott 52
Gawronski, William 58
Gemignani, Nathan 61
Gendler, Anne 131
Georgi, Sara 194
Gering, Shannon 135
Gernenz, Heather 79
Gershenowitz, Deborah 47, 220
Gettman, Joyce 121
Gevaert, Mallory 52
Gibson, Angela 115, 221
Gichuru, Dorcas 55
Gieling, Saskia 33
Gill, Craig W. 109
Gillespie, Carmen 43
Gillooly, Diana 47
Ginder, Rachel 145
Ginsburg, Erica 143
Gipson, Kyle 113
Gleason, Laura 93, 94
Glemot, Suzanne 84
Glover, Elizabeth 143
Gnerlich, Ingrid 149
Go, Michael 83
Godlewski, Cynthia 74
Gold, Heather 199
Goldberg, David 113
Golden, Katherine 199
Goldstead, Catherine 86
Goldstein, Alrica 122
Golub, Sophie 116
Gonokami, Makoto 177
Gonsalves, Charles 59
Gonzales, Pat 90
Gonzalez, Anibal 43
Gonzalez, Carmen Torrado 61
González, María Victoria 34
Goodman, Eleanor 145
Goodman, Robert White 86
Goodwin, Abigail 120
Goranescu, Elena 100
Gordon, Ariel 96
Gosnell, Jason 97
Goss, Heather 113
Goto, Kensuke 177
Gottshall, Jon 145
Gotwals, Hannah 112
Gough, Peggy 172
Goussy, Patrick 104
Grainger, Jeremy 158
Grande, Scott 141
Grandstaff, Emily 187
Grant, Donna 153
Grant, Paul 196
Grathwohl, Casper 140, 141, 142
Gray, Kelly 171
Greco, Debbie 149

Green, Joanna	40	Halverson, Pete	110
Green, Nicholas	112	Ham, Scott	104
Greenberg, Jonathan	126	Hamblen, Carol	86
Greenhalgh, Adam	118	Hamblet, Bill	119
Greig, Justine	93	Hames, Charles	126
Grench, Charles	127	Hamilton, Emily	108
Gresham, Zach	186	Hamilton, Liz	131, 221
Greyson, Brent	135	Hamlin, Mona	167
Gribbin, Laura	127	Hamm, Lisa	57, 220
Griffin, Don	63	Hammack, Brice	158
Griffith, Drew	111	Hammer, Jennifer	125
Griffith, Glenn	119	Hammer, Melissa	90, 221
Grodsky, Larry	47	Hamrick, David	172
Gross, Abby	140	Hansard, Patrick	29
Grosse, Diane	63	Hansen, Kathleen	115
Grossman, James R.	28	Haproff, David A.	157
Grossman, Sarah E.M.	61	Harper, Allie	25
Grote, Molly	113	Harpster, Kristin	191, 220
Grotophorst, Wally	70	Harrington, Marjorie	102
Grzan, Lisa	141	Harrington, Sarah	140
Guagnini, Valeria	47	Harris, Amy	113, 221
Guerra, Margie	221	Harris, Jake	183
Guerra, Paul	173	Harrison, Aimee	166
Guerrero, David	173	Harrison, Joyce	88, 222
Guinta, Kimberly	158	Harrison, Kristen	42
Guiod, Suzanne E.	167	Hart, Chris	95, 222
Gulino, Louis	140	Hart, Gary	52
Gunderson, Maryann	133	Harvey, Alan	164
Gunnison, Toni	196, 221	Hashimoto, Hiroki	177
Guo, Janalyn	185	Hashman, Mary	104
Guo, Meide	165	Haskell, Michael	58
Gurganus, Cynthia	64	Hatch, James C.	115
Gusinde-Duffy, Mick	72	Hatfield, Ed	73
Gutierrez, Romi	66	Hawkins, Kevin	220
Guttman, Joseph	144	Hayden, Jeffrey	80
Guttormsen, Kate	37	Haydon, Brett	125
Guynes-Vishniac, Sean	104	Haydon, Roger	60
Gydus, M.F.	113, 221	Hayes, Stacey	73
Haav, Julia	149	Hayes, Todd	142
Hadley, Patrick	185	Haynes, Zachary	141
Haenisch, Julie	149	Headrick, Jeri	73
Hagerman, Liza	151	Headrick, Marianne	48
Haggerty, Thomas	48	Hearn, Aaron	191
Hagman, Lorri	189	Hearne, Shivaun	193
Haire, Timothy	199	Heath, Mary	109
Hajnoczky, Helen	44	Hebel, Brad	57
Hale, Charles	112	Hebert, Hannah	145
Hall Marie	67	Heck, Emma	49
Hall, Charles	66	Hegeman, Anne	187
Hall, Emily	116	Heineke, Mark	121, 220
Hall, Jonathan	61	Heinzelmann, Jaqueline	155
Hall, Julia	149	Heise, Laura DiPonzio	154
Hall, Megan	38	Heiser, Chris	51, 221
Halley, Brian	99, 220, 221	Helba, Steve	141
Halliday, Dorothea	199	Helke, Katie	112
Halliday, Mark	125	Helms, Derek	88
Halpern, Eric	143	Henderson, John	108
Halter, Theresa	82	Hendricksen, Sara	122

Henry, Christie	148, 221	Hudson, Tricia	141
Henry, Tricia	100	Hull, Stephen	123
Hensley, Heather	64	Hulsey, Dave	82
Hensley, Kate	113	Humme, Adelia	123
Henson, Kristi	25	Humphreville, Sarah	140
Heo, Inae	179	Humphrey, Taylor	23
Hernandez-French, Anna	142	Hunt, Jenny	39
Hernandez, Aurelia	165	Hunt, Val	75
Hernandez, Terika	106	Hunter, Sian	66
Herrera-Diaz, Maritza	58	Hunter, Stephanye	66
Hershbein, Brad	184	Husband, Len	178
Hetherington, David	207	Hutchinson, Emma	125
Hicks, Savannah Grace	35	Hwa, Karen T.	61
Hildebrand, Douglas	27	Hyzy, Karen	53
Hill, Amanda	47	Iaffa, Elena	57
Hill, Mindy	64	Iarrera, Linda	100
Hindley, Victoria	112	Idell, Sacha	94
Hirashima, Steven	77	Igali, Monika	27
Hirata, Kari Ann	77	Iguchi, Yasuyo	113
Hirschberg, Adam	47	Ikeda, Masako	77
Hirschy, Norm	140	Imbornoni, Ann-Marie	199
Hirst, Bethan	95	Imperio, Irene	170
Hiscox, Abbie	113	Inkei, Peter	50
Hitchens, Clare	195	Ireland, Brad	118
Hitt, Gretchen	155	Irvin, Margo	164
Hivnor, Margaret	52	Itkin, Beth Kressel	186
Hnatow, Andrew	172	Jackson-Whyte, Debra	169
Hoagland, Nancy	64	Jackson, Erika	184
Hoak, Michael	199	Jackson, Joe	149
Hobbs, Catherine	57, 222	Jackson, Rhodri	141
Hodorowicz, Cate	127	Jackson, Zoë	28
Hoff, Alexandra	123	Jacob, Mary Ann	174
Hoffman, Robert	52	Jacobs, Donald	71
Hogan, Angie	187	Jacobs, Joanna	25
Hogeland, Kim	88, 220	Jacobson, Tanjam	49
Hohman, Laura	82	Jacobson, Tony	86
Holden, Oliver	207	Jacqmin, Hilary S.	86
Hole, Brian	211	Jacques, Kelly Chrisman	88
Holland, Claudia	70	Jain, Anne Fuzellier	164
Holmes, Jack	86	Jajuga, Elise	106
Holmes, Nathan	130	Jankowski, Marianne	131, 220
Holway, Pamela	38	Janssen, Karl	88
Holway, Richard	187	Jansz, Winston	79
Hoogerwerf, Jeroen	33	Jarrad, Mary Beth	126
Hooper, Clare	93, 221	Jarrell, Cade	39
Hooper, Niels	45	Javsicas, Aaron	170
Hop, Kristen	25	Jemison, Lisa	179, 221
Hope, Katie	113	Jennings, Genny	174
Horst, Ines ter	148	Jensen, Michael	213
Houlihan, Connor	38	Jerome, Jennifer	57
Howard, Meredith	57	Jestis, Cheryl	79
Howells, Richard	75	Jimenez-Moreno, Ana	134, 221
Huard, Ricky S.	133	Jimenez, Anja	66
Hubbard, John	143	Johnson, Aaron	47
Hubbart, Dustin	79	Johnson, Claudette	95
Huber, Tasha	90	Johnson, Erin-Elizabeth	152
Hudson, Christopher	116	Johnson, Harmony	41
Hudson, Liz	41	Johnson, Kimberly F.	86

Kramer, Gary	170	Lay, Thomas	67
Kraus, Dennis	53	Lazaro, Arvin	137
Kraus, Donald	140	Lazarus, Todd	57
Krause, Amanda	35, 220	Leach, Kaitlyn	47
Krause, Tom	185	Leach, Vicki	161
Krebs, Paula M.	115	Leary, Dan	107
Kressel Itkin, Beth	220	LeBien, Thomas	75
Kretzer, Kyle Howard	86	Leboff, Katelyn	61
Kriesel, Leslie	57	Ledendecker, Thea	24
Krissoff, Derek	194	Lee, Chang Jae	57
Krouse, Young-hee	97	Lee, Katie	68
Krum, Jeff	47	Lee, Kristie	174
Kuehm, Scot	148, 220	Lee, Marie	112
Kuehm, Scot	220	Lee, Milenda	57
Kuerbis, Lisa	167	Lee, Pahnia	196
Kull, Matthew	208	Lee, Su-Mei	165
Kumler, Katie	155	LeGro, Hope	71
Kunos, Linda	50	Leichner, Kim	143
Kuny, Greg	29	Leichum, Laura	52
Kuroda, Takuya	177	Lemmons, Thom	174
Kurtz, Kevin	58	Lenz, Scott	196
Kushnirsky, Julia	57	Leonard, Alexandria	221
Kutsko, John F.	159	Leonard, Benjamin	140
La Mantia, Katherine	72	Leonard, Kristy	199
LaBrenz, Marcia	104	Leone, Sara	64
Lage, Amy	121	Leppig, Angela	68
Laity, Susan	199	Lerner, Mark	67
Lamb, Cynthia	48	Leshan, Larry	66
Lambert, Allison	173	Lester, Liz	36
Lambert, Julie	145	Levay, Rachael	56
Lambert, Ray	64	Leventhal, Josh	107
Lamm, Gigi	143	Leventhal, Philip	57
LaMorte, Gianna	172	Levine, Karen	74
Lance, James	60	Levine, Scott	61
Landerholm, Savanah	39	Levinson, Meagan	149
Lane, Victoria	167	Levy, Rachel	117
Langlois, Dennis	149	Lewchuk, Jodie	178
Lanick, Colleen	222	Lewek, Tom	115
Lanne-Camilli, Amanda	166	Lewis, Dorothy	117
Lape, Todd	110	Lewis, Jeremy	140
Lara, Greg	57, 58	Li, Lingxi	148
Larkin, Sheniqua	57	Lichtenstein, Alex	28
LaRose, Charley	178	Liese, Debra	149
Larsen, David	96	Lightfoot, Nancy	81
Larsen, Wayne	163	Lilly, Nick	52
Larson, Alodie	140	Lin, Ying	54
Laska, Elizabeth	26	Lindenfeldar, Maria	149
Latture, Richard	119	Lindsay, Nick	113
Lauer, Chloe	196	Ling, Jessica	164
Laughlin, Philip	112	Linker, Damon	143
Laun, Karen	61	Lipinski, Michelle	164
Laur, Mary	52	Lipp, Michelle	44
Laurent, Amy	47	Lipscombe, Trevor	49
Laut, Julie R.	78, 221	Litkey, Jozsef	50
LaVela, Casey	196, 221	Litt, Neil	149
Lawrence-Hunt, Jessica	112	Little, Geoffrey	59, 221
Laws, Andrea	88	Little, Nadine	45
Lawton, Caryn	190		

Little, Stephen	132	Maisner, Elaine	127
Littlefield, Kyle	174	Malar, Gregory	156
Liu, Amy	135	Malashewsky, Megan	41
Liu, Katherine	60	Malcolm-Clarke, Darja	81
Lloyd, Alice	51	Malcolm, Ian	75
Lloyd, Dennis	196, 219, 220	Malcolm, Reed	45
Lloyd, Kathryn	174	Maloney, Karen	47
Lloyd, Matt	47	Manaktala, Gita	112, 219, 221
Lobkowicz, Michelle	179	Manion, Deborah	167
Lochner, Wendy	57	Manko, Cliff	40
Locke, Elizabeth	173	Manning, Linda	25
Lockhart, Robert	143	Manning, Shaun	104
Lockwood, Karen	167	Marambio, Josefina	34
Loe, Cheryl	77	Marchenkova, Maria	116
Loehr, Julie L.	106	Marcus, Rachel	117
Loerke, Ellen	203	Marguy, Kathryn	86
Long, James	94	Mark, Gigi	164
Long, John	118	Markell, Amanda	113
Long, Linda	80	Marks, Rachael	40
Lonie, Tonia	110	Marney, Tim	29
Loo, Patricia	80	Marshall, Demi	172
Lopez-Torres, Angelica	172	Marshall, Kate	45
Losh, Lacey	121	Marsland, Joanna Ruth	127
Lou, Loretta	33	Marson, Rosie	125
Louth, John	140	Martin, Annie	191
Love, Alexa	41	Martin, Carolyn	161
Lovecraft, Margaret	94	Martin, Dawn	106
Lowenthal, Marc	112	Martin, Elyse	28
Luber, Joel	64	Martin, Jan	64
Luchsinger, Amy	141	Martin, Katherine	140
Luciano, Bessie	179	Martin, Larisa	88
Ludwick, Cameron	172, 222	Martin, Mike	174
Lui, Mary	220	Martin, Miranda	57
Lumenello, Susan	40	Martin, Pieter	108
Lundgren, Eric	108	Martinelli, Theresa	191
Lunsford, Stacy	123	Martinez, Bryan	158
Luttrell, Marsha	103	Marting, Bill	141
Lutz, Bryan	66	Martino, John	49
Lutz, Kimberly	221	Maselli, Elisabeth	158
Luu, Kathryn	145	Masi, Alexa	112
Ly, David	41	Mason, Jacqueline	100
Lykke, Kristina	86	Mason, Tony	95
Lynch, Haley	40	Massabrook, Jessica	222
Lynley, Cason	64, 221	Matheson, Laurie	78, 220
Lyons, Christie	113	Mathias, Ashley	161
MacBrien, Nathan	131	Mathrubutham, Sankaran	210
MacColl, Pamela	40	Mattern, Margaret	120
MacDonald, Alphonse	117, 221	Matthews, Jermey	112
Macdonald, Jane	52	Mattox, Daniel	55
Machado, Ralph	88	Maxfield, Marcela	164
Mackie, Rob	100	Mayer, Mary	199
Macklem, Ann	41	Mazo, Carolina	34
MacNeil, Mary	187	Mazzarra, Chris	64
MacNevin, James	41	Mazzocchi, Jay	127
Madden, Kyla	100	McAdam, Matthew	85
Mahalek, Gina	127	McAnespie, Elena	46
Maher, Sylvia	31	McArdle, Jeff	79
Mainville, Lara	138, 221	McBride, David	140

McCallum, Heather	200	Mennel, Timothy	51
McCarthy, Juliana M.	86	Menzies, Elspeth	125
McConkey, Jill	96	Merzlak, Paul	118
McCormack, Marilyn	178	Meszaros, Abel	50
McCormick, Mack	90	Meyer, Astrid	145
McCormick, Wynona	174	Meyer, Caitlin	40
McCoy, Jim	84	Meyers, Adrienne	52
McCraney, Tricia	212	Micic, Vesna	179
McCreary, Courtney	110	Mickulas, Peter	158
McCollough, Aaron S.	70	Midgley, Peter	27
McCullough, Michael	64	Milberger, Kurt	106
McDermott, Kathleen	75	Miles, Terry	128
McDonald, Leigh	35	Miller, Allison	28
McDonnell, Julia	141	Miller, David	81
McDougall, Kelly	112	Miller, Janice	112
McDuffie, John J.	29	Miller, Jon	24
McEntire, Ila	90	Miller, Kim	219
McFee, Mollie	52	Miller, Robert	141
McGandy, Michael J	60.	Miller, Robyn L.	63
McGandy, Michael J.	220	Miller, Sarah	199
McGann, Michael	169	Miller, Stephani	97
McGaughey, Tyler	52	Milliken, Leif	120
McGavick, Sarah	172	Mills, Eric	119
McGlone, Jonathan	104	Miniard, Kathi	55
McGraw, Tom	52	Mink, Sarah	183
McGregor, Bridget	181	Mitchell, David	61
McGregor, Heidi	206	Mitchell, Jim	113
McGuinness, Phillipa	125	Mitchell, Nicole	189, 219, 220
McHugh, Elise	123	Mixon, Jennifer	110
McIntyre, Jennifer	162	Miyasato, Terri	77
McKay, Vicky	48	Modi, Akshay	80
McKenna, Anne	196	Moeller, Rachel	108
McLaughlin, Brenna	219	Moen, Jeff	108
McLaughlin, Larin	189, 221	Moffat, Fiona	137
McLean, Julie	209	Mogollón, Abby	35, 221
McLeod, John	127, 221	Moldvai, Marta	140
McMahon, Don	116	Mones, Mark	187
McMahon, Sheila	196	Monggae, Matselane	197
McMenemy, Siobhan	195	Montano, Dawn	26
McMillen, Wendy	132	Moore-Swafford, Angela	163
McMurray, Heather	160	Moore, Beth	113
McMurtray, Lisa	109	Moore, Nathan	64
McNamara, Sara	142	Moos, Katja	64
McShane, Daniel	166	Morales, Ruth	150
McTigue, Karen	200	Moravetz, Jeff	97
Means, Allison Thomas	85	Morgan, Dan	45
Meehan, Erin	141	Morris, Michael	61
Meekers, M'Bilia	189	Morris, Ryan	166
Mehring, Adam	196	Morrison, Bailey	172, 221
Meijer, Margreet	91	Morrison, Richard W.	67
Meikle, Barry	179	Morrone, Cathy	113
Melina, Valerie	66	Morse, Jeremy	104, 220
Melton, Mardee	77	Mortensen, Dee	81
Melvin, Terrence J.	86	Mortimer, Rebecca	95
Mendez, Jose Antonio	48	Mortis, Steffanie	181
Mendlik, Haley	121	Mosser, Gianna	131
Mendonça, Megan R.M.	30	Motieram, Sati	156
Mendoza, Cristian	48	Muccie, Mary Rose	170

Owen, Susan	45	Phillips, Lauren	66
Owens, Kathryn	71	Phillips, Peter	47
Pahwa, Ankit	179	Philpott, Brooke	64
Pakiela, James	57	Piché, Mireille	138
Palladino, Lily	143	Pickett, Duncan	187
Pan, Jennifer	157	Pickett, Vanessa	178
Pancholi, Rumit	80	Pidgeon, Sean	140
Pandya-Lorch, Rajul	83	Pierre, Stephanie	199
Panetta, Jackie	66	Pimm, Matthew	116
Pankratz, Sherith	141	Pinchefsky, Andrew	100
Panner, Craig	140	Pinckney, Joel	172
Paredes, Julio	34	Pingel, Ryan	196, 220
Park, Josh Hyoun Woo	80	Pinnone, Daniela	32
Parker, Erika	29	Pintaudi-Jones, Rose	141
Pastel, Sara	115	Pisano, Joanne	100
Pasti, Mary	199	Pitts, Kathryn	132, 221
Patnaik, Gayatri	40	Pitts, Melissa	41
Patrick, Richanna	61	Plant, Alisa	120
Patterson, Meg	178	Platter, Clara	125
Pattishall, Roy	64	Plummer, Herbert	58
Patton, Susan	219	Poe, Marshall	32
Paul, Hannah	149	Poggione, Mary	107
Paul, Tammy	53	Pogrebin Saltz, Carole	169
Paulson, Jennifer	86	Pohlod, Anna	104
Payne, Topher	48	Poirier, Jacqueline	149
Payton, Tom	181	Polivka, Raina	45
Pazik, Steven	52	Pop, Antonia	179
Pearson, Janie	82	Pope, Barbara Kline,	85
Pedersen, Nadine	41	Poss, Marielle	57
Peeler, Denis	79	Post, Tom	171
Pellien, Jessica	113	Potter, Jane	141
Pelton, Elizabeth	199	Potter, Jonathan	160
Peltz, James	165	Powell, Joseph B.	193
Penfold, Chris	182	Power, Danielle	47
Pennefeather, Shannon	107	Power, Nancy	169
Pennywark, Leah	164	Powers, Carol	161
Pensak, Susan	57	Powers, Emily	40
Perales-Estoesta, Noah	77	Powers, Jane	113
Perez, Peter	46	Pranzatelli, Robert	199
Perkins, Kirsten	197	Pratt, Beth	133
Perri, Trevor	131, 221	Pratt, Dan	56
Perry, Linsey	171	Pratt, Darrin	56, 220, 221
Pervin, David	140	Price, B. Byron	135
Pesek, Diana	145	Price, Destini	30
Peters, Susan	145	Priday, Caroline	149
Petersen, Lorna	156	Priddy, Kristine	163
Peterson, Bob	53	Prieto, Stephanie, Elliott	192
Peterson, Joseph	52	Prior, Robert	112
Peterson, Ryan	145	Procopio, Joseph	80
Petilos, Randolph	52	Proe, Tony	202
Petrik, Katrina	41	Proefrock, Jim	79
Petrucci, Ashely	170	Proia, Brandon	127
Petrylak, Ashley	141	Prpick, Sean	153
Petty, Jill	221	Puchalla, Joel	121, 221
Pfeiffer, Alice R.	167	Puckett, Mary	66
Pfund, Niko	139, 140	Pullano, Michelle	113
Phillips, Betsy	186	Pulvirenti, Teodoro	156
Phillips, Jenna	186	Purcell, Finn	100

Purple, Katherine	151, 221	Ridge, Sam	36
Putens, Nathan	121	Rimer-Surles, Cathy	63, 221
Pyle, Dan	81	Rinella, Michael	166
Queen, Wendy J.	86	Ringblom, Jenny	52
Quick, Pam	112	Ringo, Tad	78
Quimba, Cheryl	61	Rittenhouse, Rose	52
Quinlan, Daniel	178	Ritter, Devon	53
Quinn, Michele	25	Rivera, Carlos	48
Quinn, Yelba	42	Roach, Brian	49
Race, Justin	151	Roane, Kari	52
Raddatz, Kristen	52	Robert Croce, Carmen	159
Rafert, Samara	133	Roberts, Conrad	88
Ramirez, Linda	173	Roberts, Jennifer	101
Ramos, Alex	145	Roberts, Laura	29
Ranalli, Kathy	144	Roberts, Lisa	75
Rancourt, Suzanne	178	Roberts, Rebecca	116
Randall, Lucy	140	Roberts, Tony	135
Rankin, Charles E. (Chuck)	135	Robinson, Chris	47
Ratcliff, Blake	140	Robinson, Christopher	64
Ratzlaff, Richard	100	Robinson, Kim	45
Rauch, Reba	185	Robinson, Morris (Dino)	131
Rawls, Tiffany	123	Roche, Thomas	72
Read, Cynthia	140	Rodrigue, Sylvia Frank	163
Reaman, Micki	136	Rodriguez, Anna Maria	135
Reaume, Julie	106	Rodríguez, John Mario	34
Recter, Petra	141	Roessner, Maura	45
Rector, Molly	36	Rogers, Jennifer Manley	69
Reed-Morrisson, Laura	145	Rogers, Kelly	85, 221
Reed, Chris	179	Rold, Alison	120
Reed, Ken	149	Rolfs, Erin	100, 221
Reedy, Nora	85	Rollins, Leslie	74
Reeser, Tara	191	Roman, Steven	42
Regan, Ann	107	Romeo-Hall, Ange	61
Regoli, Michael	81	Roosa, Deste	99
Rehl, Beatrice	47	Roper, Sarah	95
Reid, Chris	141	Rose, Amber	196
Reid, Marcia E.	115	Rosenbaum, David	111, 220
Reilly, Eileen	149	Rosenfield, Abigail Schott	164
Reiser, Beth	201	Rosolina, Rachel	81
Reitmeier, Ami	79	Ross, Briana	75
Rennells, Kevin	104	Ross, Marsha	52
Rennison, Robin	111	Ross, Rachel	191, 220
Renteria, Rey	173	Ross, Simon	95
Renwick, Devon	86	Rossetti, Chip	125
Renwick, Simon	172	Rossi, Janet	113
Repeta, Kasia	65	Rotella, Giuseppe	48
Repetto, David	47	Rothko, Mark	118
Repino, Robert	140	Routon, Anne	31
Repta, Bob	79	Roux, Michael	79
Reshota, Olga	155	Rowley, Kristen Elias	134, 220
Reynolds, Victoria	66	Rowley, Linda	105
Rheault, Sonia	138	Roy, Mary Lou	27
Rice, Dawn	209	Roy, Michael	29
Richards, Alun	95	Royal, Chad	64
Richards, Melanie	95	Rubeck, Levi	113
Richards, Michael	155	Ruccia, Dan	65, 220
Richards, Todd	191	Rude, Pam	81
Richardson, Jerry	163	Rudy, Gordon	52

Ruiz, Marcia	169	Schuetz, Richard	123
Runia, Rixt	33	Schuster, Emily	135
Runyon, Ashley	81	Schutjer, Karin	43
Rusko, Joe	86	Schwaiger, Elizabeth	138
Russell, Bonnie	191, 220	Schwartz, Barry L.	120
Russell, Richard A.	118, 119	Schwartz, Eric I.	57
Russo, Sarah	141	Schwarz, Jessica	57
Ryan, Jessica	64	Schwinck, Claire	121
Ryan, Ray	47	Schynert, Kendra	164
Ryan, Suzanne	140	Scobie, Charles	139, 141
Rye, Olivia	96	Scollans, Colleen	140, 141
Ryman, David	113	Scott, Iain	58
Sacher, Jennifer	30	Scott, Rachel	137
Safer, Rachel	141	Scott, Rebecka	23
Saffel, Than	194	Scrivener, Brian	44
Sagara, Mike	164	Scudder, Dean	141
Sain, Elizabeth	132	Seagram, Andrew	52
Sala, Edward	190	Searl, Patricia	187
Salas, Lauren	52	Seburyamo, Kate	166
Salisbury, Leila W.	90	Seger, Rebbeca	141
Salling, Stacey	173	Sekora, Rosemary	121
Saltus, Iris	122	Sell, Laura	64, 222
Saltzman, Glenn	71	Sells, Dianna	174
Salvatore, Laurea	140	Sen, Sharmila	75
Sampson, Nancy	64	Sery, Doug	112
Samuel, Patrick	131	Sewall, Martha	86
Sanders-Buell, Sara	118	Sewell, David	187
Sanfilippo, Tony	134	Seyl, Emily	174
Santella, Anna-Lisa	140	Shaffer, Bryan	151
Santiago, Carlos	150	Shah, Vijay	109
Sapir, Marc	116	Shahan, Andrea	120
Sapire, Sara	199	Shanahan, Mary	52
Sarratt, Blanche	25	Shanholtzer, Joshua	146
Satrom, Ellen	187	Shanklin, Serenity	107
Sattler, Maggie	108	Shanley, Maxwell	164
Saunders, Kat	89	Shannon, Jennifer	155
Saunders, Mark H.	187, 222	Shannon, Kate	173
Savage, Lisa	64	Shapiro, Stephen	178
Savarese, Anne	148	Shaw, Laura	152
Sayre, Dan	141	Shay, Alison	127, 221
Scallan, Amanda	94	Shay, Mariah	118
Scanlon, Sonia	199	Shayegan, Leyli	169
Scarpelli, Elizabeth	55, 221	Shea, Brian	86, 221
Scecina, Lisa	199	Shear, Donna A.	120, 219, 220, 221
Schaffner, Melanie B.	86	Shepherd, Danielle	95
Schaper, Jennifer	64	Sher, Richard B.	43
Schier, Jeffrey	199	Sherer, John	127
Schleicher, Wendy	118	Sherman, Amy	146
Schlesinger, Laurie	149	Shidlauski, Tamara	79
Schmelzinger, Kim	221	Shields, Charlie	36
Schmidt, Eric	45	Shimabukuro, Jill	52
Schmidt, Karen	74	Shirley, Melissa	153
Schmidt, Randy	41	Shoemaker, Susannah	149
Schnaufer, Wendi	25	Shojaie, Rosemary	155
Schneider, James	222	Shor, Deborah	141
Schneider, Naomi	45	Shoup, Jeff	141
Schrader, Rebecca	189	Shull, Brigitte	47, 221
Schreiber, Meighan	156	Siewers, Alfred	43